ADVANCE PRAISE FOR

The United States Involvement in the South China Sea Dispute

"With the rise and expansion of China's economy, the importance of the South China Sea to China's geo-strategy and development consideration has also increased. And it has also severely challenged the core interests of the United States in the South China Sea where China and the United States have started hegemony competition and security rivalry. Facing this hot issue, what is even more special and precious on this book is from the standpoint, angle, and strategy of the United States in the South China Sea. It definitely allows readers to have a full glimpse of the long-term U.S. strategic involvement and engagement in the South China Sea."

—Jenn-Jaw Soong, Distinguished Professor, National Cheng Kung University

"As China's presence in the maritime realm increases, academics, area experts, practitioners and politicians need to understand China's perspectives. Professor Ma's book is therefore timely, as it sets out to show and explain the Chinese position on the South China Sea in a forthright manner."

—Mark Hoskin, Historian, University of London

"The inspirational value of this book mainly lies in the fact that it prompts us to think deeply about the history and future trend of the U.S. South China Sea policy from the framework of academic foundation and realistic concern, which provides a new space for studying the relationship between other countries and the South China Sea issue."

—Guo Yuan, Professor, Jinan University

The United States Involvement in the South China Sea Dispute

The Belt and Road Initiative
Interdisciplinary Perspectives

Wenshan Jia
Series Editor

Vol. 1

The Belt and Road Initiative: Interdisciplinary Perspectives series
is part of the Peter Lang Regional Studies list.
Every volume is peer reviewed and meets
the highest quality standards for content and production.

PETER LANG
New York • Bern • Berlin
Brussels • Vienna • Oxford • Warsaw

Jianying Ma

The United States Involvement in the South China Sea Dispute

PETER LANG
New York • Bern • Berlin
Brussels • Vienna • Oxford • Warsaw

Library of Congress Cataloging-in-Publication Data

Names: Ma, Jianying, author.
Title: The United States involvement in the South China Sea dispute / Jianying Ma.
Description: New York: Peter Lang, 2022.
Series: The belt and road initiative: interdisciplinary perspectives; vol. 1
ISSN 2689-7970 (print) | ISSN 2689-7989 (online)
Includes bibliographical references and index.
Identifiers: LCCN 2021047348 (print) | LCCN 2021047349 (ebook)
ISBN 978-1-4331-8518-2 (hardback)
ISBN 978-1-4331-8519-9 (ebook pdf) | ISBN 978-1-4331-8520-5 (epub)
Subjects: LCSH: South China Sea—International status. | United States—Foreign relations.
Classification: LCC KZA1692 .M349 2022 (print) | LCC KZA1692 (ebook) | DDC 341.4/480916472—dc23/eng/20211220
LC record available at https://lccn.loc.gov/2021047348
LC ebook record available at https://lccn.loc.gov/2021047349
DOI 10.3726/b17976

Bibliographic information published by **Die Deutsche Nationalbibliothek**. **Die Deutsche Nationalbibliothek** lists this publication in the "Deutsche Nationalbibliografie"; detailed bibliographic data are available on the Internet at http://dnb.d-nb.de/.

Peter Lang Publishing, Inc., New York
80 Broad Street, 5th floor, New York, NY 10004
www.peterlang.com

Contents

List of Tables

Acknowledgments

I received generous help from many people in writing this book and would like to acknowledge them here.

I am deeply grateful to Dr. Jia Wenshan, Dean of Global Engagement Academy at Shandong University (Weihai), China, and Professor of Communication and Global Studies at Chapman University for his enthusiastic encouragement and recommendation to publish this book and include it in the Belt & Road Initiative: Interdisciplinary Perspectives series edited by him. I am also very grateful to Prof. Jenn-Jaw Soong at the Department of Political Science of National Cheng Kung University, Taiwan, for giving his insightful and constructive comments of the manuscript. I have been inspired by various exchanges with them.

I owe my sincere appreciation to a number of individuals for their invaluable support. This goes especially to Dr. Mark Hoskin, Department of History, SOAS, University of London, UK, and Ms. Hui Siyuan of Beijing International Studies University, China, for their wonderful language correction and polishing. Thanks to these scholars for their great help to me. They are Prof. Christopher Len of National University of Singapore, Prof. GuoYuan of Jinan University, Dr. Hu Bo of Peking University, Dr. Zhang Mingliang of Jinan University, Dr. PanYue of Jinan University, Prof. Zhao Weihua of Fudan University, Dr. Zeng Huansheng of National Taiwan Ocean University, Prof. Pang Zhongying of Ocean University of China, Prof. Shen Dingli of Fudan University, Prof. Tang Yi of National Chengchi University, Dr. Ma Bin of Fudan University, and Dr. Liu Yanhua of China National Institute for South China Sea Studies.

I would also like to thank the anonymous reviewers for their valuable insights and all people at Peter Lang Publishing who participated in the process for their highly efficient, professional, and friendly cooperation. This applies specifically to the production editor Malini, editorial assistant Suma George, the production manager Jackie Pavlovic and the commissioning editor Li Na. Their academic and editing advice undoubtedly improved the quality of the final version of the text.

Last but not least, I am very thankful to my parents, Ma Jingxun and Zhao Longjun, and my mother-in-law, Liu Chuancai, for their unconditional love and support. I owe my deepest gratitude to my wife Wang Shuzhen and my daughter Ma Junru, for their dedication to and faith in me. Their love and care have given me the courage to pursue my dream.

List of Abbreviations

ADF	Australian Defense Force
ADIZ	Air Defense Identification Zone
AMM	ASEAN Foreign Ministers' meeting
APEC	Asia Pacific Economic Cooperation
ARF	ASEAN Regional Forum
ASEAN	Association of Southeast Asian Nations
ASEM	Asia-Europe Meeting
BRI	Belt and Road Initiative
CAFTA	China-ASEAN Free Trade Area
CCG	China's Coast Guard
COC	Code of Conduct in the South China Sea
CRS	Congressional Research Service
CUES	Code for Unplanned Encounters at Sea
DOC	Declaration on Conduct of Parties in the South China Sea
DoD	Department of Defense
DoS	Department of State
EEZ	Exclusive Economic Zone
EIA	Energy Information Administration
FON	Freedom of Navigation
FONOPs	Freedom of Navigation Operations
FRUS	Foreign Relations of the United States

FTA	Free Trade Agreement
G7	Group of Seven
GDP	Gross Domestic Product
GPO	U.S. Government Printing Office
JCS	Joint Chiefs of Staff
MAGTF	U.S. Marine Air Ground Task Force
MDA	Maritime Domain Awareness
MLE	Maritime Law Enforcement
NCCPC	National Congress of the Communist Party of China
NDMC	National Defense Mobilization Committee
NSC	National Security Council
NSD	National Security Directive
NSDD	National Security Decision Directives
PAFMM	People's Armed Forces Maritime Militia
PDD	Presidential Decision Directive
PLA	People's Liberation Army of China
PLAN	People's Liberation Army Navy of China
PRC	People's Republic of China
QUAD	Quadrilateral Security Dialogue
RAN	Royal Australian Navy
ROC	Republic of China
ROK	Republic of Korea
SCS	South China Sea
TPP	Trans-Pacific Partnership
UNCLOS	United Nations Convention on the Law of the Sea
USCC	U.S.-China Economic and Security Review Commission
USCG	U.S. Coast Guard
WPNS	Western Pacific Naval Symposium
WTO	World Trade Organization
WWII	World War II

Introduction

The Chinese descriptive Nanhai (南海) is commonly recognized in the international community as the South China Sea (SCS).[1] It is a marginal sea adjoining the Western Pacific Ocean between 23°27' north latitude and 3° south latitude, and between 99°10' east longitude and 122°10' east longitude, encompassing an area of around 3,500,000 square kilometers. In China's official and public discourse, it is bounded in the north by Guangdong's southern coastline and the southern Taiwan Strait (23° N), in the south by James Shoal (4° N) and the Natuna Islands in Indonesia, southern Vietnam's coastline (108° E), and in the east by Sarawak, Sabah in Malaysia and Palawan, Luzon in the Philippines (120° E). China's Nanhai Zhudao (the South China Sea Islands) consists of Dongsha Qundao (Pratas Islands), Xisha Qundao (Paracel Islands), Zhongsha Qundao (Macclesfield Bank), and Nansha Qundao (Spratly Islands).[2] Like the Mediterranean Sea and the Caribbean Sea, the SCS is mostly surrounded by continents and islands, placing it alongside them as one of the three major inland seas in the world.[3]

The SCS islands and their adjacent waters have been China's territory since ancient times. China is not only the first country to discover and name islands and reefs, but also the first to exercise sovereignty and jurisdiction over the SCS.[4] Therefore, China has sufficient historical and legal support to justify its sovereignty claims. In fact, China's sovereignty over the SCS islands was not widely challenged until the end of World War Two (WWII). The disputes in the SCS during this period were mainly derived from French aggression and Chinese resistance, while the other colonial masters of now independent countries around the SCS did not make any claims to sovereignty. With the development of international law of the sea since the 1950s, especially the discovery of undersea oil and gas resources in the SCS, some Southeast Asian countries began to claim sovereignty over the SCS islands one after another, resulting in the emergence of the SCS issue. In the evolution of disputes in the SCS, intervention by powers outside the region, especially the United States, has become the most important international factor in any prospect of a dispute resolution.

Significance of the Book

The United States plays a pivotal role in the SCS issue. Historically, the United States is not only the initiator of the unresolved sovereignty over the Paracel and Spratly Islands in the SCS after WWII, but also the State that directly interferes in the SCS by frequently sending military forces on patrols without justifiable reasons, thereby disregarding China's sovereignty. Throughout the Cold War, the SCS was a key area of great strategic and geopolitical importance in the U.S. Asia-Pacific strategy that is assigned to the Seventh Fleet. Consequently, the SCS issue is utilized as an excuse and a tool to contain China and the Soviet Union in a bid to encircle the Soviet bloc in East Asia.

After the Cold War, the SCS was regarded by the United States as a potential source of conflict affecting the stability of the Asia-Pacific region, endangering its interests, and also as an ideal location to carry out its containment strategy against China. Therefore, after the Cold War the United States became actively involved in the SCS dispute. It has repeatedly reaffirmed that the peace, stability, and freedom of navigation in the SCS are in the fundamental interests of the United States. The United States opposes the use or threat of force and maintains that all disputing parties should resolve their differences through diplomatic efforts and abide by the recognized principles of international law, in particular the provisions of the United Nations Convention on the Law of the Sea (UNCLOS), despite the fact that the Congress has not ratified the UNCLOS, and remains unlikely to do so.

In terms of practical development, the United States has become the most critical external factor affecting the situation in the SCS. With the rapid rise of China, the United States has attached more importance to the geopolitical importance of the SCS and listed it as the southern frontier as it seeks to contain China's rise. On the one hand, the United States accuses China of being belligerent and threatening the freedom of navigation in the region, sending warships in the vicinity of the islands and flying fighters over them to conduct freedom of navigation operations (FONOPs), directly challenging China's sovereign rights and interests in the SCS.

On the other hand, in the process of competing with China for sovereignty and maritime rights in the SCS, some disputing countries in the SCS have also tried to drag in the United States to create a confrontation between it and China so that they reap the rewards without physical exposure. American treaty allies (such as the Philippines) and potential strategic partners (such as Vietnam) show they intend to exert continual pressure on China through joint efforts, attempting to force China into making concessions on the SCS issue. This provides a perfect opportunity for the United States to intervene in the SCS issue: The overlapping identities of the U.S. Asia-Pacific allies/partners and the States with territorial claims in the SCS continually prompt the United States to intervene in the SCS issue on the grounds of maintaining the alliance system created in the post-colonial era and assuming partnership obligations that suit its own interests. Although the United States is not a direct party to the SCS dispute, it cannot be ignored in the near future when the management and mitigation of relevant disputes are considered.

Given the importance of the United States in the SCS dispute, this book is devoted to providing a comprehensive, accurate, and up-to-date analysis of the U.S. policy in the SCS, and its involvement and impact on potential dispute-solving processes, mainly from a historical and realist perspective. It endeavors to answer the following questions: What influence has the United States had in the SCS dispute? What policy and stance has the United States adopted in the SCS dispute and how has the United States shifted its policy from neutrality to proactive engagement? What is the strategic motive behind it? Also, has the United States, as it claims, taken no position on the competing sovereignty claims in the SCS? The United States has intervened strongly in the SCS during recent years. What is the orientation of its intervention? What prospects are there for U.S. policy in the SCS in the future?

The disputes in the SCS not only concern China's territorial sovereignty and integrity, but also the security of China's sea lanes and its core maritime rights and interests. It is a major strategic issue involving China's sovereignty, security, and future development. As an outsider, the United States is not a direct disputant in the SCS issue, so the SCS dispute should not be a stumbling block to China-U.S. relations. But the United States has intensified its interference in the SCS issue under the pretext of safeguarding freedom of navigation in recent years, in response to the rapid rise of China. Consequently, the SCS issue has become an important strategic issue in China-U.S. relations. In this regard, studies of the SCS dispute between the United States and China are significant for the following reasons.

First, the oceans are strategically important for a high-quality development of China as a state. As China accelerates its pace to develop its maritime space, the priority is to handle current maritime disputes properly. This research provides policymakers with some understanding of the origin and development of related disputes, enabling them to grasp the ever-changing connotations and orientation of U.S. policy on the SCS, before it recommends additional policy approaches aimed toward generating a more peaceful, stable, non-confrontational, and law-abiding environment in the SCS. It also helps deepen China's understanding of international maritime dispute settlement, maritime diplomatic contest, global maritime politics and theories of maritime rights, and brings insights into the study of marine research.

Second, the U.S. policy on the SCS is closely related to its overall strategic layout in the Asia-Pacific region. Through the discussion of the content, means, characteristics, and influence of the U.S. policy in the SCS since WWII, the structure and process of the United States involvement in the SCS dispute will be deeply studied. This is not only conducive to revealing the essence and trend of the U.S. Asia-Pacific strategy from historical and realist aspects, but is also helpful in enabling a better understanding of how the United States integrates its national security, economic, geopolitical, and other interests in the SCS dispute into its entire Asia-Pacific strategy at both macro and micro levels.

Third, the surrounding region is an important strategic area for China's steady development. In October 2013, China held its first meeting on its neighborhood diplomacy, at which President Xi Jinping stressed that China should make more efforts to advance neighborhood diplomacy, strive for a favorable neighborhood environment for its own development, and make its development more beneficial to neighboring countries, thereby creating a common development path.[5] In the same year, China put forward the Belt and Road Initiative (BRI), which provides Chinese technical knowledge to promote economic prosperity and regional economic cooperation among countries along the BRI, strengthening exchanges at all levels of society, and cultivating mutual learning among different civilizations, thereby promoting global peace and development. Given the tremendous value of the SCS in both the regional geostrategic environment and international trade, the implementation of neighborhood diplomacy and the BRI, especially the construction of the 21st-Century Maritime Silk Road, cannot be implemented fully without proper handling of the SCS issue and China-US relations. Therefore, this study will provide intellectual support for China's legitimate efforts to promote its neighborhood diplomacy and the construction of the 21st Century Maritime Silk Road.

Fourth, a study of the SCS dispute between the United States and China is also necessary for the implementation of a maritime power strategy. With the deep integration of China and the world in the new century, the role of the oceans in China's strategic design has risen significantly. China needs to understand and manage the oceans more than ever before. Against this background the 18th National Congress of the Communist Party of China (NCCPC) in November 2012 put forward for the first time the strategic guideline for improving the capacity of marine resource exploitation, developing marine economy, protecting marine ecological environment, and resolutely safeguarding national maritime rights and interests, with the goal of building China into a maritime power.[6] In his report to the 19th NCCPC in October 2017, China's President Xi Jinping called for coordinated efforts on land and sea, and accelerated the building of the components necessary for China to be a maritime power, which once again sounded the trumpet for China to emerge as a modern maritime power.[7] For an understanding of China's response, which is geared toward protecting her rights and interests through the implementation of a national security strategy, a study of US policies and activity in the SCS is of great significance.

Previous Literature

As one of the three famous marginal continental seas in the world, the SCS, with its outstanding strategic position and abundant resources, was called by some strategists as "the Mediterranean Sea in Asia," "the second Persian Gulf,"[8] and "the third hottest sea area."[9] Especially after the Cold War, there are now extra-regional countries, led by the United States, who have actively intervened in this strategic area and kept a cautious eye on the direction of China's policy towards territorial and jurisdictional disputes in the SCS. As a result, the SCS dispute, which was only a territorial dispute, has evolved into a highly complex issue of global significance.[10] It not only covers the traditional ownership of islands, maritime delimitation, and competition for energy resources, but also involves the so-called freedom of navigation and great power competition. So far, research on the United States in the SCS dispute have mainly focused on its strategic interest in the SCS, the significance and influence of its intervention, the evolution of its policy, and the China-U.S. competition on maritime rights in the Asia-Pacific region.

Research Literature in China

At present, a representative point of view in Chinese academic circles holds that in order to construct a grand strategy to contain the Soviet Union during the Cold War, the United States did not form a long-term and stable policy on the SCS, but held an opportunistic attitude. Although unwilling to accept that sovereignty of the SCS belongs to China, the United States did not publicly and vehemently oppose China's sovereignty over the SCS when it was threatened by the Soviet Union, with China as its ally.[11] After the Cold War, however, the United States gradually rediscovered the geopolitical value of the SCS, especially after the Mischief Reef Incident in 1995. The United States began to pay special attention to the SCS issue and used it as a stepping stone to guard against China's rise and balance the unreasonable demands of neighboring countries to ensure that the situation in the SCS evolves in accordance with U.S. interests.[12] Wang Chuanjian and Deng Fan believe that the United States' strategic demands in the SCS are to maintain its dominance in the region, which is consistent with its Asia-Pacific strategic goals.[13] Wu Shicun points out that the United States will continue to intervene in the SCS issues in such areas as non-traditional security, economic exchanges, political exchanges, military presence, infiltration in the Strait of Malacca, and maritime intelligence investigation.[14]

Since Barak Obama came to power in 2008, the United States has significantly increased its involvement in the SCS dispute. Scholars such as Ju Hailong and Song Yanhui believe that, compared with previous statements, the Obama administration has shown two phenomena of expansion in terms of "national interests" and "international interests" in the SCS: (a) The "national interests" arena expands to include the use of public space in the SCS (including the sky), the maintenance of legal business practices, and respect for international law. (b) Expand the number of stakeholders to those with international interests to Japan, India, Russia, Australia, EU and other peripheral countries and regions, and attempt to further internationalize and multilateralize the SCS dispute.[15]

After Donald J. Trump took office in 2017, U.S. policy on the SCS has maintained a certain degree of continuity, although it has also made new breakthroughs in action and authorization.[16] From a military alliance treaty perspective, Zhang Lei compares the possibility of U.S. military intervention in the China-Japanese and China-Philippine territorial disputes and concludes that the United States is more likely to intervene in the China-Japanese Diaoyu/Senkaku Islands dispute, and military intervention in the China-Philippine SCS dispute is less likely. For this reason, China should adopt a proactive policy on the SCS dispute while avoiding military frictions over the Diaoyu/Senkaku Islands issue.[17] It is worth noting that, as an important driving force in the decision-making process of the U.S. SCS policy, the United States Congress has become even more prominent in its interference in the SCS issue in recent years, which has also attracted the attention of the academic community.[18] After the ruling in the SCS arbitration case in 2016, China's academic circles have analyzed the responses to the SCS arbitration and criticized its legality.[19]

According to Li Jinming, the United States has not changed its Cold War mentality, and its excuse for continuing to intervene in the SCS issue has just changed from containing the expansion of communism to maintaining freedom of navigation in the SCS.[20] Zhang Mingliang points out incisively that the United States' public intervention in the SCS dispute in the name of upholding the freedom and safety of shipping routes is only a facade, and its hidden purpose is to contain China through the SCS issue.[21] Cao Yunhua and his associates believe that, as the most active participant outside the region, the United States has repeatedly stressed that all parties to the SCS dispute must be resolved in accordance with international law and the relevant provisions of the UNCLOS. In fact, the United States has not only ignored the divergences in the understanding of the rights and interests in the SCS between itself, as a non-party to the UNCLOS, China and other signatories, but also ignores the limitation of the Southeast Asian States' claims based on long-standing principles of international law.[22]

The United States intervention in the SCS dispute will undoubtedly cause certain challenges to China's efforts to resolve the SCS dispute, but this does not mean that the United States can do whatever it wants. Guo Yuan believes that the United States is also constrained by some factors, including the continuous development of regional and sub-regional multilateral mechanisms on the SCS issue in recent years; Southeast Asian countries' conceiving of establishing a region of peace, freedom, and neutrality to pursue independence and autonomy; the strong appeal of the SCS issue; the relationship between China and its neighboring countries in the SCS issue, etc. All these factors determine the extent and depth of U.S. involvement in the SCS issue.[23] Liu Jianfei believes that the U.S. strategy towards China under the framework of the new global strategy and the Asia-Pacific strategy still has two sides. There is no fundamental conflict of interests between China and the United States in the SCS, and the interests of the United States and some claimants in the SCS are not uniform in nature. There are still broad common interests and space for cooperation between China and the United States.[24]

Based on the new reality of the international power structure, current academic circles tend to believe that the substantive problem reflected by U.S. intervention in the SCS dispute is the competition between China and the United States for dominance in the Western Pacific. Yang Yi points out that the SCS issue is essentially a strategic game between China and the United States.[25] Zhong Feiteng believes that as the United States continues to intervene in the SCS dispute, the rivalry between China and the United States in the SCS is heading towards a sea power competition.[26] In light of China-U.S. bilateral relations, although Chinese President Xi Jinping has repeatedly stated to the United States that the Pacific Ocean is wide enough to accommodate China and the United States,[27] China pursues its own sovereignty and territorial integrity, not maritime expansion. However, the United States still uses such political cliché as "to ensure the freedom of maritime navigation and safeguard the alliance system." Its attempt to challenge China's maritime sovereignty reflects U.S. anxiety over China's rise and its determination to maintain its hegemony in the Asia Pacific. In other words, the sea power game between China and the United States in the Asia-Pacific region is, in essence, the contradiction between China's claims for maritime sovereignty and the continuance of the U.S. maritime hegemony.

With respect to the SCS dilemma between China and the United States, Liu Zhongmin recommends that China should proceed from the multiple needs of China's national grand strategy and strive to avoid conflict with the United States. Furthermore, it is necessary to strengthen the China-U.S. maritime military security consultation mechanism, and increase mutual understanding and trust in the field of maritime security. Meanwhile, China should promote the development of its maritime force in a prudent and orderly manner and realize peace through strength.[28] Zhang Wenmu advocates that China should avoid being hampered by the SCS issue in developing its maritime rights. When it comes to safeguarding its maritime rights and interests in its neighborhood, China should adopt a strategy with certain priorities rather than strike out from all directions and exert its power in a balanced way. He suggests that China should adopt a proactive defensive and restrictive stance in the SCS, while adopting an offensive posture in the East China Sea.[29] Ling Shengli believes that the key to avoiding conflicts between China and the United States in maritime power lies in whether the two sides can do a good job in conflict prevention and crisis management, and if China can establish the general direction of the maritime power strategy of "promoting peace through strength."[30]

The maritime power competition between China and the United States is a typical competition between a continental power and a maritime power, a rising power and a hegemonic power.[31] China and the United States have substantial disputes over rights and interests in the waters of the Western Pacific and obvious divergences in understanding relevant provisions of the international law of the sea. However, the contradictions between China and the United States are not irreconcilable, and the likelihood of a direct armed conflict is slim. Wang Jisi writes that the United States has challenged China in strategy and security, but it is still risky to assume that the United States is China's main enemy and to base China's grand strategy on this perception. China must convince other countries, including the United States and its Asian neighbors, that it is considering the concerns of others as it builds up its defense capabilities, especially its Navy.[32] Xin Qiang believes that the United States has contained the expansion of China's maritime power; meanwhile, it actively seeks pragmatic maritime cooperation with China to prevent China-U.S. relations from falling into confrontation. In his opinion, the sea power game between China and the United States has dual characteristics with the coexistence of strategic conflict and tactical cooperation, offshore conflict and far-sea cooperation, and conflict in traditional security field and cooperation in non-traditional security field.[33] While it may be too early to say how China-U.S. relations will unfold, these academic discussions at least indicate that only coexistence and cooperation between China and the United States can meet the expectations and interests of bilateral relations. What matters is not the breadth of the Pacific, but if Chinese and American strategists are broad-minded enough to accommodate each other.

Research Literature in Foreign Academic Circles

Historically, the cognition and involvement of the United States in the SCS dispute has undergone a long process of evolution. Kimie Hara, a researcher in the Centre for International Governance Innovation, found in the relevant historical archives that as early as the drafting stage of the San Francisco Peace Treaty in 1951, the United States blurred sovereignty aspects in the SCS, and arbitrarily included an ambiguous treatment of the Paracel and Spratly Islands in the treaty while blocking China's participation. Worse still, the treaty merely renounced

Japan's rights to the Paracel and Spratly Islands without explicitly restoring them to China as promised in the prior negotiations, thus sowing the seeds for later territorial disputes.[34] Bob Catley and Makmur Keliat believe that with the growing shadow of the Cold War between East and West, the United States began to put the SCS issue under the overall strategic layout of containing communism, and its policy on the SCS issue was mainly aimed at following and serving the security strategy of the Asia-Pacific region.[35] Zhang Xiaoming of the U.S. Air Force University points out that the United States has always believed that China's historical claims to the SCS are untenable, and the United States opposes the Spratly Islands as part of China's territorial claims on the grounds that any Chinese actions in the SCS will pose a threat to regional security.[36]

In the eyes of Western scholars, the United States has actively intervened in the affairs of the SCS region and repeatedly called on relevant countries to settle disputes in the SCS through peaceful means, which, of course, includes its declared national interests, such as freedom of navigation and economic objectives.[37] But the underlying reason is that the SCS issue provides the United States with a rare opportunity and a starting point for its new Asia-Pacific strategy. Robert D. Kaplan, a senior fellow at the Center for A New American Security, wrote in 2011 that "East Asia can be divided into two general areas: Northeast Asia, dominated by the Korea Peninsular, and Southeast Asia, dominated by the SCS." "East Asia, or more precisely the Western Pacific, which is quickly becoming the world's new center of naval activity, presages a fundamentally different dynamic."[38] Bronson Percival, a senior adviser at the Center for Naval Analyses, also notes that "the SCS may not be a 'litmus test' of China's intentions or of U.S. consistency in Asia. Nonetheless, it is a good issue for the United States . . . it simultaneously strengthens U.S. alliances and partnerships with other states in Asia."[39]

Lee Lai To, a professor at the National University of Singapore, holds that the United States has been constantly playing China off against Southeast Asian countries, creating tensions in the SCS, and increasing its military presence and influence in Southeast Asia through arms sales, military assistance pacts, joint military exercises, and cooperation in non-traditional security fields, with a view to maintaining its dominance in the region.[40] M. Taylor Fravel, an expert on China's oceans at the Massachusetts Institute of Technology, admits that the United States has significantly increased its involvement in the SCS issue in the past few years, mainly in response to China's actions, which makes the maritime security issues in the SCS a crux in China-U.S. relations.[41] Patrick M. Cronin and Robert D. Kaplan wrote a research paper in January 2012 that the United

States needs to develop a correct China policy to safeguard the interests of the United States and its allies in the SCS. This strategy must be based on the strong military and economic strength, and the United States must seek rules-based cooperation and avoid unnecessary military conflicts with China through flexible diplomatic and economic means. Meanwhile, the United States needs to reverse its decline in naval power, consolidate security ties with ASEAN countries, promote consensus-building multilateral cooperation, establish an open regional trading system, and forge a realistic relationship with China.[42]

To a fair number of American scholars, China's foreign policy, including its behavior in the SCS, has become increasingly assertive as its power has grown in recent years.[43] In particular, the accelerated modernization of the Chinese Navy has made Beijing increasingly inclined to use coercive means to safeguard its sovereignty, maritime rights, and interests in the SCS. In this regard, M. Taylor Fravel and Michael D. Swaine believe that China's threat to U.S. oil companies in the SCS in 2007–2008, the increase of China's law enforcement activities in the SCS in 2009–2010, and the expansion of military exercises and friction with Vietnam and the Philippines are the best proof of China's coercive behavior.[44] Alastair Iain Johnston pointed out in his research in 2013 that China did show more aggressive rhetoric and behavior in maritime disputes.[45] The Center for Strategic and International Studies (CSIS), a U.S. think tank, published a report entitled "Countering Coercion in Maritime Asia: the Theory and Practice of Gray Zone Deterrence" in May 2017, which put forward policy proposals in response to China's establishment of an Air Defense Identification Zone (ADIZ) in the SCS and China's militarization of the SCS by changing its topography.[46]

In recent years, the U.S. Congressional Research Service (CRS) has also conducted studies on China's island construction in the SCS,[47] the issue of exclusive economic zone (EEZ) in China's maritime disputes,[48] and China's naval modernization,[49] etc., and put forward U.S. policy recommendations. Carl Thayer of the Center for New American Security Studies (CNAS) advocates an indirect cost-imposing strategy for the United States in the SCS.[50] Joel Wuthnow of National Defense University in the United States, however, believes that U.S. policy in the SCS, which is focused on imposing political, economic, and military costs on China, has failed to address two problems: China's continuing buildup of military and paramilitary power in the region, and the risk of an incident at sea escalating into major conflict.[51] A study by the Center for Strategic and International Studies in August 2017 has also pointed out that China continues to carry out similar activities in Paracel Islands after completing its artificial island-building program in the Spratly Islands.[52] Weston S. Konishi of the

Chicago Council on Global Affairs (CCGA) has argued in January 2018 that the Trump Administration's main response to China in the SCS is to intensify FONOPs in the waters around the islands and reefs in the SCS. Although this measure has aroused great concern in China, there is no evidence that it has any substantive impact on China's island construction process.[53]

In response to China's expansion of maritime power in the Western Pacific, Robert Ross, a professor of political science at Boston College, attributes China's ambitious naval buildup to nationalism rather than national security necessity. Robert believes that recent developments in Chinese politics and defense policy indicate that China will soon embark on an ambitious maritime policy that will include construction of a power-projection navy centered on an aircraft carrier.[54] In his view, widespread nationalism, growing social instability, and the leadership's concern for its political legitimacy drive China's naval ambition. Naval nationalism is the combination of China's governmental demand for maritime power and nongovernmental nationalism, as it seeks to wipe out the century-old humiliation by modern naval aggression by means of developing a strong navy. Michael A. Glosny and Phillip C. Saunders, at the Center for Strategic Studies at the National Defense University, hold that naval nationalism cannot fully and objectively explain the expansion of China's naval power.[55] Conversely, they argue that increasing China's maritime power is merely a reflection of protecting its expanding overseas interests when its national interests expand around the world and it becomes more deeply integrated into the global economy. China has developed a moderate and limited naval projection capability, instead of the "naval nationalism."

A research report by the United States Air Force University stated in 2000 that the current passive neutrality of the United States in the SCS could neither prevent unrest and conflicts between China and ASEAN nor within ASEAN countries. Additionally, the U.S. overt political and military intervention in the region would alienate itself from ASEAN and China. To this end, the report recommends that the United States adopt a proactive, neutral policy—non-threatening but consistent—to engage effectively in Southeast Asia, particularly in the SCS.[56] In recent years, as China and other claimant parties around the SCS have intensified their disputes over sovereignty and rights in the SCS, some Western analysts and scholars believe that this will eventually lead to the deterioration of the situation in the SCS and instability in the Asia-Pacific region.[57] Some Western scholars regard the SCS dispute as a power competition between China and the United States.[58] Other scholars even argue that the United States and its allies are in danger of losing the SCS in this power competition.[59] After the SCS arbitration in 2016, Western academic circles have conducted in-depth analysis on the legal status, subsequent impact, and reactions of the arbitration.[60] Considering the huge divergences between China and the United States on the SCS issue, the United States Government and academia believe that China's claims in the SCS have no legal support and thus call on all parties to respect and implement the arbitration ruling.[61] Given its consistent posture as suppressing China's claims on the SCS issue, the above-mentioned American stance on the SCS arbitration case is not surprising.

According to the existing research results, although the academic circles have different research perspectives and focuses, most of them believe that the United States intervention in the SCS has become a new focus affecting China-U.S. relations and the security situation in the Asia-Pacific region. Due to the complexity and dynamic nature of disputes in the SCS, there is still a long way to go to make refinements and improvements in the current researches, which is highlighted as follows:

First, the U.S. policy towards the SCS dispute since WWII is inconsistent and unstable. In fact, the U.S. policy has been modified and shifted according to the changing international situation and its own interests. In this regard, academia should examine the continuity and transformation of the U.S. involvement in the SCS dispute, and distinguish long-standing policy from the variable, which is of great significance for evaluating the direction of the U.S. policy in the SCS.

Second, in face of the U.S. proactive involvement in the SCS dispute, the attitude and response of neighboring countries are of critical importance, which is an important influential factor for China to formulate its neighborhood diplomacy and the SCS policy. Considering the various interests, it is hard to expect that the neighboring countries respond to the American involvement in the same way. Therefore, it is necessary to analyze the attitudes and reactions of the major neighboring countries in recent years.

Third, new changes have taken place in the U.S. involvement in the SCS issue. For example, the U.S. Congress has played an increasingly prominent role, differences between China and the United States on the issue of freedom of navigation have become increasingly fierce, and China's maritime militia has gotten much attention. Therefore, it is necessary to make an in-depth analysis of the U.S. policy concerning the SCS and China-U.S. relations in the SCS in recent years. Ultimately, the latest developments of the situation in the SCS and the latest interpretations of the U.S. SCS policy after the Trump administration took office also require follow-up investigations.

Organization of the Book

This book is divided into three parts: introduction, main body, and conclusion. The introduction mainly establishes research issues and their significance, a literature review describing the academic debate, and the research framework. The concluding chapter summarizes the major findings of this research, followed by three pairs of "positive correlation" between the United States and the SCS issue. The main body consists of the following nine chapters.

Chapter One analyzes the historical origin and realistic development of the SCS issue. The SCS not only has a prominent geostrategic position with rich oil and gas reserves, but also an important international shipping sea lane, which has irreplaceable military value. The SCS islands have been China's territory since ancient times. China is the first country in history to discover and manage the islands and reefs in the SCS and their adjacent waters, and has indisputable historical and legal basis for sovereignty of the SCS. During WWII, some islands and reefs in the SCS were occupied by Japanese invaders. After WWII, according to the *Cairo Declaration* and *Potsdam Proclamation* and other international legislative documents, China's territory occupied by Japan, including the SCS, should be restored to China. Accordingly, the Nationalist government took over and managed the SCS Islands. With the discovery of oil and gas resources in the SCS in the 1950s and 1960s, however, the countries around the SCS began to put forward claims over the sovereignty of the islands and reefs in the SCS. Taking advantage of China's weak military strength and political turmoil, some countries tried to legalize and realize their vested interests on the basis of the modern international law of the sea. During this period, extra-regional powers led by the United States constantly intervened, and consequently, the SCS has evolved from a geographical concept to an international issue involving politics, economy, military, law, history, geography, and many other fields, with maritime sovereignty as the core and island sovereignty, maritime division, and resource allocation as the main issues.

Chapter Two reviews and explores the U.S. policy on the SCS during the Cold War. Before WWII, the U. S. interests in the SCS were quite limited. The SCS was merely a commercial sea lane for the United States, therefore it attached more importance to the Philippines as a raw materials source, consumer base, and a springboard for expansion into China. The SCS, located in the west of the Philippines, had not entered the strategic horizon of the United States. After WWII, the United States reexamined the strategic value of the SCS. Due to the rapid disintegration of U.S.-Soviet wartime cooperation, coupled with ideological competition and divergence in national interests, the East and the West gradually fell into the abyss of the Cold War. In the context of the bipolarity, the SCS has become a frontier for the United States to contain socialist China and compete for hegemony with the Soviet Union. Throughout the Cold War, U.S. policy on the SCS revolves around the Cold War. For the need of anti-China and anti-Communist in the early and middle stages of the Cold War, the United States ignored the SCS issue and deliberately blurred the sovereignty of the SCS. In the final stages of the Cold War, the United States pursued the "reluctant neutrality" on the SCS issue for the sake of uniting China to resist the Soviet Union.

Chapter Three discusses and analyzes the adjustment of U.S. policy on the SCS in the post-Cold War era. The collapse of the Soviet Union and the drastic changes in Eastern Europe led to the end of the Cold War and the collapse of the bipolar structure of the international system. In the post-Cold War era, the Asia-Pacific region has become one of the most economically vibrant regions in the world, and its political status has also been significantly enhanced. The security situation in the Asia-Pacific region tended to ease, but the unstable factors still existed. The interaction between China and the United States became a key factor affecting the regional order. In this context, while strengthening its political, economic, and security ties with countries in the Asia-Pacific region, the United States adjusted its Asia-Pacific security strategy. In line with changes in the situation in the Asia-Pacific region and the reshaping of its Asia-Pacific security strategy, the U.S. SCS policy has been modified accordingly. During this period, the promulgation of the Law of the People's Republic of China (PRC) on the Territorial Sea and the Contiguous Zone in 1992, the entry into force of the UNCLOS in 1994 and the Mischief Island Incident in 1995 greatly promoted a transformation of U.S. SCS policy. Entering the new century, the incidents of 9/11 prompted the rapid transformation of the U.S. national security strategy to anti-terrorism. Focusing on the war against terrorism, the United States has adopted a strategy of continuous involvement while not allowing itself to be trapped in the SCS issue. Thus the situation in the SCS was relatively stable.

Chapter Four studies the U.S. strong intervention in the SCS issue under the background of the "rebalancing" strategy in Asia Pacific. After Obama took office, the United States changed the Bush Jr. administration's neoconservative thinking, declaring that the United States would shrink from the quagmire of the global war on terrorism, and proposing a "rebalancing" strategy in the Asia Pacific. The introduction of such strategy was not only an instinctive response to an increasingly multipolar world and the relative decline of the United States, but also a strategic option to comply with the geopolitical strategic focus of the

Asia-Pacific region and to cope with the growing rise of China. In this context, the SCS issue has become an important starting point for the United States to promote the "rebalancing" strategy, and the United States has taken a tough stand, intervening in the SCS dispute. It not only vigorously hypes the SCS issue and frequently condemns China's territorial claims, but also constantly questions the legitimacy of China's intermittent line in the SCS, opposes to changing the status quo in the SCS by force or coercion, and opposes China's historical claim of sovereignty in the SCS. At the same time, the United States has repeatedly demanded that China cease its land reclamation activities in the SCS and has sent warships and aircraft into the waters and airspace of the SCS in the name of freedom of navigation to challenge China's maritime claims. In addition, the United States also enhances its military strength by enhancing its security cooperation agreements with Southeast Asian countries involved in the SCS dispute, and actively encourages and solicits foreign powers to form a multilateral alliance to intervene, to jointly exert pressure on China and promote its self-imposed perception of a liberal international order.

Chapter Five studies the attitude and reaction of the major neighboring countries to the U.S. "rebalancing" strategy in the Asia Pacific and its involvement in the SCS issue. This chapter separates China's neighboring countries into five categories, namely ASEAN, Japan, India, Russia, and Australia. ASEAN takes a relatively contradictory stand. It invites the United States to play an active role in the regional issues, but is unwilling to see the U.S. strategy in the Asia Pacific become too militarized, with its potential to bring conflicts and tensions to the region. Japan applauds the implementation of the "rebalancing" strategy and takes the initiative to cooperate with the United States to boost its involvement in the SCS issue. India maintains a cautious attitude towards the U.S. pivot to the Asia-Pacific region. On the one hand, India emphasizes that its activities in the SCS do not have political implications; on the other hand, it pays attention to freedom of navigation and potential commercial interests in the SCS. The official response of Russia is relatively "silent." In light of the U.S. intervention in China's maritime disputes, Russia acts as a regional power balancer and gives China limited support on the relevant issues. As an important ally of the United States, Australia has actively cooperated and supported the U.S. "rebalancing" strategy and its intervention in the SCS in diplomatic, security, and economic aspects. However, the Australian government's responses have invoked a variety of criticisms and controversies from China.

Chapter Six makes a comprehensive analysis of the influence of the U.S. Congressional intervention in the SCS issue and its methods. Congress is a driving force and has a huge impact on the U.S. government's foreign policy-making behavior. This function is vividly manifested in the SCS issue. The main methods for Congressional intervention in the SCS issue include proposing Bills, holding Hearings, deliberating Reports, Speeches, Statements, and Letters from Members. Congressional intervention in the SCS issue shows the following characteristics: First, it has gradually formed a cross-party consensus that supports intervention in the SCS issue. Second, physical intervention varies in different periods, while remaining closely related to the overall U.S. strategy toward China and the situation in the SCS. Third, there is a policy consensus between the Executive and the Congress, but Congress is more robust than the Executive. Fourth, Members of Congress are frequently asking questions about the SCS. There are biases and unfair tendencies in their views on China, which reflect their worries and wariness about China's rapid rise. U.S. Congressional intervention in the SCS issue will not only influence the U.S. government's decision-making and promote the administration's active intervention in the SCS issues, but also worsen the situation in the SCS. These actions intensify the SCS issue and hinder China-U.S. relations, which is not conducive to peace and stability in the Asia-Pacific region.

Chapter Seven analyzes the freedom of navigation and China-U.S. power game in the SCS. With the rapid rise of China and its greater investment in areas that contribute to a maritime power status, China-U.S. competition for sea power in the Asia-Pacific region has become increasingly fierce, especially in the SCS. In order to maintain its maritime hegemony, the strategic reputation of its alliance and its dominance in the Asia-Pacific region, the United States frequently challenges China's maritime sovereignty and rights on the ground of defending so-called freedom of navigation. Looking through the maritime disputes between China and the United States in recent years, however, it is not difficult to find that the implementation of freedom of navigation in Chinese waters has become one of the most important means for the United States to intervene in the SCS issue. This chapter makes an in-depth study of U.S. FONOPs, the introduction and development of the freedom of navigation program, and the general situation and characteristics of the FONOPs carried out in respect of China. This chapter holds that China-U.S. contention on the freedom of navigation in the SCS is not based on disrupted navigation, instead, it serves as an excuse to constrain China's rise and maintain American hegemony in the region. This is the essence of China-U.S. maritime contests and the fundamental reason for China-U.S. confrontations in the SCS.

Chapter Eight focuses on the U.S. understanding and evaluation of China's maritime militia. In order to accelerate the implementation of its maritime power strategy and effectively safeguard China's maritime rights and interests, China has not only strengthened the construction of traditional naval and air forces, but also integrated and upgraded the maritime militia force. In the context of fierce competition between China and the United States over the SCS issue, China's maritime militia has attracted close attention from American academic circles, political circles, think tanks, and the media. On the whole, the academic and political circles of the United States highly value the status of China's maritime militia, regarding it as the third maritime force. The role and function of China's maritime militia force, the impact assessment of the United States on China's maritime militia force, and the policy response of the United States to China's maritime militia force are thoroughly explored. However, due to the wariness and worry about the rise of China's maritime power in the new era, the limited understanding with China, and the misunderstandings and biases of some researchers themselves, there are shortcomings in U.S. research. There is a lack of objective evaluations on the development of China's maritime militia force, and some conclusions are even speculative, controversial, and over exaggerated.

Chapter Nine is a comprehensive interpretation of the U.S. SCS policy since Trump came to power in 2017. Since then, the U.S. SCS policy has attracted the attention of all parties. From the perspective of policy discourse, the SCS issue is one of the topics frequently mentioned by the United States, whether in unilateral statements, bilateral talks, or multilateral occasions. From the perspective of policy, the Trump administration has partially inherited and followed the previous SCS policy, while it has also modified recent policies, such as increasing patrols in the SCS and revising the approval process, combining strategies of "linkage" and "destabilizing," accelerating militarization of the SCS through military power, and imposing constraints on China with American definitions of order. The Trump administration's involvement in the SCS issue is not only a reflection of the growing anxiety over China's rapid rise, but also a practical need to promote its Indo-Pacific strategy. At the same time, the Trump Administration's continuous intervention in the SCS also has strategic considerations, that is, to appease U.S. allies in the Asia-Pacific region, ensure its strategic credibility, and to safeguard U.S. maritime hegemony and limit China's maritime expansion. Looking forward to the future, the United States will continue to intervene in the SCS issue via various means. Therefore, to prevent military friction and even conflict between China and the United States in the SCS, these two sides need to enhance their crisis management framework.

Notes

1 In most Chinese expressions, Nan Hai (南海) and Nan Zhong Guo Hai (南中国海) are used interchangeably and in roughly the same range. For simplicity, this book uses the SCS. To be clear, Vietnam calls the SCS the Bien Dong (or East Sea in English), and the Philippines and Malaysia commonly refer to it as the SCS, though the Philippines has intentionally used the term "Philippine Sea" since 2011. As an important part of the SCS, the Spratlys are commonly known in the English-speaking world as the Spratly Islands, the Trung Sa Quan Dao in Vietnam, and part of the Kalayan Islands in the Philippines.

2 Li Jinming, *Research on the SCS Territory,* Harbin: Heilongjiang Education Press, 2014, pp.3–4.

3 Li Guoqiang, *Studies on SCS: History and Current Situation,* Harbin: Heilongjiang Education Press, 2003, p.2.

4 See Zhang Liangfu, *Let History Tell the Future: A Centennial Record of China's Jurisdiction of the SCS Islands*, Beijing: China Ocean Press, 2011; Li Caixia, *The Historical Events Chronicle of the SCS Islands,* Beijing: Social Sciences Academic Press, 2017.

5 "Xi Jinping delivers an important speech at the forum on neighborhood diplomacy," People's Daily Online, October 25, 2013, http://politics.people.com.cn/n/2013/1025/c70731-23332292.html

6 See the Report to the 18th National Congress of the Communist Party of China.

7 Ibid.

8 Scott Snyder, *The SCS Dispute: Prospects for Preventive Diplomacy*, Washington, D. C.: United States Institute of Peace, 1996, p.4.

9 SCS is one of the strategic hotspots. The other two are the Mediterranean Sea and the Caspian Sea. See Dai Xu, "'Attacking the Enemy before It is Fully Prepared': A Petition for Changing SCS Strategy," *Frontiers*, No. 7 (I), 2012, p.13.

10 Wang Chuanjian, "U.S. Policy in the SCS: History and Reality," *Foreign Affairs Review*, No. 6, 2009, p.87.

11 For related studies, see Zheng Zemin, "American Policies towards SCS during the Cold War," Southeast Asian Affairs, No.4, 2015, pp.13–18; Wang Chuanjian, "U.S. SCS Policy: History and Reality," Foreign Affairs Review, No.6, 2009, pp.91–94; Li Jinming, "The Status quo of SCS Disputes and the Intervention of Major Powers Outside the Region," Contemporary International Relations, No.7, 2011, p.7; Guo Yuan, "U.S. Policy on the SCS and Its Impact in the Early Cold War," Pacific Journal, No.7, 2012, pp.35–43; Zheng Zemin, Major Powers in the SCS Issue: America, Japan, India, Russia and the SCS Issue, Beijing: World Affairs Press, 2010, pp.35–44.

12 For recent Chinese studies on the evolution of U.S. policy in the SCS after the Cold War, please refer to Ge Hongliang, "America's SCS Policy in the Post-Cold War and

Its Influence on Sino-U.S. Relations," Southeast Asia & South Asian Studies, No.2, 2012, pp.16–21; Wang Chuanjian, "U.S. Policy in the SCS: History and Reality," Foreign Affairs Review, No.6, 2009, pp.87–100; Wang Yiwei, "Rethinking of SCS Issue: A Perspective of Sino-U.S. Relations," Fudan American Review, No.1, 2006, pp.81–103; Guo Yuan, "The US Policies of SCS after the Cold War," Academic Exploration, No.1, 2008, pp.54–58; Lu Fanghua, "The US Factor in SCS," Southeast Asia & South Asian Studies, No.4, 2009, pp.6–10; Cai Penghong, "Analysis of the US policy in the SCS," Contemporary International Relations, No.9, 2009, pp.1–7; Wang Xiangyu and Li Wenlong, "The Analysis of American Element in the Dispute of SCS," Journal of Guizhou Normal University(Social Science Edition), No.3, 2001, pp.25–28; Jiang Yang and Wang Yiwei, "SCS in US Asia-Pacific Security Strategy," Southeast Asian Studies, No.5, 1998, pp.33–37; Deng Fan, "The Trend of US Policy of Interference with Issues Related to SCS," Pacific Journal, No.11, 2011, p.83; Long Xinggang and Liang Dongxing, "The U.S. Factor in SCS Issue," Around Southeast Asia, No.9, 2010, pp.16–19; Wang Chuanjun, "The infiltration and influence of Extra-regional Powers to the SCS," Journal of Contemporary Asia-Pacific Studies, No.11, 2011, pp.14–18; Zhou Qi, "The Origin and Evolution of the U.S. SCS Policy in the Post-Cold War Era," World Economics and Politics, No.6, 2014, pp.35–40; Shi Yongming, "The U.S. Policy in the SCS: Target and Strategy," Southeast Asian Affairs, No.1, 2015, pp.1–9; Ju Hailong, "A Historical Analysis on the SCS Policies of the USA: Based on the Declassified Documents of FRUS, DDRS, and DNSA," Academic Exploration, No.6, 2015, pp.106–115.

13 Wang Chuanjian, "US Policy on SCS: History and Reality," *Foreign Affairs Review*, No.6, 2009, p.100; Deng Fan, "The Trend of US Policy of Interference with Issues Related to SCS," *Pacific Journal*, No.11, 2011, pp.83–91.

14 Wu Shicun, *The SCS Dispute: Origin and Development*, Beijing: China Economic Press, 2010, pp.172–180.

15 See Ju Hailong, "Research on the Obama Administration's SCSs Policy," *Journal of Contemporary Asia-Pacific Studies*, No.3, 2011, p.99; Song Yanhui, *The United States and the SCS Dispute,* Taipei: Angle Publishing Co., Ltd, 2016, pp.91–93; He Zhigong and An Xiaoping, "The American Factor and its Influence in the Disputes in SCS," *Journal of Contemporary Asia-Pacific Studies*, No.1, 2010, pp.132–145; Wang Gonglong, "The Adjustment of US Policy toward the SCS and the Room for Cooperation across the Taiwan Straits on This Issue," *International Forum*, No.6, 2011, pp.1–5; Sun Xiaoling, "The U.S. Factor in the SCS Dispute between China and Vietnam," *Southeast Asian Studies*, No.3, 2012, pp.32–37.

16 Su Xiaohui, "Study on Developments of the SCS Policies under the New U.S. Administration," *Pacific Journal*, No.7, 2017, pp.36–43; Wei Zongyou, "A Preliminary Study of Trump's Government SCS Policy," *Southeast Asian Studies,* No.2, 2018, pp.124–137; Ma Jianying and Jiang Bin, "The Trump Administration's

SCS Policy: Initiatives, Motivations and Prospects," *The Journal of SCS Studies*, No.2, 2018, pp.36–44; Zhang Ye, "Analysis of US Freedom of Navigation Operation in SCS under the Trump Administration," *Pacific Journal*, No.9, 2018, pp.94–100.

17 Zhang Lei, "The Possibility Of the United States to Intervene by Military Means in the Island Disputes Between China and Japan and Between China and the Philippines: A Comparison From the Perspective Of the Military Alliances Treaties," *Fudan American Review*, No.1, 2012, pp.47–68.

18 See Zhang Mingliang, "The U.S. Congressional Involvement in SCS Issue: Approaches and Implications," *The Journal of SCS Studies*, No.3, 2015, pp.26–34; Zhao Yang and Gong Honglie, "The Reaction of the U.S. Congress to China's Land Reclamation in the Nansha Islands," Pacific Journal, No.5, 2016, pp.41–51; Li Guizhou, "America's Attitude towards the SCS: A Perspective based on American Congressional Acts," *Contemporary Asia-Pacific Studies*, No.5, 2016, pp.112–134; He Weibao, "Characteristics and Causes of Legislation on the SCS Issue in the US Congress," in Zheng Bingwen and Huang Ping, ed., *American Studies Report (2015)*, Beijing: China Social Sciences Academic Press, 2015, pp.179–195; Guo Yonghu and Song Jianxin, "US Congress Legislation on Maritime Disputes Involving China and its Implications," *China International Studies*, No.5, 2018, pp.103–114; Song Yanhui, *The United Stated and the SCS Dispute,* Taipei: Angle Publishing Co., Ltd, 2016, pp.149–212.

19 Department of Boundary and Maritime Affairs of the Ministry of Foreign Affairs of the People's Republic of China (ed.), *Compilation of Documents Responding to the SCS Arbitration Case*, Beijing: World Affairs Press, 2016; China Society of International Law, *China Annual Review of International Law: Special Issue on Jurisdiction in the SCS Arbitration*, Beijing: Law Press, 2016; Zhu Feng and Yu Mingcai, ed., *The Philippines' SCS Arbitration Case: Perspective*, Beijing: World Affairs Press, 2018; China Society of International Law, *Criticism of the Award of the SCS Arbitration*, Beijing: Foreign Languages Press, 2018; Huang Yao and Huang Jingwen, *The SCS Arbitration Case by the Philippines: Legal Analysis of the Core Issues*, Hong Kong: Joint Publishing (HK) Co. Ltd., 2019.

20 Li Jinming, "The Status quo of SCS Disputes and the Intervention of Major Powers Outside the Region," *Contemporary International Relations*, No.7, 2011, pp.1–8.

21 Zhang Mingliang, *America's Involvement in the SCS: Process, Drives, and Implications,* Hong Kong: Hong Kong Press for Social Sciences LTD., 2011.

22 Cao Yunhua and Ju Hailong, ed., *Report on SCS Situation From 2011 to 2012*, Beijing: Current Affairs Press, 2012, p.104.

23 Guo Yuan, "The US Policies of SCS after the Cold War," *Academic Exploration*, No.1, 2008, pp.57–58; Guo Yuan: *Geopolitics and the SCS Dispute*, Beijing: China Social Sciences Press, 2011, pp.179–182.

24 Liu Jianfei, "The Situation in the SCS and Sino-US Relations Under the Background of the US Strategic Focus Shifting Eastward," *Journal of University of International Relations*, No.4, 2012, pp.93–98.
25 Yang Yi, "Peripheral Environmental Dilemma and Security Policy Paradox," *World Affairs*, No.1, 2012, p.30.
26 Zhong Feiteng, "Three Strategic Issues in the Study of the SCS: Review and Reflection Based on Relevant Literature," *Foreign Affairs Review*, No.4, 2012, p.32.
27 Du Shangze and Wen Xian, "Xi Jinping and President Obama Hold Meeting," *People's Daily*, June 9, 2013, 1st edition.
28 Liu Zhongmin, *World Maritime Politics and Ocean Development Strategy of China*, Beijing: Current Affairs Press, 2010, pp.410–414; "Sea- power Issues and Post- cold-war Sino- US relations: Contradictory Perceptions and Difficult Options," *Foreign Affairs Review*, No.6, 2005, pp.55–60.
29 Zhang Wenmu, "Paradise Is Faraway, But China Is Nearby: A Study on Geopolitics between China and Its Neighboring Countries and Regions and the Law of their Interaction," *World Economics and Politics*, No.1, 2013, pp.16–21.
30 Ling Shengli, "A Strategic Analysis of Sino-U.S. Maritime Competition in the Asia Pacific Region," *Journal of Contemporary Asia-Pacific Studies*, No.2, 2015, pp.61–81.
31 Yang Zhen and Zhou Yunheng, "On the Contradiction of Sea Power between China and America," *Contemporary International Relations*, No.2, 2011, p.8; Hu Bo, "Peaceful Power Shift Between China and the U.S. on the Seas of East Asia: Risks, Opportunities and Strategies," *World Economics and Politics*, No.3, 2013, pp.31–32.
32 Wang Jisi, "China's Search for a Grand Strategy: A Rising Great Power Finds Its Way," *Foreign Affairs*, Vol.90, No.2, Mar/Apr 2011, pp.72–77.
33 Xin Qiang, "On the 'Duality' of Sea Power Game between China and the U.S.," *Conmilit*, No.6, 2016, pp.32–40.
34 Kimie Hara, *Cold War Frontiers in the Asia-Pacific: Divided Territories in the San Francisco System*, London and New York: Routledge, 2007, pp.146–153.
35 Bob Catley and Makmur Keliat, *Spratlys: the Dispute in the SCS*, Farnham: Ashgate Publishing Limited, 1997, p.112.
36 Zhang Xiaoming, "U.S. SCS Policy: Origin and Evolution," *American Studies Quarterly*, No.1, 2016, pp.34–51.
37 Bonnie S. Glaser, "Armed Clash in the SCS," Report of Council on Foreign Relations, April 2012.
38 Robert D. Kaplan, "The SCS Is the Future of Conflict," *Foreign Policy*, Sept/Oct 2011, Issue188, pp.1–8.
39 Bronson Percival, "America 'Returns' to Asia: The SCS," Conference on "The SCS: Cooperation for Regional Security and Development," Hanoi, Vietnam, November 3–5, 2011.
40 Lee Lai To, "China, the USA and the SCS Conflicts," *Security Dialogue*, Vol.34, No.1, March 2003, pp.25–39.

41 M. Taylor Fravel, American Policy Towards the Disputes in the SCS: 1995–2017, trans. Qi Hao, *Contemporary American Review*, No.1, 2017, pp.41–56.
42 Patrick M. Cronin & Robert D. Kaplan, "Cooperation from Strength: U.S. Strategy and the SCS," in Patrick M. Cronin, ed, *Cooperation from Strength: The United States, China and the SCS*, report of CNAS, Jan 2012, http://www.cnas.org/files/documents/publications/CNAS_CooperationFromStrength_Cronin_1.pdf
43 The representative comments and research is as follows: Michael Swaine, "Perceptions of an Assertive China," *China Leadership Monitor*, No.32, 2010; Andrew Small, "Dealing with a More Assertive China," *Forbes*, February 18, 2010; Thomas J. Christensen, "The Advantages of an Assertive China: Responding to Beijing's Abrasive Diplomacy," *Foreign Affairs*, Vol.90, No.2, March/April 2011, pp.54–67; Alastair Iain Johnston, "How New and Assertive is China's New Assertiveness?," *International Security*, Vol.37, No.4, Spring 2013, pp.7–48; Michael Yahuda, "China's New Assertiveness in the SCS," *Journal of Contemporary China*, Vol.22, No.81, May 2013, pp.446–459; Dingding Chen, Xiaoyu Pu, Alastair Iain Johnston, "Debating China's Assertiveness," *International Security*, Volume 38, Number 3, Winter 2013/2014, pp.176–183.
44 M. Taylor Fravel, "China's Strategy in the SCS," *Contemporary Southeast Asia*, Vol.33, No.3, 2011, pp.302–303; Michael D. Swaine, M. Taylor Fravel, "China's Assertive Behavior-Part Two: The Maritime Periphery," *China Leadership Monitor*, No. 35, Summer 2011, pp.16–17.
45 Alastair Iain Johnston, "How New and Assertive is China's New Assertiveness?" *International Security*, Vol.37, No.4, Spring 2013, pp.7–48.
46 Michael Green, Kathleen Hicks, Zack Cooper, John Schaus, Jake Douglas, "Countering Coercion in Maritime Asia: the Theory and Practice of Gray Zone Deterrence," Center for Strategic and International Studies (CSIS), May 2017.
47 Ben Dolven, Jennifer K. Elsea, Susan V. Lawrence, Ronald O'Rourke, Ian E. Rinehart, "Chinese Land Reclamation in the SCS: Implications and Policy Options," CRS report, June 18, 2015.
48 Ronald O'Rourke, "Maritime Territorial and Exclusive Economic Zone (EEZ) Disputes Involving China: Issues for Congress," CRS report, September 15, 2017.
49 Ronald O'Rourke, "China Naval Modernization: Implications for U.S. Navy Capabilities—Background and Issues for Congress," CRS report, September 18, 2017.
50 Carl Thayer, "Indirect Cost Imposition Strategies in the SCS: U.S. Leadership and ASEAN Centrality," Report of Center for A New American Security, April 24, 2015.
51 Joel Wuthnow, "Beyond Imposing Costs: Recalibrating U.S. Strategy in the SCS," *Asia Policy*, No.24, July 2017, pp.123–138.
52 "Update: China's Continuing Reclamation in the Paracels," Asia Maritime Transparency Initiative, Updated August 9, 2017, https://amti.csis.org/paracels-beijings-other-buildup/

53 Weston S. Konishi, "China's Maritime Challenge in the SCS: Options for US Responses," Report of the Chicago Council on Global Affairs, January 2018, p.2.
54 Robert S. Ross, "China's Naval Nationalism: Source, Prospects, and the U.S. Response," *International Security*, Vol. 34, No. 2, Fall 2009, pp.46–81.
55 Michael A. Glosny and Phillip C. Saunders, Robert S. Ross, "Debating China's Naval Nationalism," *International Security*, Vol. 35, No.2, Fall 2010, pp.161–175.
56 David R. Stilwell, "A More Active Neutrality: The Need for a Long Range U. S. Security Strategy in the SCS," Report of the U.S. Air University, 2000.
57 Robert D. Kaplan, *Asia's Cauldron: The SCS and the End of a Stable Pacific*, New York: Random House, 2014.
58 Evelyn Goh and Sheldon W. Simon, *China, the United States, and South-East Asia: Contending Perspectives on Politics, Security, and Economics*, New York: Routledge, 2008; Enrico Fels, Truong-Minh Vu, *Power Politics in Asia's Contested Waters: Territorial Disputes in the SCS*, New York: Springer, 2016; Michael Fabey, *Crashback: The Power Clash Between the U.S. and China in the Pacific*, New York: Scribner, 2017; Anders Corr, *Great Powers, Grand Strategies: The New Game in the SCS*, Maryland: Naval Institute Press, 2018; James C Hsiung, *The SCS Disputes and the US-China Contest: International Law and Geopolitics*, World Scientific Publishing, 2018; Huiyun Feng, Kai He, *US-China Competition and the SCS Disputes*, Routledge, 2018.
59 James M. Fones, *China, United States and Its Allies: How the United States and Its Allies are Losing the SCS*, CreateSpace Independent Publishing Platform, 2016.
60 Stefan Talmon and Bing Bing Jia, *The SCS Arbitration: A Chinese Perspective*, Oxford: Hart Publishing Ltd, 2014; Shicun Wu, Keyuan Zou, eds., *Arbitration Concerning the SCS: Philippines versus China*, New York: Ashgate Publishing, 2016; Fu-Kuo Liu and Jonathan Spangler, "SCS Lawfare: Legal Perspectives and International Responses to the Philippines v. China Arbitration Case," Report of SCS Think Tank/Taiwan Center for Security Studies, January 29, 2016; Fu-Kuo Liu, Keyuan Zou, Shicun Wu, and Jonathan Spangler, eds., "SCS Lawfare: Post-Arbitration Policy Options and Future Prospects," Report of SCS Think Tank/Taiwan Center for Security Studies, April 2017; S. Jayakumar, Tommy Koh, Robert Beckman, Tara Davenport, Hao Duy Phan, *The SCS Arbitration: The Legal Dimension*, Edward Elgar Pub, 2018; Alfredo Robles Jr., *The SCS Arbitration: Understanding the Awards and Debating with China*, Sussex Academic Press, 2019.
61 Fu-Kuo Liu and Jonathan Spangler, "SCS Lawfare: Legal Perspectives and International Responses to the Philippines v. China Arbitration Case," Report of SCS Think Tank/Taiwan Center for Security Studies, January 29, 2016.

1 Origins and Development of the SCS Issue

"The Philippine is not concerned about the islands since the islands are not in the territorial waters of the Philippines, hence the issue has nothing to do with the interests of the Philippines."

—American Philippines Government's statement on "Incident of Nine Islets" in 1933

"The Government of the Democratic Republic of Vietnam recognizes and agrees with the statement of the Government of the People's Republic of China on the declaration of the territorial sea on September 4th, 1958 and the Democratic Republic of Vietnam respects this decision."

—From the diplomatic note of Prime Minister of the Democratic Republic of Vietnam Phạm Văn Đồng to Chinese Prime Minister Zhou Enlai on September 14, 1958

The so-called SCS issue refers to disputes over the sovereignty and maritime rights of the islands, reefs, and adjacent waters in the SCS among China and neighboring countries around the SCS, including Vietnam, the Philippines, Malaysia, Brunei, and Indonesia. These disputes include the ownership of islands, the delimitation of the continental shelf and EEZ, and the exploitation of oil, gas resources, and fisheries, among which the core of the problem is the sovereignty of the Spratly Islands. In ancient times, the SCS was "a sea of peace, life and culture," on which the coastal residents lived a relatively calm life, engaging in exploitation activities, while communications between the East and the known West prospered. Since Western colonialism swept the world, with its attendant ocean partition and the blatant intervention of foreign Powers in domestic and regional affairs, the SCS has gradually changed from a natural geographical concept to an international issue involving politics, economy, military, law, history, geography, and many other fields, with maritime sovereignty as its core problem and island sovereignty, sea division, and resource allocation as its focus.[1]

Geostrategic Importance of the SCS

Geographical environment is an important perspective through which international issues can be observed, determining the position of a country or region in the world and its foreign strategic options. In this regard, Spykman, a well-known American geopolitical theorist, pointed out that geography "is the most fundamental conditioning factor in the formulation of national policy because it is the most permanent."[2] Patrick O'Sullivan, a British geopolitical scholar, also believed that "be they friendly or hostile, the strength of sympathetic and influential ties between the governments of nations is as much a matter of geographic distance as of political and cultural distance. Certainly in tracing both the causes and courses of wars, distance and space count for a lot at the grand strategic level."[3] Hans J. Morgenthau, an expert on political realism, once warned that the geographical location "remains a fundamental factor of permanent importance which the foreign policies of all nations must take into account, however different its bearing upon political decisions might be today from what it was in other periods of history."[4] Hence it can be seen that geographical environment is the key point to study a country or region. To analyze the strategic position of a country or region, the importance of its geographical environment cannot be ignored.

From a global perspective, those areas that play prominent roles or become the "hot spot" in international geopolitical strategy have one or all of the following characteristics. First, it is in a "geo-fragmented" zone, with complex topographic and geomorphological characteristics. This can particularly occur in areas with smaller developing countries, which can act as flashpoints in regional conflicts and political disputes that spiral out of control or provoke attention from larger powers.For example, the Balkans, known as "Europe's political powder barrel," was directly involved in two world wars. Second, it is an area rich in energy resources which are coveted by various Powers, such as the Caspian Sea and other oil-rich areas. Third, it is located near a transportation hub with key passageways, such as the Suez Canal and the Strait of Hormuz. The turbulent regions in West Asia and North Africa further enclose these two shipping routes, creating a long-term and fierce geopolitical competition, with external Powers occupying military bases to fulfill their national interests, such as those on Crete and in Turkey, leftovers of the Cold War and the Balkans Crisis.[5] Fourth, it has military value which is favorable to defenders and acts as a deterrent to other countries. The Balkans is an area that has much in common with the SCS, with its own U.S. military bases in Guam and Okinawa. Overall, the SCS meets all the requirements exhibited in the example of the Balkans.

First, from a geopolitical perspective, the SCS is a semi-enclosed sea[6] surrounded by China, the Philippines, Malaysia, Vietnam, Indonesia, and Brunei, with fragmented geographical characteristics. As a marginal sea in the west of the Pacific Ocean, the SCS appears to be a "rhombic basin" extending from northeast to southwest. Due to its location in the convergence zone of Eurasia, Indian Ocean, and Pacific Ocean, the geological structure and topography of the SCS is extremely complex.[7] More importantly, a series of island chains such as the Japanese Home islands, the Ryukyu Islands, the islands that make up the Philippines, and the Greater Sunda Islands are scattered from north to south in the Western Pacific Ocean. At the same time, the SCS is located in Southeast Asia, where the geographical structure is equally complex. There are numerous small- and medium-sized countries in the region, whose religious beliefs are inconsistent, political structure types are diverse, and economic development is uneven. Political turbulence and internal conflicts in some countries also take place from time to time. In addition, there are a large number of islands, reefs, and shoals in the SCS, surrounded by a number of stakeholders who have made claims after WWII. Among these parties, the countries situated on the rim, like China and Malaysia, as well as the archipelagic countries, like Indonesia and the Philippines, have made overlapping claims to sovereignty and defended their maritime rights and interests in the SCS. Through the above facts, it is not difficult to find that the SCS is located in the debris belt of East Asia, and its geographical environment is complicated and its topographic fragmentation is also evident.

Second, there are abundant resources in the SCS. As one of the four major marine oil and gas accumulation centers in the world, there are abundant oil and gas resources in its submarine strata. According to preliminary estimates, the total geological oil reserves in the SCS are approximately 23–30 billion tons, with an optimistic estimate of 55 billion tons and natural gas reserves of 20 trillion cubic meters, hence known as the "second Persian Gulf."[8] According to an assessment report on oil and gas resources in the SCS issued by the U.S. Energy Information Administration (EIA), energy potential in the SCS amounts to approximately 11 billion barrels of oil and 190 trillion cubic feet of natural gas in proved and probable reserves, believing that the SCS is a potential source of hydrocarbons, particularly natural gas.[9]

Third, the SCS has large reserves of exploitable resources. These include coastal mineral sand, manganese nodules, hydrothermal minerals, and other mineral resources, with 650 million tons of dissolved salt, 310 billion tons of magnesium, 17 billion tons of tin and copper, 2.9 billion tons of nickel and manganese, 500 million tons of silver, 8 million tons of gold, 6 billion tons of uranium, and 25 billion tons of heavy water.[10] What's more, it is predicted that the total reserves of combustible ice in the SCS will be 70 billion tons of oil equivalent.[11] Besides, there are all kinds of aquatic resources in the SCS, such as fish, shrimps, crabs, shellfish, algae, and thousands of others, with more than 2000 kinds of marine fish and more than 200 kinds of economically viable fish living on the bottom of its continental shelves. The annual fish production in the middle-upper reaches of the SCS is 1.4 tons per square kilometer, and in the deep sea area is 0.7 tons per square kilometer. If the maritime area in the SCS is 3.5 million square kilometers, the annual total output can reach 9.45 million tons, and the maximum sustainable catch is 4.72 million tons.[12] As the land-based resources are being exploited in an exhaustive manner every day, the strategic value of marine resources in the SCS becomes particularly significant.

Fourth, the SCS is also an important maritime route and holds significant strategic and political importance. It is known that China's seas are basically closed or semi-closed, which is a negative aspect when China wishes to make global connections via its connecting waterways. Compared with other maritime powers in the world, China's seas are significantly less open. Thus, in the outward looking Chinese perception, the maritime channels around China are precious golden waterways that connect China with the world.[13] As to the SCS, it connects China with three continents (Asia, Africa, and Oceania) and two oceans (the Pacific Ocean and the Indian Ocean), therefore, it is known as the strategic pivot of the sea. Furthermore, the SCS is constrained by the strategic throat of the Strait of Malacca. It was not only a gateway on the ancient maritime Silk Road, but also an important lifeline for modern Asia-Pacific countries to carry out maritime trade and transportation. Especially after the end of the Cold War, the SCS has become even more prominent as an international trade channel as trade contacts among Asia-Pacific countries have become increasingly frequent. It has become the maritime lifeline of the world's major trading powers/groups, such as the Middle East with China, Japan, ASEAN, and so on. Therefore, it is honored as the "third Golden Waterway in the world."[14]

At present, the SCS is one of the busiest waterways in the world. Each year, more than a quarter of the cargo ships and one-third of the seaborne trade in goods passes through the SCS. Nearly 70,000 merchant ships carrying more than $5.3 trillion worth of goods pass through the SCS. It is estimated that nearly 270 cargo ships pass through this area every day, and half of the world's super tankers, which carry a quarter of the world's oil and two-thirds of natural gas, must pass through this area, with the traffic volume three times that of the Suez Canal and five times that of the Panama Canal. For all countries in the world, especially the global economic powers and hegemonic powers like the United States, 80 % of the oil imports and transportation of large quantities of raw materials must go through the SCS, which highlights the extremely important commercial and strategic value of the SCS and its great significance to relevant countries.[15] José Almonte, a former national security adviser to the Philippines, has argued that whoever controls the sea will "ultimately control both archipelagic and peninsular Southeast Asia and play a decisive role in the future of the Western Pacific and the Indian Ocean -- together with the strategic sea lanes to and from the oil fields of the Middle East."[16]

In terms of the islands and reefs in the SCS, especially in the Spratly Islands, though the isolated reefs have limited military value and modern weapons and monitoring systems, such as nuclear submarines and satellites, greatly reduce the strategic significance of the islands concerned, still there is no reason to ignore the strategic position of the SCS. From a military strategic perspective, by occupying these islands and reefs, it is possible to monitor and disrupt the normal navigation of passing ships and aircraft, giving "direct or indirect control from the Strait of Malacca to Japan . . . even most of the sea routes from East Asia to West Asia, Africa and Europe."[17] In fact, during WWII, Japan built naval bases in the Paracel and Spratly Islands, and used them as springboards for large-scale attacks on the Indo-China Peninsula, the Philippines, Singapore, and Indonesia. During the Cold War, the United States and the Soviet Union also conducted military activities in and around the SCS, and both sides set up military bases, in Subic Bay in the Philippines and Kinan Bay in Vietnam, stationing large numbers of naval forces in them. The Spratly Islands and its surrounding waters have been closely monitored in the United States and the Soviet Union for a long time, making the SCS the forefront of the Cold War at that time. After the end of the Cold War, although the threat of the Soviet Union has been eliminated, the United States still adjusts and strengthens its military presence in Singapore, Thailand, and the Philippines in various ways to maintain its influence in the SCS. It can be seen that no matter how the world changes, the outstanding military strategic value of the SCS cannot be easily changed.

Origins and Evolution of the SCS Issue

The SCS issue has undergone a long-term development and evolution process. Historically, China had indisputable sovereignty over the SCS islands and adjacent waters, and was the first country to discover, name, develop, and manage the islands in the SCS and place them into an administrative territory.[18] As early as the Qin and Han Dynasties, the SCS was an important route for China to carry out large-scale ocean navigation and commerce and the main location for fishery production.[19] Since then, China had produced a large number of books and maps covering and recording the SCS in different historical periods. Moreover, the Chinese were the first to carry out economic activities in the SCS. Since the Song and Yuan Dynasties, there were relevant descriptions and records of the islands in the SCS. By the Qing Dynasty, the territory of the SCS has been clearly stated, and the islands in the SCS have been clearly recorded in the State, Provincial, and County annals, therefore compiled by successive Governments at all levels.[20] Although China is the first to have discovered, named, explored, and exploited the Spratly Islands and relevant waters, and the first to have exercised sovereignty and jurisdiction over them, history has not tipped the scales towards China. With decline in the middle and late Qing Dynasty, the gateway and borders of the SCS became outposts for foreign invaders to open the door to China on their terms, eventually leading to the islands in the SCS being claimed by Western colonialists.

Early Occupation of the SCS by Foreign Powers

Among those foreign powers, Britain was at the forefront of its invasion in the SCS. In order to facilitate navigation in the SCS and prepare for the future, the British ships conducted surveys on more than 30 occasions in the second half of 19th century, covering Pratas, the Paracel Islands, Macclesfield Bank, and the Spratly Islands.[21] In 1901, Chen Shoupeng compiled a book, "Xin yi zhong guo jiang hai xian yao tu zhi," which translated the parts in Volume III of the *China Sea Directory* compiled by the British Navy's Hydrographic Office in 1868 that detailed China's rivers and seas. The book records that Chinese fishermen have been engaged in fishery production and living the year round on Islands of the SCS and its surrounding waters. In the second picture of the first volume "from China's coastal areas and Yangtze River to the China seas and the South Seas islands," the Pratas Islands and Paracel Islands were clearly marked out.[22] In this period, the British also renamed islands and reefs in the SCS, while some islands were left with the original names that the Chinese fishermen had used long before Westerners had arrived in these waters.[23]

For the same purposes, Germany has also surveyed the Paracel and Spratly Islands on the SCS shipping route,[24] which was later discovered by the Qing government in 1883. The Qing government telegraphed the Governor-General of Kwangtung-Kwungsi (Liang Guang Zong Du) to figure out the situation, followed by negotiation and representations that caused Germany to cease their operations.[25] As another European power, France also coveted the islands and reefs in the SCS. After the end of the Sino-French war, France and China signed the "Convention Concerning the Delimitation of the Border between China and Tonkin (northern Vietnam)" and "Treaty on the Border Line of Kwangtung and Vietnam" in 1887 and 1890, respectively, which recognized that the Paracel and Spratly Islands belong to China, but still sought to establish a stronghold in Paracel Islands and nibble away China's territory. From 1898 to 1899, France twice made attempts to establish a Chinese and Vietnamese fishermen supply station and lighthouse in Paracel Islands, but they failed in the end.[26]

If the surveys of the SCS by Western Powers in the 19th century were a test run, then in the 20th century, with the deepening of Western infiltration and influence in Asia, the invasion would be even more intensified. By this point a rising power, Japan turned its attention to the SCS Islands soon after it occupied Taiwan. Since 1908, Japanese organized groups conducted illicit investigations of the Paracel and Spratly Islands, mining the phosphate resources on the islands without seeking permission first.[27] During this period, China's Government made continuous representations and Chinese people made strong protests by boycotting Japanese goods, merchants, and shipping. After the global economic crisis began, Japan had to withdraw from Paracel Islands in 1929. However, Japan's development of resources in the SCS area, added to national security aspects, aroused France's interest. In order to safeguard its geographical interests in Southeast Asia, France tried to prevent Japan's expansion in the SCS, on the one hand, and intensified its encroachment in the SCS, on the other hand, with the intention of turning it into its own sphere of influence.[28]

When Japan was invading Northeast China in 1931, France claimed that Annam (French protectorate in Vietnam) had a "prior right" over the Paracel Islands on December 4, 1931, and sent a note to the Chinese Embassy in France in 1933, and the government of the Republic of China (ROC) immediately filed a protest against France's Embassy.[29] On April 7–12, 1933, France sent warships to occupy nine small islets in the Spratly Islands, creating the "Incident of the Nine Islets,"[30] and announced on December 12 that these islets would be under the jurisdiction of Ba Ria Province, Vietnam.[31] The French move not only aroused strong protests from China's government and people from all walks of life, but also caused Japan's wariness. Japan also made the sovereignty claim over the Spratly Islands, rejecting French actions on the ground that the relics of the phosphate mine company of Japan on the islands means that they still have the intention to come back again, and claimed that the sovereignty of the islands should naturally belong to Japan.[32] The French side retorted that the Japanese consul had asked the Annamese government to mine phosphate ore on the island in 1930, which inferred Japan had long acquiesced in French sovereignty over the island. France also claimed that the occupation of the island was only for the installation of buoys to facilitate navigation and was not intended to construct a new military base.[33] Still, Britain was apprehensive that once France built military fortifications such as airbases and submarine berths on the occupied islands, sea lane control in the SCS would fall completely into the hands of France, thus causing the maritime traffic from Singapore to Hong Kong to be blocked by France at any time.[34] During the Anti-Japanese War, Japanese occupied the SCS Islands in 1938–1939. On April 9, 1939, Japan formally announced that the three islands, including the Spratly Islands, were renamed the Sinnan Islands (New South Islands) and were under the jurisdiction of the Governor of Taiwan.

The SCS Returned to China after WWII

During WWII, China, the United States, and Britain signed the *Cairo Declaration* on December 1, 1943. In accordance with its provisions that "the territory stolen by Japan from China, such as Manchuria, Taiwan and Penghu Islands, shall be restored to the Republic of China,"[35] and the requirements in the *Potsdam Proclamation* signed on July 26, 1945, that the terms of the *Cairo Declaration* shall be carried out,[36] China formally recovered Taiwan on October 25, 1945, and then officially recovered the Paracel and Spratly Islands. It can be said that

China's resumption of sovereignty over the islands in the SCS has a legal basis at this point. Following these acts, in March 1947, the government of the ROC published *Nan Hai Zhu Dao Wei Zhi Lue Tu* (Location Map of the SCS Islands) on which the dotted line is marked, that is, the "traditional maritime boundary line" or "eleven-dashed line" of the SCS.[37] In February 1948, the Chinese government officially published *Zhong Hua Min Guo Xing Zheng Qu Yu Tu* (Map of the Administrative Districts of the ROC) including *Nan Hai Zhu Dao Wei Zhi Tu* (Location Map of the SCS Islands), exhibiting China's sovereignty and jurisdiction over the SCS to the international community.[38]

In spite of the amount of resistance in the process of recovering the sovereignty of the SCS, the ROC government insisted on the diplomatic struggle and strove to defend China's maritime sovereignty rights and interests within the "eleven-dashed line."[39] After the founding of the PRC in 1949, *Nan Hai Zhu Dao Tu* (the Map of the SCS Islands) and the *Map of the PRC* published by the government also mark the intermittent boundary lines of the SCS. However, in 1953, the number of U-Shaped Lines in the SCS is reduced from 11 to 9, which is commonly known as the "nine-dashed line" of the SCS.[40] After that, the Chinese government issued the *Declaration of the Government of the PRC on the Territorial Sea*[41] and the *Law of the PRC on the Territorial Sea and Contiguous Zone* on September 4, 1958, and February 25, 1992, respectively, which further exhibited the legal status of the "nine-dashed line" in the SCS.

It is safe to say that before the 1950s, there was no so-called SCS issue since the neighboring countries did not ever question China's defensive measures or declaration of sovereignty over the SCS. For example, before its independence, the American Philippines Government made its position clear on the "nine islets" issue among China, Japan, and France in 1933, by stating "the Philippines is not concerned about the islands since the islands are not in the territorial waters of the Philippines, hence the issue has nothing to do with the interests of the Philippines."[42] Another example is that the Philippines government did not raise any objection when the government of the ROC drew a map of the Spratly Islands in November 1946, announcing the landmarks and names of islands as well as carrying out naval inspections, which is tantamount to acknowledging China's sovereignty over those islands.[43]

The SCS Issue Began to Rise in the 1950s

Since the 1950s, with the beginning of the Cold War and the changes in the internal political situation of some countries, the attitude of the countries concerned on the SCS began to undergo subtle changes. For example, after independence, the Philippines began to raise a dissenting voice on the sovereignty of the SCS, before making attempts to occupy the Spratly Islands under Cloma, which were disavowed at the time. On April 10, 1950, the Chairman of the Foreign Affairs Committee of the House of Representatives of the Philippines proposed that the Philippine government acquire the West and Southwest of Palawan Island. In May, after China's People's Liberation Army (PLA) entered Hainan Island, the Philippines media called on the Philippine government and the United States to send troops to occupy the Paracel and Spratly Islands to ensure Philippines' security.[44] On May 17, 1950, the then President of the Philippines, put forward the so-called proximity is sovereignty theory based on the "red threat," that is, the Philippines is closest to the Spratly Islands, thus according to international law, the archipelago should belong to Philippines.[45] Since then, the Philippines has also created the "Cloma incident,"[46] and fabricated the "trust territory,"[47]etc., which revealed its intention to muddy the waters before it attempted to occupy the islands and reefs in the SCS.

In the 1950s, Vietnam was split into two political entities: the Democratic Republic of Vietnam (North Vietnam) and the Republic of Vietnam (the Saigon regime of South Vietnam). Under the leadership of the Communist Party of Vietnam, North Vietnam respected and recognized China's sovereign, rights, and interests in the SCS.

For example, on June 15, 1956, North Vietnamese Deputy Minister of Foreign Affairs Ung Van Khiem reportedly informed Mr. Li Zhi-ming, Chargé d'Affaires ad Interim of the Chinese Embassy in Vietnam, that "according to Vietnamese data, the Paracel and Spratly Islands are historically part of Chinese territory."[48] Mr. Li Lu, Deputy Director of the Asia Division of the Vietnamese Foreign Ministry, who was present at the meeting, added that "judging from history, these islands were already part of China at the time of the Song Dynasty."[49] What is worth mentioning is that in his diplomatic note to Chinese Prime Minister Zhou Enlai on September 14, 1958, the Prime Minister of the Democratic Republic of Vietnam Pham Van Dong also unequivocally wrote that "the Government of the Democratic Republic of Vietnam recognizes and agrees with the statement of the government of the PRC on the decision of territorial sea on September 4th, 1958" and "the Democratic Republic of Vietnam respects this decision."[50]

In contrast, the Saigon regime of South Vietnam, on the pretext of inheriting the rights of French Indo-China, claimed to be a party to the SCS dispute and continued to fight with China for sovereignty over the Paracel and Spratly

Islands.[51] During the San Francisco Conference held in June 1951, which was held without the official presence of China due to the position of the U.S., the Prime Minister of South Vietnam, Tran Van Hu, issued a statement saying that " . . . as we must frankly profit from all the opportunities offered to us to stifle the germs of discord, we affirm our right to the Spratly and Paracel Islands, which have always belonged to Vietnam."[52] Neither the Chinese Mainland nor the Taiwan authorities attended the meeting, which resulted in an untimely rebuttal and resistance to the Vietnamese government's words and deeds. Moreover, the Saigon regime of South Vietnam sent troops to occupy the islands and plunder resources, beginning predatory exploitation of the resources on the islands, as well as driving China's fishermen away through intimidation, issuing statements, announcements, and setting up a county system to legitimize its appropriation of the Paracel Islands.[53] Although the claims made by the governments of Philippines and South Vietnam in the 1950s to the Spratly and Paracel Islands brought the SCS issue on the horizon, it did not develop into broad territorial disputes, and the SCS was still regarded as China's territory globally. For example, on the first ICAO Pacific regional flight conference held in Manila (capital of the Philippines) on October 27, 1955, the participating countries adopted a resolution demanding China Taiwan authorities to build a meteorological observatory in the Spratly Islands, and no country, including the Philippines and South Vietnam, raised any objections or voiced any reservations.[54] In addition, the 1958 *Haider Atlas*, published in the Federal Republic of Germany, specifically marked the Pratas Islands (Dongsha Islands) and the Paracel Islands (Xisha Islands) in German as Pratas, Paracel, and in Chinese transliteration as Tungsha Tao, Hsisha Chüntao, and clearly marked the Paracel Islands as Chinese territory.[55]

The SCS Issue Has Become Increasingly Prominent since the 1960s

In the 1960s and 1970s, the SCS issue became prominent, with two decisive factors highlighting the importance of the area. One is the discovery of oil and gas resources in the SCS and the other is the incubation and development of the new international law of the sea.[56] Since 1966, the Coordination Committee for Mineral Resources Exploration in the Offshore Area in Asia of the UN Economic and Social Council carried out preliminary exploration in some sea areas, including the SCS. In 1968, a multinational joint investigation team headed by Emery, an American biologist, explored the surrounding waters of China and published the famous "Emery Report" (fully known as the "Technical Report of the Coordination Committee for Mineral Resources Exploration in the Offshore

Areas in Asia"). The report holds that the continental shelf of the SCS, including the Vietnam coast and its adjacent waters, the eastern and southern part of the Spratly Islands, is likely to contain abundant oil resources.[57]

As soon as the Emery Report was published, it aroused widespread concern in the international community, and it became a widespread perception that the SCS is "another Persian Gulf." The surrounding countries in the SCS became more agitated, initiating a wave of seizing the islands or reefs and exploring oil or gas resources in the SCS. After the outbreak of the first oil crisis, the economic and strategic value of oil and gas resources in the SCS has been greatly highlighted. In order to obtain potential oil and gas resources, neighboring countries began to compete for the sovereignty and maritime rights and interests of the islands and reefs in the SCS.

In this period, the new international law of the sea provided a new impetus for all countries to expand their maritime rights and interests. Since the Third United Nations Conference on the Law of the Sea in December 1973, the international community went through 11 rounds of arduous negotiations, lasting for 10 years, and eventually passed the UNCLOS on April 30, 1982. According to the principles of the international law of the sea, a country's acquisition of a maritime territory means that it has an EEZ extending 200 nautical miles based on the outer edge of the territory.

As far as the SCS is concerned, it is surrounded by several countries and they are very close geographically, although only some are neighboring countries. As a result of the UNCLOS, if the EEZ is divided by 200 nautical miles, there will be overlapping areas, causing an additional area of dispute. Considering the numerous islands and reefs scattered in the SCS, the division of maritime rights and interests in the SCS will become even more complicated on the ground that these islands can be used as the basis for delimiting the EEZ. Although the UNCLOS also introduces a dispute settlement mechanism, its role in the settlement of maritime boundary disputes is quite limited since the mandatory provisions for disputes are powerless. In fact, the dispute settlement clause of the Convention has only part of judicial power in essence, which emphasizes flexibility rather than legal certainty. The Convention only recognizes the right of each coastal state to delimit the EEZ, but it does not provide a solution for any disputes arising from the EEZ, which would undoubtedly intensify the contention over islands among those countries, a factor that the Conference did not consider.[58]

In addition, the provisions of the UNCLOS on the continental shelf have loopholes. It defines the continent as "the whole natural extension of the land territory" and stipulates that "to a distance of 200 nautical miles from the baselines from which the breadth of the territorial sea is measured where the outer edge of the continental margin does not extend up to that distance." Since the coastal distance among the Southeast Asian countries around the SCS is within 400 nautical miles, the continental shelf division among the relevant countries will inevitably result in conflict according to this regulation.[59] Although the international law of the sea has "inherent deficiencies," since the 1970s and 1980s, the countries around the SCS have occupied the islands, reefs, and sea areas of the SCS on the basis of relevant provisions, such as dividing the continental shelf and EEZ, even occupying via military means.

After the end of the Cold War, as Southeast Asian countries made claims on the SCS, their occupation of islands and reefs in the SCS and the exploitation of marine resources constantly occurred, and the relationship between China and some Southeast Asian countries has become rather tense. So far, the SCS has become one of the only areas in the world where there are disputes over the sovereignty of islands and reefs, maritime jurisdiction, EEZ, and the delimitation of the outer continental shelf. Moreover, under the influence of traditional and non-traditional security factors, and under the interaction of forces inside and outside the region, the SCS has become one of the most dangerous areas in the world, and the SCS dispute has become one of the most difficult problems to resolve in the field of global ocean affairs.[60]

The Nature of the SCS Issue and the Status Quo of the Disputes

After the end of the Cold War, though the tension between the East and the West has been greatly reduced, the SCS issue, which is between China and some Southeast Asian countries, has not been fundamentally eased. In order to safeguard their vested interests in the SCS, some countries continue to strengthen their control over the occupied islands and reefs, speed up the exploitation of energy resources in the SCS, and try their best to find legal support for their encroachment.[61] In order to protect their immediate interests, some countries have even launched measures to internationalize and complicate the SCS issue. On the ground of regional security, certain countries have strengthened their security cooperation with foreign countries such as the United States and Japan, to achieve the purpose of checking and balancing China's rise. The SCS issue is far more than simple territorial sovereignty disputes between China and some

Southeast Asian countries; however, judging from the geopolitical importance of the SCS, the development of the SCS issue, and the orientation of the United States, Japan, India, and other foreign powers in recent years, there are many disputes about maritime rights and interests in the SCS.

Cao Yunhua, a Chinese scholar, divides the SCS issue into four levels: first, the issue of the SCS's waterway safety and free passage of international public goods; second, the demarcation dispute among China, Indonesia, and Brunei in EEZ; third, the dispute between China and Philippines on the Scarborough Shoal and its adjacent waters; and fourth, disputes over the sovereignty of the Spratly Islands and its adjacent waters.[62] In these classifications, the disputes focused on the Spratly Islands are undoubtedly the most complicated and difficult to resolve, and it also constitutes the core of the SCS issue. Based on the abovementioned division and the practical significance of the SCS dispute in the political, economic, and security fields, the nature of the SCS issue can be summed up in four dimensions: (a) the dispute over the sovereignty of islands and reefs, (b) maritime delimitation dispute, (c) competition for energy resources, and (d) waterway security and free passage. Among all, sovereignty is the core problem while oil and gas are the focus.[63]

At present, the disputed sea area in the SCS is 1.43 million square kilometers, and China's actual control area is less than 620,000 square kilometers.[64] From the perspective of the reef occupation, apart from the Chinese mainland's control of seven reefs, the Taiwan authorities control Itu Aba Island, which is the largest island in the Spratly Islands,[65] and the remaining 46 islands and reefs were all occupied by countries around the SCS in different periods.[66] Up to now, the many disputes in the SCS are a complex situation, with separation and confrontation among China, Vietnam, the Philippines, Malaysia, Indonesia, Brunei, and Taiwan. Among them, Vietnam, the Philippines, and Malaysia occupy most of the islands and reefs. Although Indonesia does not occupy the islands and reefs, there is a maritime delimitation disputes with China. Brunei also has maritime demarcation issues with China. At the same time, Brunei also claims sovereignty over some islands and reefs in the SCS, but has not sent troops to occupy them. Moreover, the abovementioned countries in the SCS dispute have exploited the oil and gas resources in the SCS to varying degrees, regardless of ongoing disputes.

Besides China, Vietnam is the only country that claims sovereignty over the Spratly and Paracel Islands and their surrounding waters. It is the only country claiming to have "historical evidence" that exhibits sovereignty of the islands and reefs. As mentioned above, before the reunification of Vietnam, the Democratic Republic of Vietnam (North Vietnam) once recognized China's sovereignty over the Spratly and Paracel Islands. The Saigon regime of South Vietnam attempted to inherit the rights of French Vietnam and vied with China for sovereignty over the Spratly and Paracel Islands. On February 14, 1974, the regime of Nguyễn Văn Thiệu in South Vietnam issued a white paper after defeat in the naval battle in the Paracel Islands, claiming that "they have enough historical evidence to justify Vietnam's sovereignty over Hoang Sa and Truong Sa,"[67] which are actually China's Paracel Islands (Xisha Islands) and Spratly Islands (Nansha Islands). In January 1975, *History and Geography*, a quarterly magazine in Saigon, also echoed the white paper by launching a special issue called "special examination of Hoang Sa and Truong Sa," with maps and photocopies attached, to prove its claim that Vietnam has been the "master" of the two island groups since ancient times.[68]

After unification in 1975, the New Socialist Republic of Vietnam began to break its implicit promises and infringe on the sovereignty of the islands and reefs in the SCS. For example, after the reunification of Vietnam, the North Vietnamese army not only took over some Spratly Islands and reefs previously controlled by South Vietnam, but also increased the number of troops stationed there, killing the South Vietnamese troops to do so.[69] By the end of the 1970s, Vietnam began to claim sovereignty over the Paracel and Spratly Islands. On August 7, 1979, Vietnam declared in a statement on Huangsha islands and Changsha islands that Vietnam was the first country in history to occupy, organize, control, and explore these islands, and it had a full historical and legal basis for its sovereignty over the two islands.[70] Since then, Vietnam has published two white papers, respectively, on September 28, 1979 and January 18, 1982, and claimed to have complete sovereignty over the Paracel and Spratly Islands. So far, Vietnam has occupied 29 islands and reefs, strengthened the construction of island and reef facilities, overexploited oil and fishery resources, planned a so-called local government and declared its sovereignty, becoming the largest entrenched interest in the SCS dispute.

The Philippines is also a dispute party among Southeast Asian countries, one whose occupation of the islands and reefs in the SCS comes second after Vietnam. It has privately referred to some of the islands in the Spratly Islands as "Kalayaan" in an attempt to separate them in international perspectives.[71] From 1970 to 1999, the Philippines successively occupied nine reefs in the Spratly Islands through five military operations that involved loss of life, including the second largest island, Thitu Island. At present, the Philippines has built several military bases, airport runways, lighthouses and radar stations, and strengthened actual control by sending troops and paid immigration on the occupied islands and reefs. Meanwhile, the Philippines has unilaterally promulgated some marine legislation documents and cited the concept of 200 nautical miles EEZ to include China's sea areas surrounding Scarborough Shoal and Spratly Islands in its EEZ. It can be said that the Philippines is second only to Vietnam in terms of the scope of claim and the degree of infringement on China's rights and interests in the Spratly Islands.[72]

Malaysia's occupation of some Spratly Islands follows a path of both occupying territory and exploiting resources. As early as 1968, the Malaysian government designated more than 80,000 square kilometers of sea area within the Spratly Islands as a mining area. By the end of 1979, the Malaysian continental shelf map also incorporated the southern area of the Spratly Islands into Malaysia's territory, such as Glasgow Shoal and North East Shoal. In 1995, Malaysia sent troops to occupy Investigator Shoal and Erica reef.[73] At present, Malaysia has occupied five islands and reefs in the SCS, and continues to take various measures to strengthen its control and management. It is worth noting that, as the second largest oil and gas producer and the third largest natural gas exporter in Southeast Asia, most of Malaysia's oil and gas resources come from the SCS, it is the largest exploiter of oil and gas resources in the Spratly Islands, and its output is far higher than that of Vietnam, the Philippines, and Brunei.[74] In addition, most of Malaysia's oil fields and drilling platforms in the SCS are located within China's nine-dashed line.

Indonesia and China have no direct dispute over the ownership of islands and reefs in the SCS, but in the Natuna islands, Indonesia has maritime delimitation disputes with China, Vietnam, and other countries. For a long time, Indonesia has been actively promoting the settlement of the SCS issue, and tried to gain a voice in the SCS issue by playing the role of "honest broker."[75] In order to achieve this goal, Indonesia has constantly expanded its naval construction in order to use force to backup its maritime interests. Moreover, it has actively used the ASEAN organization to unite with other Southeast Asian countries to put pressure on China, expecting that China would make concessions.[76] In recent years, with the SCS dispute heating up, Indonesia has attempted to act as a mediator and constantly emphasizes the importance and core position of the UNCLOS in solving the SCS issue.[77] For example, after Indonesia and the Philippines reached an agreement on the eastern side of the Sulawesi sea in 2014,

Indonesia's ambassador to the European Union, Oegroseno, wrote an article claiming that since the Philippines and Indonesia can no longer adhere to the demarcation line drawn 115 years ago, while solving problems in accordance with the Convention, China should accordingly seek sovereignty over the SCS based on international law, not on the historical nine-dashed line.[78] In 2015, the Center for Strategic and International Studies of Indonesia claimed in a long report that this act was a "model" for the peaceful settlement of maritime delimitation disputes and the maintenance of maritime security in East Asia.[79]

Since its national independence in 1984, Brunei has promulgated the system of 200 nautical miles EEZ through legislation,[80] and issued a new map showing the jurisdiction of the sea area. Meanwhile, Brunei claimed sovereignty over the Louisa Reef, which is in the south of the Spratly Islands, and clearly stated its sovereignty claims to the Foreign Ministry of China in 1987 and 1988. Unlike Vietnam and Malaysia, however, Brunei has no military presence on the relevant islands and reefs.[81] At present, Brunei occupies about 50,000 square kilometers in the Spratly Islands waters, which is 8.6 times of Brunei's domestic area, and two of Brunei's eight oil fields are within China's nine-dashed line.[82] As oil and gas resources are the pillar of Brunei's national economy, its output value accounts for 60 % of GDP, 97.8 % of export trade, and 90 % of national income.[83] Therefore, the essence of Brunei's rights and interests in the SCS is more embodied in safeguarding the development and utilization of marine oil and gas resources: On the one hand, efforts should be made to expand the exploitation and utilization of oil and gas resources to promote national economic growth. On the other hand, through cooperation with foreign enterprises, the interests of all countries are bound together, thus increasing their joint influence in the SCS.[84]

Overall, Vietnam, the Philippines, Malaysia, Indonesia, and Brunei constantly make claims to maritime rights and interests within China's "nine-dashed line" in the SCS, which in China's view violates her territorial sovereignty. These countries originally took advantage of China's weak naval forces, and fished in troubled waters during the confrontation between the two sides across the Taiwan Strait, stepping up efforts to occupy islands and reefs by sending troops, paid immigration, building runways and lighthouses, tourism development, and exploiting energy resources in their relevant maritime areas, all in attempts to create established facts by virtue of the "first come, first served" principle. For the assertions, relevant basis and the status quo of occupation in the SCS, please refer to Table 1.1.

Table 1.1. Status quo of occupation in the SCS and relevant basis of certain Southeast Asian countries

Parties to the dispute	Primary claim	Status quo of occupation	Basis
Vietnam	Sovereignty over the Spratly Islands, Paracel Islands, and related sea areas.	Currently occupying 29 islands and reefs: Southwest Cay (Apr.14,1975), Sand Cay (Apr.25, 1975.), Namyit Island (Apr.27,1975), Sin Cowe Island (Apr.27,1975), Spratly Island (Apr.29,1975), Amboyna Cay (Apr.29,1975), Sin Cowe East Island (Mar.23,1978), Central London Reef (Apr.2,1975), Pearson Reef (Apr.10,1987), Barque Canada Reef (Feb 1987), West London Reef (Dec.30,1987), Tennent Reef (Jan.26,1988), Ladd Reef (Feb.5,1988), Discover Reef (Feb.6,1988), East London Reef (Feb.19,1988), Alison Reef (Feb.27,1988), Cornwallis South Reef (Mar.2, 1988), Petley Reef (Mar.15,1988), South Reef (Mar.24,1988), Collins Reef (June.28,1988),	(1) Historical basis: relevant records of Vietnamese historical documents. (2) Provisions of the UNCLOS concerning the continental shelf and EEZ. (3) Sovereignty succession: Annan, French colonial government, and the Saigon government have sovereignty over the Spratly Islands and the Paracel Islands. Vietnam has the right to inherit relevant rights.
		Lansdowne Reef (June.28, 1988), Bombay Castle (June.30,1989), Prince of Wales Bank (June.30,1989), Vanguard Bank (July.5,1989), Prince Consort Bank (Nov.4,1990), Grainger Bank (Nov.3,1991), Renjun Tan (Nov.30,1993), Kingston Shoal (June 1998), Orleana Shoal (June 1998)	(4) Although the *Cairo Declaration* requires Japan to abandon China's territory, it does not mention the Spratly Islands. (5) Vietnam's sovereignty statement at the San Francisco Peace Treaty meeting was not opposed or reserved.

Table 1.1. *Continued*

Parties to the dispute	Primary claim	Status quo of occupation	Basis
The Philippines	Sovereignty over the so-called Karajan islands composed of 33 islands and reefs in the Spratly Islands and its sea area	Currently occupying nine islands and reefs: Nanshan Island (Sept.11, 1970), Flat Island (Sept. 1970), Thitu Island (May 9,1971), Loaita Island (July 14,1971), Northeast Cay (July 30,1971), West York Island (July 30,1971), Loaita Southwest Reef (Mar.4,1978), Commodore Reef (July 28,1980), Second Thomas Shoal (1999)	(1) "Trust territory": it is not explicitly stated that the Spratly Islands should be returned to China, and the islands are a "trust territory" according to the Peace Treaty with Japan on the San Francisco Conference in 1951. (2) In 1956, the Philippines discovered the "terra nullius" and took possession of it first.
			(3) Contiguity or proximity: the Spratly Islands is closer to the Philippines. (4) The provisions of the UNCLOS concerning the continental shelf and EEZ. (5) The needs of the Philippines' national security and economic lifeblood.
Malaysia	Sovereignty over 12 Spratly Islands and reefs and their sea areas within its continental shelf	Currently occupying five islands and reefs: Swallow Reef (Aug.20,1983), Ardasier Reef (Oct.9, 1986), Mariveles Reef (October 1986), Investigator Shoal (April 1999), Erica Reef (April 1999)	The provisions of the UNCLOS concerning the continental shelf and EEZ.

Continued

Table 1.1. *Continued*

Parties to the dispute	Primary claim	Status quo of occupation	Basis
Indonesia	No claim of sovereignty over islands and reefs, but the delimitation disputes over the exclusive marine economic zone with China	No invasion or occupation over the contested islands and reefs.	The provisions of the UNCLOS concerning the continental shelf and EEZ.
Brunei	Sovereignty over Louisa Reef and related sea areas	No troops were sent to occupy Louisa Reef.	The provisions of the UNCLOS concerning the continental shelf and EEZ.

Source: The table was drawn by the author according to relevant literature.

The Development Trend of the SCS Issue

It is known that the SCS issue is a complex dispute involving the territorial sovereignty and the division of maritime rights and interests among China and Southeast Asian countries. Although relations between China and Southeast Asian countries have become closer with the Declaration on the Conduct of Parties in the SCS in November 2002, and China's accession to the Treaty of Amity and Cooperation in Southeast Asia in 2003, it seems that the complexity of the issue has not been minimized, and the internationalization of the SCS dispute has not been fundamentally mitigated and tackled. Especially in recent years, with the implementation of the marine strategies of the countries around the SCS, they have made significant progress in promoting the construction of marine legislation, strengthening maritime law enforcement and marine jurisdiction. On this basis, strengthening their effective jurisdiction over the occupied territory of the SCS has become an important option for relevant countries to protect the rights and interests of the SCS. At the same time, since the turn of the century, the United States, Japan, India, Australia, and other extraterritorial forces have often intervened in the SCS dispute to safeguard their own interests and implement the "Asia-Pacific strategy," resulting in deterioration of the security environment in the SCS region. It can be said that the SCS issue has not been effectively alleviated under the joint influence of both internal and external factors. On the whole, the SCS issue in this new period presents the following trends.

New Changes Have Taken Place in the Dispute Pattern and Power Balance in the SCS Issue

In China's view, neighboring countries have wantonly occupied and trampled on China's territorial sovereignty, maritime rights and interests, regardless of historical facts and international law, constantly stirring up trouble in the SCS and creating the SCS issue. This dispute could have been settled through "one-to-one" bilateral negotiations between China and the countries in Southeast Asia, but with the deepening of ASEAN's internal integration and the changes of the SCS situation in recent years, Southeast Asian countries have gained an advantage through the political platform of ASEAN, which virtually increases their political chips in the contest that has been created with China, turning the situation from "one-to-one" to "many-to-one."

From a power balance perspective, there are three forces functioning in the SCS dispute. First, the single stance from the Chinese mainland; second, the group with ASEAN as its platform and Vietnam-Philippines-Malaysia playing a leading role; and third, the group headed by the United States, which includes Japan, Australia, and India. Among the three forces, the second has a political advantage and the third has distinct military advantages. Based on the common aim of fighting against China in a variety of arenas, the latter two forces have a tendency to unite, which is manifested in the following aspects: Southeast Asian countries welcome the United States, Japan, Australia, and other countries to intervene in SCS issues on various occasions and through various channels, such as inviting companies from those States to participate in the exploitation of oil and gas and fishery resources, and to provide political reasons for their intervention in the SCS issue. In addition, the foreign Powers are eager to hype the SCS issue in attempts to realize their strategic goals of containing China, which echoes the strategic and political attempts of Southeast Asian countries.[85] Needless to say, a new alliance led by the United States aimed at China can be formed, and will obviously put China in a disadvantaged position.

The SCS Issue Tends to Be Multilateral and Internationalized

The SCS was a front line during the Cold War, and the relevant countries experienced friction and even sporadic conflicts around issues of sovereignty, ownership, and resource development. However, the situation in the SCS was relatively calm and its influence on the international community was relatively limited. During this period, the SCS dispute was more of a regional issue.[86] Along with the intensification of geopolitical competition in the SCS after the Cold War, the SCS issue has become "multilateral" and "internationalized" under the influences of countries both in and outside the region. For example, Southeast Asian countries have actively welcomed foreign powers to intervene in the SCS issue in recent years, and have successively introduced more than 200 oil companies from the United States, the United Kingdom, Japan, Russia, Italy, and other countries for resource development in the SCS, in addition to putting forward proposals to internationalize the SCS issue, including submitting the SCS issue to the United Nations or international conferences, advocating "demilitarization" in the Spratly Islands and co-management by neighboring countries, even making efforts to rename the SCS.[87]

Additionally, in October 2010, Vietnam took advantage of its rotating presidency of ASEAN to actively promote the SCS issue to be included in the agenda of the ASEAN Summit for the first time.[88] In January 2013, the Philippines unilaterally submitted its SCS dispute between China and the Philippines to an international arbitration tribunal under UNCLOS, which revealed its political intent by promoting internationalization of the SCS issue and exerting pressure on China with the help of a third-party organization.[89] What is more noteworthy is that in the statement on maritime security adopted by the Foreign Ministers' meeting of the Group of Seven (G7) on April 15, 2015, the situation in the South and East China Sea's was involved for the first time.[90] On April 11, 2016, the statement on maritime issues made by the Foreign Ministers' meeting of the Group of Seven once again mentioned issues related to the East and SCS's, which aroused strong dissatisfaction from China.[91] Since the Trump administration came to power in 2017, the United States, together with Japan, Australia, and India, has been involved in the SCS issue more frequently. The abovementioned cases show that the SCS issue has gone beyond the "region" under the deliberate promotion of relevant countries inside and outside the region, and the trend of accelerating internationalization is quite obvious.

ASEAN Plays a Prominent Role in the SCS Issue

Speaking of the internationalization of the SCS issue, ASEAN's discussion on SCS issue and its "counter-leadership" are noteworthy. The SCS issue was originally a dispute between China and some Southeast Asian countries. However, the countries involved in the dispute are also members of ASEAN, which leads to the connection between China and ASEAN on the SCS issue. In recent years, two new phenomena have emerged around the three-dimensional relationship among the SCS, ASEAN, and China.

One is the ASEANization of the SCS issue. It means that the SCS issue is initiated or led by ASEAN (countries) and discussed on the platform of ASEAN meetings (occasion). The SCS issue was originally between some ASEAN Member States and China, while by ASEAN's participation, it now becomes an issue between ASEAN and China through the initiatives of a few States that wish to intensify an aura of conflict at the diplomatic and public perception levels. Overall, it has become one of the main tools used to deal with the SCS issue for ASEAN countries.[92] Another phenomenon is ASEAN assertion of counter-leadership over China, which influences or even decides China's behavior in the SCS, that is, as a relatively weak party, ASEAN gradually guides and influences China's attitudes and actions in the SCS with the strategy of "showing weakness" and "moderate obedience," so as to realize their specific political goals.[93] These two phenomena are similar in essence, effectively putting China in a passive position on the SCS issue, which should be highly valued by China.

The SCS Is Increasingly Militarized

In the face of an intensified competition for rights and interests in the SCS in recent years, neighboring countries have begun to vigorously implement a strategy of "seeking sea power with military force" to promote a transformation of military modernization, thus intensifying the arms race in the SCS and increasing the risk of a local conflict. According to the annual report of strategic assessment 2012, issued by the national defense policy research center of the Chinese Academy of Military Sciences on May 28, 2013, in recent years some countries making claims in Southeast Asia have increased their procurement of maritime combat weapons to reverse their domestic situations of backward equipment and weak combat capability. Among them, Vietnam bought two Gepard class frigates from Russia in 2011, and the six Kilo-class submarines were also ordered before 2016. The Philippines revised Modernizing the Philippines Armed Forces at the end of 2012 and plans to allocate $1.8 billion for defense procurement in the following five years. Currently, the Philippines is planning to purchase 10 patrol boats and several submarines from Japan.[94] In addition, according to construction plans, the number of submarines in the Asia-Pacific region will increase from 56 to 78 in the near future. It can be predicted that as countries in the Asia-Pacific region compete to develop submarines, China's surrounding waters will become "extremely crowded" and the situation is extremely complicated. The pressure of military preparation has never been as urgent as it is today.[95] As a result, the fierce arms race situation in the SCS will inevitably lead to the possibility and uncertainty of local armed conflicts.

From "Dispute over Claim" to "Dispute over Jurisdiction"

If the disputes among the parties to the overall dispute over the SCS mainly remained at the diplomatic level in the 1990s, then after entering the 21st century, countries began to take more specific actions, with the help of legal, economic, military, and other means to expand the actual space in the SCS, that is, from "dispute over claim" to "dispute over jurisdiction." In terms of law, some countries have enacted domestic legislation to increase their domestic legal claims in the SCS during recent years. For example, the "territorial sea baseline act" passed by the Philippines in 2009 and Vietnam's maritime law passed by Vietnam's parliament in 2012 have included certain islands, reefs, and sea areas in the SCS under the so-called jurisdiction of the country. In terms of economy, some countries have also significantly accelerated the pace of oil and gas resource exploitation in the SCS. For example, by means of independent development, cooperation with foreign oil companies and bids, Malaysia and Vietnam have been expanding their areas of oil and gas resources exploitation and intruding into China's traditional boundary line in the SCS in recent years.[96] It can be said that at present, the disputes in the SCS have changed from a simple diplomatic competition to an all-round contest in the fields of diplomacy, economy, law, and military, therefore, the contest for the relevant rights and interests has been complicated by different sides taking various concealed measures, which increases the difficulty for the dispute to be resolved peacefully.

Great Powers Outside the Region, Especially the United States, Have Significantly Stepped Up Intervention in the SCS

The superior geographical position of the SCS provides the coastal countries with the opportunity to become a maritime country, and in the meantime, the semi-enclosed sea and its complicated geographical locations and geomorphological characteristics result in a series of disputes among countries to exert influence and control over the maritime areas, including the United States, Japan, India, and other countries outside the region. These countries are extremely concerned with the transportation of industrial raw materials, the safety of free navigation, the exploration and development of oil and gas resources, and the change of regional power structure in the SCS. Therefore, they are highly sensitive to the development trend of the SCS issue, and even attempt to directly participate in the settlement of disputes since they have signed oil exploration and exploitation contracts with relevant countries in the region.[97]

Among all of the countries outside the region, the United States, as the world's maritime hegemony and long-term dominant country in the Asia-Pacific region, has the largest impact on the SCS issue. In fact, the United States has been a major player in the SCS both in post-WWII history and in practice.[98] Even though the United States claimed that it would not take a position on the sovereignty of the islands and reefs in the SCS, Washington has always been concerned about the unimpeded maritime activities in the SCS, stressed the freedom of navigation, and attempted to maintain the power balance in the region. In addition, many American oil companies have signed agreements with parties to the dispute, and the U.S. government has also signed defense contracts with some Southeast Asian countries, thus the United States believes that it has extensive commercial and security interests in the region.[99] With the shift of its strategic focus from the West to the East in the new century, the United States is bound to step up its interference in the SCS issue in an attempt to check and balance the rise of China.

Notes

1 Guo Yuan, *Geopolitical Study of the SCS,* Harbin: Heilongjiang University Press, 2007, pp.35–46.
2 Nicholas J. Spykman, "Geography and Foreign Policy," *American Political Science Review,* Vol.32, No.1, February 1938, p.29.
3 O'Sullivan, *Geopolitics,* New York: Routledge, 1986, p.1.
4 Hans Morgenthau, *Politics Among Nations: The Struggle for Power and Peace,* New York: Alfred A. Knopf, Inc., 1948, p.80.
5 Liu Feng, *SCS Development and National Security,* Beijing: Xue Xi Publishing House, Hainan Publishing House, 2013, p.7.
6 Enclosed and semi-enclosed sea means "a gulf, basin or sea surrounded by two or more States and connected to another sea or the ocean by a narrow outlet or consisting entirely or primarily of the territorial seas and exclusive economic zones of two or more coastal states." Based on this definition, the main closed or semi-closed seas in the world include the Black Sea, the Mediterranean Sea, the North Sea, the

Bering Sea, the Gulf of Mexico, the Baltic Sea, the Caribbean Sea, the Okhotsk Sea, the Gulf of Aden, the Sea of Japan, the Persian Gulf, the Andaman Sea, the Red Sea, the Celebes Sea, the East China Sea, and the SCS. Please refer to United Nations Convention on the Law of the Sea, Dec.10, 1982, 1833 U.N. T.S. 396.

7 Feng Wenke and Bao Caiwang, "Topographic and Geomorphological Characteristics of SCS," *Marine Geological Research*, No. 4, 1982, p.80.

8 "SCS is Rich in Oil and Gas Resources and Will Become a New Economic Growth Pole," *Hainan Daily*, July 9, 2012, p.A2.

9 U.S. Energy Information Agency, "SCS Region," February 7, 2013, available at: http://www.eia.gov/beta/international/analysis_includes/regions_of_interest/South_China_Sea/south_china_sea.pdf

10 Wu Yi et al., *Economic Impact Assessment of SCS*, Beijing: Economic Science Press, 2013, p.89.

11 Wu Yi et al., *Economic Impact Assessment of SCS*, Beijing: Economic Science Press, 2013, p.108.

12 Wu Yi et al., *Economic Impact Assessment of SCS*, Beijing: Economic Science Press, 2013, p.39.

13 Li Guoqiang, *Study of the SCS: History and Current Situation*, Harbin: Heilongjiang Education Press, 2003, p.90.

14 Guo Yuan, *Geopolitics and the SCS Dispute*, Beijing: China Social Sciences Publishing House, 2011, p.59.

15 Qi Kai, "The Cause of the SCS Dispute: Energy or Geopolitics?," Guangming.com, December 30, 2012, http://int.gmw.cn/2012-12/30/content_6194499_2.htm

16 Aileen S. P. Baviera, "Security Challenges of the Philippine Archipelago," *Southeast Asian Affairs*, 1998, p.226.

17 Wu Shicun, *The SCS Dispute: Origin and Development*, Beijing: China Economic Press, 2010, p.3.

18 Lin Jinzhi, "The History of China's Earliest Discovery, Management and Jurisdiction of the SCS Islands," edited by Lu Yiran, *The SCS Islands: Geography, History, Sovereignty,* Harbin: Heilongjiang Education Press, 2012, pp.55–84.

19 Shen Keqin. *A Review of the Disputes Over the Sovereignty of the SCS Islands.* Taipei: Taiwan Student Book Publishing House, 2009, pp.40–41.

20 Shen Wenzhou. China's Coastal Waters: *space and geography.* Beijing: China Ocean Press, 2006, p.152. For the research on the literature records of the SCS in ancient Chinese historical books, please refer to: Zheng Ziyue, *A Brief Geographic Record of the Islands in the SCS*, Beijing: Commercial Press, 1947; *Collection of the Islands of the SCS*, Taipei: Taiwan Student Book Publishing House, 1974; Chen Tianxi, *Compilation of the Cases of Pratas Islands and Paracel Islands*, Beijing: Commercial Press, 1982; Zeng Zhaoxuan, "A Preliminary Analysis of the Ancient Documents of the SCS Islands," *Collections of Essays On Chinese Historical Geography*, Vol. 1, 1991, pp.133–160; Li Jinming, Records of the SCS Territory in China's Historical

Writings, *China Borderland History and Geography Studies*, Vol. 3, 1996, pp 28–36; Han Zhenhua edit, *Compilation of Historical Materials of the SCS Islands*, Beijing: The Oriental Publishing House, 1988; Lin Jinzhi, "The History of China's Earliest Discovery, Management and Jurisdiction of the SCS Islands," edited by Lu Yiran, *The SCS Islands: Geography, History, Sovereignty*, Harbin: Heilongjiang Education Press, 2012, pp.55–84; Lin Jinzhi, "The Chinese people have a long history of the development of Paracel Islands and Spratly Islands," edited by Lu Yiran, *The SCS Islands: Geography, History, Sovereignty*, Harbin: Heilongjiang Education Press, 2012, pp.85–102; Lin Ronggui and Li Guoqiang, Comprehensive Study of the History and Geography of Spratly Islands, edited by Lu Yiran, *The SCS Islands: Geography, History, Sovereignty*, Harbin: Heilongjiang Education Press, 2012, pp.103–122; Li Jinming, *Research on the Territory of the SCS*, Harbin: Heilongjiang Education Press, 2014, chapter two, chapter three, and chapter four.

21 Han Zhenhua, ed., *Compilation of Historical Materials of SCS Islands*, Beijing: The Oriental Publishing House, 1988, pp.692–694.

22 *Atlas and records of the SCS Islands (foreign volume)*, edited by China Frontier Literature Research Center of the National Library of China, Beijing: National Library Press, 2016, pp.46–47.

23 Wu Shicun, *The SCS Dispute: Origin and Development*. Beijing: China Economic Press, 2010, pp.22–23.

24 Han Zhenhua, ed., *Compilation of Historical Materials of SCS Islands*, Beijing: The Oriental Publishing House, 1988, p.694; Philip Joseph, *Foreign Diplomacy in China, 1894–1900: A Study in Political and Economic Relations with China*, New York: Routledge, 2019, pp.191–193.

25 Han Zhenhua, ed., *Compilation of Historical Materials of SCS Islands*, Beijing: The Oriental Publishing House, 1988, p.143.

26 Han Zhenhua, ed., *Compilation of Historical Materials of SCS Islands*, Beijing: The Oriental Publishing House, 1988, p.637.

27 Han Zhenhua, ed., *Compilation of Historical Materials of SCS Islands*, Beijing: The Oriental Publishing House, 1988, pp.235–236.

28 Guo Yuan, *Geopolitics and the SCS Dispute*, Beijing: China Social Sciences Publishing House, 2011, p.88.

29 France claims to be in possession of the Paracel Islands for the following reasons: (1) Annan had built a monument on this island, and this fact was recorded in Annan's history. (2) In Chinese history, two British ships sank near the island due to collision with Chinese fishing boats. At that time, Britain protested to China. In the reply of the Qing government, Qizhou islands were not Chinese territory, so it was not responsible. The government of the Republic of China also sent a note to the Embassy in Paris to protest: (1) The longitude and latitude of the island belong to China's territorial waters, and the geographical situation is very obvious; (2) In history, Li Zhun was sent to the island at the end of the Qing Dynasty, firing guns and

raising the flag to reiterate that it was Chinese territory; (3) There was a call for the Far East Meteorological Association in Hong Kong. At that time, the director of the meteorological observatory in France and the director of the Xujiahui Observatory in Shanghai attended the meeting, at which the French side asked the Chinese government for a weather station in the Paracel Islands. See Zheng Ziyue, *Geography of the Islands in SCS*, Beijing: Commercial Press, 1947, pp.77–78.

30 The nine islands are: the Spratly Islands, Itu Aba Island, Thitu Island, Loaita Island, Amboyna Cay, Namyit Island, Lankiam Cay, Northeast Cay, and Southwest Cay. However, the existence of French and Japanese forces in the Spratly Islands is not long, which does not constitute the historical or legal basis of territorial ownership. See Guo Yuan, "The Spratly Islands Affairs and the Negotiations among China, France and Japan," *World History*, No. 3, 2015, pp.87–97.

31 Research and Design Committee of the Ministry of Foreign Affairs of the Republic of China (Taiwan), *Compilation of Archives of SCS Islands of Ministry of Foreign Affairs*, II (1), 1995, p.097.

32 Xu Gongsu, "The French Occupation of Nine Islets," *China's Frontier Issues*, Taiwan Student Book Publishing House, 1975, p.158.

33 Wu Shicun, *The SCS Dispute: Origin and Development*, Beijing: China Economic Press, 2010, p.28.

34 Xu Gongsu, "The French Occupation of Nine Islets," *China' Frontier Issues*, Taiwan Student Book Publishing House, 1975, p.160.

35 The U.S. Department of State Bulletin, Washington D.C. Office of Public Communication Bureau of Public Affairs, Vol. 9, No. 232, December 4, 1943, p.393.

36 World Affairs Press, ed., *International Treaties Collection (1945–1947)*, Beijing: World Affairs Press, 1959, p.78.

37 For a detailed study of the "intermittent line" in the SCS, please refer to Peter Kien-Hong Yu, "The Chinese (Broken) U-Shaped Line in the SCS: Points, Lines, and Zones," *Contemporary Southeast Asia*, Vol.25, No.3, 2003, pp.405–430; Malek, Melda, "A Legal Assessment of China's Historic Claims in the SCS," *Australian Journal of Maritime & Ocean Affairs*, Vol.5, Issue 1, March 2013, pp.28–36; Zou Keyuan, "The Chinese Traditional Maritime Boundary Line in the SCS and Its Legal Consequences for the Resolution of the Dispute over the Spratly Islands," *The International Journal of Marine and Coastal Law*, Vol.14, No.1, 1999, pp.27–55; Gau, Michael Sheng-Ti, "The U-Shaped Line and a Categorization of the Ocean Disputes in the SCS," *Ocean Development & International Law*, Vol.43, Issue1, Jan-Mar2012, pp.57–69; Miyoshi, Masahiro, "China's 'U-Shaped Line' Claim in the SCS: Any Validity Under International Law?" *Ocean Development & International Law*, Vol. 43 Issue 1, Jan-Mar2012, pp.1–17; Hossain, Kamrul, "The UNCLOS and the US-China Hegemonic Competition over the SCS," *Journal of East Asia & International Law*, Vol.6 Issue1, Spring 2013, pp.107–133; Keyuan, Zou, "China's U-Shaped Line in the SCS Revisited," *Ocean Development & International Law*, Vol. 43 Issue

1, Jan-Mar 2012, pp.18–34; Chung, Chris P. C., "Drawing the U-Shaped Line," *Modern China: An International Journal of History and Social Science*, Vol. 42 Issue 1, Jan 2016, pp.38–72; Mcdorman, Tedl, "The SCS: The U-Shaped Line, Islands and the Philippine-China Arbitration," *German Yearbook of International Law*, Vol.56, 2013, pp.33–62; Wang Zheng, "Chinese Discourse on the 'Nine-Dashed Line' Rights, Interests, and Nationalism," *Asian Survey*, Vol.55, Number 3, 2015, pp.502–524; United States Department of State, Bureau of Oceans and International Environmental and Scientific Affairs, *Limits in the Seas, China: Maritime Claims in the SCS*, Report No.143, December 5, 2014; M. Sheng-Ti Gau, "The U-Shaped Line and a Categorization of the Ocean Disputes in the SCS," *Ocean Development & International Law*, Vol.43, No.1, 2012, pp.57–69; K-H. Wang, "The ROC's Maritime Claims and Practices with Special Reference to the SCS," *Ocean Development & International Law*, Vol.41, 2010, pp.237–252; L. Jinming and L. Dexia, "The Dotted Line on the Chinese Map of the SCS: A Note," *Ocean Development & International Law*, Vol.34, 2003, pp.287–295. Guan Jianqiang, A Study on the Legal Status of the Nine-Dashed Line in the SCS, *International Review*, No. 4, 2012; Xu Zhiliang, Li Lixin, Pan Hong, Zhou Xin, Self-evident State Boundary Implication of "Nine-Dashed Line" in Historical Maps of China, *Pacific Journal*, No. 2, 2013; Zhang Lei, Rethinking the Ways to Solve the Dispute about Nine-dashed Line, *Pacific Journal*, No. 12, 2013; Jia Yu, The Historical Right in the SCS, *China Legal Science*, No.3, 2015; Jia Yu, On the Law Status of Duanxuxian (nine-segmented line) of SCS, *China's Borderland History and Geography Studies*, No.2, 2005; Li Jinming, The Chinese U-shaped Line in the SCS: Its Background and Effectiveness, *Southeast Asian Studies*, No.1, 2011; Jia Yu, The Jurisprudential Meaning of the Nine-Dashed Line in the SCS, *Social Science Front*, No.4,2015; Jin Yongming, Nature of the Dashed Line and Legal Status of Internal Water Areas in SCS, *China Legal Science*, No.6, 2012; Li Jinming, "The Legal Status of the U-shaped Line in the SCS: Historic Waters, Maritime Boundary or A Line of Islands Ownership?" *Southeast Asian Affairs*, No.4, 2010; Li Jinming, "An Overview of Reviews on the Legal Status of the U-shaped Line in the SCS," *Southeast Asian Affairs*, No.2, 2011; Li Jinming, "The U-Shaped Lines in the SCS: Background and Legal Status," *Contemporary International Relations*, No.9, 2012; Jia Yu, "International Law Theory of SCS Issues," *China Legal Science*, No.6, 2012; Huang Yao, Huang Jingwen, "A Commentary and Refutation of the US State Department's report on China's Dashed-Line in the SCS," *Chinese Review of International Law*, No.3, 2015; Zhang Jie, "The Perception Gap on the "U-Shaped Line" in the SCS and China's Strategic Choices," *The Journal of International Studies*, No.2, 2014; Sourabh Gupta and Leonardo Bernard, "Comments of Foreign Scholars on U. S. State Department Nine-Dashed Line Report," *Asia-Pacific Security and Maritime Affairs*, No,6,2015; Gao Zhiguo, Jia Bingbing, *The Nine Dash Line in the SCS: History, Status and Implications*, Beijing: China Ocean Press, 2014; Li Jinming, *Research on the SCS*, Harbin: Heilongjiang Education Press, 2014, pp.203–260; Chen Hongyu, *The Decision-making Process and Implications of the "Republic of China" Government's Drawing the Boundary Line of the SCS Islands, Bulletin of Academia Historica*, No. 47, 2016, pp.91-118; Li Woteng, *From Map Drawing to Artificial Islands Building: Centennial History of Disputes in the South China Sea*, Taipei: Wu-Nan Culture Enterprise, 2017, pp.706–740. *Atlas and Records of the SCS Islands (Modern volume)*, edited by China Frontier Literature Research Center of the National Library of China, Beijing: National Library Press, 2016, pp.184–185.

38 China Frontier Literature Research Center of the National Library of China, ed., *Atlas and Records of the SCS Islands (Modern Volume)*, Beijing: National Library Press, 2016, pp.184–185.

39 For example, China encountered gross interference and aggression from France when taking over the islands in the SCS. See Li Jinming, China's Government's Struggle to Safeguard the Sovereignty Over Paracel Islands and Spratly Islands Before and After the War of Resistance Against Japan, *China's Borderland History and Geography Studies*, No.3, 1998, pp.72–74.

40 The reason for the decrease in the number of U-Shaped Lines is to deal with the two lines in the Beibu Gulf between China and Vietnam. At that time, the relations between the two countries were close, and both advocated three nautical miles of territorial sea. Although the situation changed later, the nine-dashed line became the standard for China to publish maps since then. See Gao Zhiguo and Jia Bingbing, *The Nine Dash Line in the SCS: History, Status and Implications*, Beijing: China Ocean Press, 2014, p.11.

41 *Foreign Relations Documents of the People's Republic of China (Volume V)*, Beijing: World Affairs, 1959, pp.162–163.

42 Han Zhenhua, ed., *Compilation of Historical Materials of the SCS Islands*, Beijing: The Oriental Publishing House, 1988, p.264.

43 "The Origins of the Paracel and Spratly Islands Disputes," *People's Daily*, 5th edition, May 15, 1979.

44 Chen Hongyu, *The Territorial Sovereignty of Taiwan and its Neighboring Islands*, Taipei: Taiwan Student Book Publishing House, 2018, p.559.

45 *Foreign Relations Documents of the People's Republic of China (Volume IV)*, Beijing: World Affairs, 1958, p.61.

46 On May 11, 1956, Tomas A. Cloma, a Filipino, organized a private expedition to some islands and reefs of the Spratly Islands and unlawfully named them "Freedomland." Afterwards, the Philippine government did not stop Cloma's arbitrary violation of the sovereignty of other countries, but connived and acquiesced his actions and even expressed support for Cloma's activities. See Marwyn S. Samuels, *Contest for the SCS*, New York and London: Methuen, 1982, pp.81–86.

47 The Philippines claims that the San Francisco Peace Conference only stipulates that Japan renounces all right, title, and claim to the Spratly Islands and Paracel Islands,

but does not specify which country gains the right. Therefore, the Spratly Islands is considered to be "trust territory," which are under the trust of the victorious countries of the Second World War and should be jointly decided by these countries or the United Nations. See Fu Kuncheng, Sovereignty and Mineral Resources in the SCS: History and Law, Taipei: Youth Cultural Enterprise, 1981, p.85.

48 "The Origins of the Paracel and Spratly Islands Disputes," *People's Daily*, 5th edition, May 15, 1979.

49 Jianming Shen, International Law Rules and Historical Evidence Supporting China's Title to the SCS Islands, 21 H ASTINGS INT 'L & COMP . . . L. REV. 1–75 (1997–1998), p.54.

50 The Ministry of Foreign Affairs published a note by the former Vietnamese Prime Minister, which showed that the Paracel Islands belongs to China. people.cn, June 9, 2014, http://world.people.com.cn/n/2014/0609/c1002-25122321.html

51 Wu Shicun, *The SCS Dispute: Origin and Development*, Beijing: China Economic Press, 2010, p.81.

52 White Paper On the Hoang Sa (Paracel) & Truong Sa (Spratly) Islands, Republic of Vietnam, Ministry of Foreign Affairs, Saigon, 1974.

53 Guo Yuan, *Geopolitics and the SCS Dispute*, Beijing: China Social Sciences Publishing House, 2011, p.101.

54 SCS Islands in Foreign Records: Official Records, http://www.thesouthchinasea.org/2016-07/20/c_53282.htm

55 China Frontier Literature Research Center of the National Library of China, *Atlas and Records of the SCS Islands (Modern Volume)*, Beijing: National Library Press, 2016, pp.296–297.

56 Ju Hailong, *China's Maritime Power and Strategy*, Beijing: Current Affairs Press, 2009, p.262.

57 K. O. Emery et al., "Geological Structure and Some Water Characteristics of East China Sea and Yellow Sea," *UNECAFE/CCOP Technical Bulletin*, Vol. 2, 1969.

58 Bob Catley and Makmur Keliat, *Spratlys: The Dispute in the SCS*, England: Ashgate Publishing Limited, 1997, p.68.

59 Li Jinming, *Research on the SCS Territory*, Harbin: Heilongjiang Education Press, 2014, pp.175–176.

60 Ian Townsend-Gault, "Preventive Diplomacy and Proactivity in the SCS," *Contemporary Southeast Asia*, Vol.20, No.2, 1998, p.171

61 An Yingmin et al., *Security Strategy in the SCS and Marine Administration Strengthening*, Beijing: China Economic Press, 2011, p.7.

62 Cao Yunhua and Ju Hailong, ed., *SCS Situation Report (2012–2013)*, Beijing: Current Affairs Press, 2013, pp.15–16.

63 Li Guoqiang, *Prospecting and Developing SCS Oil and Gas Resources*, China International Studies, No.6, 2014, p.104.

64 Zhang Shiping, *China's Sea Power*, Beijing: People Daily Press, 2009, p.223.

65 It is also reported that the Fiery Cross Reef controlled by China mainland has replaced the Itu Aba Island controlled by the Taiwan authorities and become the largest island in the Spratly Islands after reclamation, but this information has not yet been confirmed by Chinese authorities. At the same time, it is also necessary to point out that the Fiery Cross Reef is an artificial island after expansion, and Itu Aba Island is still the largest natural island in the Spratly Islands.

66 Guo Yuan, *Geopolitics and the SCS Dispute*. Beijing: China Social Sciences Publishing House, 2011, p.141.

67 For the critical analysis of the white paper, see Chen Hongyu, "The Review of Vietnamese Official Historic Arguments on the Paracel and Spratly Islands," *Prospect and Exploration*, Vol.12, No.10, 2014, pp.42–75. In fact, the so-called Hoang Sa Islands and Truong Sa Islands recorded in historical and geographical documents of Vietnam are islands and beaches in the offshore waters of Vietnam. They have nothing to do with the Paracel Islands and the Spratly Islands. The Vietnamese Government after reunification is obviously obfuscating the history. For relevant research, please refer to Dai Kelai, Yu Xiangdong, "'Fu Bian Za Lu' and the so-called 'Huangsha' and 'Changsha' issues," *International Studies*, No. 3, 1989, pp.24–28.

68 See [Viet] Ruan Ya et al., *A Special Examination of Hoang Sa and Truong Sa*, trans. Dai Kelai. Beijing: Commercial Press, 1978.

69 Li Jinming, *SCS Waves: Southeast Asian Countries and the SCS Issue*, Nanchang: Jiangxi Universities and Colleges Press, 2005, p.45.

70 Wu Shicun, ed., *A Collection of Documents on the SCS Issue*, Haikou: Hainan Publishing House, 2001, p.211.

71 That is, in the "Cloma incident," the name of the so-called terra nullius. As a matter of fact, these "terra nullius" were not discovered by Cloma for the first time. Before that, there were Chinese fishermen living and producing on the islands, which were actually "islands of ownership." Australian scholars pointed out that it is totally inaccurate to say the Spratly Islands is "terra nullius." As long as the Philippines occupied some of the islands in the Spratly Islands, Chinese mainland, Taiwan, and Vietnam had already debated over the sovereignty of the islands. Taiwan and Vietnam had occupied part of the reefs in the Spratly Islands. Taiwan has also been stationed on the largest island since 1956. It means that the Philippines' claim of "terra nullius" obviously deviates from the principle of "terra nullius" recognized by international law. See Bob Catley and Makmur Keliat, *Spratlys: The Dispute in the SCS*, England: Ashgate Publishing Limited, 1997, pp.37–38.

72 Wu Shicun, *The SCS Dispute: Origin and Development*. Beijing: China Economic Press, 2010, p.118.

73 Wu Shicun, *The SCS Dispute: Origin and Development*. Beijing: China Economic Press, 2010, pp.143–147.

74 Li Guoqiang, "Prospecting and Developing SCS Oil and Gas Resources," *China International Studies*, No.6, 2014, p.107.

75 Chang Shu, "Evolution of Indonesia's SCS Policy," *International Data Information*, No. 10, 2011, pp.25–28.
76 Guo Yuan, *Geopolitics and SCS Dispute*, Beijing: China Social Sciences Publishing House, 2011, p.159–160.
77 Liu Chang, "Unsolved Delimitation of Indonesia's Maritime Boundaries: Current Situation, Characteristic and Outlook," *Southeast Asian Studies*, No.5, 2015, p.38.
78 Arif Havas Oegroseno, "How Indonesia and the Philippines Solved Their Maritime Dispute," *The Diplomat*, June 14, 2014, http://thediplomat.com/2014/06/how-indonesia-and-the-philippines-solved-their-maritime-dispute.
79 Rizal Sukma, Shafiah F. Muhibat, Lina A Alexandra, and Rocky Intan, "The Future of The Seas in East Asia: Toward a Comprehensive Maritime Cooperation," in Shafiah F. Muhibat and Audrey Stienon., *The Future Of The Seas In East Asia: Forging A Common Maritime Future For Asean And Japan*, Jakarta: Centre for Strategic and International Studies, Indonesia, 2015, p.19
80 Kent G, Valencia M J, *Marine Policy in Southeast Asia*, University of California Press, May, 1985, pp.171–173.
81 Gordner L G, The Spratly Islands Disputes and the Law of the Sea, 25 Ocean Dev. & Int's l L. 61, 1994, p.68.
82 Wu Shicun, *The SCS Dispute: Origin and Development*. Beijing: China Economic Press, 2010, pp.150–151.
83 "Many countries successively purchase Brunei crude oil and natural gas," published in Asia Pacific Daily, August 6, 2012 http://www.apdnews.com/business/economy/434.html
84 Wu Yan, "Brunei's SCS Policy," in Ju Hailong, ed., *The SCS Situation Report (2013–2014)*, Beijing: Current Affairs Press, 2015, p.332.
85 See Gong Jianhua, "The Causes, Current Situation and Internal Characteristics of the SCS Issue," *Theory and Reform*, No.2, 2010, p.145.
86 Wu Shicun, "Thinking on Challenges and Countermeasures of the SCS Issue," *Administration Reform*, No.7, 2012, pp.15–16.
87 Wu Shicun, *The SCS Dispute: Origin and Development*. Beijing: China Economic Press, 2010, pp.160–162.
88 Deng Yingwen, "On Vietnam's Measures to Internationalize the SCS Issue," *Southeast Asian Studies*, No.6, 2010, p.30.
89 Mao Junxiang, "Political and Legal Analysis of Philippines' Submission of SCS Dispute to International Arbitration," *Law Review*, No. 2, 2014, p.109.
90 Statement of G7 concerning the situation in the East China Sea and the SCS for the first time, People's Daily, April 17, 2015, http://world.people.com.cn/n/2015/0417/c157278-26862666.html
91 Official website of China's Ministry of Foreign Affairs: Foreign Ministry spokesman Lu Kang answers reporters' questions on the ocean issues made by the G7 foreign

ministers, April 12, 2016, http://www.fmprc.gov.cn/web/fyrbt_673021/t1354750.shtml

92 Zhang Mingliang, "ASEAN's Approaches for SCS Issue: Process, Background and Implications," *Southeast Asian Affairs*, No.1, 2016, p.2.

93 Nie Wenjuan, "How Does ASEAN Assert 'Counter-Leadership' over China in the SCS?" *Contemporary Asia-Pacific Studies*, No.4, 2013, pp.85–106.

94 China's military think tank: Countries around the SCS compete for arms to intensify the arms race, People's Daily, May 29, 2013, http://mil.news.sina.com.cn/2013-05-29/1747726299.html

95 Liu Kui and Li Yan, Submarine arms race is making China's surrounding waters "extremely crowded," published in China Youth Daily, June 19, 2015, 9th edition.

96 See Wu Shicun, "Thinking on Challenges and Countermeasures of the SCS Issue," *Administration Reform*, No.7, 2012, p.16.

97 Wu Shicun, *The SCS Dispute: Origin and Development*. Beijing: China Economic Press, 2010, p.162.

98 Zheng Zemin. *Great Powers in the SCS Issue*. Beijing: World Affairs Press, 2010, pp.30–104.

99 Jurgen Schwarz, Wilfried A. Herrmann, and Hanns-Frank Seller, ed., *Maritime Strategies in Asia*, trans. Ju Hailong and Wu Yan, Beijing: People's Publishing House, 2014, p.81.

2 The U.S. SCS Policy during the Cold War

"It is their purpose that Japan shall be stripped of all the islands in the Pacific which she has seized or occupied since the beginning of the First World War in 1914, and all the territories Japan has stolen from the Chinese, such as Manchuria, Formosa, and the Pescadores, shall be restored to the Republic of China."

—Cairo Declaration

"It should be made certain that there be no basis, either stated or implied, written into the Treaty which might provide for the possible legal claim of Communist China to sovereignty over Formosa, the Pescadores, Paracel, and Spratly Islands."

—Memorandum for the Secretary of Defense Marshall, June 26, 1951

After WWII, the Chinese National Government dispatched officials and warships to the Paracel and Spratly Islands to resume exercise of authority over islands in the SCS in November 1947. This was in accordance with the provisions in the *Cairo Declaration* and the *Potsdam Proclamation*—that Chinese territory occupied by Japan, including the islands in the SCS, should be returned to China.[1] The warships were provided by the United States under the wartime *Lend Lease Act*,[2] which indicated that the United States recognized China's recovery of the islands in the SCS at that time. Since then, official documents, such as *A Supplementary Key to Accompany the V.K. Ting Atlas of China* published by the Library of Congress Reference Department Division of Maps in 1949,[3] and the *Sailing Directions for the Western Shores of the China Sea from Singapore Strait to and Including Hong Kong* published by the U.S. Government Printing Office (GPO) in 1957,[4] all recognized the Paracel and Spratly islands in the SCS as China's territory, and adopted the names the Chinese government gave to those islands, reflecting American acquiescence to China's effective jurisdiction over the islands in the SCS.[5]

With the breakdown of cooperation between the U.S. and Soviet Union, the iron curtain between the communist East and the capitalist West was erected. During this period, the SCS became a front line as the United States sought to contain socialist China and compete with the Soviet Union for global hegemony, and the U.S. SCS policy was formulated, revolving around the Cold War per the Memorandum quoted above. In the early stage of the Cold War, the United States disregarded its prior stance on the SCS issue, developing instead an ambiguous strategy on the sovereignty issue to suit its anti-China and anti-communism stance. In the middle and late period of the Cold War, the United States took a "reluctant neutral" position on the SCS issue in order to unite with China as it strove to resist the Soviet Union's development.

American Connection with the SCS in the Early Times

Though geographically far apart, the earliest connection between the United States and the SCS can be traced back to the end of the 18th century. In August 1784, the American merchant ship "Empress of China" sailed through the SCS and arrived at Guangzhou port, opening a trade route to China, which is commonly recognized as the starting point of China-U.S. ties.[6] By 1786, American merchant ships sailed across vast oceans to the offshore of China and trade exchanges began to rise between China and the United States; however, early communications between the two countries were carried out by American businessmen for pure commercial interests, in which the SCS was only regarded as a shipping route.[7] In the 19th century, with the development of domestic capitalism after the Civil War, the United States developed a strong desire to seize overseas colonies, and began to follow in the colonial footsteps of Britain and France in the East. The first target of U.S. aggression in the East was Japan instead of Southeast Asia or the SCS. In July 1853, Matthew Calbraith Perry, commander of the American East India Squadron, "persuaded" Japan to open its market to outside markets due to its display of military power and forced it to sign the *Treaty of Kanegawa* in February 1854 and the *Japan-U.S. Treaty of Amity and Commerce* in July 1858, thus obtaining extraterritorial and other privileges.

Domestically crisis-ridden Japan awakened from its isolation and underwent tremendous transformations through the self-strengthening movement—Meiji Restoration—after which, Japan not only successfully realized its national rise to "equality" with Western states, and developed rapidly towards a militarized and industrialized nation, but also followed the steps of the Western powers, undertaking foreign aggression, and growing into a powerful competitor in East Asia in a short time. The United States had to prepare for the southward aggression targeting Taiwan, China. In 1867, the United States dispatched warships to invade Taiwan, the *Rover* Incident, but in the end nothing was achieved. After the Meiji Restoration, Japan and France made Taiwan their target of aggression. Eventually, Taiwan was ceded to Japan after the First Sino-Japanese War from 1894 to 1895. As a result, the United States had to move its aggressive target southward once again.[8]

It should be pointed out that the United States, like other Western powers, also dispatched vessels to conduct surveys on sea routes and hydrology in the SCS. For example, the U.S. survey ship David Scott intruded into the Owen Shoal of the Spratly Islands to conduct a survey in 1835, and the Vincennes research ship intruded into the central part of the Spratly Islands to conduct a survey in 1842.[9] Considering these activities were carried out for the safety of all navigators, it should be counted as public survey which is essentially different from the reconnaissance surveys conducted by American military aircraft and vessels in the SCS during and after the Cold War.[10] Nonetheless, frequent American surveys conducted in the SCS implied that the sea routes and navigation safety in the SCS had attracted certain attention at that time.

With the continuous southward movement of American colonial conquest, the Philippine islands became the next target. In 1898, the United States launched their first foreign imperialist war, Spanish-American War, which successfully replaced Spain in the Philippines, allowing the United States to gain its foothold in the Western Pacific for the first time. The United States and Spain signed the *1898 Treaty of Peace between the United States of America and the Kingdom of Spain* (the *Treaty of Paris*) and the *1900 Treaty between the United States of America and the Kingdom of Spain for Cession of Outlying Islands of the Philippines* (the *Treaty of Washington*). According to Article III of the *Treaty of Paris*, the island attribution line of the western Philippines extends along the line formed using the coordinates 4°45′North Latitude and 119°35′East Longitude to the north 7°40′North Latitude, and then to the west 118°East Longitude, and then to the north 20°North Latitude;[11] the Spratly Islands are not within the boundary line, therefore they do not belong to the Philippines according to the law of treaties. In accordance with the provisions of the treaty in 1900, Spain relinquished islands belonging to the Philippine Islands outside the area of Article III of the 1898 treaty. The Spratly Islands does not belong in the Philippines archipelago, nor were they included in the treaty of 1900.[12] These points can be determined from the actions of the United States while it was the colonial power; there were surveys made of islands in the Spratly's, but they were never recorded as part of the Philippines territory, nor were any attempts made to exploit them by Filipino fishermen or others.

The reason why the two treaties did not extend the territory of the Philippines to the SCS was that the strategic goal of the United States at that time was to occupy the Philippines and use it as a "springboard" for entering Asia, especially China, rather than targeting the SCS.[13] Therefore, the United States just took the SCS as high sea where it can transit through, without any concept of sovereignty over the islands in the South China Sea during this period. What's more, American ships could navigate freely and even enter the adjacent waters in the SCS when the Qing government was in turmoil at home and couldn't spare efforts to attend to these islands. In addition, the international law on territory, territorial sea sovereignty, and maritime rights and interests had not yet developed to a mature level when the contiguous zone, EEZ, and other concepts of international law of the sea had not been brought up at that time; there was no dispute or conflict in the SCS between China and the United States as the colonial power in the Philippines.[14]

By the early 1930s, the strategic value of the SCS had not been highlighted in U.S. foreign policy. In the *1930 Convention between His Majesty in Respect of the United Kingdom and the President of the United States regarding the Boundary between the State of North Borneo and the Philippine Archipelago*, the Spratly Islands was still not included in the territory of the Philippines, despite British licensed attempts to exploit them.[15] Moreover, the United States didn't support the Philippines in the Incident of Nine Islets. At that time, Kabelo de los Reyes, a former Philippine senator, believed that the nine small islets occupied by France should belong to the Philippines in accordance with the provisions of the *Treaty of Paris*. Therefore, he suggested that Frank Murphy, the then governor of the Philippines, should make efforts to make representations. The governor directly conveyed this proposal to Washington without any personal comments attached. But the suggestion was not adopted by Washington due to the lack of legal basis, as the nine islets were not within the territory of the Philippines delineated in the *Treaty of Paris*. Additionally, the influence of the Great Depression meant the United States had no time or intent to pay any form of attention to the question.[16] Besides, U.S. surveyors stationed on the Philippine Coast also confirmed that the island was located outside the territorial sea line stipulated in the *Paris Treaty*,[17] that is, it was not within the internationally recognized territory of the Philippines in any way.

For a long time before WWII, American interests in the SCS were quite limited. On the one hand, the scale of commercial trade between the United States and the countries surrounding the SCS was not large, and its proportion of the total foreign trade volume of the United States was not high. For the United States, the SCS was just a maritime channel for commercial use, whose strategic importance was not that crucial. On the other hand, the Philippines before independence was just a raw material–producing country, commodity market, and a rapidly increasing drain on U.S. finances. The United States paid more attention on how to expand to China through the "springboard" of the Philippines. Moreover, the main threat faced by the Philippines at that time came from Japan in the north, rather than Britain, France, or the Netherlands in the SCS to its west. Therefore, the SCS did not get any strategic attention from the United States and the Philippines until the outbreak of WWII.[18]

WW II and the Change of American Recognition towards the SCS

After the Marco Polo Bridge (Lukouchiao) Incident broke out on July 7, 1937, China entered a full-scale war with Japan that had been rumbling on since 1931. In order to apply a blockade of China, thereby restricting foreign military supplies shipped to China, Japan seized the Pratas Islands on September 3. On March 1, 1939, Japan dispatched troops to occupy the Paracel Islands; on March 30, Japan occupied the Spratly Islands. On April 9, Japan formally announced the occupation of the three archipelagos, including the Spratly Islands, and renamed them as the Sinnan Islands (New South Islands), which was placed under the jurisdiction of the governor of Taiwan. Japan also announced that the Sinnan Islands had been a land without owners since the ancient times, and it was first managed and developed by Japanese businessmen.[19] On May 17, 1939, the U.S. Secretary of State put forward three propositions to the Japanese occupation of the three islands: First, the United States believed that international disputes should be settled through international negotiations and arbitration; second, it was improper to regard a large range of islands and reefs as an archipelago; third, the jurisprudential basis of the Japanese government's claim to sovereignty was groundless. The actions of the Japanese government didn't have international validity. The United States didn't recognize the Japanese government's sovereignty over the Sinnan Islands.[20] It can be seen that the United States had made reservations and declared opposition to Japan's occupation of the islands in the SCS at that time.

Japan's occupation of islands in the SCS was to serve as an important base for pushing forward the "southward strategy" and as an "outpost for Japanese troops to invade Southeast Asia from Taiwan."[21] D. G. E. Hall, a British historian in Southeast Asia, pointed out that Formosa (Taiwan) is far away from Singapore's naval base. Once Japan occupied Hainan Island, the distance could be shortened to 1300 nautical miles, and the occupation of the Spratly Islands could be further shortened by 700 nautical miles.[22] Japan's occupation of islands in the SCS had two largely unexpected impacts. First, it revealed the importance of the Spratly Islands to Philippines' national security, which was one of the reasons why the Philippines made demands on the Spratly Islands soon after the end of WWII. Second, it inspired the United States to reexamine the strategic value of the SCS.[23] By occupying the islands, it was convenient to monitor ships sailing between Singapore and the Far East, which gave Japan a favorable position in the war. For this reason, the United States not only paid close attention to Japan's every move in the Far East, including the construction of military facilities,[24] but protested against Japan's unilateral invasion.[25]

During WWII, the strategic position of the SCS was further highlighted. On the one hand, Japan built military facilities on the islands and used them as military bases to enter Southeast Asia. On the other hand, Japan invaded Southeast Asia through the SCS. Especially in wartime, whoever controls the SCS will take the initiative in strategic material transportation, maritime traffic blockade, and merchant fleet protection. Therefore, the strategic value of shipping routes in the SCS during WWII was shown to be significant. With the outbreak of the Pacific War in 1941, the SCS also became an important area for the United States to fight against Japan. During the war, the U.S. military frequently destroyed the Japanese traffic lines in the SCS, launched submarine warfare against Japanese merchant ships, and attacked Japanese troops stationed on Itu Aba Island.[26] These military actions played an important role in the final defeat of the Japanese army, and it also brought into being a concrete connection between the United States and the SCS. The SCS shipping lines were no longer only of commercial significance, but also of immeasurable strategic value.

As WWII came to an end, the top priority for the Allied forces was to engage in dialogue and consultation for the proper handling of the postwar issues and the establishment of the postwar order, including how to deal with the Japanese occupation of Chinese territory. The Spratly and Paracel Islands, as part of the occupied territory, are also included in the territorial separation issue. As the outsized winner of WWII and the establisher of the postwar world order, the United States undoubtedly played a vital role in dealing with the sovereignty of the islands in the SCS. China, the United States, and the United Kingdom stipulated in the *Cairo Declaration* in December 1943 that "Japan shall be stripped of all the islands in the Pacific which she has seized or occupied since the beginning of the First World War in 1914, and all the territories Japan has stolen from the Chinese, such as Manchuria, Formosa, and the Pescadores, shall be restored to the Republic of China."[27] In accordance with the provisions, the Spratly and Paracel Islands and other islands in the SCS, which were occupied by Japan and were placed under the jurisdiction of Taiwan during WWII, should be restored to China.

The islands in the SCS are not specifically referred to in the declaration, but whether or not the treaty contains provisions on the SCS and no matter how these provisions are worded, there is no doubt that the islands in the SCS should be included in the returned Chinese territory, since they were Chinese territory in history and were illegally occupied by Japan during the war with China. Some countries hold that the *Cairo Declaration* does not specify the SCS, thus coming to the conclusion that the Paracel and Spratly Islands are lands of uncertain ownership after WWII, which is evidently groundless and untenable.[28] Whether the United States, the United Kingdom, and other countries deliberately undermined China's rights and interests in the process of dialogue and consultation, the simple and crude approach to resolving the postwar territorial issue undoubtedly brought adverse effects to China's handling of the SCS issue.

After Japan's surrender in 1945, its remaining troops successively withdrew from the SCS. The then Allied Supreme Commander Douglas Macarthur ordered all Japanese troops north of 16 degrees North Latitude to surrender to China, which meant that the territory in the north of the Paracel Islands in the SCS would be recovered by the ROC. Although Macarthur's command didn't refer to the Spratly Islands, the Japanese army stationed in the Spratly Islands, along with that of the Paracel Islands, followed these orders and surrendered to the Chinese troops stationed in Yulin, Hainan Island. After full preparations, the then national government troops recovered the SCS islands from October 1946 to February 1947, and established the Office of Administration in the Pratas

Islands, the Paracel Islands and the Spratly Islands, respectively. In 1946, the Kuomingtang government dispatched military officials and personnel to take over the islands in the SCS, utilizing warships which were provided by the United States on the basis of the *Lend Lease Act*, and officers and sailors who also received training from the United States, which indicated that the United States, to a certain extent, recognized and supported China's exercise of authority over the islands in the SCS at that time.[29] China's taking over the islands in the SCS not only conforms with international law, but also establishes China's actual jurisdiction over the SCS.

It is safe to say that WWII changed the U.S. recognition towards Southeast Asia and the SCS in some degree. During the war, Japan's military activities on the islands in the SCS posed a great threat, making the United States realize the high strategic value of the SCS and the wider Southeast Asia,[30] as is pointed out in the memorandum "American Far East Policy" issued by the U.S. Council on Foreign Relations in January 1941 that "The Philippine Islands, the Dutch East India and British Malaya are the main sources of important raw materials for the United States in peacetime and wartime. If these places are controlled by a potential hostile force, our freedom of movement will be greatly restricted."[31] Due to the ongoing reconstruction of regional order in the Far East after WWII and the readjustment of American East Asian policy, the position of the SCS in the U.S. foreign strategy was not clear-cut in the early postwar era.

Intentional Ambiguity over the Issues of Sovereignty in the SCS

The anti-fascist war victory did not bring a permanent peace. On the contrary, with the resulting rupture of the cooperation between the United States and the Soviet Union in wartime, the international community soon fell into a Cold War, based upon an ideological struggle. Under its containment strategy, the strategic focus of the United States and the Soviet Union was mainly in Europe. In Asia, it followed an "Island Chain Strategy" to avoid taking more responsibilities on the mainland. For example, MacArthur, the commander-in-chief of the U.S. Pacific Command, said in March 1949 that "our line of defense runs through the chain of islands fringing the coast of Asia. It starts from the Philippines and continues through the Ryukyu Archipelago, which includes its main bastion, Okinawa. Then it bends back through Japan and the Aleutian Island chain to Alaska."[32] On January 12, 1950, U.S. Secretary of State Acheson also pointed out that the

U.S. defense line in the Western Pacific Ocean started from the Aleutian Islands in the north, crossed the Japanese islands and Ryukyu Islands in the middle, and extended to the Philippines in the south.[33] It can be seen that in the early postwar period, not only did the Korean Peninsula not attract American attention in the Western Pacific defense line, but also the SCS in the west of the Philippines was not included in the American defense line.

The outbreak of the Korean War in June 1950 greatly changed the American view on the international situation in the Far East. In order to suppress the expansion of Communist forces in Asia and prevent the Korean peninsula from falling into the hands of the Soviet Union,[34] The United States not only actively intervened in the Korean War, and dispatched the Navy Seventh Fleet to the Taiwan Straits, it also signed the *Agreements on the Common Defense Assistance in Indo-China* with France and Indochina in December to provide necessary military assistance.[35] At the same time, the United States also came up with the "Domino Theory," reiterating the importance of Indochina's geographical location and its rich resources when it did so.[36] It indicated that the United States raised awareness to the importance of Indochina's status at this moment. With the deepening of U.S. involvement in Indochina issues, the strategic significance of the SCS, which is geographically close to this area, was becoming prominent. It was now placed within the American strategic defense line since any strategy implemented in Indochina cannot be achieved without transiting the SCS.[37]

In this context, with the requirement of an Asian anti-Communist strategy, the United States deliberately blurred prior sovereignty awareness over the islands in the SCS. For example, declassified archives show that in the process of drafting the *San Francisco Peace Treaty with Japan*, the U.S. Joint Chiefs of Staff (JCS) Chairman clearly instructed the Department of Defense (DoD) to ensure that the text of the *Peace Treaty* does not contain any content invoking Communist China's rights or sovereignty over the Paracel and Spratly Islands.[38] Since the United States had the intention of "preventing the SCS from falling in the hands of China (mainland)," the final provisions on the peace treaty only stipulate that Japan renounces all right, title, and claim to the Paracel and Spratly Islands, but does not clearly specify who has sovereignty over these islands.[39] Although the United States did not deny the sovereign rights of the Taiwan authorities to the two islands, it deliberately blurred the sovereignty of the islands in the SCS, which created the "undecided sovereignty" of the Paracel and Spratly Islands, and laid the framework for the sovereignty disputes to arise in the SCS.[40]

Meanwhile, the United States stepped up its formation of a strategic encirclement to deal with the expansion of communism in Asia. During this period, the United States signed a series of military and alliance agreements with relevant countries, including *Agreement on the Expansion of Military Bases Between the United States and the Philippines* in 1950, *U.S.-Thailand Joint Defense Assistance Agreement* in 1950, *Australia, New Zealand and the United States Pacific Security Treaty* in 1951, *Treaty of Mutual Cooperation and Security Between the United States and Japan* in 1951, etc. It is noteworthy that the United States also pushed Japan and Taiwan to conclude the so-called Japan-Taiwan Treaty in 1952 to make up for the Taiwan authorities not being invited to the San Francisco Peace Conference.[41] Through a series of treaties, the United States initially established a crescent-shaped strategic encirclement in Asia, creating a strategic frontier in the SCS.

These treaties, however, made those countries focus solely on bilateral relations with the United States and neglected the possibilities for multilateral cooperation among countries in the region.[42] Worse still, the 1954 Dien Bien Phu battle pushed the Indochina war to a climax and struck a heavy blow to U.S. intervention strategies.[43] Since then, the Geneva Conference aimed at discussing the peaceful resolution of the North Korean issue and the restoration of Indochina's peace was another major victory for the Communist Party,[44] which caused serious consequences, threatened America's security position in the Far East, and consolidated the strength of the Communist Party in the local area.[45] All of the signs showed that it was high time to adjust the U.S. Asian policy and to establish a collective security system against China in Southeast Asia.[46]

In order to put the military forces in Southeast Asia under the wing of the United States, after several months of negotiations, the *Southeast Asia Collective Defense Treaty* (also known as the *Manila Pact*) led by the United States was officially implemented on September 6, 1954. So far, the United States had established a defense line in Southeast Asia, which, together with the two defense lines already drawn in the Taiwan Strait and the Korean Peninsula, constituted three frontlines[47] or a "three-pronged rake"[48] to resist China's expanding influence. As used in the treaty, the "treaty area" is specified in Article VIII, which is the general area of Southeast Asia, including also the entire territories of the Asian parties, and the general area of the Southwest Pacific not including the Pacific area north of 21 degrees 30 minutes North Latitude.[49] It means that most of waters in the SCS, which is in the Pacific area south of 21 degrees 30 minutes North Latitude, is included in the treaty area. Meanwhile, the protocol attached designated the States of Cambodia and Laos and the Free Territory under the jurisdiction of the State of Vietnam as to which provisions are applicable. It indicated that the treaty was also applicable to the SCS, which was located in Indochina Peninsula and the Philippines.[50] Overall, the treaty demonstrated that although the SCS was not explicitly referred to in the *Southeast Asia Collective Defense Treaty*, it had actually been included in the treaty area, thereby becoming an important part of the American containment strategy in Asia.

With the support of the abovementioned bilateral and multilateral security treaties, the United States became increasingly involved in Indochina affairs. In May 1961, the Kennedy administration dispatched a special force to Vietnam, which was a prelude to direct participation in the Vietnam War. Meanwhile, the United States turned a blind eye to China's protests, and recklessly navigated freely in the SCS, and violated China's sovereignty through passage into her waters and territorial overflights, particularly with U-2 reconnaissance aircraft. It can be said that from the mid-1950s to the end of the 1960s, the SCS to some extent had become an externally positioned "Inner Lake" of the United States. The United States not only conducted military exercises, but also used the sea routes to transport military power to Vietnam, making the SCS a shortcut for military reconnaissance, provocative actions, and even invasion.[51] For example, in July 1954, a U.S. carrier-based aircraft fleet not only directly intruded into China's airspace and waters near Hainan Island, but also attacked two Polish merchant ships and Chinese frigates bound for Chinese ports.[52] Afterwards, it became common for U.S. military aircraft to invade the airspace over the SCS, sometimes even flying as low as 200 or 300 meters off the ground.[53] Throughout the 1960s, U.S. aircraft and U.S. Navy invaded China's airspace and territorial sea off the Paracel Islands more than 230 times.[54] Besides, in April 1965, Johnson defined the entire Vietnam and its adjacent waters as a "combat area" for the U.S. armed forces, and dispatched military forces to inspect incoming and outgoing ships.[55] It showed that the United States had taken the SCS as its front line to engage in the Vietnam War and contain China.

In addition to its acts in the SCS, the United States was also very sensitive to the actions of China (mainland), using its powerful military force to stop China (mainland) from recovering the islands in the SCS. As a contrast, for the activities of the Taiwan authorities, South Vietnam, the Philippines, and other allies in the SCS, the United States just sat out and played dumb.[56] When CPC forces landed on Robert Island in 1956,[57]the U.S. Department of State (DoS) immediately held an emergency meeting, and Secretary of State Dulles dispatched an aircraft reconnaissance to confirm the reports. It displayed that the United States attached a great importance to the event and was getting sensitive when learning that China (mainland) had the capability to go to the Paracel Islands. For the United States, such actions exemplified the "Communist expansion," which would directly threaten U.S. interests.[58]

In contrast, the United States made a passive response to the "Cloma Incident" during the same year, believing that China (the mainland) was obviously unable to advance to the Spratly Islands, and would not affect their strategic interests. Therefore, the United States did not care about the war of words among China (mainland) and American allies (the Philippines, South Vietnam, and Taiwan authorities). American strategic opinion was obviously unfavorable to China (mainland), and its containment policy had become the main factor in restraining China from taking effective action in this region, and it provided the Taiwan authorities, South Vietnam, and the Philippines with the opportunity to fill the political and legal vacuum left by Japan's defeat.[59] It can be concluded that the U.S. SCS policy in this period was mainly to contain the expansion of communism and met the need of its anti-Communist and anti-China policies. Its main task was to reject China's claim for sovereignty over the SCS and prevent relevant islands from falling into the hands of the Communist Party of China.

Reluctant Neutrality

In the 1970s, new changes had taken place in the international strategic situation, which were unfavorable to the United States. During this period, the military strength of the Soviet Union was greatly enhanced, and it took an offensive global posture. On the contrary, the United States not only encountered domestic economic stagflation and recession, but also suffered strong commercial competition internationally from Western Europe and Japan. Therefore, the struggle between the United States and the Soviet Union appeared to be a trend of "the Soviet Union attacking and the United States defending." In this context, the Nixon administration attempted to deal with the strategic pressure from the Soviet Union by making efforts at reconciliation between China and the United States. At the same time, the division within the Eastern bloc and the rising contradictions between China and the Soviet Union also made it possible to ease the tensions between China and the United States. Therefore, China was no longer the objective of American containment strategy in this period, but a partner of the United States against the Soviet Union. U.S. recognition of China changed from "the most dangerous enemy" in the past to a "quasi-ally."[60]

The foundation of China-U.S. relations was still fragile; however, from Nixon, Reagan to the Bush administration,[61] the United States regarded China as a partner in joint confrontation with the Soviet Union. From Nixon's visit to China in 1972 to the end of the 1980s, China-U.S. relations developed rapidly in the face of common challenges from the Soviet Union, making exchanges and cooperation not only in the field of economy and culture, but also in strategy and military affairs.[62] Due to the heavy casualties and high costs it was subjected to in the Vietnam War during this period, the United States had to sign the *Paris Agreement on Ending the War and Restoring Peace in Vietnam* on January 27, 1973, and soon withdrew all its troops from Indochina Peninsula, and thus the United States and South Vietnam alliance was just an empty title,[63] indicating that American domination in the SCS gradually declined.

After the United States withdrew from the Indochina Peninsula, it also lost an important bridgehead in the Southeast Asia. In contrast, with the unification of Vietnam and the formation of the Soviet Union-Vietnam alliance, the Soviet Union acquired the Cam Ranh Bay military base in Vietnam in the late 1970s, which formed a cross-sea confrontation with the U.S. military bases Subic Bay and Clark Airbase in the Philippines on the opposite side of the SCS. The strategic value of the Cam Ranh Bay military base may be limited in the bipolar confrontation, but it is of great significance in terms of regional conflicts, including the conflict over the sovereignty of islands in the SCS.[64] As some American strategists have said, the base would serve the Soviet Union's SCS and Indian Ocean Strategy, and help the Soviet Union break through the strategic and geopolitical encirclement established by the United States and its allies in the Western Pacific Ocean.[65] Furthermore, the base also greatly enhanced the Soviet Union's military offensive capability. In various senses, the threat in this region was increasing, and a strong response was needed.[66] Thus the SCS became an important field for the United States and the Soviet Union to compete for hegemony, and it also became a strategic frontier for the United States to resist the expansion of the Soviet Union. For example, a Soviet aircraft carrier fired a signal flare at an American warship on a tracking and reconnaissance mission in April 1984, which was a manifestation of the tense confrontation between the United States and the Soviet Union in the SCS.[67]

Due to its preference to China in the global hegemonic confrontation with the Soviet Union, the United States was less involved in the SCS dispute during this period, and basically held a position of "getting out of disputes and maintaining neutrality" to avoid irritating China on such sensitive issue as its sovereignty in the SCS.[68] In the battle of the Paracel Islands between China and South Vietnam in January 1974, although the United States retained a strong military presence in the SCS and the conflict area was within the control of the Seventh

Fleet of the United States, an American was captured by China in the conflict, and the United States still refused to take sides when South Vietnam had repeatedly asked the United States for help after their military failure.[69] Moreover, John F. King, U.S. DoS spokesman, also issued a statement on the battle, saying that the United States would not support any party and hoped that the two sides in the conflict would settle the dispute peacefully, but the United States had no intention of getting involved.[70]

The United States took the same position in the battle of the Spratly Islands between China and Vietnam.[71] On April 10, nearly a month after the battle, the then Assistant Secretary of State for Far East Affairs stated publicly that the United States would not support any party and was not going to help ease tensions.[72] On April 29, Ronald Hays, commander of the U.S. Pacific Fleet, also claimed that the conflict between China and Vietnam in the SCS was very serious, but U.S. warships did not intend to intervene, and hoped both sides could find a solution that will no longer result in bloodshed.[73] General Liu Huaqing, the father of the modern Chinese Navy, as a witness in the conflict, confirmed in his memoir that the United States showed a "cautious and detached attitude in the SCS conflict between China and Vietnam, hoping to solve the dispute peacefully."[74] Obviously, Vietnam, as an ally of the Soviet Union, became the objective of American containment strategy in the 1980s, thus the United States chose not to intervene in the China-Vietnam conflict or show support to the weaker side.

It is worth pointing out that in order to avoid unnecessary entanglements, the United States also took a selective self-restraint posture on certain issues related to the SCS. For example, U.S. policy was extremely astute on the issue of oil and gas resources development in the disputed areas of the SCS, and announced that it was not to participate in the exploitation activities of private enterprises in the disputed areas. From the middle to late 1970s, U.S. government still required domestic companies to take a hands-off approach, thereby not provoking China due to activity such as oil exploitation on the disputed continental shelf and the SCS. But in this period, six oil companies from the United States and Europe obtained contracts from China for geological surveys of the coastal areas of the SCS continental shelf. Vietnam protested against an exploration area to the west of China's Hainan Island, believing that the area belonged to its territorial waters, but Washington did not raise any objections to the contract.[75]

Similarly, the United States takes an ambiguous stance when it comes to the Spratly Islands issue in the *U.S.-Philippines Mutual Defense Treaty.* Since 1970, the Philippines began to dispatch troops to occupy some islands and reefs in the Spratly Islands, which caused strong protest from China. There are some divergences of views on whether or not the *Mutual Defense Treaty* is applicable to the Spratly Islands. Kissinger, the then Secretary of State, denied that the United States had volunteered to help the Philippines in the Spratly Islands, and suggested that the United States should not show its excessive support for the Philippines when the Philippines did not ask to counter against China. The United States made its decision in consideration of two factors: On the one hand, with the easing of tensions between China and the United States, the latter did not want to be involved in the China-Philippine dispute in the Spratly Islands. If the United States rashly took hasty action without figuring out China's intentions, it was bound to undermine the process of normalization China-US relations were undergoing. Additionally, under the influence of the Nixon Doctrine the United States urgently needed to carry out a strategic retrenchment in Asia instead of undertaking more defense obligations. For the United States at that time, it was more important than anything to avoid the risk of repeating the Vietnam War by supporting the Philippines' claim for sovereignty over the Spratly Islands and reefs.[76]

In 1976, the Philippines took advantage of the adjustment of U.S. military bases in the Philippines, demanding the United States to make a clear statement of responsibility for the *Mutual Defense Treaty Between USA and Philippines.* The Ford administration had also given ambiguous promises as to whether the treaty covers the Spratly Islands including Reed Tablemount, that is, if the treaty is applicable to Philippine aircraft and ships operating in Reed Tablemount on the premise that it obeys the rule of "peaceful settlement of disputes and restraint of the application of force" as stipulated in Article 1.[77] In the end, the United States made a difference between Philippines' land security and disputed island waters. The Spratly Islands as a "disputed" area was excluded from the treaty, and Philippines also publicly stated that it would not implicate the United States in the disputed waters of the SCS.[78]

Since then, in response to Vietnam's invasion of Cambodia and the signing of the military alliance treaty with the Soviet Union in 1978, the United States and the Philippines reinforced their defense ties and enhanced Article V in the treaty in January 1979; however, the United States specifically added that the treaty was to be "consistent with international law" in the provisions. In Article V, it stipulated that "an armed attack on either of the Parties is deemed to include an armed attack on the metropolitan territory of either of the Parties, or on the island territories under its jurisdiction in the Pacific or on its armed forces, public vessels or aircraft in the Pacific," whilst the boundary of the Pacific region is not clearly defined in the treaty. Although there is room for the United States to stand with the Philippines to intervene in the SCS dispute, it is certain that the United States has always been reluctant to give a clear and supportive commitment to the Philippines' territorial claims in the Spratly Islands.[79]

It should be pointed out that U.S. policy during this period made the situation in the SCS develop in favor of China, but the friendliness was only temporary. It was only a strategic option of the United States in face of the full-scale expansion of the Soviet Union at that time, and did not mean that the United States recognized or even supported China's position on the SCS issue.[80] In fact, during the Cold War, the U.S. position on the SCS issue followed a basic principle that the SCS sovereignty dispute could not deviate from the global strategic layout of the United States, and it should keep in alignment with and contribute to this strategic layout. The global strategic goal of the United States during the Cold War was to contain the expansion of Communist forces led by the Soviet Union. Therefore, the attitude and position of the U.S. to many specific international issues, including the SCS issue, was be subject to the strategic competition between the United States and the Soviet Union to a great extent, fluctuating and changing accordingly. In other words, the United States publicly or secretly supported or acquiesced in any move that was conducive to resisting the Soviet Union on the SCS issue.[81]

However, it does not mean that the United States itself will stop its aggression against China in the SCS. As a matter of fact, the United States has never completely ceased a series of secret reconnaissance activities against China in the SCS. In April 1989, an American spy plane crashed in the SCS. Although the United States refused to disclose the specific mission and the specific country the aircraft was targeting, it can be inferred that the target country must be China judging from the flight route along the coastal area of South China.[82] It is safe to say that against the background of "strategic triangle" among China, the United States, and the Soviet Union, the United States had to moderate its behaviors on the SCS issue, and maintained a "neutral" position in the armed conflicts and sovereignty disputes regarding the SCS for the strategic requirement of "uniting with China and resisting the Soviet Union." But these moderate behaviors didn't reflect its actual strategic intentions. In fact, the United States never wanted China to exercise sovereignty over the SCS. In this regard, the so-called neutral attitude held by the United States during this period was a kind of "reluctant neutrality" in reality.

Notes

1 Han Zhenhua, ed., *Compilation of Historical Materials of the SCS Islands*, Beijing: The Oriental Publishing House, 1988, pp.180–181.
2 Zhang Mingliang, *America's Involvement in the SCS: Process, Drives, and Implications,* Hong Kong: Hong Kong Press for Social Sciences LTD., 2011, pp.79–82.
3 L. W. Wadsworth, *A Supplementary Key to Accompany the V.K. Ting Atlas of China* (edition of 1934), Washington, the Library of Congress Reference Department Division of Maps, 1949, p.19.
4 United States Hydrographic Office, *Sailing Directions for the Western Shores of the China Sea from Singapore Strait to and Including Hong Kong*, Washington: United States Government Printing Office, 1957, p.77.
5 Hui Ming, "Retracing the Sovereignty of the SCS Islands Through Modern American Documents," *Journal of Chinese Humanities*, No.4, 2016, pp.17–22.
6 For the records of the "Empress of China" sailing to China and the early trade between China and the United States, please refer to John W. Swift, P. Hodgkinson, Samuel W. Woodhouse, "The Voyage of the Empress of China," *The Pennsylvania Magazine of History and Biography*, Vol.63, No.1, Jan. 1939; Smith, Philip Chadwick Foster, *The Empress of China*, Philadelphia, Pa.: Philadelphia Maritime Museum, 1984; Philip Chadwick Foster Smith, *The Empress of China*, translated by International News Department and Law Office of Guangzhou Daily, Guangzhou: Guangzhou Publishing House, 2007; Chang Jiu and Shi Lujia, ed. *Two Hundred Years of Sino-US Relations*. Beijing: Xinhua Publishing House, 1984, p.3; Qi Wenying, " On the Issue of the 'Empress of China'," edited by the editorial board of the series of books on the history of Sino-US Relations, *A Collection of Essays on the History of Sino-US Relations (Volume I)*, Chongqing: Chongqing Press, 1985; Qi Wenying, "A Preliminary Analysis of the Reasons for the Success of the First Voyage of the 'Empress of China'," edited by the editorial board of the series on the history of Sino-US Relations, *Essays on the History of Sino-US Relations (Volume II)*, Chongqing: Chongqing press, 1988; Li Dingyi, *Early Sino-American Diplomatic History*. Beijing: Peking University Press, 1997, pp.1–13.
7 Zheng Zemin, *Great Powers in the SCS Issue*, Beijing: World Affairs Press, 2010, p.32.
8 Zheng Zemin, *Great Powers in the SCS Issue*, Beijing: World Affairs Press, 2010, pp.32–33.
9 Han Zhenhua, ed., *Compilation of Historical Materials of the SCS Islands*, Beijing: The Oriental Publishing House, 1988, pp.691–692.
10 Zhang Mingliang, *America's Involvement in the SCS: Process, Drives, and Implications,* Hong Kong: Hong Kong Press for Social Sciences LTD., 2011, pp.56–57.
11 See article III, *Treaty of Peace between the United States of America and the Kingdom of Spain (Treaty of Paris)*, signed in Paris, December 10, 1898.

12 Han Zhenhua, ed., *Compilation of Historical Materials of the SCS Islands*, Beijing: The Oriental Publishing House, 1988, pp.524–525.
13 In the second year of its occupation of Philippines, the United States put forward the "open door" policy for great powers' division of China, which achieved great success. It demonstrated the American strategic focus was in Chinese mainland, not the SCS.
14 Zheng Zemin, *Great Powers in the SCS Issue*, Beijing: World Affairs Press, 2010, p.34.
15 Policy Research Office of the State Oceanic Administration, *A Collection of International Maritime Delimitation Treaties*, Beijing: Ocean Press, 1989, p.301.
16 Zhang Mingliang, *America's Involvement in the SCS: Process, Drives, and Implications.* Hong Kong: Hong Kong Press for Social Sciences LTD., 2011, pp.64–65.
17 "Nine Islets Are Included into French Territory," *Shun Pao*, August 23, 1933.
18 Zhang Mingliang, *America's Involvement in the SCS: Process, Drives, and Implications.* Hong Kong: Hong Kong Press for Social Sciences LTD., 2011, p.65.
19 Tatsuo Urano, *International Conflict over the SCS: the History, Analysis and Documents*, Tokyo: Tosui Shobo Publishers, 1997, pp.330–336.
20 Tatsuo Urano, *International Conflict over the SCS: the History, Analysis and Documents*, Tokyo: Tosui Shobo Publishers, 1997, pp.345–346.
21 Chen Xinzhi, "ROC-PRC Relations and the SCS Dispute," *Issues and Studies*, Vol. 38, No. 7, July 1999, pp.23–41.
22 D. G. E. Hall, *A History of Southeast Asia*, translated by Institute of Southeast Asian History of Sun Yat-Sen University, Beijing: Commercial Press, 1982, pp.920–921.
23 Wang Chuanjian, "American Policy in the SCS: History and Reality," *Foreign Affairs Review*, No. 6, 2009, pp.89–90.
24 The U. S. Department of State, *Foreign Relations of the United States Diplomatic Papers*, 1939, The Far East, Vol.III, pp.113–116.
25 Stein Tonnesson, "The History of the Dispute," in Timo Kivimaki, ed., *War or Peace in the SCS*, Copenhagen: NIAS Press, 2002, p.10.
26 Zhang Mingliang, *America's Involvement in the SCS: Process, Drives, and Implications.* Hong Kong: Hong Kong Press for Social Sciences LTD., 2011, pp.75–79.
27 Press Communiqué Regarding Conference of President Roosevelt, Generalissimo Chiang Kai-Shek, and Minister Churchill at Cairo, *FRUS*, 1943, China, pp.176–177.
28 For example, in order to support its claim for sovereignty, Vietnam has made different interpretations on whether the Cairo Declaration involves the two islands. See Zhang Mingliang, *America's Involvement in the SCS: Process, Drives, and Implications.* Hong Kong: Hong Kong Press for Social Sciences LTD., 2011, pp.73–75.
29 Zhang Mingliang, *America's Involvement in the SCS: Process, Drives, and Implications.* Hong Kong: Hong Kong Press for Social Sciences LTD., 2011, pp.79–82.
30 Guo Yuan, "U.S. Policy on the SCS and Its Impact in the Early Cold War," *Pacific Journal*, No.7, 2012, p.36.

31 Laurence H. Shoup and William Minter, *Imperial Brain Trust: The Council Foreign Relations and United States Foreign Policy,* translated by Yi Li and Wei Liang et al., Shanghai: Shanghai Translation Publishing House, 1981, p.126.

32 Henry Alfred Kissinger, *Diplomacy,* New York: Simon & Schuster, 1994, p.475.

33 Acheson, "Crisis in Asia: An Examination of U.S. Policy," *The Department of State Bulletin*, January 23, 1950, p.116.

34 Yonosuke Nagai and Akira Iriye, *The Origins of the Cold War in Asia*, New York: Columbia University Press, 1977, p.281.

35 *International treaties* (1950–1952), Beijing: World Affairs Press, 1959, p.735.

36 Dwight D. Eisenhower, *The White House Years: Mandate for Change (1953–1956)*, New York: Doubleday & Company, Inc., 1963, pp.332–333; *Public Papers of the Presidents of the United States: Dwight D. Eisenhower, 1954,* Washington: Government Printing Office, 1960, pp.382–384, 387–388.

37 Zhang Mingliang, *America's Involvement in the SCS: Process, Drives, and Implications.* Hong Kong: Hong Kong Press for Social Sciences LTD., 2011, p.126.

38 "The Secretary of Defense (Marshall) to the Secretary of state," Washington, June 28, 1951, *FRUS*, 1951, Asia and the Pacific, Vol.VI, Part 1, Washington, D. C: United States Government Printing Office, 1977, p.1157.

39 V. K. Wellington Koo, *V. K. Wellington Koo papers,* translated by Institute of Modern History of Chinese Academy of Social Sciences, Vol.9, Beijing: Zhonghua Book Company, 1989, p.693; Kimie Hara, "The San Francisco Peace Treaty and Frontier Problems in The Regional Order in East Asia, A Sixty Year Perspective," *The Asia-Pacific Journal*, Vol.10, Issue 17, No.1, April 23, 2012, p.4.

40 For scholars who hold this view, please refer to Zhang Mingliang, *America's Involvement in the SCS: Process, Drives, and Implications.* Hong Kong: Hong Kong Press for Social Sciences LTD., 2011, pp.102–103; Li Jinming, "The Chinese U-shaped Line in the SCS:Its Background and Effectiveness," *Southeast Asian Studies*, No.1, 2011, p.41; Guo Yonghu, "Historical Investigation on the U. S. Policy to Sino-Philippine Nansha Islands Disputes--Interpretation based on the U. S. Recent Declassified Diplomatic Files," *Contemporary China History Studies*, No.2, 2013, p.107. However, some scholars believe that the Peace Treaty with Japan of 1951 only stipulated Japan's relinquishment of the Paracel Islands and Spratly Islands, but did not stipulate the sovereignty of these islands, mainly because: (1) the United States believed that there were disputes over the sovereignty of these islands between China and France, and it was difficult to define these disputes; (2) there are serious differences between the United States and Britain on the issue of the peace conference and the peace treaty with Japan, which constrains the choice of the United States; (3) the United States did not realize the strategic and economic value of the islands in the SCS. Therefore, preventing these islands from falling into the hands of new China is not the main reason for the ambiguous words in the treaty. The Peace Treaty with Japan is not the "root" or "curse" of the SCS dispute. It is inappropriate to exaggerate

the negative impact of the relevant provisions of the Peace Treaty with Japan. See He Weibao, "New Arguments on the Arrangement of the Xisha (Paracel) and Nansha (Spratly) Islands in the Treaty of Peace with Japan and its Impact," *The Chinese Journal of American Studies*, No.4, 2014, pp.68–89. The book holds the view that "the fuzzy attitude of the United States is intentional and has led to the subsequent sovereignty disputes."

41 Rao Geping, "A Legal Perspective on 'the Uncertain Status of Taiwan'," in Zi Zhongyun and He Di, ed., *Forty Years of US-Taiwan Relations: 1949–1989*, Beijing: People's Publishing House, 1991, pp.78–107.

42 Guo Yuan, "U.S. Policy on the SCS and Its Impact in the Early Cold War," *Pacific Journal*, No.7, 2012, p.38.

43 R.H. Fifield, *Southeast Asia in American Policy,* translated by Qun Li, Beijing: World Affairs Press, 1965, p.19.

44 Coral Bell, *Survey of International Affairs 1954,* translated by Yunting et al., Shanghai: Shanghai Translation Publishing House, 1984, p.92.

45 *FRUS*, 1952–1954, Vol.12, Washington, D. C: United States Government Printing Office, 1984, pp.696–709.

46 Robert J. Mcmahon, *The Limits of Empire: The USA and the Southeast Asia since the World WarII*, New York: Columbia University Press, 1999, p.64.

47 Wang Jisi, "US China Policy From 1945 to 1955 and its Consequences," *The Chinese Journal of American Studies*, No.1, 1987, pp.44–45.

48 In 1953, Dulles declared that the United States was implementing the "three-pronged seizure of the dragon" strategy in Asia, that is, one prong emerging from Korea, another from Taiwan, and the third from India, to jointly contain Red China. See Maxwell D. Taylor, *Swords and Plowshares*, New York: Da Capo Press, 1972, p.137.

49 *Southeast Asia Collective Defense Treaty (Manila Pact),* September 8, 1954, Article VIII.

50 Zhang Mingliang, *America's Involvement in the SCS: Process, Drives, and Implications.* Hong Kong: Hong Kong Press for Social Sciences LTD., 2011, pp.129–130.

51 Zheng Zemin, *Great Powers in the SCS Issue*, Beijing: World Affairs Press, 2010, pp.39–41.

52 World Affairs Press, ed., A Collection of Materials on Sino-US Relations (Part 2), Beijing: World Affairs Press, 1960, pp.1927–1930.

53 "The 100th Warning to US imperialism that the Chinese people cannot be bullied, US aggression must be liquidated," *People's Daily,* May 27, 1960, edition 1.

54 Han Zhenhua, ed., *Compilation of Historical Materials of the SCS Islands*, Beijing: The Oriental Publishing House, 1988, p.484.

55 "Vietnamese government warns against American banditry acts in Vietnam and its adjacent waters, also condemns its barefaced provocations of war," *People's Daily*, May 10, 1965, edition 1.

56 Chi-Kin Lo, *China's Policy towards Territorial Disputes: The Case of the SCS Islands*, London and New York: Routledge, 1989, pp.32–33.
57 On June 10, 1956, South Vietnamese soldiers manning a meteorological station in Coral Island of the Paracel Islands sent a message to the Ministry of Foreign Affairs of South Vietnam, saying the Chinese army had already reached Robert Island, and everyone was in danger, demanding immediate withdrawal. The U.S. embassy in Saigon immediately reported the news to the DoS, which led to an "emergency response" from the U.S. side. However, it turned out to be false intelligence. See Zhang Mingliang, "The United States and Robert Island Affairs," *Southeast Asian Studies*, No.2, 2005, pp.60–64.
58 Zhang Mingliang, *America's Involvement in the SCS: Process, Drives, and Implications*. Hong Kong: Hong Kong Press for Social Sciences LTD., 2011, pp.158–159.
59 Marwyn S. Samuels, *Contest for the SCS*, New York and London: Methuen, 1982, pp.92–93.
60 Wang Jisi, "The 'Strategic Triangle' in US Policy Towards China," *The Chinese Journal of American Studies*, Vol.6, No.2, p.9.
61 Harry Harding, *A Fragile Relationship: The United States and China Since 1972*, Washington D.C.: The Brookings Institution, 1992.
62 Jia Qingguo, "New Understanding of China-US Relations," *The Chinese Journal of American Studies,* No.1, 1995, p.43.
63 For the changes of the alliance between the United States and South Vietnam in this period, see Shao Xiao: "Looking at the US–South Vietnam Alliance in the Nixon Administration from the Signing of the Paris Agreement," *History Research and Teaching*, 2010, No. 1, pp.99–104.
64 Bob Catley and Makmur Keliat, *Spratlys: The Dispute in the SCS*, England: Ashgate Publishing Limited, 1997, p.114.
65 The Views of Admiral Ronald Hay and David Winterfold in Susumu Awanohara, "Crusading Navigator," *Far Eastern Economic Review*, June 18, 1987, pp.34–35.
66 Interview with Caspar Weinberger, "View from Pentagon," *Far Eastern Economic Review*, June 20, 1985, p.46.
67 "The Soviet aircraft carrier fired signal flares hitting the US frigate in the SCS," *People's Daily*, April 6, 1984, edition 6.
68 Ang Cheng Guan, "The SCS Dispute Re-visited," *Australian Journal of International Affairs*, Vol.54, No.2, 2000, p.203; Wang Chuanjian, "American Policy in the SCS: History and Reality," *Foreign Affairs Review*, No. 6, 2009, p.94.
69 Shao Xiao, "The Battle of the Paracel Islands and Nixon's Policy in the SCS," *Southeast Asian Studies*, Issue 3, 2012, pp.25–30.
70 "U.S. Says It Is not involved," *The New York Times*, January 20, 1974, L.10.
71 Lee Lai To, "China, the USA and the SCS Conflicts," *Security Dialogue*, Vol.34, No.1, March 2003, p.28.

72 Liu Liandi and Wang Dawei, *The Track of Sino-US Relations: An Overview of Major Events Since the Establishment of Diplomatic Relations*, Beijing: Current Affairs Press, 1995, p.246.
73 Guo Ming, ed., *The Evolution of Sino-Vietnam Relations in the Past 40 Years*, Nanning: Guangxi People's Publishing House, 1992, p.199.
74 Liu Huaqing, *Memoirs of Liu Huaqing*, Beijing: Chinese People's Liberation Army Publishing House, 2004, p.541.
75 Wu Shicun, *The SCS Dispute: Origin and Development*, Beijing: China Economic Press, 2010, p.164.
76 Guo Yonghu, "Historical Investigation on the U. S. Policy to Sino-Philippine Nansha Islands Disputes-- Interpretation based on the U. S. Recent Declassified Diplomatic Files," *Contemporary China History Studies*, Issue 2, 2013, pp.105–107.
77 Guo Yonghu, "Historical Investigation on the U. S. Policy to Sino-Philippine Nansha Islands Disputes-- Interpretation based on the U. S. Recent Declassified Diplomatic Files," *Contemporary China History Studies*, Issue 2, 2013, pp.107–108.
78 FRUS, 1969–1976, Volume E-12, Documents on East and Southeast Asia, 1973–1976, Document 354 [DB]
79 Mark J. Valencia, "The Spratly Islands: Dangerous ground in the SCS," *The Pacific Review*, Vol.1, Issue 4, 1988, pp.438–443.
80 Wang Chuanjian, "The SCSs and Sino-U.S. Relations," *Contemporary Asia-Pacific Studies*, Issue 2, 2014, p.6.
81 Zheng Zemin, *Great Powers in the SCS Issue*, Beijing: World Affairs Press, 2010, p.44.
82 Zheng Zemin, *Great Powers in the SCS Issue*, Beijing: World Affairs Press, 2010, p.43.

3

The U.S. Policy Adjustment on the SCS after the Cold War

"The territorial sea and the contiguous zone of the People's Republic of China promulgated by China may lead to the escalation of sovereignty disputes over the Spratly Islands. It seems that it is out of place for China to pass this law at this time."
—U.S. Assistant Defense Secretary James Roderick Lilley, March 1992

"Maintaining freedom of navigation is a fundamental interest of the United States. The United States takes no position on the legal merits of the competing claims to sovereignty over the various islands, reefs, atolls, and cays in the SCS. The United States would, however, view with serious concern any maritime claim or restriction on maritime activity in the SCS that was not consistent with international law, including the 1982 United Nations Convention on the Law of the Sea."
—U.S. Statement through the State Department spokesman on May 10, 1995

With the Soviet flag, which has been flying in the Kremlin for nearly 70 years, falling slowly, the Cold War between the United States and the Soviet Union finally ended with the collapse of the Soviet Union and the resultant upheaval in Eastern Europe. With the breakdown of the bipolar confrontation that had consumed the world for decades, the world entered the post-Cold War era. Despite positive progress in the political and economic status as well as the regional security situation, the Asia-Pacific region still faced uncertainty. The interaction between China and the United States has become a key factor, further affecting the regional order. In the face of the new situation in the Asia Pacific after the Cold War, the United States has constantly strengthened its political, economic, and security ties within the Asia-Pacific region and adjusted its Asia-Pacific security strategy. In line with the changes of the situation in this region and the reshaping of the U.S. security strategy to Asia Pacific, the U.S. policy to the SCS has also been adjusted accordingly after the Cold War. In particular, the Third United Nations Conference on the Law of the Sea and the Mischief Reef incident in 1995 have greatly prompted the change of U.S. policy towards the SCS dispute. In this century, the United States has adopted the strategy of continuous intervention but not being trapped in the SCS dispute due to its engagement in anti-terrorism, therefore the situation in the SCS has been relatively stable.

The Situation in the Asia-Pacific Region after the Cold War

The SCS, connecting the Indian Ocean and the Pacific Ocean, is an important route in the Asia-Pacific region and occupies prominent strategic position. Therefore, the security and stability of the SCS is directly related to the overall situation in the Asia-Pacific region, and vice versa. As a part of the Asia-Pacific strategy, U.S. strategy on the SCS is bound to be subordinate to the layout of Asia-Pacific strategy. For this reason, it is necessary to examine the overall situation in this region in the post-Cold War era while studying U.S. policy adjustments on the SCS.

First, as the most vigorous economic market in recent decades, the Asia-Pacific region is full of strategic interests and economic opportunities for the United States. The scientific and technological revolution sweeping the world in the 20th century has provided strong technical support for the economic development of the Asia-Pacific region. The major countries seized the opportunity of industrialization and modernization, and undertook a global industrial transformation by actively introducing foreign capital and foreign aid, and finally established an export-oriented economic structure. From the perspective of the economic development track, Japan took the lead in achieving high-speed economic growth by using the funds, technology, and market of the United States in the 1960s, followed by the "four little dragons," including South Korea, Singapore, Hong Kong, and Taiwan, which realized industrialization in the 1970s. In the 1980s, the "three tigers," including Indonesia, Thailand, and Malaysia, stood out in development, and later China took off rapidly in the 1990s. Some Japanese scholars summarized the developing structure of East Asia as the "flying geese" model, which means that one economy, like the first goose in a V-shaped formation, can lead other economies toward industrialization, passing older technologies down to the followers as its own incomes rise and it moves into newer technologies. Apart from Japan's desire to dominate the East Asian economy, there is a hierarchy of development, that is, the United States, Japan followed by "the Four Asian Tigers" ASEAN, China, India, and Indochina (especially Vietnam).[1]

The end of the Cold War created favorable external circumstances for the economic growth of Asia-Pacific countries. In addition to Japan's relative recession, most other emerging industrial economies and developing countries have achieved rapid economic growth. On the whole, compared with those outside the Asia-Pacific region, the growth rate of the developed countries in the region is slightly higher than that of the European developed countries, while the growth rate of the developing countries in the Asia-Pacific region is much higher than that of the developing countries in other regions. Therefore, if the early rise of Japan was only a special case of the development of non-Western countries, and the achievements of the "four little dragons" in Asia was not of universal significance due to their relatively small scale, then the ability of China, Vietnam, and other countries to catch up after the Cold War persuaded people to recognize the miracle growth of East Asia.[2] In short, the economic growth, investment and trade, technology transmission, and personnel exchanges in the Asia-Pacific region have become more frequent after decades of accumulation, and it has become the most vibrant economic region in the world. Therefore, the Asia Pacific was a region full of interests and opportunities for the United States.[3]

Second, the overall political status of the Asia-Pacific region has risen significantly, which has attracted American strategic attention. After the Cold War, this region has become the gathering place of major powers in the world, and presents an asymmetric multipolar architecture.[4] There are not only the traditional powers like the United States, Japan, and Russia, but also emerging powers like China and India, which undoubtedly play a decisive role in the division and reorganization of the international pattern in the post-Cold War era. The Asia-Pacific region is also the intersection of capitalist and socialist systems, Eastern and Western civilizations, and developed and developing economies. Coupled with its inherent particularity and complexity in politics, economy, and culture, it has become one of the most prominent areas of confrontation and conflict in the world.

Europe was at the center of the world political arena for hundreds of years before WWII. In the Cold War, even though it was impacted by the rise of the third world and the Non-Aligned Movement, the main focus of the U.S.-Soviet struggle for hegemony was still in Europe. However, with the sustained economic development of the Asia-Pacific countries in the post-Cold War era, the rise of the Asia-Pacific region, especially the East Asian countries, has become a reality, which not only broke the traditional "four centers theory," namely, Atlantic center, European strategic center, Western civilization center, and developed country center,[5] but also produced a global focus with the North Atlantic as the center since Columbus and Dagama, which then began to shift to the Western Pacific.[6] The rise of the Asia-Pacific region cannot but arouse the great attention of the United States. In this regard, Winston Lord, then Assistant Secretary of State for Asia-Pacific Affairs, said in the early 1990s that strengthening relations with the Asia-Pacific region would be placed at the top of its foreign policy by the U.S. government, and in the long-term economic and security planning of the United States, East Asia will be given more attention than Europe.[7]

Third, despite positive progress in the overall security situation, the Asia-Pacific region still faces uncertainty. The United States began to regard the SCS as a potential tipping point of conflicts. During the Cold War, the Asia-Pacific region was an important location for confrontation between the United States and the Soviet Union. Two "hot wars," the Korean War and the Vietnam War, also took place in this region, which demonstrated the tense situation at that time. After the end of the Cold War, the collapse of the Soviet Union led to the dissolution of the confrontation between the great powers in the Asia-Pacific region, and peace and development became the theme of the times. Against this background, the security situation in Asia Pacific has generally tended to ease. But it does not mean that security issues in the Asia-Pacific region have been substantially solved in the post-Cold War era, since the potential sources of conflict still exist. Among them, the SCS sovereignty dispute is regarded by the United States as one of the factors affecting peace and stability in the Asia-Pacific region.

In April 1990, the U.S. DoD submitted to Congress a report entitled "A Strategic Framework for the Asian Pacific Rim: Looking Toward the 21st Century." In addition to listing the potential conflicts caused by the nuclear issue on the Korean Peninsula and the expansion of Taiwan independence forces, the SCS dispute is also regarded as a long-standing factor endangering regional stability. In the eyes of U.S. strategic analysts, the unresolved territorial disputes of the Spratly and Paracel Islands are likely to bring many Southeast Asian countries into a regional conflict and affect the freedom of navigation across the main channel in the SCS.[8] In May 1997, the U.S. DoD issued the "Report of the Quadrennial Defense Review" concerning the security situation in Asia, in which Iraq, Iran, and North Korea were listed as the sources of threat.

Meanwhile, it also pointed out that sovereignty and territorial disputes in other Asian regions were still potential sources of conflict.[9] Obviously, it is the SCS sovereignty dispute that the report implies. In the "2001 Report of the Quadrennial Defense Review," the United States paid more attention to the security issues in the periphery of Western Pacific, believing that the East Asian coastal area from southern Japan to Australia to the Bay of Bengal is a particularly challenging region. It is a vast area with rising powers, "failed states," and potential regional conflicts. Furthermore, the density of U.S. military bases and facilities in the region is lower than that in other key areas. To this end, the United States needs to strengthen its military front deployment forces in the region.[10] Since the SCS is located at the center of the East Asian periphery, the SCS naturally becomes the potential area for military confrontation and conflict.

Fourth, the interaction between China and the United States has become the key to shaping the order in the Asia-Pacific region. As the only superpower after the Cold War, the United States undoubtedly occupies a dominant position in shaping the order of the Asia-Pacific region. After the Cold War, the United States not only maintained a considerable number of allies and military bases in the region and deployed more than 100,000 troops, but it also greatly strengthened its economic ties with East Asia and the Western Pacific region. Its total trans-Pacific trade with Asian countries has exceeded nearly one-third of the transatlantic trade volume with Western European countries. In addition, the close ties between the United States and Asia are also reflected in the number of immigrants. Asian Americans have become the fastest growing immigrant group in the United States.[11] Therefore, in the post-Cold War era, the United States attached more importance to its participation in Asia-Pacific affairs. As James A. Baker, then Secretary of State, said, "the end of 1991 should see the closing off of several tragic, defining episodes of the American experience in Asia and open a new chapter of U.S. engagement in the region as we approach the 21st century."[12]

As a power in East Asia, China has made great achievements after the reform and opening up, and has increasingly become influential in the Asia-Pacific region.[13] Since reform and opening up, China has not only created a rapid economic growth rate of about 10 % per year, but also played a vital role in global and regional affairs. China's participation is indispensable to the resolution of the North Korean nuclear issue, the containment of non-proliferation, and the response to global issues such as the global financial crisis and climate change. To some extent, after the Cold War, China was rapidly rising in a peaceful way, becoming one of the leading forces in East Asia.[14] As a result, the changes in the balance of power between China and the United States and the shared responsibilities to cope with global problems and challenges have not only promoted the re-internationalization of China-U.S. relations,[15] but also made these two countries become the key forces in shaping the order of the Asia-Pacific region after the Cold War.

Shaping U.S. Security Strategy in the Asia-Pacific Region after the Cold War

With the advent of the post-Cold War era, the U.S. Asia-Pacific security strategy, which mainly served to fight against the Soviet Union, has obviously been unable to adapt to the new situation in the Asia-Pacific region. In order to ensure the "balance" of global strategy, the United States urgently needs to change the long-term "single track" strategy with Europe as the priority during the Cold War to a "dual track" strategy with equal emphasis on Europe and Asia so that the two regional strategies can develop in harmony. As Robert A. Scalapino has said, "Despite the natural attention recently given to Europe and the U.S.S.R., it is time for America to cease merely reacting and to start innovating in its policies in Asia."[16]

George H. W. Bush Administration's Concept of "Pacific Community"

In 1989, President George H. W. Bush Senior put forward the "New Pacific Partnership" initiative. In July of the same year, Secretary of State James A. Baker wrote an article, which for the first time elaborated the idea of building a "Pacific Community" to expand and strengthen the extensive and in-depth participation of the United States in the region, and the New Asia Pacific Security Strategy of the United States was thus taking shape. The set-up of a flexible and strong Asia-Pacific security framework constitutes one of the "three pillars" of the "Pacific Community" vision.[17] In order to establish a new Asia-Pacific security architecture and meet the diversified security needs of different countries in the region, the United States needed to change and adjust its mission and structure while maintaining its military presence in the Asia-Pacific region. Meanwhile, the United States urged Japan and other allies to reasonably share more security obligations. In view of specific security issues in the region, the United States attempted to resolve them through multilateral consultations. Specifically, the United States took the following measures:[18]

First, the United States advocated the establishment of a new "global partnership" between the United States and Japan based on the U.S.-Japan alliance, urging Japan to shoulder more defense responsibilities. At the same time, the United States put pressure on Japan to open its domestic market.

Second, the United States adjusted its policy on the Korean Peninsula and promoted the development of the situation in favor of the United States. Specifically, on the basis of building a more equal partnership, the United States continued to adjust and optimize the military alliance between the United States and South Korea, and appropriately reduced the number of U.S. troops stationed in South Korea. The United States also promoted the denuclearization of the Korean Peninsula and reduced its level of military confrontation in the region. In addition, the United States explored the establishment of a "multilateral mechanism" between China, the United States, Japan, Russia, and the north and south of the Korean Peninsula to promote a lasting solution for the Korean Peninsula nuclear issue.

Third, the United States adopted a strategy of both "containment" and "contact" with China to pursue its interests regarding the security strategy and ideological diplomacy patterns it pursued regarding China. The collapse of the Soviet Union caused the triangular relationship between China, the United States, and the Soviet Union to disintegrate after the Cold War. Coupled with the "Tiananmen Square Incident" in Beijing in 1989, China-U.S. relations entered an "era of strategic consensus dissolution."[19] On the one hand, the George H. W. Bush administration took the lead in imposing pressure and sanctions on China, and on the other hand, it did not want to see China-U.S. relations slide into an abyss. Therefore, it maintained high-level political contacts with China while imposing sanctions, mainly for the sake of safeguarding its strategic and economic interests, and at the same time, pushing China to "make changes and start reforms" by maintaining contact with Beijing.

Fourth, the United States invested more strategic resources in Southeast Asia to expand its influence. It included strengthening relations with ASEAN countries, reaching a series of military cooperation plans with Singapore and the Philippines, and discussing the possibility of using military facilities "on a commercial basis" with Malaysia and Indonesia. At the same time, the United States also adjusted the Indochina policy, and no longer recognized the United Nations seat of the Kampuchea resistance force coalition government, actively improved relations with Vietnam, and had dialogues and cooperation with Vietnam on Kampuchea issue and missing American soldiers in Vietnam.

Clinton Administration's Concept of "New Pacific Community"

Since Clinton took office in the White House in January 1993, the United States has paid more attention to Asia-Pacific affairs. In addition to continuing part of the foreign and security policies of the George H. W. Bush administration in the Asia-Pacific region, the Clinton administration also believed that the Pacific region would become a center of employment, cooperation, and economic growth. The future of the United States depended on its extensive, full, and in-depth participation in Asia-Pacific affairs.[20] Therefore, in order to establish an order under "American rule" in the Asia-Pacific region, Clinton administration put forward the strategic concept of "New Pacific Community" in July 1993, which was based on common strength, shared prosperity, and common recognition of democratic values.[21] The "New Pacific Community" strategy was undoubtedly a new development in U.S. strategy, shaping the Asia Pacific in the post-Cold War era. It indicated that the U.S.-Asia-Pacific security policy would usher in a turning point. To this end, the Clinton administration made strategic adjustments around the following three aspects.

First of all, it emphasized the importance of economic security and sought to establish a free and open economic and trade system in the Asia-Pacific region. Since Clinton took office, the trade volume between the United States and the Asia-Pacific region accounted for 36 % of the total U.S. global trade, which was 40 % higher than that of the United States and Europe, and was still rising. At the same time, the trade deficit between the United States and countries in the Asia-Pacific region was also increasing sharply. By 1996, the total trade deficit had reached 164.7 billion US dollars, of which Japan and China were the top two countries.[22] For the United States, there is a "paradox" in the new situation of the vigorous development of the Asia-Pacific economy after the Cold War. On the one hand, the United States provided a security guarantee for the Asia-Pacific allies, and on the other hand, these allies, especially Japan, had built up what was now a strong economic competition with the United States. As Edward N. Luttwak put it, geopolitics is changing into geo-economics in the post-Cold War era. The U.S. allies in the past are becoming adversaries.[23] To this end, the Clinton administration declared that "it is time to take economy and trade as the primary factor of American security."[24] While emphasizing "free trade," the Clinton administration put forward the principle of "fair trade," requiring Asia-Pacific countries to open their markets and reduce their trade surplus with the United States. In addition, the United States has also actively promoted the transformation of Asia Pacific Economic Cooperation (APEC) into a regional multilateral trade negotiating platform, so as to promote trade and investment liberalization in the Asia-Pacific region and increase the opportunities for American enterprises to enter the Asian market.

Second, the United States maintained military strength in the Asia-Pacific region and supported the establishment of a multilateral security dialogue mechanism. In February 1995, the Clinton administration issued its first report "United States Security Strategy for the East Asia -Pacific Region," which pointed out that the core interest of the United States in the Asia-Pacific region was to prevent the political and economic control of the region from falling into the hands of a competitive and hostile country or alliance.[25] The report marked a new round of adjustment for U.S. security strategy in the Asia-Pacific region. In terms of garrisoning, the report proposed to maintain the U.S. military force in East Asia at about 100,000 men, which was equivalent to the quantity of Europe. It meant that the Clinton administration had abandoned the plan proposed by the former government in 1990 and 1992 to reduce the scale of U.S. military force in East Asia in stages.[26] Accordingly, in face of the fact that "the Far East is already becoming—after the Eurasian oblong of violence—the world's second-most intense concentration of modern weaponry . . . The paradox of the region is that it is becoming the world's center in economic activity while lacking any multilateral structure of security."[27] According to Clinton, "Some in the United States have been reluctant to enter into regional security dialogues in Asia, but I see this as a way to supplement our alliances and forward military presence, not to supplant them. These dialogues can ensure that the end of the Cold War does not provide an opening for regional rivalries, chaos and arms races."[28] Therefore, on the basis of maintaining the bilateral alliance, the Clinton administration attached great importance to multilateralism, preventive diplomacy, and collective security, although these measures were aimed at maintaining the dominant position of the United States in the Asia-Pacific region and ensuring the strategic interests and economic security of the United States.

Finally, the United States paid more attention to the promotion of American democratic system and values, and raised awareness of its ideology. In advocating the strategic concept of the "New Pacific Community," Clinton reiterated the importance of promoting democracy, and took it as one of the four priorities to promote the security of the "New Pacific Community."[29] In his view, "one of the important goals of the New Pacific Community is to promote universal democracy and human rights for the people of Asia Pacific countries, which are also an important means for the United States to seek lasting peace, prosperity and stability in the region." Only by promoting and establishing American style democracy in the Asia-Pacific region can it be "most in line with the security and economic interests of the United States."[30] In addition, the Clinton administration's concept of "democratic promotion" was also reflected in "A National Security Strategy For A New Century in 1997," in which expanding democracy was listed as one of the three core goals of the U.S. national security strategy, together with promoting security and enhancing prosperity.[31] Under its guidance, the U.S. practice in the Asia-Pacific region during the Clinton administration paid high attention to democracy and human rights. For instance, in the APEC forum, the United States had constantly promoted the values of democracy and human rights; on the issues of trade, investment, and technology transfer to Asia-Pacific countries, it had always been linked with democracy and human rights issues; it had attached human rights conditions to the MFN treatment of China, and had repeatedly put forward anti-China bills at the UN human rights conferences.[32]

Recalibrating U.S. Strategy in the SCS in the Post-Cold War Era

In line with the change of the situation in the Asia-Pacific region and the shaping of the U.S. Asia-Pacific security strategy, the U.S. policy on Southeast Asia and the SCS also underwent readjustment. On the one hand, the strength of the Soviet Union and its successor Russia in Vietnam's Cam Ranh Bay military base had been greatly reduced, and Vietnam had gradually completed the withdrawal of troops from Cambodia, which eliminated the direct "threat" faced by the United States in the region. On the other hand, the financial difficulties of the United States in the post-Cold War era, the rise of nationalism in Southeast Asia, and the destruction of U.S. military bases by natural disasters also prompted the United States to believe that its military presence in this region was no longer as important as it was during the Cold War. For this reason, the George H. W. Bush administration once planned to reduce its military strength in the Asia-Pacific region,[33] and decided to close the naval base in Subic Bay and the Clark air force base in 1991.[34] It can be said that the end of the Cold War and the U.S. military contraction in Southeast Asia helped deescalate geopolitical tensions in the SCS.

Domestic Debates on the SCS Policy

After the collapse of the Soviet Union, heated debates on the Asia-Pacific security strategy had been launched in the United States around the U.S. policy option in Asia Pacific in the post-Cold War era. Although analysts put forward different strategic plans, their basic consensus was that there was shared interest interdependency between the United States and the Asia-Pacific region. Therefore, most of them advocated that the United States should continue to intervene in Asian affairs, only varying in the degree of intervention and commitment responsibilities.[35] There were also controversies on the SCS issue. Although officials and academicians generally made unclear statements on the sovereignty of the islands in the SCS, most of them were skeptical about China's claim of sovereignty over the SCS. On the relationship between the SCS and the U.S. Asia-Pacific security strategy, there are two different views in the United States.

Some people, represented by Major General William Crowe, believed that after the Cold War, the strategic importance of the SCS was seriously overestimated, and the oil resources in the SCS region were not as rich as estimated. Therefore, the United States should not pay too much attention to the maritime disputes in the region, and its security commitments to its partners in the SCS should also be restricted to diplomatic support. While some people headed by Richard Solomon, Assistant Secretary of State, firmly believed that the SCS issue was a major source of tension in the region, just like the Korean Peninsula issue in East Asia, Cambodia issue, and the dispute over the northern territories between Russia and Japan. In particular, China's claim of sovereignty over the islands in the SCS posed a potential threat to the interests and security of the United States. Therefore, the United States needed to be involved in the defense of Southeast Asia as a stabilizing force and strengthen its security relations with Southeast Asian countries.[36]

In February 1992, the Chinese government promulgated the *Law of the PRC on the Territorial Sea and the Contiguous Zone*, and once again confirmed China's sovereignty over the Paracel and Spratly Islands in the legislature. This legislative act not only aroused the wariness of the countries around the SCS, but also immediately caused wide concern in the United States. In early March, James Lille, Assistant Secretary of Defense, expressed his concern when attending the first Asia-Pacific Defense Conference in Singapore. As he said, the United States is concerned that the dispute over sovereignty over the Spratly Islands would probably escalate after the action taken by China, and it seemed inappropriate for China to pass the law on the Spratly Islands for the time being, although it was originally codified in the 1958 Declaration.[37] Frank Wisner, the U.S. ambassador to the Philippines, also claimed in an interview that the United States opposed any country's claim to sovereignty over the Spratly Islands by force. If there was a threat to peace in this region, the United States would respond. The United States would not stand idly by, especially when it affects American alliances.[38]

Despite the abovementioned "concerns" until the end of George H. W. Bush administration, there has been no substantial change in the U.S. policy stance on the SCS. According to U.S. Deputy Secretary of State Robert B. Zoellich, the United States did not hold a position on the territorial sovereignty of the SCS, but called for ensuring freedom of navigation in the region, and that all parties should resolve their differences by peaceful means.[39] It is the first time that the United States has publicly and partially clarified its position and expressed its demands on the SCS issue after the Cold War.

After the Clinton administration came to power in 1993, the debate on the SCS issue in the United States began to converge. Regarding the SCS dispute as a regional security threat entered the mainstream voice in the U.S. political circles. For instance, at the ASEAN ministerial meeting in July 1994, Deputy Secretary of State Talbott said that regional security challenges in the SCS were looming. The United States didn't hold a position on the territorial claims of all parties, but strongly opposed the use of force to resolve relevant disputes. The United States supported Indonesia-led efforts to resolve disputes and develop resources peacefully.[40] In August, U.S. Ambassador to Japan Walter Mondale also believed that although the Cold War had ended and resolution on some regional disputes had made significant progress, there were still many security threats in East Asia. Among them, North Korea's nuclear weapons issue was the most representative, but the competitive territorial disputes in the SCS should not be ignored.[41] In October, Secretary of Defense William Perry also stressed in a speech at the China National Defense University that, among the regional security challenges facing Asia, the SCS issue was the third most important challenge besides the nuclear program on the Korean Peninsula and nuclear proliferation in South Asia. As a long-standing regional tension, the SCS dispute had brought potential dangers for the future of the region. If the territorial disputes lead to the outbreak of regional conflicts, it will have a fatal impact on the security of the region and threaten the maritime routes of the United States and other countries in the world.[42] Compared with its former attitude, U.S. senior officials' recognition on the SCS issue is clear and the expressions are explicit.

Changes of the U.S. SCS Policy

In this context, the U.S. SCS policy has undergone significant changes. Among them, two events had a huge impact on the behavior of the United States. One is the UNCLOS, which entered into force on November 16, 1994. The UNCLOS was adopted at the Third United Nations Conference on the Law of the Sea, which entered into force on 16 November 1994. The primary objective is "recognizing the desirability of establishing through this convention, with due regard for the sovereignty of all States, a legal order for the seas and oceans which will facilitate international communication, and will promote the peaceful uses of the seas and oceans, the equitable and efficient utilization of their resources, the conservation of their living resources, and the study, protection, and preservation of the marine environment."[43] However, in spite of the fact that China has sovereignty over the SCS, Southeast Asian countries around the SCS have cited the relevant provisions of the Convention on territorial sea, EEZ, and continental shelf to claim so-called maritime sovereignty and jurisdiction over the SCS. To some extent, the Convention provides a legal "basis" for the Southeast Asian States disputing China's sovereignty in the SCS, and encourages them to constantly increase their contention for the delimitation of islands in the SCS. These actions have intensified the sovereignty disputes in the region, undoubtedly creating better conditions for the United States to intervene in SCS issues.

The other is the Mischief Reef incident in February 1995.[44] Mischief Reef is located in the east of the Spratly Islands. The reef is about 135 nautical miles away from western Philippines and 240km from the western part of Palawan, Philippines. Mischief Reef is part of China's Spratly Islands, while the Philippines has incorporated the island into its so-called Kalayaan islands group, creating a perception of separation that wasn't known historically. In the early of 1995, the Philippines claimed to have found Chinese warships "invading" the waters of Mischief Reef and building military facilities on Mischief Reef. Chinese side responded that China constructed a civil production facility to protect the life safety of fishermen working in the sea area of the Spratly Islands of China.[45] China and the Philippines had a diplomatic debate on this issue, triggering a military crisis. Although the Mischief Reef incident finally subsided, it caused the United States to become more vigilant, believing that China was the biggest threat in the SCS, and showed an obvious tendency to interfere. In this regard, Mark J. Valencia, an American scholar on ocean issues, once pointed out that China's behavior in Mischief Reef has caused the United States to be wary of China because they took the safety of the air route linking Europe and East Asia into consideration.[46]

Shortly after the Mischief Reef incident, the U.S. House of Representatives passed Resolution 114 on March 10. The resolution not only uses the word "aggression" to describe China's behavior in safeguarding its rights in the SCS, but also declares "the right of free passage through the SCS to be in the national security interests of the United States, its friends, and allies," further claiming that "any attempt by a nondemocratic power to assert, through the use of force or intimidation, its claims to territory in the SCS to be a matter of grave concern to the United States." Nonetheless, it calls upon the government of the PRC to adhere faithfully to its commitment under the *Manila Declaration of 1992*, and calls upon the President of the United States to review the defense needs of democratic countries with claims to territory in the SCS.[47] On March 30, the U.S. Senate Foreign Relations Committee also proposed Senate Resolution 97, it urged the Executive Branch to reiterate to the claimants in the SCS that the United States does not take a position on any individual claim, and called upon all of the claimants to refrain from using military force to assert or expand territorial claims in the SCS. In additions, it urges the Executive Branch to declare the active support of the United States for the *1992 Manila Declaration of the Association of South East Asian Nations*, and calls upon all the claimants to observe faithfully its provisions. It also offers criticism, stating that the response of the United States to the entire issue has been less than adequate.[48]

Statements on the U.S. SCS Policy

Considering the rapid escalation of the SCS situation, and in response to the concerns of both houses of Congress on the SCS issue, Christine Shelly, spokesman of the U.S. DoS, issued a formal statement on the SCS issue on 10 May 1995. The contents are as follows:

(a) The United States strongly opposes the use of force or the threat of force to resolve territorial disputes, and urges all parties to the dispute to exercise restraint and avoid actions that may worsen the situation. (b) The United States has a lasting interest in maintaining peace and stability in the SCS, and calls on all parties involved in the dispute to deal with relevant disputes in a diplomatic manner, taking into account the interests of all countries. The United States is willing to help as much as it can if the disputing state considers it useful. The United States welcomed ASEAN's statement on the SCS issue in 1992. (c) It is in the fundamental interest of the United States to safeguard the freedom of navigation in the SCS. The unimpeded passage of all ships and aircraft in the SCS is crucial to the peace and prosperity of the entire Asia-Pacific region, including the United States. (d) The United States does not hold a position on the sovereignty of various islands and reefs in the SCS. However, it is seriously concerned about any maritime claims or restrictions on marine activities in the SCS that are inconsistent with international law, including the 1982 UNCLOS.[49] It is the first time that the United States has systematically clarified its policy essentials in the SCS. It not only expresses the interests and concerns of the United States in detail on the SCS issue, but also clearly shows its intention to target China.

Meanwhile, the United States also showed its partiality for the Philippines in the Mischief Reef incident. During the incident, Philippine President Ramos and U.S. Presidential Special Envoy Ross held a meeting. Both sides agreed that a series of mechanisms was needed to continue to implement the security-related provisions in the defense treaty between the two countries. The U.S. Secretary of State Christopher also reminded China that the United States had an obligation to protect the security of the Philippines in accordance with the U.S.-Philippines treaty. In addition, the U.S. military also showed support for the Philippines. The Pentagon soon discussed the military needs of the Philippines and the assistance that the United States may provide, going on to dispatch U.S. Special Forces to train the Philippine army on how to garrison the Spratly Islands for long periods.[50] On June 16, 1995, Joseph Nye, then Assistant Secretary of Defense, claimed that if the freedom of navigation at sea was damaged by military conflicts in the SCS, the United States would prepare military escorts. It was the first time that a U.S. political figure proposed direct military intervention in the SCS dispute.[51]

Since then, the United States took even more robust stance on the SCS issue. On August 21, 1996, the United States issued a diplomatic note to China, accusing China of a failure to comply with international law in the SCS. It claimed that China should use the "low water line" principle rather than the straight line principle to delineate the territorial claims of the coastal area, Hainan Island and the Paracel Islands.[52] In March 1997, the U.S. Naval Analysis Center proposed in its report that the Seventh Fleet of the United States should play a responsible role in protecting the freedom of navigation in the SCS.[53] In December 1998, Dana Rohrabacher, a member of the U.S. House of Representatives, took a Philippine transport plane to reconnoiter Mischief Reef regardless of dissuasion, and issued an "investigation report" after. The report describes China's actions in the SCS in terms of "expansion" and "aggression." It severely criticizes the silence of the U.S. DoS and the Pentagon on China's actions as an "ostrich policy," and calls on the U.S. government to take practical actions to support democratic friendly countries and resist China's military expansion in the SCS.[54]

It is notable that during this period the United States also terminated its plan to reduce East Asian garrisons, and decided to maintain its troops in the Far East and the Pacific region at 100,000, basically equal to that in Europe.[55]

In this regard, Christopher, then Secretary of State, once said incisively that the Spratly Islands dispute was a reason for the United States to maintain a stronger influence in the Asia-Pacific region. Although no big country regarded any other country as a military threat in the near future, there was still a danger that old contradictions would revive or new ones may grow. Additionally, the United States normalized its relations with Vietnam during this period. Some commentators believed that it was certainly related to Vietnam's increasingly important position, but playing a "Vietnam card" and exerting pressure on China over the increasingly intensified SCS issue was also a major factor for the United States to promote the normalization of U.S.-Vietnam relations.[56]

Continuous Intervention but Not Falling into the Dispute Trap

After President George W. Bush took office in 2001, he enacted a series of unilateral policies with a strong neo-conservatism inclination, trying to realize the so-called absolute security and continue the unipolar hegemony of the United States. The Bush administration attached great importance to the Asia-Pacific region in the global strategic layout of the United States, and actively promoted the shift of U.S. security focus into the Asia-Pacific region, so as to strengthen the existence of the United States, stabilize its allies, reconstruct its order, and ensure its leadership. In order to maintain its leading position in the Asia-Pacific region, the Bush administration changed the formulation of the "constructive strategic partnership" between China and the United States in the Clinton administration, repeatedly claiming that China is a "strategic competitor" of the United States,[57] and the number one imaginary enemy, thus it is necessary to contain China.[58] In this context, the SCS has naturally become an ideal place for the United States to contain China, and the game between China and the United States in the SCS started to increase in ferocity.

Reconnaissance Aircraft Crash Incident

At the turn of the century, the United States frequently carried out military reconnaissance activities against China in the SCS, which directly triggered the China-U.S. aircraft crash incident in the SCS. On April 1, 2001, a US EP-3 surveillance plane flew over the southeast of Hainan Island of China and made a low-altitude reconnaissance in the sea off Sanya. China dispatched two Shenyang

J-8 fighters to track and monitor the U.S. surveillance aircraft, one of which collided with it, causing the Chinese fighter to crash. The U.S. surveillance plane entered China's airspace and landed at Hainan Lingshui airport without receiving Chinese permission. After the incident, China and the United States negotiated over responsibility, the nature of the area where the incident occurred, the compensation for China's losses by the U.S. side, whether the U.S. military aircraft landed at China's airport without the consent of the Chinese side, whether the Chinese side has the right to board the U.S. military aircraft, and how the U.S. aircraft and personnel could leave China. The China-U.S. aircraft incident triggered unprecedented levels of tension, especially when the Bush administration publicly announced China as a strategic competitor, the United States showed an arbitrary and unscrupulous attitude overall. The United States maintained that its aircraft was flying over the SCS in international airspace and enjoyed the right to freedom of flight and "complete immunity," leading to its refusal to pay any compensation for the incident caused.[59]

Although the aircraft crash incident is only a small probability event, it was by no means accidental. It demonstrated that the United States has been on guard against China for a long time, and frequent military activities against China in the SCS are only a microcosm.[60] In other words, there has been an "undercurrent surge" and constant in-fighting between China and the United States in the region. In fact, before the incident, the United States maintained high-frequency reconnaissance rates of China in the SCS, which was very rarely reported in the media. In his meeting with foreign guests on April 3, 2001, China's President Jiang Zemin asked, "Why does the United States often conduct reconnaissance flights so close to China?" He used the word "often" here to show the frequency of U.S. aircraft reconnaissance.[61] A month after the incident, the United States resumed its military reconnaissance activities along the coast of China. During the crisis management phase, the United States also used the "Taiwan issue" to suppress China. On April 24, the Bush administration announced that it had approved the sale of advanced weapons to Taiwan, including eight diesel-powered submarines, four Kidd-class destroyers, 12 P-3C long-range anti-submarine patrol aircraft, MH-53E mine sweeping helicopters, and other advanced weapons.[62] Considering that the decision on arms sales to Taiwan happened shortly after the China-U.S. aircraft incident, and the U.S. government has repeatedly said that the arms sales to Taiwan have nothing to do with the incident, the statement is obviously unconvincing.[63]

In order to strengthen its strategy of military deterrence against China in the SCS, the United States launched frequent military exercises and military exchanges after the incident. In April 2001, the United States held a joint military exercise code named "2001 shoulder to shoulder" in the waters off Luzon Island, the Philippines. In the same month, the USS Blue Ridge also visited Malaysia and Singapore. In May, the United States held a joint military exercise code named "Cobra Gold" with Thailand. From July 2001 to June 2001, the United States cooperated with the Philippines and Singapore, respectively, to conduct naval training. In August, the United States conducted a large-scale exercise code named "Passing Exercise" alone in the SCS, and sent military forces including two aircraft carriers Constellation and Calvin, a large number of cruisers, frigates, destroyers, and 150 aircraft, with 15000 participants. As a matter of fact, the name "passing exercise" itself is intended to declare that the U.S. military is still, as always, dominating the peace and stability of the SCS and safeguarding the freedom of navigation in the SCS.[64] In September, the U.S. Navy and air force were also granted the right to freely use Philippine ports and fly over Philippine airspace.

The United States Turns to "Counter-Terrorism" Strategy

On September 11, 2001, three airliners hijacked by terrorists collided with the World Trade Center building in New York City and the DoD building in Washington, D.C., leading to the collapse of the buildings. After the 9/11 incident, terrorism became the most present threat the United States faced. The Bush administration had to shift the strategic focus of the United States to the "war on terror." Since the beginning of the Afghanistan and Iraq wars, the United States has focused on the Middle East, and reduced its strategic attention towards the Asia-Pacific region, including the SCS. For example, Condoleezza Rice, Secretary of State, was absent from the ARF twice in 2005 and 2007, respectively, and refused to hold the U.S.-ASEAN summit. However, the Asia-Pacific region was not removed from the U.S. strategic agenda. In fact, while busy with the war on terrorism, the Bush administration also made appropriate adjustments to the U.S.-Asia-Pacific security strategy to meet the global strategic needs of the "anti-terrorist."

Specifically, while maintaining and strengthening the Asia-Pacific bilateral alliance system with the U.S.-Japan alliance as the core, the Bush administration has established various Issue Alliances or Temporary Alliances in response to the complex and changeable security situation in the Asia-Pacific region and the need to establish a global anti-terrorism "United Front." During this period, the United States dealt with the North Korea nuclear crisis, cooperated with

Southeast Asian countries in anti-terrorism and anti-proliferation through these flexible alliances.[65] From the perspective of military deployment, U.S. troops stationed in the Asia-Pacific region began to weaken "permanent strength" and consolidate "smart entry." On September 30, 2001, the Pentagon proposed in its Quadrennial Defense Review Report that the deployment of U.S. military forces in the Asia-Pacific region must change the traditional way of expanding the size of its garrison or adjusting its military bases. It should be based on the principle of expanding potential security partners and reach more access or infrastructure contracts through negotiation and treaties to obtain temporary access to foreign military facilities.[66]

The U.S. SCS Policy in the Anti-terrorism Era

After the 9/11 incident, Southeast Asia was opened up as the "second anti-terrorist battlefield" by the United States. For the need of joint anti-terrorism, China-U.S. relations have also improved, but the U.S. military reconnaissance activities in the SCS have not been correspondingly restrained. On the contrary, under the banner of anti-terrorism and route security, the United States frequently sent advanced military reconnaissance planes and ocean survey ships to the SCS to collect intelligence, and took the opportunity to spy on China's military capabilities and deployment in the region. At the same time, the United States has strengthened its presence in Southeast Asia in various ways to maintain its influence on the SCS issue. It was mainly manifested in the following aspects.

First, the United States strengthened the military presence around the SCS in the name of anti-terrorism. In the two Quadrennial Defense Review Reports issued by the Bush administration, it is clearly stated that the U.S. military strategic focus should be tilted to the Asia-Pacific region,[67] and continuously enhance the military presence and response capability in the SCS through signing military agreements with the Philippines, Thailand, Singapore, Malaysia, Indonesia, and Vietnam and other neighboring countries in the SCS, and carrying out military cooperation activities, such as joint military exercises, military assistance, and military training.[68] In order to prevent terrorist attacks, the United States also put forward the Container Security Initiative, Non Proliferation Security Initiative, and Regional Maritime Security Plan, so as to strengthen cooperation and strength in maritime security with Southeast Asian countries. At the same time, the United States also took part in non-traditional security activities in the SCS, such as maritime disaster relief, anti-piracy, and anti-terrorism, to demonstrate the responsibility of a great power, improve its international image, and enhance its influence in Indonesia, the Philippines, Myanmar, and other countries. For example, when meeting with Philippine President Arroyo at the White House on June 24, 2008, Bush said that the United States would send the Reagan aircraft carrier battle group to participate in the rescue operations in the Philippine disaster area. In this regard, most military observers believed that the United States was actually carrying out its military strategic deployment in the Philippines and even the whole SCS under the banner of disaster relief.[69]

Second, in the middle and late period of the Bush administration, the White House realized the importance of economic issues, and began to implement the "fair trade policy" by means of "multi track system" through developing unilateral, bilateral, and multilateral relations, so as to promote trade and investment liberalization in the Asia-Pacific region, and strive to open up "emerging markets" in the region. During this period, the United States negotiated bilateral free trade agreement (FTA) with Singapore and South Korea in 2004 and 2007, respectively. At the same time, the United States has strengthened its economic and trade relations with Thailand, Malaysia, Indonesia, the Philippines, Vietnam, and Cambodia by signing a framework agreement on trade and investment, providing economic and technical assistance and promoting relevant countries' entry into the WTO. In addition, the United States has also launched free trade negotiations with ASEAN, promoting the signing and implementation of The Framework Document for the Plan of Action to Implement the ASEAN-U.S. Enhanced Partnership, Enterprise for ASEAN Initiative, and U.S.-ASEAN Trade and Investment Framework Agreement. The United States has regularly held U.S.-ASEAN economic ministerial consultation meetings, and used economic means to influence the foreign policies of Southeast Asian countries, using its economy as a "carrot" and the threat of withdrawal as a "stick."[70]

Third, the United States supports the SCS dispute parties in Southeast Asia in various ways. During the period of George W. Bush's administration, the main means for the United States to take sides in the SCS issue in Southeast Asia were to provide military intelligence to Southeast Asian countries, actively carry out bilateral or multilateral military interaction, and foster new leading forces of ASEAN countries to strengthen ASEAN's unity, so as to enhance ASEAN's centripetal force and ability to resist China.[71] It is worth noting that the Bush administration acquiesced in the participation of American oil companies in the development of oil and gas resources in the disputed waters of the SCS. In addition to the original U.S.-Philippine cooperation in development, the United States increased its cooperation with Vietnam during this period. In June and November 2007, Chevron Corporation and Exxon Mobil Corporation, respectively, signed cooperation and development agreements with Vietnam on oil and gas resources exploitation in the SCS. While they are private companies, these agreements could not be enacted without the tacit authorization and support of the U.S. government.

Fourth, the United States strengthened its relations with Japan, Australia, and other allies to coordinate its activities in the SCS. Japan and Australia are, respectively, regarded as the "north anchor" and "south anchor" of the United States in the Pacific region, while Southeast Asia and the SCS are the bridges connecting the two anchors. After the 9/11 incident, bilateral and trilateral cooperation between the United States, Japan, and Australia were strengthened. Since 2003, the three countries have held ministerial level security dialogues and informal consultations on issues of common concern, such as security and counter-terrorism in the Pacific Rim region. In February 2005, during security consultations with Japan, the United States also listed Southeast Asia as a common strategic goal, intending to draw Japanese military forces into Southeast Asia. By strengthening the trilateral security cooperation among the United States, Japan, and Australia, and combining with Southeast Asia cooperation, and establishing the Pacific Rim security network, the United States can not only greatly improve the flexibility and mobility to deal with the Asia-Pacific and even global threats, but also avoid the emergence of new powerful countries that can challenge the interests of the United States in the Asia-Pacific region.[72]

Overall, during the Bush administration, the United States maintained its continuous involvement in the SCS issue, but it did not fall into a dispute trap. Instead, the United States implemented a set of principles of balance of power to prevent the situation in the SCS from sliding into a situation beyond the control of the United States. The main reasons are as follows:

First, the United States quickly turned its strategic focus towards "anti-terrorism" after the 9/11incident, and had no time to consider the development of the situation in the SCS. Second, in the anti-terrorism era, the United States needed China's support to join the global anti-terrorism fight, so there was no desire to offend China on the SCS issue. At the same time, maintaining peace and stability in the SCS was in line with the regional strategic interests of the United States at that time. Third, although the United States attached importance to the safety of navigation and freedom of over flight in the SCS, and strengthened its military presence in Southeast Asia through joint military exercises, the anti-terrorism strategy occupied too much strategic energy of the United States, causing the diplomatic influence of the United States in Southeast Asia to decline.[73] Fourth, in order to correct the excessive dependence of the

United States on unilateralism and force, Condoleezza Rice, Secretary of State, began to advocate "transformational diplomacy" after 2006, recognizing that the possibility of war between great powers in the future is very slim, and cooperation among big powers will become a trend. In order to meet the global and regional challenges, and to solve the failure of existing international mechanisms, it is necessary for the United States to strengthen its cooperation with other powers.[74] The change of diplomatic perception was also conducive to the improvement of China-U.S. relations, thus reducing the probability of friction and conflict between the two sides in the SCS.

Notes

1 Yu Xintian, "The Prospect of East Asian Modernization and its Impact on the World," *Pacific Journal*, No.2, 1994, p.69.
2 Yu Xintian, "The Prospect of East Asian Modernization and its Impact on the World," *Pacific Journal*, No. 2, 1994, p.66.
3 The U.S. Department of Defense, *A Strategic Framework for the Asian Pacific Rim: Report to Congress*, 1992, p.2.
4 Richard J. Ellings and Edward A. Olsen, "Asia's Challenge to American Strategy," *Analysis*, The National Bureau of Asian Research, Vol.3, No.2, 1992, p.8.
5 Chen Fengjun, "The Global Significance of the Rise of the Asia Pacific Region—A Challenge to the 'Four Centers Theory'," *Journal of Contemporary Asia-Pacific Studies*, No.1, 1994, pp.12–32.
6 Luo Rongqu, "Modern Historical Significance of the Rise of East Asia and its Prospects in the 21st Century," *Tianjin Social Sciences*, No. 2, 1992, p.6.
7 Chen Fengjun, ed., *An Analysis of Asia Pacific Security*, Beijing: China International Broadcasting Press, 2004, p.9.
8 The U.S. Department of Defense, *A Strategic Framework for the Asian Pacific Rim: Looking Toward the 21st Century*, April, 1990, p.3–4; Donald S. Zagoria, "The Changing U.S. Role in Asian Security in the 1990s," in Sheldon Simon, ed., *East Asian Security in the Post-Cold War Era*, M .E . . . Sharpe, New York, 1993, pp.51–52.
9 The U.S. Department of Defense, *Report of the Quadrennial Defense Review*, April, 1997.
10 The U.S. Department of Defense, *the Quadrennial Defense Review Report*, September 30, 2001.
11 James A. Baker, III, "America in Asia: Emerging Architecture for a Pacific Community," *Foreign Affairs*, Vol.70, 1992, p.4.
12 James A. Baker, III, "America in Asia: Emerging Architecture for a Pacific Community," *Foreign Affairs*, Winter 1991/1992, Vol.70, No .5, p.1.

13 For China's growing influence in East Asia, see Evelyn Goh, "Meeting the China Challenge: The U.S.in South east Asian Regional Security Strategies," *Policy Studies Monograph*, No.16, Washington, D. C., East-West Center, 2005; Robert S. Ross, "Balance of Power Politics and the Rise of China: Accommodation and Balancing in East Asia," *Security Studies*, Vol.15, No.3, 2006, pp.355–395.

14 Robert S. Ross, "China's Rise, Regional Power Transfer and East Asian Security: from 1949 to the 21st century," translated by Shen Peng, *World Economics and Politics*, 2009, No. 11, pp.36–43.

15 Wu Xinbo, "The Re-internationalization of Sino-American Relations," *World Economics and Politics*, No. 8, 2009, pp.21–29.

16 Robert A. Scalapino, "The United States and Asia: Future Prospects," *Foreign affairs*, winter 1991, pp.39–40.

17 The other two are to build the framework of economic integration and promote the process of democratization.

18 James A. Baker, III, "America in Asia: Emerging Architecture for a Pacific Community," *Foreign Affairs*, Vol.70, 1992, pp.9–17; Wang Wei, ed., *Evolution of U.S. Asia Pacific Policy (1776–1995)*, Jinan: Shandong People's Publishing House, 1995, pp.404–417;Wu Guifu, "The Trend of US Asia Pacific Strategic Adjustment," *Contemporary Asia Pacific*, No. 5, 1992, pp.64–65.

19 Tao Wenzhao, *U.S. China Policy in the post-Cold War Era*, Chongqing: Chongqing Press, 2006, pp.15–22.

20 Wang Wei, ed. *Evolution of U.S. Asia Pacific Policy (1776–1995*), Jinan: Shandong People's Publishing House, 1995, p.419.

21 "Clinton in Korea: A Call for a Pacific Community," *The New York Times*, July 11, 1993, p.A8.

22 Xin Benjian, "The Asia Pacific Region: The First Focus of the U.S. Global Strategy in the 21st Century--Examples, Reasons and China's Foreign Policy." *World Economics and Politics*, 2001, No. 8, p.29.

23 Edward N. Luttwak, "From Geopolitics to Geo-Economics: Logic of Conflict, Grammar of Commerce," *The National Interest*, No.2, Summer 1990, pp.17–23.

24 Lin Xiaoguang, "American Asia Pacific Strategy: From Bush to Clinton," *Foreign Social Sciences Studies*, No. 2, 1994, p.21.

25 U.S. Department of Defense, *United States Security Strategy for the East Asia-Pacific Region*, February 1995, p.7.

26 U.S. Department of Defense, *United States Security Strategy for the East Asia-Pacific Region*, February 1995, p.2.

27 Zbigniew Brzezinski, *Out of Control: Global Turmoil on the Eve of the 21st Century*, New York: Collier Books, 1993, p.199.

28 U.S. Department of Defense, *United States Security Strategy for the East Asia-Pacific Region*, February 1995, p.13.

29 The other three are: undertaking military obligations to the Asia-Pacific region, curbing weapons of mass destruction, and conducting dialogue on regional multilateral security. See Office of the Press Secretary, "Remarks by the President in Address to the Korean National Assembly," The White House, July 10, 1993; Wu Xinbo, *Turbulent Water: U.S. Asia-Pacific Security Strategy in the post-Cold War Era,* Shanghai: Fudan University Press, 2006, p.39.

30 Wang Wei, ed. *Evolution of U.S. Asia Pacific Policy (1776–1995)*, Jinan: Shandong People's Publishing House, 1995, p.423.

31 "A National Security Strategy For A New Century," May 1997, available at: http://nssarchive.us/NSSR/1997.pdf

32 For the contest on human rights between China and the United States during the Clinton Administration, please refer to Tao Wenzhao, *U.S. China Policy in the post-Cold War Era*, Chongqing: Chongqing Press, 2006, pp.186–193.

33 U.S. Department of Defense, *A Strategic Framework for the Asia Pacific Rim: Looking Toward the 21st Century*, April 1990, pp.7–8.

34 Some scholars have pointed out that it has not fundamentally shaken the U.S. military influence in the SCS, because the United States has not completely abandoned the forward deployment strategy, the US-Philippines Joint Defense Treaty is still in force, and the alliance between the two countries still exists. Meanwhile, after the withdrawal, the United States also retained a series of unknown facilities in the Philippines, including the naval communication terminal in San Miguel, the large-scale communication and signal transmitting station at camp o'donnay, the air defense radar system and reserved communication circuit equipment of Wallace air force base, which still play a huge reconnaissance function. See Derek Da Cunha, "The 5th Colum, US Navy Politics," *Far Eastern Economic Review*, 3 May, 1990, p.25.

35 For contents of the debate, please refer to Wu Xinbo, *Turbulent Water: U.S. Asia-Pacific Security Strategy in the post-Cold War Era*, Shanghai: Fudan University Press, 2006, pp.9–14.

36 See Zheng Zemin, *Great Powers in the SCS Issue*, Beijing: World Affairs Press, 2010, pp.45–47.

37 United Press International Manila, March 2, 1992. Quoted from Zhang Mingliang, *America's Involvement in the SCS: Process, Drives, and Implications*, Hong Kong: Hong Kong Press for Social Sciences LTD., 2011, p.247.

38 "Work with China on Spratly Row, U.S. Urges ASEAN," *Straits Times*, March 28, 1992, p.19.

39 Susumu Awanohara, "Washington's Priorities: US Emphasizes Freedom of Navigation," *Far Eastern Economic Review*, Vol.155, No.32, August 13, 1992, p.18.

40 *US Department of State Dispatch*, Vol.5, No.32, August 8, 1994, available at: http://dosfan.lib.uic.edu/ERC/briefing/dispatch/1994/html/Dispatchv5no32.html

41 *US Department of State Dispatch*, Vol.5, No.38, September 19, 1994, available at: http://dosfan.lib.uic.edu/ERC/briefing/dispatch/1994/html/Dispatchv5no38.html

42 *US Department of State Dispatch*, Vol.5, No.44, October 31, 1994, available at: http://dosfan.lib.uic.edu/ERC/briefing/dispatch/1994/html/Dispatchv5no44.html
43 See the preamble to the *United Nations Convention on the Law of the Sea*.
44 For a detailed analysis of the Mischief Reef incident, please refer to Li Jinming, "Overview on the Mischief Reef Incident," *Southeast Asian Affairs*, No. 1, 2000, pp.66–74.
45 Nayan Chanda, "Territorial Imperative," *Far Eastern Economic Review*, February 23, 1995, p.15.
46 Mark J. Valencia, *Sharing the Resources of the SCS*, London: Martinus Nijhoff Publishers, 1997, p.87.
47 The 104th Congress 1st Session "H.RES.114," "Expressing the sense of the House of Representatives that the United States should support peace and stability in the SCS," in the House of Representatives, March 10, 1995, available at: https://www.congress.gov/104/bills/hres114/BILLS-104hres114ih.pdf
48 Congress, Senate resolution 97- Relative to the SCS, Congress Record, March 30, 1995, available at: https://www.congress.gov/crec/1995/03/30/CREC-1995-03-30-pt1-PgS4932.pdf
49 "Hearings before the subcommittees on international economic policy and trade and Asia and the Pacific of the committee on international relations," House of Representatives, 104th Congress, 2ed session, May 30 and June 19, 1996, p.157.
50 Zheng Zemin, *Great Powers in the SCS Issue*, Beijing: World Affairs Press, 2010, pp.45–47.
51 Nigel Holloway, "Jolt from the Blue: U.S. Prodded to Firm up its Policy on Spratlys," *Far Eastern Economic Review*, August 3, 1995, p.22.
52 Lee Kim Chew, "US keen to limit China's Claims to SCS Territory," *The Strait Times*, September 10, 1996, p.27.
53 Eduardo Lachica, "Southeast Asian Sea Lanes Vital to U.S.: Navy Study Stresses Need for Washington to Help Routes Open," *The Asian Wall Street Journal*, March 19, 1997, p.16.
54 Zhang Mingliang, *America's Involvement in the SCS: Process, Drives, and Implications*. Hong Kong: Hong Kong Press for Social Sciences LTD., 2011, pp.273–277.
55 Chalmers Johnson and E.B. Keehn, "The Pentagon's Ossified Strategy," *Foreign Affairs*, July/August, 1995, p.103.
56 Zheng Zemin, *Great Powers in the SCS Issue*, Beijing: World Affairs Press, 2010, p.53.
57 "George W. Bush on China," available at: http://www.ontheissues.org/celeb/George_W__Bush_China.htm; Condoleezza Rice, "Promoting the National Interests," *Foreign Affairs*, January/February, 2000, p.57.
58 Zalmay Khalilzad et al., *The United States and Asia: Toward a New U.S. Strategy and Force Posture*, Rand, 2001, pp.16–23.
59 P. M. Cronin., *Cooperation from Strength: The United States, China and the SCS*, Report of Center for a New American Security, 2012, pp.69–79.

60 Wang Chuanjian, "American Policy in the SCS: History and Reality," *Foreign Affairs Review*, No. 6, 2009, p.97.
61 Zhang Mingliang, *America's Involvement in the SCS: Process, Drives, and Implications.* Hong Kong: Hong Kong Press for Social Sciences LTD., 2011, p.305.
62 "Weapons the U.S .Will Sell Taiwan," *Associated Press*, Apr.23, 2001, available at: http://taiwansecurity.org/AP/2001/AP-042301.htm
63 Zhang Qingmin, "US-Taiwan Military Relations in Bush's First Term: Seen from the Implementation of Bush's Decision of Arms Sale to Taiwan," *American Studies Quarterly*, No.4, 2004, pp.19–21.
64 S. Yann-Huei, "The Overall Situation in the SCS in the New Millennium: Before and After the 9/11 Terrorist Attacks," *Ocean Development & International Law*, 2003, 34 (3–4), pp.237–238.
65 Zheng Yingping, "The Thought of Bush Administration's New Alliances Strategy," *Contemporary International Relations*, No. 11, 2002, pp.43–47; Zheng Yingping, "On New Advantages of American's Asian and Pacific Security Strategy and its Effects on Surrounding Countries of China," *Pacific Journal*, No. 2, 2004, p.58; Ma Junping, "The Asia-Pacific Security Strategy of Bush Administration: Adjustments and Trends," *Journal of PLA University of Foreign Languages*, No.5, 2005, p.115.
66 U.S. Department of Defense, *Quadrennial Defense Review Report*, September 30, 2001, pp.4–5.
67 U.S. Defense Department, *Quadrennial Defense Review Report*, September 30, 2001; U.S. Defense Department, *Quadrennial Defense Review Report*, February 6, 2006.
68 Cao Xiaoyang, "The US Military Presence in Southeast Asia After the 9/11 Incident and its Influence," *Contemporary Asia Pacific Studies*, No. 3, 2006, p.27; Guo Yuan, *Geopolitics and the SCS Dispute*, Beijing: China Social Sciences Press, 2011, p.185.
69 See Wang Chuanjun, "What is the intention of the US aircraft carrier battle group to go to the Philippine disaster area," *Guangming Daily*, June 27, 2008.
70 Wu Shicun, *The SCS Dispute: Origin and Development*. Beijing: China Economic Press, 2010, pp.172–173.
71 Zheng Zemin, *Great Powers in the SCS Issue*, Beijing: World Affairs Press, 2010, pp.81–92.
72 Cao Xiaoyang, "The US Military Presence in Southeast Asia After the 9/11 Incident and its Influence," *Contemporary Asia Pacific Studies*, No. 3, 2006, p.27.
73 Song Yanhui, *The United States and the SCS Dispute*, Taipei: Angel Publishing Co., Ltd., 2016, pp.81–82.
74 Condoleezza Rice, "Transformational Diplomacy," January18, 2006, available at: http://www.state.gov/secretary/rm/2006/59306.htm.

4 The U.S. Strategic Rebalance and the SCS Dispute

"As a Pacific nation and resident power we have a national interest in freedom of navigation, open access to Asia's maritime domain, the maintenance of peace and stability, and respect for international law in the SCS."

—Secretary of State Hillary Clinton

"I reiterated that the United States will stand with allies and partners in upholding fundamental interests, among them the freedom of navigation and overflight, lawful commerce that is not impeded and peaceful resolution of disputes."

—President Barack Obama

Casting himself as a reformer, Barack Obama began to reorient American foreign policy and lay out a new national security strategy after he took office in 2009. One of the important measures made was to pivot the U.S. strategic focus to Asia and implement a rebalancing strategy. The main goal of the rebalancing strategy was to redistribute the global strategic resources and military power through strategic withdrawal in the Middle East and strategic expansion in the Asia-Pacific region, to maintain American political leadership and military primacy under the new domestic and international situation. The rebalancing strategy was mainly aimed at China and Indo-Pacific, stretching from the Western Pacific Ocean to the Indian Ocean, thus naturally including Southeast Asia and the SCS. In order to implement the new Asia-Pacific strategy, the United States persistently interferes in the SCS issue.

The Background of the Rebalancing Strategy

After taking office, Obama changed the neo-conservative thinking of former President Bush Junior's administration, declaring that the United States would get out of the quagmire of the global war on terrorism. Instead, he proposed a strategy of rebalancing towards Asia Pacific. The shift of foreign strategy is based on its domestic political ecology, as well as its cognition and response to the external environment. The U.S. rebalancing strategy towards the Asia-Pacific region also has its specific international and domestic background. It is not only an instinctive response to the increasingly multipolar world and the relative decline of the American power, but also a strategic option to refocus on the Asia-Pacific region as a strategic and economic center, enabling the United States to meet the challenges of emerging powers.

Global Level: An Emerging Multi-polarity

After eight years of war against terror, and the impact of the global financial crisis in 2008 when the Obama administration took office, the U.S. national strength has declined in real terms. Although there has been a constant debate in the United States about the decline of the United States, it is an indisputable fact that the capability of the United States to lead the global economy and international finance has been questioned by the international community.[1] In this regard, some American elites admit that the United States is losing its global dominance, its superior position in politics, economy, security and other fields, and that past glory is hard to resume when one country's economic scale once occupied more than one third of the world.[2] At a time when the United States was focusing on the war against terrorism, emerging powers like China and India were rising rapidly, changing the global political landscape. The collective rise of emerging powers not only enhanced their international influence, but also brought forth calls for the reform of the long-term international order dominated by Western countries and for the construction of a new world order. Newly emerging states have advanced their own interests and want a fair world order.

The change in the balance of power has attracted the attention of the United States. Fareed Zakaria, a well-known political commentator, points out that we are now in a post American Era, in which power is being transferred from the United States to other countries or other actors.[3] Richard N. Haass, President of the American Institute of Foreign Affairs, describes the spread of power and the decline of American international hegemony as the advent of a "non-polarity." In his view, the principle characteristic of 21st-century international relations is turning out to be non-polarity: a world dominated not by one or two or even several states but rather by dozens of actors possessing and exercising various kinds of power. This represents a tectonic shift from the past.[4] Both Zakaria's post American era and Haas's non-polarity reveal a reality: The world is undergoing major changes unseen in a century, and its essence is to bid farewell to the post-Cold War period and move towards a new multipolar era.

The decision-makers of the United States are obviously not fully prepared for the upcoming multipolar world. They are worried that "as wealth and power become less concentrated in the United States' hands, the country will be less able to shape world politics."[5] To a certain extent, they are becoming frightened that the United States will lose its leadership role and be unable to sit at "the head of the table." Such anxiety rises with China's growing power and increasing confidence, and the pessimists who believe in American decline get more support.[6] In order to rebuild the image of the United States, regain American confidence, and reshape the leadership of the United States, the Obama administration decided to withdraw some forces from Iraq and adjust the global strategic layout.

Regional Level: Asia-Pacific Region as the Geopolitical Center

The world's geostrategic situation has undergone unprecedented changes since the 21st century. The rapid economic rise in the Asia-Pacific region and the power shift lead to the "rise in the East and fall in the West," and the Asia-Pacific region once again becomes the geo-economic center. At present, the Asia-Pacific region is not only one of the most economically dynamic regions, but also the largest emerging market in the world, and incorporates the top three economies—the United States, China, and Japan. Moreover, the region also accounts for two thirds of the total foreign exchange reserves, 30 % of the total global exports, and more than 50 % of the economic scale.[7]

In addition, the Asia-Pacific region is home to 40 % of the global population, 2.7 billion consumers, and 44 % of world trade. The large economies in the Asia-Pacific region not only play an indispensable role in participating in global economic governance, but also in promoting high-tech research and development, product innovation, and technology diffusion.[8] According to the prediction of

Goldman Sachs, in the future the global geo-economic focus will shift to the Asia-Pacific region. It is expected that China will replace the United States as the world's largest economy by 2027. By 2050, most of the top 10 economies in the world will be in the Asia-Pacific Region.[9] In the context of the global financial crisis, the booming economy in the Asia-Pacific region was in sharp contrast to the debt-ridden situation of Western countries.

The strategic importance of the Asia-Pacific region to the United States has become increasingly prominent, both in economy and in security. China and Japan are the first and second largest creditors of the United States, and China, Japan, and South Korea are among the seven major trading partners of the United States. At the same time, the region is also one of the most important export destinations for the United States. According to statistics from the U.S. Department of Commerce in 2015, 7 of the top 15 U.S. export markets are located in the Western Pacific region.[10] Considering the economic growth of the United States has not improved significantly since the global economic crisis in 2008, the booming market demand in the Asia-Pacific region was thought of in the United States as a region that would undoubtedly help the United States to expand exports, create employment opportunities, and help to drive the U.S. economy out of the economic trough as soon as possible.[11]

It is worth noting that the Asia-Pacific region is also the only region where legacies of the Cold War remain. The Korean Peninsula issue, the Taiwan issue, and the rising maritime sovereignty dispute in East Asia in recent years are all closely related to the post WWII security interests of the United States. The long-standing non-traditional security issues in the region, such as terrorism, nuclear proliferation, resource competition, frequent natural disasters, and transnational epidemic diseases, also pose potential challenges to the United States.[12] More importantly, alliances in the Asia-Pacific region are the cornerstone for the United States to implement strategy in Asia and even in the world, which is of decisive significance to U.S. national security. As former Secretary of State Hillary Clinton said, "the United States cannot economically separate itself from the Asia Pacific region," "our enterprises export $320 billion in goods and services to Asia Pacific countries every year, creating millions of jobs. At the same time, thousands of U.S. military personnel are serving to maintain security in the region, a work that has continued for generations."[13] To sum up, the geostrategic significance of the Asia-Pacific region as a geopolitical center and the economic and security interests of the United States in the region determine the Obama administration's strategic direction in its pivot to the Asia-Pacific region.

Domestic Level: Militarism and Its Consequences

For a long time, the United States has been self-proclaimed as the "freedom beacon" and "model of democracy," but it has always preferred to use force. It is not difficult to find that the United States is not only an "armed America" (its military power has been outstanding for a long time), "a warrior America" (various military strategic ideas emerge in endlessly), but also a "militaristic America" (daring to use force frequently abroad).[14] Some scholars attribute the behavior of attaching importance to war preparation at home and inclining to use force abroad as "militarism."[15] There is no doubt that after the end of the Cold War, especially after the 9/11 incident, the Bush Junior's administration was gravitating towards unilateralism in the name of anti-terrorism, and successively launched the wars in Afghanistan and Iraq, and used force to preempt and subvert the regime, which is the vivid reflection of the American militarism.

The reason why militarism prevails in the United States, on the one hand, stems from the self-confidence of American policy makers and elite groups on the national strength and global status of the United States. Brzezinski, a famous American geostrategic scholar, once made a classic comment on America's status after the Cold War. As he put, "the scope and pervasiveness of American global power today are unique. Not only does the United States control all of the world's oceans and seas, but it has developed an assertive military capability for amphibious shore control that enables it to project its power inland in politically significant ways."[16] Due to its unparalleled military strength, American policy makers showed an aggressive posture in foreign policy and became confrontational without fear when launching a war. On the other hand, it also stems from the acquiescence of the American people to overseas military intervention. With a superior geographical position and advanced modern technology supporting national strength, Americans rarely experience the destruction and fear of war, thus they lack a negative historical memory of war. As a result, Americans are more likely to support government military interventions abroad.[17]

However, the "militarism" under the Bush Junior's administration has brought serious domestic and foreign consequences. When Obama took office in the White House in 2009, American national power was seriously weakened and its international image was badly damaged. Therefore, international strategic resources urgently needed to be redistributed. It can be said that the United States has overdrawn its national strength due to its lust for profit and abuse of power. The situation has flared up in the United States, and the contradictions and problems have been intensified at home and abroad, leading to Washington's new experience of mounting international criticism.[18] President Obama depicted this situation in his inaugural speech that "we are in the midst of crisis is now well understood. Our nation is at war against a far-reaching network of violence and hatred. Our economy is badly weakened, a consequence of greed and irresponsibility on the part of some, but also our collective failure to make hard choices and prepare the nation for a new age . . . that the challenges we face are real."[19] The "lost decade" began to haunt the United States, becoming a new memory for Americans. It can be seen that the militarism pursued by Bush Junior's administration and its serious consequences have led to a profound self-examination for the elite leadership of the United States. It forced the United States to change its course and restore its diplomatic strategy to the normal track.

Shadow of China: The Key River behind U.S. Rebalancing Strategy

The Obama administration has repeatedly stressed that the United States welcomes a rising China to shoulder a responsible leadership under U.S. leadership; encourages China to make greater contributions to peace, security, and prosperity; and hopes that the United States and China can carry out steady and pragmatic cooperation.[20] Some people of insight also believe that it is obviously too superficial to interpret the U.S. policy as containment against China. The new Asia-Pacific strategy of the United States, which is based on strategic, economic, and political basis, is the reflection and continuation of its long-term focus on the interests of the Asia-Pacific region, rather than "tailor-made" for China.[21]

However, it is undeniable that China is indeed closely related to the formulation of the new Asia-Pacific strategy.[22] As Zhao Suisheng, director of the U.S.-China Cooperation Research Center at Denver University, said, China is an important factor in the Obama administration's new Asia-Pacific strategic layout. This is not only because cooperation with Beijing is the key to the success of this strategy, but also to cope with the changes in regional power patterns caused by China's rise and American concerns about Beijing's rising influence.[23] In other words, the rebalance is not "only" about China, while it is certainly "also" about China.[24]

In fact, the rapid rise of China in the new century shocked the United States. In 2010, China surpassed Japan to become the world's second largest economy following the United States, while its total industrial output value surpassed that of the United States and leaped to first in the world, and its total export volume surpassed that of Germany and ranked first in the world. The trade volume of China-Japan, China-ROK (Republic of Korea) is also more than that of the U.S.-Japan, U.S.-ROK. All of these changes suggest an accelerating power shift towards China.[25] According to the Carnegie Endowment for International Peace, China will surpass the United States as the world's largest economy in a generation. If China's economy grows at an average annual rate of 5.6 % from 2009 to 2050, its GDP will jump from 3.3 trillion U.S. dollars in 2009 to about 46.3 trillion U.S. dollars in 2050. At that time, China's total economic volume will exceed that of the United States by more than 20 %.[26] In view of the great prospect of China's economic growth, C. Fred Bergsten, director of the Peterson Institute for International Economics, once put forward a "G-2" approach between the United States and China to steer global governance process, which aroused strong international repercussions.[27] More importantly, according to the estimation of the Stockholm International Peace Research Institute, in line with the momentum of economic development, China's military rise will be inevitable, and its military expenditure will exceed that of the United States in 2035.[28] With China's strength enhancement, its interaction with the external environment is changing from the past "passive response" to a more "active shaping," and appears more confident in safeguarding its own core interests,[29] rather than endless compromising.

Changes in the balance of power between China and the United States have undoubtedly increased the anxiety of the United States about its own decline. Americans generally regard China as a competitor and have great concerns about China's strategic options.[30] For instance, in his 2011 State of the Union address, Obama repeatedly mentioned China's leading position in the fields of solar energy utilization, high-performance computer production, and high speed railways. Taking the launch of the first human satellite by the Soviet Union half a century ago as an example, Obama declared that the United States was facing a new "Sputnik moment," thus in order to win back control of the future, the United States must redouble its efforts.[31] At the same time, through the results of surveys conducted by several American institutions, it is found that the ordinary American has more awareness of China's rise. Compared with the past, people who recognize "China rises," "China is extremely important," "China surpasses the United States," "China is the first," "the United States is declining," and "China's threat" have increased significantly.[32] In combination, the speeches of the President, the work of institutions and the media combined to create awareness, if not a growing fear, among the general population.

What is more challenging is that China's development model is different from the "liberal" political and economic model of the United States, but it still has achieved great success.[33] If some developing countries follow China's development, it will undoubtedly overshadow the once dazzling American model.[34] In fact, China's success has attracted extensive attention in many developing countries, and its fruitful achievements brought by reform and opening up have also provided a roadmap for other countries, which has increased the pressure on the United States. Thus, it is not difficult to find that U.S. rebalancing toward the Asia-Pacific region is not completely directed against China, but there is still the China shadow behind it.

Strategic Initiatives of the Rebalancing Strategy

Since the end of the Cold War, the United States has constantly modified the strategy towards Asia Pacific. Both the "Pacific Community" of the Bush Senior's administration and the "New Pacific Community" of the Clinton administration exemplify the increasing importance of the Asia-Pacific region in the post-Cold War era. Bush Junior's administration relatively neglected the importance of Asia due to its focus in the war on terror. Compared with previous administrations, the Obama administration stepped up and broadened U.S. engagement in the Asia-Pacific region, and its rebalancing strategy is a multidimensional strategy, covering political, diplomatic, military, economic, and wide-ranging fields.

Strengthening Political and Diplomatic Alliances and Partnerships

There are many allies and partners of the United States in the Asia-Pacific region. It was vital to reestablish a dominant structure for the American alliance system in the Asia-Pacific region, and a network of bilateral alliances and partnerships and multilateral relationships. In this regard, the 2010 U.S. National Security Strategy report pointed out that "Alliances are power multipliers: through cooperation and coordination with multiple allies, collective power is much better than the United States acting alone." In view of the fact that "the U.S. allies with Japan, South Korea, Australia, the Philippines and Thailand are the cornerstones of maintaining Asian security and the foundation for the prosperity of the Asia Pacific region," the United States will "continue to deepen and update these alliances to reflect the dynamics of regional change and the strategic trend of the 21st century."[35] Specifically, the United States has strengthened the alliance with Japan, South Korea, Australia, and the Philippines, as well as its partnerships with India and Vietnam.

In terms of bilateral alliance relations, the Obama administration attached particular importance to strengthening its relations with Japan and South Korea. The United States sees the U.S.-Japan alliance as a foundation of the regional security architecture and critical to the rebalancing towards the Asia Pacific, so the first foreign leader that President Obama met with in the Oval Office was the Prime Minister of Japan. Secretary of State Hillary Clinton also chose Japan as the first stop of her Asian trip. At the U.S.-Japan Foreign and Defense Ministers' Meeting in June 2011, the two governments outlined their common strategic objectives and reaffirmed the commitment to strengthen alliance cooperation in a regional and global setting. In response to the new changes in the global strategic situation, the two countries extended their cooperation fields to global concerns such as oceans, space, and the internet in the "United States-Japan Joint Statement: A Shared Vision for the Future" issued on April 30, 2012.[36] In November 2012, U.S. Deputy to National Security Advisor Donilon once again reiterated that the key to the implementation of the strategy of rebalancing toward Asia Pacific is security cooperation with Japan. The United States will vigorously enhance bilateral cooperation in the field of security and promote Japan to play its due role in regional security.[37] In the U.S.-Japan Joint Vision Statement issued in April 2015, the two governments also stressed close cooperation through the U.S. rebalancing strategy and Japan's "proactive contribution to peace" to maintain peace and prosperity in the region and the world.[38]

As the bridgehead of the United States in Northeast Asia, South Korea is undoubtedly an important fulcrum for the United States to promote the rebalancing strategy in the Asia-Pacific region. With China's rapid economic development in recent years, South Korea has recently become closer to China, mainly for economic reasons. However, the "Cheonan" incident in March 2010 increased South Korea's security dependence on the United States, resulting in unprecedented cooperation in foreign policy and military defense.[39] Since then, the landmark Korea-U.S. FTA entered into force on March 15, 2012, underscoring the depth of bilateral political and economic ties. The agreement not only helps Korean enterprises to enter the U.S. market, but also brings closer the political and military relations between the two sides. It goes beyond economic ties and became an important political consideration.[40] On June 14, U.S. Secretary of Defense Panetta reiterated at the second U.S.-Korean Ministerial Dialogue 2+2 Meetings that South Korea is extremely crucial in the rebalancing strategy being formulated by the U.S. DoD, and the alliance with South Korea is one of the cornerstones of the implementation of this strategy.[41] Under the influence of the U.S. rebalancing strategy, the U.S.-ROK alliance has undergone two changes: one is the transformation from the bilateral operation of the United States and South Korea to the trilateral cooperation between the United States, Japan, and the ROK; the other is the transformation from a single deterrence to a dual deterrence against North Korea and China.[42]

Australia is an important springboard in the U.S. rebalancing strategy, which provides strategic surveillance for the United States in Southeast Asia: the Indian and the Pacific Oceans. With the in-depth implementation of the rebalancing strategy, both the Australia-New Zealand-America Security Alliance mechanism and the Australia-U.S. Ministerial Conference mechanism have been strengthened to varying degrees.[43] Meanwhile, the United States and Australia continue to expand cooperation in counter-terrorism, space, internet, and other fields.[44] In September 2011, the Foreign Ministers and Defense Ministers of the United States and Australia met and reached two important achievements on strengthening bilateral security cooperation: First, the U.S. military was allowed to enter Australia for the first time, which was the biggest breakthrough in the past 30 years since the establishment of the U.S.-Australia alliance; second, cyber warfare was included in bilateral defense treaties, which is the first time that the United States has carried out cooperation in this field outside of NATO.[45]

As to U.S.-Philippine relations, American focus on China and the rising tensions in the SCS between China and the Philippines have energized the U.S.-Philippine alliance. In January 2011, the United States and the Philippines held the first Bilateral Strategic Dialogue in Manila, setting up four working groups including the legislature and the rule of law, economy and trade, territorial defense and maritime security, and regional and global relations. In April 2012, the two sides held the first 2+2 meeting for Foreign Ministers and Defense Ministers in Washington, D.C., reaffirming the strategic value of the U.S.-Philippines alliance as "an anchor" for peace, stability, and prosperity in the Asia-Pacific region.[46] Besides, the United States has also increased economic assistance and disaster relief to the Philippines, and made efforts to enhance the cooperation between the two countries in non-military fields.

While strengthening bilateral alliances, the United States has also strengthened its partnership with India, Vietnam, and other countries in the region. As an emerging power, India's geostrategic importance is self-evident. Taking advantage of India's increasing economic strength and its function to check and balance China, the United States has increased its attention towards India in promoting the rebalancing strategy. In July 2009, Secretary of State Hillary Clinton said on her visit to India that she sought to launch the third phase of the U.S.-India relationship "upgrade" to a new version she dubbed "U.S.-India 3.0," recognizing

India as a global partner of the United States. Additionally, in the 2010 National Security Strategy Report, the Obama administration declared that the strategic relationship between the United States and India was based on shared interests. It was intended to be the embodiment of the common values of the two largest democratic countries in the world.[47]

In order to promote the development of the strategic partnership between the two countries, the United States restarted U.S.-India strategic dialogue in June 2010. In October, Secretary of State Hillary Clinton used "India Pacific" in her speech for the first time in Hawaii, pointed out the importance of this region, and stressed the need to strengthen maritime military cooperation with India and other countries.[48] In November, President Obama took the opportunity of his visit to India to further ties between the two countries. He not only publicly expressed his support for India to be elected a permanent member of the UN Security Council, but also announced the relaxation of U.S. technology export restrictions to India since India's nuclear test in 1998, and lifted the ban on India's purchase of U.S. military and civilian technology.[49] Moreover, in the strategic guidance released by the Pentagon in January 2012, Washington also claimed that it would focus on developing a long-term strategic partnership with India, to enhance India's capability as an anchor for the regional economy and a broader provider of security in the Indian Ocean region.[50] For the first time, India was promoted by the U.S. as a key partner in its global security aims.

The United States has also begun to attach importance to Vietnam under the rebalancing strategy. In the 2010 Quadrennial Defense Review Report, Vietnam was listed as the potential member for a "new strategic relationship."[51] On August 17, the first U.S.-Vietnam Defense Policy Dialogue was held in Hanoi, which finalized regular military exchange and policy cooperation between the two sides.[52] In September 2011, the United States and Vietnam established a Memorandum of Understanding (MOU) on defense cooperation, which clearly outlined that cooperation between the two sides would be extended to maritime security, maritime search and rescue, United Nations' peacekeeping operations, humanitarian relief and exchanges by defense, science, and education institutions.[53] In June 2012, U.S. Defense Secretary Leon Panetta visited Cam Ranh Bay, the deep water port and former American military base, as part of an effort to promote a closer military partnership with the Vietnamese and reassert the U.S. presence in Asia. The visit had deep historical significance, in that Mr. Panetta is the first U.S. Defense Secretary to visit Cam Ranh Bay since the end of the Vietnam War. Panetta also expressed the desire of the U.S. military to use Cam Ranh Bay base in future, saying that "it will be particularly important to work with partners like Vietnam to use harbors like this as we move our ships from our ports on the west coast to our stations here in the Pacific."[54] After the fourth defense policy dialogue between Vietnam and the United States at the deputy ministerial level on October 28, 2013, the two sides had more in-depth interaction in security, and promised to strengthen dialogue and cooperation on issues left over from the Vietnam War, maritime security, the SCS issue, and the ASEAN Defense Ministers Meeting.[55] On May 6, 2014, the two countries signed an Agreement on the peaceful use of nuclear energy, marking significant progress in nuclear energy cooperation and moving Vietnam away from its dependence on Chinese and Korean coal.

Strengthen the Military Security Presence and Military Strength Construction

It is an important means for the United States to continuously strengthen its military presence and military strength build-up in the Asia-Pacific region to promote its rebalancing strategy. In fact, military and security constitute the most preeminent and practical part of the Asia-Pacific rebalancing strategy.[56] In his speech to the Australian Parliament in November 2011, President Obama said that the United States had begun a review that identified the most important strategic interests and guided its defense priorities and spending over the coming decade. As the wars in the Middle East ended, the government had directed its national security team to make its presence and mission in Asia Pacific a top priority. As a result, reductions in U.S. defense spending would not "come at the expense of Asia Pacific."[57] On January 5, 2012, the U.S. DoD also pointed out in its strategic report that the United States was facing severe budget pressure, but it would strive to maintain its status as the premier military power. At the same time, the report also advocated strengthening military presence in the Asia-Pacific region and turning the U.S. military focus to the Asia-Pacific region.[58]

On the whole, the Obama administration's rebalancing in the Asia-Pacific region stressed geography and capability: On the one hand, the United States shifted global strategic resources to the Asia-Pacific region, extending from Northeast Asia to Southeast Asia, South Asia and Oceania. On the other hand, it will continue to strengthen the size of the Asia-Pacific garrison and seek to maintain absolute military superiority.[59]

First, the United States has increased its military deployment in the Asia-Pacific region. In June 2012, Defense Secretary Panetta announced at the Shangri La Dialogue held in Singapore that although a number of U.S. warships would be decommissioned in the following five years, the United States would replace them with more than 40 warships that possessed new military technologies and upgraded combat power capabilities. Moreover, in the following years, the U.S. military would increase its activities in the Asia-Pacific region, including increasing the scale and frequency of joint military exercises, and the frequency of warships visiting ports in the region. At present, the U.S. Navy's deployment in the Pacific and Atlantic Ocean's is roughly equal. By 2020, the United States will deploy 60 % of its surface ships in the Asia-Pacific region, including six aircraft carriers, the majority of its cruisers, destroyers, littoral combat ships, and submarines.[60] At the same time, nearly 60 % of available U.S. F-22 fighters and 70,000 soldiers will be deployed in the Asia-Pacific region in the future, including the First U.S. Army, the main U.S. ground force.[61] In addition, the United States intends to prioritize deployment of the latest and most advanced weapons, including the F-35 joint attack aircraft, new electronic and communication technologies, improved precision-guided weapons, and cruise missiles, to the Indo-Pacific region.[62]

Second, the United States has expanded its military presence in the Asia-Pacific region. To cope with tensions on the Korean Peninsula and the Taiwan Strait, U.S. military deployment in the Asia-Pacific region is mainly concentrated in Northeast Asia. In the context of its rebalancing in the Asia-Pacific region, the United States has expanded its military presence in Oceania, Southeast Asia, and the Indian Ocean.[63] For example, in the summer of 2012, the first 250 U.S. Marines arrived in Darwin, Australia, and the number was expected to reach 2500 within five years. The United States and Australia have also agreed that Australia will operate a U.S. Air Force C-band ground-based radar system and establish the Space Surveillance Telescope in Australia to jointly build a space defense line to monitor the Pacific Ocean, the Indian Ocean, and the entire continent of Asia.[64] On March 1, 2013, the first U.S. Navy's Littoral Combat Ship officially left for Singapore, starting an 8-month deployment rotation. In addition, the United States has strengthened its military relations with the Philippines, Indonesia, Malaysia, Thailand, Myanmar, and other Southeast Asian countries through arms sales, joint training, port visits, optimized deployment, and restoration of military relations.[65] The United States also attaches great importance to India in the Asia-Pacific rebalancing strategy regarding that State as possessor of a key role in shaping regional security and prosperity in the 21st century. The two countries not only expanded their arms trade, but also carry out frequent joint military exercises. In the past few years, the United States has become the country with the largest number of military exercises in partnership with India.[66] In addition to strengthening bilateral alliances, the United States has continued to encourage Indo-Pacific allies and partners to strengthen mutual security cooperation, leading and promoting the "small trilateral" relations, namely, U.S.-Japan-ROK, U.S.-Japan-Australia, U.S.-Japan-India, and U.S.-India-Australia.[67]

Third, the United States has renewed its military operational concepts and increased its military technological innovation. To cope with the anti-access and area-denial capabilities of China and Iran, and to ensure its military intervention and free action in the world are not challenged, the United States actively updates its operational concept and continuously developed the integrated operation capabilities by coordinating action in sea, land, air, network, and electricity. Among them, Air-Sea Battle, launched by the U.S. DoD in 2010, is the vivid reflection of this innovative concept, which constitutes the core of the U.S. rebalancing strategy in the aspect of military.[68] In January 2012, U.S. DoD issued Joint Operational Access Concept 2012 to outline the concept in detail.[69] Air-Sea Battle mainly tries to deal with the threat of anti-access and area-denial of other countries through use of superior naval and air forces, and by improving joint operations, military deterrence, and long-distance delivery capabilities in the global public domain, so as to ensure American global leadership and strategic interests.[70] The Pentagon also clearly proposed in Defense Budget Priorities and Choices Fiscal 2014 that it would increase the investment in space, Special Forces and networks, and focus on the research and development of advanced technologies such as intelligence collection, military reconnaissance, and remote monitoring, so as to provide support for improving the capability of Air-Sea Battle.[71]

Seeking to Lead Regional Integration and Regional Economic Cooperation

Economic and trade factors are the reason for the United States to put forward the Asia Pacific "rebalancing" strategy, and also important tools for the Obama administration to implement the strategy. Considering the past economic achievements, the current booming economic vitality and the optimistic developing trend in the future, the Asia-Pacific region turns out to be of great importance in the future global economic and trade pattern. For the United States, Asia is one of the most dynamic and fastest developing regions in the world, and its open markets provide unprecedented historical opportunities for the United States to invest, trade, and engage in high-end product research and development. What's more, the export of American companies to Asia and the development of the huge and growing consumer market in the region will help promote the recovery of the U.S. domestic economy.[72]

At the same time, the regional economic integration in Asian countries in recent years also puts the United States under pressure of being "marginalized." According to research, the number of FTAs in Asia has increased from 3 in 2000 to 61 in 2010, and 79 FTAs are under negotiation.[73] Besides, Asia-Pacific countries have also deepened the construction of regional integration through APEC, "ASEAN+3," and "ASEAN+6." In 2007, the ten ASEAN countries promised to establish an ASEAN economic community in 2015 to create a "single market and production base."[74] If successful, then the ASEAN economic community, together with the existing bilateral FTAs and the agreements under negotiation, will lay a foundation for economic integration in the Asia-Pacific region. Given the importance of the Asia-Pacific region to the U.S. economy, in order to avoid losing Asia and slipping into the "marginalized" situation, as well as to reverse the unfavorable situation of "export security and harvest deficit," the Obama administration tries to seek the leading role in the economic cooperation and integration of the Asia-Pacific region by promoting and leading the negotiation of the Trans-Pacific Strategic Economic Partnership Agreements.

The Trans-Pacific Partnership (TPP) is an agreement to promote mutually beneficial economic and trade cooperation. It was signed by Singapore, Chile, Brunei, and New Zealand in June 2005, and is aimed to promote trade liberalization in the Asia-Pacific region.[75] In November 2009, after the Obama administration announced that the United States had joined the TPP negotiations, the term spread widely in the international community, and Washington began to play a leading role in it. Admittedly, TPP will help to expand U.S. exports, create more employment opportunities, and promote the U.S. economic recovery, but more importantly, through participating in the TPP negotiations, the United States can obtain the following benefits at the political and strategic levels. First, the high standards of environmental protection, intellectual property protection, and labor will contribute to the improvement of the competitiveness of American enterprises and the protection of relevant intellectual property rights, and provide opportunity for the United States to maintain the America-led international trade rules. Second, the United States can disrupt the economic cooperation and integration in East Asia, and regain the leading position in Asia-Pacific cooperation. Third, TPP can help the United States to promote strategic relations with the countries concerned in Asia Pacific, especially to increase the dependence of some countries in Asia Pacific on the United States in politics and security so that the United States can maintain its superiority in the region.[76]

Since the United States announced its participation in TPP negotiations, Japan, South Korea, Australia, Vietnam, Malaysia, and other countries have followed up to join the negotiation. During this period, the United States also actively lobbied and solicited other ASEAN members to join the negotiations, claiming that this trade plan would benefit all economies, both developed and developing countries in the entire Pacific region. Douglas Paal, vice president of Carnegie Endowment for International Peace, believes that the WTO negotiations under Doha Round "seems to be really stuck" and the TPP is just trying to replace it and attempting to include more countries.[77] Kenneth Lieberthal of the Brookings Institution also points out that TPP is only a "WTO+." In other words, it contains a lot of things that the WTO already has, but adds labor standards, environmental standards, and other content that WTO does not cover.[78] In addition to having higher environmental protection and labor standards, TPP also requires a higher tariff reduction than previous world trade agreements.

As a free trade agreement, TPP has more political implications in the context of the U.S. rebalancing strategy toward the Asia-Pacific region. As Claude Barfield of the American Enterprise Research Institute has said, as a trade-centered negotiation among countries, the negotiation process of TPP is full of uncertainties, and its prospect is still not clear. However, the strategic importance has far exceeded the negotiation itself. TPP can be seen as an important symbol of the capability of the United States to pivot toward the Asia-Pacific region and to play its economic leadership in the Asia-Pacific region.[79]

On March 11, 2013, President Obama's former National Security Advisor Donilon said at the Asia Society that the centerpiece of economic rebalancing is the TPP, thus its goals are strategic as well as economic. The TPP is also "an absolute statement of U.S. strategic commitment to be in the Asia-Pacific for the long haul."[80] Therefore, TPP is the main tool for the United States to implement economic rebalancing in the Asia-Pacific region. As the United States tries to weaken the influence of East Asian trade groups by means of TPP, and at the same time, it creates a "high-standard and binding" economic and trade framework in the Asia-Pacific region, so as to consolidate the asymmetric economic status of the United States against emerging trade groups.

Rebalancing Strategy and the U.S. Policy Shift on SCS

The term "rebalancing" does not originate from the concept of "balance of power," and its underlying logic is the concept of asset redistribution in financial portfolio. When market conditions change and new business opportunities appear, it is necessary to rebalance the portfolio to maximize the return on investment. In this sense, the rebalancing strategy aims to find a balance between America's commitment to global diplomatic, economic, and military resources and its expanding political, economic, and security interests in Asia.[81] To some extent, the term "rebalancing" does reflect the main purpose of the U.S. strategic adjustment towards Asia Pacific. The original strategic pattern of the Asia-Pacific region has become "unbalanced" with the changes in regional power structures in the post-Cold War period. In order to maintain its hegemony, the United States must reestablish a new strategic balance that adapts to the profound changes of international relations in the 21st century.[82] In this regard, it is not accurate to see the rebalancing strategy as a global strategic adjustment or downsizing action, but rather a global hegemonic protection.

Rebalancing Strategy and the SCS

The rebalancing strategy in the Asia-Pacific region is an instinctive protective response made by the United States against the background of the decline of its national strength. It is also the most important reorientation of the U.S. national security strategy in the new century.[83] According to the U.S. former national security advisor Donilon, the centerpiece of this strategy includes an intensified American role in this vital region and ensures the security, prosperity and human dignity to the U.S. and its allies. To this end, security in the region requires that international law and norms be respected, that commerce and freedom of navigation are not impeded, that emerging powers build trust with their neighbors, and that disagreements are resolved peacefully without threats or coercion. All nations must play by the same rules.[84] Although the U.S. politicians have repeatedly claimed that the Asia-Pacific rebalancing strategy is not encircling China, the United States has frequently attacked China in political, diplomatic, military, economic, and other fields, which means that the strategy is tailor-made for China to a large extent. Therefore, the SCS issue, as the hot topic in the region, will naturally become a stepping stone for the United States to implement the Asia-Pacific rebalancing strategy.

First, the SCS issue is a touchstone to test whether China challenges American leadership. Most of the American strategic analysts believe that with the sustained and rapid rise of China, the United States and China have fallen into a "Thucydides trap" and will therefore encounter problems.[85] The two countries cannot avoid the "tragedy of great power politics." A strong China is bound to seek regional hegemony and challenge the leadership of the United States.[86] In their view, China's assertiveness in SCS in recent years reflected its attempt to seek regional dominance. For example, a research report released by Center for a New American Security (CNAS) in 2012 pointed out that the SCS will be a "barometer" that will determine the future leadership of the United States in the Asia-Pacific region, and it will become the world's geo-economic center to some extent. If the United States reduces its military presence in the Western Pacific due to the economic downturn, especially in the SCS, then the countries around the SCS will either be intimidated by China's rising military power or they will turn to China on their own initiative. By that time, the "free and open" world maritime order established and dominated by the United States for more than 100 years will be greatly challenged, and the leading position of the United States in the world will also be greatly weakened.[87] Therefore, some elites of the United States believe that the SCS issue has gone beyond freedom of navigation and maritime security to a certain extent, but determines whether the United States can ensure its maritime hegemony and global leadership.

Second, in recent years, China's "maritime ambition" has strengthened the determination of the United States to actively intervene in the SCS dispute, so as to ensure that China abides by its rules and prevent the United States from being "expelled" from the Western Pacific. In November 2012, the 18th NCCPC clearly put forward the strategic goal to "resolutely safeguard China's maritime rights and interests, and build China into a maritime power."[88] On July 30, 2013, when China's President Xi Jinping presided over the collective learning of the Central Political Bureau as the theme of "promoting the construction of a powerful maritime country," he pointed out that "we must keep in mind the importance of maintaining stability and safeguarding rights, uphold state sovereignty, security and development interests, and maintain the maritime rights and improve the comprehensive national strength."[89] Against this background, China has made vigorous efforts to safeguard its maritime rights, accelerated the pace of building its maritime military forces, and began to carry out reclamation operations on some islands and reefs in the SCS.

China's actions have aroused concerns from the United States. It is generally believed that China's growing maritime military strength, especially its continuously improved anti-access and area-denial capabilities, will not only break the military balance across the Taiwan Strait, but also pose a threat to the U.S. naval operations in the western Pacific region.[90] With China's actions in the SCS, it will threaten or affect the U.S. freedom of navigation in the SCS and the safety of the route from the Pacific to the Indian Ocean.[91] It can be seen that when China's maritime ambition encounters American rebalancing strategy toward the Asia-Pacific region, the SCS will inevitably become a "disputed region." For the United States, it can make waves on the SCS to contain China. Through the intervention of the SCS, the United States can form a potential deterrent to China's economy by clamping down on China's energy and trade transportation, and also restrict the continued development of China's maritime power, thus delaying or even hindering China's building into a great maritime power.[92]

Third, the U.S. involvement in the SCS issue is also subordinate to its Southeast Asian strategic layout, and is closely related to American security commitments to the region and its international reputation. During the George W. Bush administration, the United States devoted too much attention to the Middle East, resulting in the perception of relative neglect in Southeast Asia. Therefore, in order to return to Southeast Asia, the U.S. political leaders not only visited ASEAN countries, promoted the United States initiative to join the Treaty of Amity and Cooperation in Southeast Asia, but also attended the ASEAN summit, East Asia Summit, and other regional multilateral dialogues. In this context, the traditional friendly relations between the United States and its partners in the region, such as Singapore, the Philippines, and Thailand, have been consolidated, and exchanges with Vietnam, Indonesia, Myanmar, and other countries have also been strengthened. Meantime, the United States takes the SCS dispute as a stepping stone to return to Southeast Asia. The United States seemingly holds an impartial attitude towards the sovereignty dispute and pretends to be a regional arbiter, while actually taking favorable actions towards the Philippines and Vietnam. In this way, the United States not only enhances its discourse power on the SCS issue, but also achieves the goal of containing China to a certain extent.

Fourth, due to the gap in national strength among the countries around the SCS, in face of China's rise and its land reclamation in the SCS, the claimants in Southeast Asia not only choose to unify, but also "invite" the United States to intervene in the dispute and contain China. As Lee Kuan Yew, former Minister Mentor of Singapore, said at the U.S.-ASEAN Business Council in Washington on October 27, 2009, whatever challenges it faces, the core interests of the United States require it to remain a superpower in the Pacific. If the United States gives up this position, it will weaken the position of the United States in the world.[93] On May 19, 2016, Philippine President Aquino III also declared that the United States "has to maintain its ascendancy, moral ascendancy, and also the confidence of one of its allies."[94] Robert Willard, Commander in Chief of the U.S. Pacific Command, also claimed that the concerns of the United States on the SCS stems from the general concern in the region about China's maritime demands.[95]

Therefore, the United States is an "invited imperialist."[96] By supporting the SCS dispute parties of ASEAN and showing a tough stance towards China, the United States can not only pacify its Southeast Asian allies and partners, and alleviate their anxiety of being abandoned, but also maintain the credibility of the United States as a regional security upholder, thereby securing its place in the region.[97]

Major Shift of the U.S. Policy toward SCS

Under the background of rebalancing strategy in the Asia-Pacific region, the Obama administration's SCS policy tends to be tough, and has significantly increased its involvement in the SCS issue. On July 23, 2010, Secretary of State Hillary Clinton announced the Obama administration's policy on the SCS issue at the ASEAN Regional Forum (ARF) in Hanoi, claiming that the United States has extensive national interests and international interests in the SCS. The United States supports the parties to the SCS dispute to resolve issues through diplomatic consultations and oppose the use or threat of force. Although the United States claims to take no side in sovereignty claims in the SCS, those claims should comply with the UNCLOS.[98] Clinton's speech marks a new round of adjustments for the U.S. policy on SCS issues, and also indicates the new great game between China and the U.S. in the SCS. Looking through the various statements and policy statements issued by the United States on the SCS issue during the Obama administration, it is not difficult to find that, to coordinate with the adjustment of the Asia-Pacific strategy, the United States showed a robust stance on the SCS issue, and took targeted measures to contain China.

First, the United States has increased criticism and boosted pressure on China. Under the background of the rebalancing strategy in the Asia-Pacific region, the United States has constantly accused China of deteriorating the situation in the SCS with its assertive rights protection actions. On March 8, 2009, regardless of China's legitimate interests and security concerns in the SCS, the United States sent the U.S. Navy ocean surveillance ship *Impeccable* to carry out illegal survey activities in the EEZ of the SCS, which were countered by the law enforcement actions of Chinese vessels, which led to the Impeccable Incident. After the incident, the U.S. DoD issued a statement, publicly accusing China of harassment and aggressive shadowing of a U.S. Navy ocean surveillance ship in international waters, claiming that the U.S. Navy "will continue to operate in those international waters, and expect the Chinese to observe international law around there."[99] Nonetheless, Timothy Keating, head of the U.S. Pacific Command, said at a congressional hearing held on March 19 that the incident showed that China's "behavior as a responsible stakeholder has yet to be consistently demonstrated," and China's real military and strategic intentions must be taken into consideration. As he put, "the Impeccable incident is certainly a troubling indicator that China, particularly in the SCS, is behaving in an aggressive, troublesome manner and are not willing to abide by acceptable standards of behavior or rules of the road."[100] On June 27, 2011, the U.S. Senate also unanimously passed a resolution condemning China's assertiveness in the SCS, demanding that the United States strengthen its military presence in the region and make efforts to push the SCS issue towards a multilateral and peaceful settlement process.[101]

On August 3, 2012, the U.S. DoS issued the second policy statement on the SCS issue since the end of the Cold War. In this policy statement, the United States reiterated its national interests in the maintenance of peace and stability in the SCS, respect for international law, freedom of navigation and unimpeded legitimate commercial activities, and also publicly criticized the decision of the Chinese government to establish Sansha city and the stationing of new troops in the disputed areas of the SCS. The risk of escalating regional tensions runs counter to cooperative diplomatic efforts to resolve differences.[102] At the same time, China listed the sovereignty and territorial integrity of Diaoyu/Senkaku Islands as core interests during this period, and released a new version of the map illustrating China's territory in the SCS, as well as routine patrols by law enforcement vessels stationed in waters near Second Thomas Shoal. On July 29, 2013, the U.S. Senate passed a resolution accusing China of changing the territorial status quo of Diaoyu/Senkaku Islands and the SCS by threatening and using force, and continued to put pressure on China.[103] On March 31, 2015, Admiral Harris, commander of the U.S. Pacific Command, called China "provocative and expansionist," accusing China of "creating a Great Wall of sand" and "clearly militarizing" the disputed waters of the Western Pacific.[104] On May 6, 2016, Harris publicly demanded that his forces must be ready "to fight tonight."[105] Such a tough statement is undoubtedly a continuation of the U.S. tough attitude towards China on the SCS issue, and is also the latest development of American military intervention in the SCS issue.

Second, the United States opposes historic claims over the islands and maritime areas of the SCS. It is acknowledged that a country's sovereignty, sovereign rights, and jurisdiction over land has been established in the long course of history, and are solidly grounded in history. Likewise, each legal basis must be based on historical facts. Otherwise, the law will lack fairness and justice. Therefore, historical evidence in sovereignty claims cannot be ignored, and is the primary evidence to resolve territorial disputes. For this reason, China opposed ignoring historical facts and taking UNCLOS as the sole basis to determine sovereignty disputes in the SCS.[106] In addition, the current International Law of the Sea is evolved from the modern Western maritime law, which is quite different from the concept of territory in traditional Chinese culture, in which territorial sovereignty is determined by social organizations, historical traditions, and living regions of various nationalities. Therefore, if China's long-standing historic sovereignty and jurisdiction over the SCS is examined through the lenses of the international law, it has little or no legal value for China to establish its various claims, which is completely unreasonable.[107]

Nevertheless, after the Cold War, the United States has shown a tendency of attaching importance to law and neglecting history on the SCS issue. Especially since Obama came to power, the United States has held high the banner of international law, especially the UNCLOS, claiming that the settlement of the SCS dispute must be based on international law, ignoring China's historical claims, and publicly questioning China's historical rights in the SCS. On July 15, 2009, Robert Scher, Deputy Assistant Secretary of Defense, testified before the Foreign Relations Committee of the Senate that "China's territorial claims over all of the islands in the SCS is weak, in that it actually controls relatively few of them and may never, in its long history, have actually maintained effective administration and control over most of them. Thus, China's claims on the sovereignty over the SCS are not recognized by the international community."[108] On June 5, 2013, Joseph Yun, Acting Assistant Secretary for East Asian and Pacific Affairs of U.S. DoS, made a statement at a conference on the SCS issue held by the Center for Strategic and International Studies (CSIS), a Washington think tank, that the United States does not recognize the effectiveness of historical basis in territorial disputes, despite making historical rights arguments itself in the Gulf of Maine disputes with Canada.[109]

Since then, on February 5, 2014, Daniel Russel, assistant Secretary of State for East Asia and Pacific Affairs, at the Foreign Affairs Committee hearing of the House of Representatives, further declared that "the United States takes a strong position that maritime claims must accord with customary international law. This means that all maritime claims must be derived from land features and otherwise comport with the international law of the sea. So while we are not siding with one claimant against another, we certainly believe that claims in the SCS that are not derived from land features are fundamentally flawed."[110] While denying China's historic rights in the SCS, the United States has turned a blind eye to Vietnam's expansion of fishing rights to waters near Phnom Penh, the capital of Cambodia, according to the "historic waters agreement." Such sharp contrast has exposed the double standards of the U.S. policy on the SCS.

Third, the United States questions the legitimacy of China's "intermittent line" in the SCS. In 2009, the Philippine Congress passed the Baselines Bill, and Vietnam and Malaysia have made submissions to the Commission on the Limits of the Continental Shelf on the outer limits of the continental shelf beyond 200 nautical miles from the base lines. These acts have seriously violated China's sovereignty over the SCS and caused protests from the Chinese government.[111] In order to safeguard its own rights and interests, China submitted to the UN Secretary General Ban Ki Moon a nine-dashed-line map of the SCS on May 7, 2009, reiterating that "China has indisputable sovereignty over the islands in the SCS and the adjacent waters, and enjoys sovereign rights and jurisdiction over the relevant waters as well as the seabed and subsoil thereof. The position is consistently held by the Chinese government, and is widely known by the international community."[112] With regard to China's rights protection activities, the United States has frequently criticized and questioned the legitimacy and rationality of China's "intermittent line" in the SCS, claiming that the intermittent line has no legal basis and violates international rules, which threatens the freedom of navigation and commercial exchanges of countries including the United States, and also challenges the security order in the Asia-Pacific region dominated by the United States.

In her speech in July 2010, Secretary of State Hillary Clinton publicly claimed that any claim for maritime sovereignty and the acquisition of related rights and interests must be based on the provisions of the UNCLOS; in accordance with international practice, land features were the only source of legitimate claims in the SCS. Clinton's speech implies that China's "intermittent line" in the SCS is not in line with international norms.[113] On February 5, 2014, Russell, Assistant Secretary of State, also pointed out in his testimony to the Congress that there was a growing concern that China's behavior in the SCS reflected an incremental effort by China to assert control over the area contained in the so-called nine-dashed line, despite the objections of its neighbors and despite the lack of any explanation or apparent basis under international law regarding the scope of the claim itself. China's lack of clarity with regard to its SCS claims had created uncertainty, insecurity, and instability in the region. Therefore, "the international community would welcome China to clarify or adjust its nine-dashed line claim to bring it in accordance with the international law of the sea."[114]

On March 6, 2014, Samuel Locklear, the commander of the U.S. Pacific Command, made a speech on the future of Asian security at the Atlantic Council, saying that the SCS dispute is very complicated. If China believes its "nine-dashed line" claim is reasonable, it should be dealt with by the International

Court of Justice, rather than by means of coercion.[115] In April, when meeting Philippine President Aquino III, Obama also expressed his strong support for the Philippines to resort to international arbitration for the SCS dispute.[116] On December 5, 2014, the U.S. DoS published a report entitled "Limits in the Seas, China: Maritime Claims in the SCS," which specifically discussed the dashed line in the SCS. According to the report, the dashed line in the SCS is neither a national boundary nor a historic claim, but only a claim to islands within that line.[117]

Fourth, the United States opposes any bilateral negotiations and supports the multilateralism and internationalization of SCS issue. The SCS dispute involves many countries, and overlapping territorial claims to the SCS are complicated and have had a destabilizing effect. Therefore, China has advocated that the negotiation and consultation should be conducted directly by the parties concerned, while countries outside the region should not interfere in the SCS affairs. However, in the view of the United States, the comprehensive national strength of the claimants in Southeast Asia lags far behind that of China, and the ASEAN members have different interests in the region and have varying diplomatic relations with China, thus the claimants are unlikely to reach consensus on the actions and attitudes toward China on the SCS issue. To this end, the United States encourages ASEAN members to unify and coordinate their policies toward China, and actively incited the international community to pay attention to the SCS issue and to exert pressure on China with more external forces. For example, in a speech on July 23, 2010, Secretary of State Hillary Clinton called on the parties in dispute to establish multilateral solutions in accordance with international law, which was equivalent to a denial to bilateral consultation proposed by China.[118] Clinton also claimed that freedom of navigation in the SCS, the openness of Asian maritime commons, and respect for international law are in accordance with the interests of the United States and ASEAN member states, and other maritime countries and the international community also enjoy these public interests.[119] It demonstrated the United States has expanded the relevant rights and interests in the SCS to include the vast majority of countries, and made great efforts to multilateralize and internationalize the SCS issue.[120]

On August 9, 2014, China put forward a "two-track approach" to solve the SCS issue, that is, China advocated resolving the mutual differences with relevant countries in the SCS through peaceful negotiations and friendly consultations, and work actively with ASEAN countries to maintain the peace and stability of the SCS.[121] It means that the SCS issue should be solved under the framework of "ASEAN + China" and that ASEAN as a regional organization should facilitate the peaceful resolution of the dispute, and play a positive and constructive role to sustain regional harmony. In the meantime, the United States ignored China's sincerity and efforts, and persistently promoted the internationalization of the SCS issue in various ways. On September 20, 2012, U.S. Assistant Secretary of State Campbell testified in Congress, saying that the United States opposed the use of coercion, intimidation, threats, or force by any claimant to advance its claims, and believed that "claimants should explore every diplomatic and other peaceful means for dispute resolution, including the use of arbitration or other international legal mechanisms."[122] Later, the Philippines initiated arbitral proceedings against China over the SCS issue on January 22, 2013,[123] which is undoubtedly related to the implicit encouragement of the United States. In addition, in recent years, the SCS issue has constantly appeared in the agenda of regional multilateral meetings such as ASEAN, ARF, East Asia Summit and G7, which has much to do with the U.S. endeavors.

The U.S. Forceful Intervention in the SCS Issue

With the deepening of Obama's strategy of rebalancing towards the Asia-Pacific region and the intensification of conflicts among countries around SCS, the United States changed its former attitude of "taking no position" in the sovereignty dispute. This policy change encouraged some ASEAN members to take a tough stand against China. In the context of the U.S. strategy of rebalancing to the Asia-Pacific region, the SCS issue has become one of the main conflicts between China and the United States.[124] Correspondingly, from the perspective of policy practice, the United States not only frequently couches criticism towards China in world public opinion terms, but repeatedly sends warships to the area, which seriously challenged China's SCS policy. Specifically, the Obama administration has taken the following measures to intervene in the SCS issues.

Paying Close Attention to the Situation in the SCS and Constantly Hyping the SCS Issue

Since 2010, the United States has often expressed its concern about the SCS issue on various diplomatic and public occasions. Taking the Daily Press Briefings of U.S. DoS as an example, according to statistics, in the Daily Press Briefings held from 2010 to 2015, there were as many as 80 mentions of the SCS issue, and it increased year by year. In 2010, there were only 2 briefings, and in 2015, it soared to 34 briefings. In 2016, there were 49 press briefings on the SCS issue, with an average of 4 per month.[125] The high frequency of the above press briefings on the SCS issue indicates that the United States has greatly increased its diplomatic attention to the SCS issue and placed it in front of the media.

During this period, there was a sharp increase in the international media reports on the SCS issue, mainly focused on freedom of navigation in the SCS, the Declaration on Conduct of Parties in the SCS (DOC) and the Code of Conduct in the SCS (COC), and the "nine-dashed line" in the SCS. Studies have shown that such issues as a hot topic are closely related to the frequent announcement of the U.S. official and the continuous speculation of senior government officials.[126] In this way, the United States can not only "broadcast" its position on the SCS issue to the international community, but also take the opportunity to "amplify," thereby, guiding international public opinion development in its favor, thus enhancing its diplomatic influence and international discourse power on the SCS issue.

Opposing to Change the Status Quo Unilaterally and Requiring China to Halt Land Reclamation in the SCS

With the continuous infringement on China's maritime rights and interests by the countries surrounding the SCS, China has also made its endeavors to protect its maritime rights in the SCS, including land reclamation in the relevant areas. In the view of the United States, such moves demonstrate China's intention to change the status quo of the SCS by using its rising military power. Thus, the U.S. politicians have repeatedly expressed their opposition to any unilateral change of the status quo in the SCS, especially China's construction of islands and reefs in the SCS. On July 11, 2014, assistant Secretary of State Michael Fuchs criticized China's construction of islands and reefs in the SCS as a "provocative and unilateral behavior," and "has raised serious concerns about China's intentions and willingness to adhere to international law and standards." He also made three suggestions for claimants: first, claimants recommit not to establish new outposts; second, construction and land reclamation by claimants should cease; and finally, claimants could agree to refrain from unilateral enforcement measures against other claimants' long-standing economic activities that have been taking place in disputed areas.[127]

In fact, China is not the first country to reclaim land in the SCS. China's action, to a large extent, is a reluctant response. But the United States did not give an objective and impartial evaluation, but showed great anxiety about the scale and speed of China's land reclamation.[128] Moreover, on August 6, 2015, Secretary of State John Kerry criticized China at the East Asia Summit, and expressed concern to China over the pace and scope of its land reclamation efforts. As he said, "the construction of facilities for military purposes only raises tensions and the destabilizing risk of militarization by other claimant states." To this end, Kerry urged all claimants to make a joint commitment to halt further land reclamation and construction of new facilities or militarization on disputed features, and take substantive steps in the negotiations on the COC in the SCS.[129]

Defending the So-Called Freedom of Navigation and Sending Warships Directly to Intrude into the Sensitive Waters in the SCS

Due to the ambiguous provisions on passage issue in the UNCLOS, China and the United States have quite different understandings as to whether the innocent passage of the territorial sea requires the prior approval of the coastal state, whether military activities in the EEZ are applicable to freedom of navigation, which directly leads to the question of "freedom of navigation" in the SCS.[130] In the view of the United States, the Convention does not require foreign ships to obtain the prior consent of coastal states when passing through the territorial waters of one country, and its warships can enjoy the right of "innocent passage" in the territorial waters of other countries according to the existing provisions. At the same time, Article 58 of the Convention clearly stipulates that in the EEZ of coastal states, all other States, whether coastal or land locked, enjoy the freedom of navigation and overflight. Moreover, the Convention does not prohibit military surveying and reconnaissance activities outside of the territorial sea as long as permission is sought from the coastal state, so the related activities of the U.S. warships belong to "maritime freedom."[131] Therefore, the United States has accused China of violating the freedom of navigation under international maritime law and threatening the interests of the United States.

Especially since the second half of 2010, when the United States actively promoted the "pivot" strategy, return to the Asia-Pacific region, the conflict between China and the United States on the freedom of navigation in the SCS has intensified. In August 2014, a U.S. P-8 reconnaissance aircraft entered the airspace about 217km east of Hainan Island and was intercepted by Chinese fighters, which triggered a confrontation between Chinese and American military aircraft. In May 2015, the United States sent the most advanced P-8A Poseidon maritime surveillance aircraft to conduct low-altitude reconnaissance on China's islands and reefs in the SCS, and sent a warship into the disputed waters of the

SCS for the first time. Despite China's opposition, the United States dispatched the Larsen to sail within 12 nautical miles of Subi Reef on October 27, violating China's policy in the SCS. On May 10, 2016, the United States sent the destroyer Lawrence into the 12 nautical miles of territorial waters near Northwest Investigator Reef, known for several centuries as the "Dangerous Ground" to carry out a FONOP. This irresponsible behavior of the United States further increased the potential for misjudgment, and greatly aggravates the conflict between China and the United States.

Strengthening the Security Cooperation with the Parties to the SCS Dispute in Southeast Asia and Supporting them to Resist China

Among the countries surrounding the SCS, China is the most powerful in terms of comprehensive strength, especially in military strength, which is beyond the financial and industrial capacity of the Philippines, Vietnam, and other parties to the SCS dispute. Therefore, in order to prevent the Philippines, Vietnam, and other countries from suffering losses in a conflict with China on the SCS issue, the United States deliberately supports the weak to weed out the strong. On the one hand, it opposes China's use of force or threat of force in the SCS dispute. On the other hand, it continuously deepens security cooperation with the Philippines, Vietnam, and other countries, and improves their military capability to confront China. For example, in order to speed up the pace of helping the Philippines build a "minimum reliable defense force," the United States announced on June 12, 2012, that it would provide powerful land-based radar to the Philippines and assist Manila with a National Coast Watch Center to effectively detect and monitor passing ships in the SCS.[132] In December 2013, the U.S. Secretary of State Kerry announced that the United States would provide 40 million U.S. dollars to help the Philippines improve maritime security.[133] In addition, it has promised to provide 32.5 million U.S. dollars to Southeast Asia in military assistance and more than 156 million U.S. dollars in the following two years to promote and enhance marine capacity-building in the region.[134]

Meanwhile, the United States has agreed to provide 18 million U.S. dollars to invest in Vietnam's maritime security assistance.[135] More importantly, on October 2, 2014, the United States officially announced that it would partially lift the decades old arms embargo against Vietnam and allow the transfer of maritime security and defense equipment to Vietnam.[136] During his visit to Vietnam in May 2016, President Obama has announced the United States is fully lifting its embargo on sales of lethal weapons to Vietnam to remove a "lingering vestige of the Cold War."[137] In this regard, Martin E. Dempsey, chairman of the JCS of the United States, once claimed that such a move shall help Vietnam to "acquire American weapons" and "help offset the power of China."[138] In addition, the United States has also increased the frequency and scale of joint military exercises with neighboring countries in the SCS. The exercises cover various fields such as joint maritime operations, maritime patrol, amphibious landing, reconnaissance flight, intelligence sharing, and combat rescue. Through the joint military exercise, it not only strengthens the ability of relevant countries to carry out maritime operations, but also intimidates and deters China to a certain extent.

Uniting and Convincing External Forces to Form a "Multilateral Alliance" to Intervene in the SCS Dispute and Step Up Pressure on China

Connecting the Pacific Ocean and the Indian Ocean, the SCS is one of the most significant waterways in the world and aids economic activity throughout Asia. Some geopolitical theorists believe that whoever controls the SCS will control the important straits around the SCS, and the entire East Asia and Asia Pacific will be under control.[139] Therefore, in order to prevent the SCS from being "controlled" by China unilaterally, the United States not only strongly supports the Philippines, Vietnam, and other claimants in conflict with China, but also convinces Southeast Asian countries to jointly stand up against China on the SCS issue, and actively promotes countries outside the region, such as Japan, India, and Australia, to intervene in the SCS issues to contain China's "maritime expansion."

In July 2011, the United States, Japan, and Australia held a military exercise in the coastal waters of Brunei, which was the first time that the three countries held a joint military exercise in the waters near the SCS. Since then, the defense ministers of the three countries also held talks in May 2014 and issued a joint statement to express strong opposition to "the use of coercion or force to alter the status quo in the East China and SCSs unilaterally."[140] In November, the leaders of the three countries held a summit meeting, and issued a statement including "settlement of maritime disputes in accordance with international law and guarantee of freedom of passage." In February 2016, the three countries held joint military exercises in the SCS again. On March 2, Harry Harris, commander of the U.S. Pacific Command, also proposed to establish an informal U.S.-Japan-India-Australia naval alliance.[141]

In addition, in July 2014, the United States, Japan, and India held a joint military exercise in Okinawa in the Western Pacific Ocean. In October 2015, the three countries also held joint naval exercises in the Indian Ocean to ensure the "freedom and openness of the sea."[142] On March 2, 2016, Harris, head of the U.S. Pacific Command, announced that "the United States, India, and Japan will hold joint naval exercises in waters off the northern Philippines near the SCS."[143] It is worth noting that some external forces follow the steps of the United States to act on their own to interfere in the SCS issue. For example, Japan, India, and Australia held the first dialogue at vice foreign minister level in New Delhi in June 2015. Japan's Vice Minister of Foreign Affairs, Yoshiro Saiki, said that Japan, India, and Australia had reached a consensus on the SCS issue after the conference. The Indian Ocean, the Pacific Ocean, the East China Sea, and the SCS are interrelated in security, which is also crucial to the security in Indo-Pacific.[144] In other words, the initiatives proposed by the United States are leading to emboldened activities by other States, causing friction that may spill over into conflict, not only with China, but between smaller States that have used aggressive force in the past 70 years.

Notes

1 Gideon Rachman, "American Decline: This Time It's for Real," *Foreign Policy*, No.184, January/February 2011, pp.59–65; Christopher Layne, "The Waning of U.S. Hegemony—Myth or Reality? A Review Essay," *International Security*, Vol. 34, No. 1, Summer 2009, pp.147–172; Robert A. Pape, "Empire Falls," *National Interest*, No.99, January/February 2009, pp.21–34; National Intelligence Council (NIC), *Global Trends 2025: A Transformed World,* Washington, D.C.: NIC, 2008; Joseph S. Nye Jr., *The Future of Power*, New York: Perseus, 2011, chap.6; Eric S. Edelman, *Understanding America's Contested Primacy*, Washington, D.C.: Center for Strategic and Budgetary Assessments, 2010, chap.3; Josef Joffe, "The Default Power: The False Prophecy of America's Decline," *Foreign Affairs*, Vol.88, No.5, September/October 2009, pp.21–35; Edward Luttwak, "The Declinists, Wrong Again," *The American Interest*, Vol.4, No.2, November/December 2008, pp.7–13; Michael Beckley, "China's Century? Why America's Edge Will Endure," *International Security*, Vol.36, No.3, Winter 2011/12, pp.41–78; Yuen Foong Khong, "Primacy or World Order? The United States and China's Rise—A Review Essay," *International Security*, Vol.38, No.3, Winter 2013/14, pp.153–175.

2 Men Honghua, "Critical Moment: China, the United States and the World in the Eyes of American Elites," *Social Sciences in China*, No. 7, 2012, p.183.

3 Fareed Zakaria, *The Post-American World: And the Rise of the Rest*, W.W. Norton&Company Incorporated, 2008.

4 Richard Haass, "The Age of Non-polarity," *Foreign Affairs*, May/June, 2008, p.14.

5 G. John Ikenberry, "The Future of the Liberal World Order: Internationalism after America," *Foreign Affairs*, 2011, May /June, Vol.90, No.3, pp.56–68.

6 Wei Hongxia, "A Close Review on Obama's Rebalancing Asia Policy," *Fudan American Review*, No. 1, 2013, p.35; Wang Hui, "The 'Hegemony Anxiety' and Strategic Eastward Movement of the United States," *Contemporary International Relations*, No. 6, 2012, pp.32–36.

7 Ralph A. Cossa, Brad Glosserman, etc., "The United States and the Asia-Pacific Region: Security Strategy for the Obama Administration," available at: http://www.cnas.org/files/documents/publications/CossaPatelUS Asia-Pacific February2009.pdf

8 Wu Xinbo, "On Obama Administration's Asia Pacific Strategy," *China International Studies*, No. 2, 2012, p.63.

9 Jim O' Neill, "Current Answers (and Questions) about Bricks and the N-11," available at: http://www2.goldmansachs.com/ideas/brics/book/BRICs-Chapter12.pdf

10 See the official website of the Bureau of Economic Analysis, U.S. Department of Commerce: http://www.bea.gov/international/index.htm#trade

11 USTR, "Trans-Pacific Partnership Announcement," available at: https://ustr.gov/about-us/policy-offices/press-office/press-releases/2009/december/trans-pacific-partnership-announcemen

12 Li Li, "Reflections on 'Asia Pacific Rebalancing Strategy' in American Academia," *Issus of Contemporary World Socialism*, No.3, 2013, p.90.

13 Hillary R. Clinton, "Remarks on Regional Architecture in Asia: Principles and Priorities," Honolulu, Hawaii January 12, 2010, available at: http://m.state.gov/md135090.htm

14 Shi Bin, "Exploring the Source of 'Militarism' in the United States," *Foreign Affairs Review*, No. 4, 2014, p.79.

15 Shi Bin, "Exploring the Source of 'Militarism' in the United States," *Foreign Affairs Review*, No. 4, 2014, p.82.

16 Zbigniwe Brzezinski, *The Grand Chessboard: American Primacy and Its Geostrategic Imperatives*, New York: Basic Books, 1997, p.23.

17 Tang Shiping and Joey S. R. Long, "America's Military Interventionism: A Social Evolutionary Interpretation," *World Economics and Politics*, No. 9, 2011, p.89.

18 Cui Liru, "The Era of Globalization and a Multipolar World," *Contemporary International Relations (the celebration special issue)*, 2010, p.2.

19 The White House, "Full Transcript: President Barack Obama's Inaugural Address," January 20, 2009.

20 The White House, *National Security Strategy*, May 2010, p.43, http://nssarchive.us/NSSR/2010.pdf

21 Robert G. Sutter, Michael E. Brown, and Timothy J. A. Adamson, with Mike M. Mochizuki and Deepa Ollapally, *Balancing Acts: The U.S. Rebalance and Asia-Pacific Stability*, August 2013, p.1.

22 Chen Yali, "The America's Rebalancing Strategy: Practical Appraisal and China's Response," *World Economics and Politics*, No.11, 2012, p.72.

23 Zhao Suisheng, "Obama Administration's Asia Pacific Strategic Rebalancing and Sino-US Relations," *Fudan American Review*, No. 1, 2013, p.2.

24 Sen. Robert Menendez, "Let's get the Asia rebalance right," *The Hill*, available at: http://thehill.com/opinion/op-ed/204858-lets-get-the-asia-rebalance-right

25 Michael J.Green, BatesGill, etc., "Strategic Views on Asian Regionalism," February17, 2009, available at: http://csis.org/files/media/csis/pubs/090217 gill stratviews web. pdf

26 Uri Dadush and Bennett Stancil, *The World in 2050*, VA: Carnegie Endowment for International Peace, April 2010, pp.9–10.

27 C.Fred Bergsten, "A Partnership of Equals: How Washington Should Respond to China's Economic Challenge," *Foreign Affairs*, July/August 2008, pp.57–69.

28 "China's Military Rise: The Dragon's New Teeth," *The Economist*, April 7, 2012, p.27.

29 In recent years, some Western public opinions believe that China is becoming "aggressive" in its maritime disputes. See Derek Watkins, "Territorial Disputes in the Waters Near China," *New York Times*, May 8, 2014; Keith Bradsher, "Philippine Leader Sounds Alarm on China," *New York Times*, February 4, 2014; "Banyan: Force Majeure," *The Economist*, May 24, 2014; "Vietnam, China Exchange Water Cannon Spray Near Disputed Oil Rig," *Voice of America News*, May 12, 2014; "Q&A: SCS dispute," *BBC*, May 8, 2014.

30 Men Honghua, "Critical Moment: China, the United States and the World in the Eyes of American Elites," *Social Sciences in China*, No. 7, 2012, pp.188–189.

31 Chris McGreal, "Obama's State of the Union Address: US Must Seize 'Sputnik Moment'," *The Guardian*, January 26, 2011.

32 These organizations mainly include the Chicago Council on Global Affairs, Gallup Corporation, Pew Center, CNN, ABC, CBS, Washington Post, etc. See Yuan Zheng, "The American Public Perception of the Rise of China," *The Chinese Journal of American Studies*, No. 4, 2013, pp.9–33.

33 Dominic Tierney, "The Dragon and the American Dream," *The Atlantic*, September14, 2010, available at: http://www.theatlantic.com/international/archive/2010/09/the-dragon-and-the-american-dream/62899/

34 Bruce J. Dickson, "Updating the China Model," *The Washington Quarterly*, Fall 2011, pp.54–55.

35 U.S. Department of Defense, *National Security Strategy*, May 27, 2010, pp.41–42, available at: http://nssarchive.us/NSSR/2010.pdf

36 The White House, Office of the Press Secretary, "United States-Japan Joint Statement: A Shared Vision for the Future," April 30, 2012, https://www.whitehouse.gov/the-press-office/2012/04/30/united-states-japan-joint-statement-shared-vision-future
37 The White House, Office of the Press Secretary, "Remarks by National Security Advisor Tom Donilon -- As Prepared for Delivery," November 15, 2012, https://www.whitehouse.gov/the-press-office/2012/11/15/remarks-national-security-advisor-tom-donilon-prepared-delivery
38 The White House, Office of the Press Secretary, "U.S.-Japan Joint Vision Statement," April 28, 2015, https://www.whitehouse.gov/the-press-office/2015/04/28/us-japan-joint-vision-statement
39 Huang Fengzhi and Liu Boran, "The Strengthening of U.S.-ROK Alliance and China's Strategic Response," *International Forum,* No.2, 2013, pp.28–29.
40 Wang Shaozhe and Hong Junjie, "US South Korea FTA: Political Considerations Outweigh Economy," *Jiefang Daily,* March 15, 2012, 6th edition.
41 Hillary Rodham Clinton, "Remarks at the U.S.-Korean Ministerial Dialogue 2+2 Meetings," June 14, 2012, available at: http://www.state.gov/secretary/20092013clinton/rm/2012/06/192390.htm
42 Zhang Jingquan, "American Asia Rebalance Strategy and the Function of U.S.-SK Alliance," *Teaching and Research,* No.9, 2013, pp.64–70.
43 For specific discussion, please refer to Chen Hongqiao, "U.S.-Australia Cooperation and U.S.'s Asia Pacific Rebalancing Strategy," *Contemporary Asia-Pacific Studies,* No.1, 2014, pp.59–68.
44 Wang Lianhe, "New Changes in the US-Australia Security Alliance," *Contemporary International Relations,* No.1, 2014, pp.37–38.
45 Zhou Fangyin, "The US Asia-Pacific Alliance System and China's Policy Options," *World Economics and Politics,* No.11, 2013, p.9.
46 Zhang Jingquan, "The Reinforcement of America-Philippine Alliance and Its Function in America Rebalance Strategy to Asia-Pacific," *Southeast Asian Affairs,* No.1, 2014, pp.3–4.
47 U.S. Department of Defense, *National Security Strategy,* May 27, 2010, http://nssarchive.us/NSSR/2010.pdf
48 Hillary Rodham Clinton, "America's Engagement in the Asia-Pacific," Honolulu, HI, October 28, 2010, http://www.state.gov/secretary/20092013clinton/rm/2010/10/150141.htm
49 Wu Xinbo, "American Asia Pacific Strategy," in Zhou Fangyin, ed., *Asia-Pacific Strategies of Major Powers,* Beijing: Social Sciences Academic Press, 2013, pp.26–27.
50 US Department of Defense (DoD), "Sustaining U.S. Global Leadership: Priorities for the 21st Century Defense," January 2012, p.2, available at: http://www.defense.gov/news/defense_strategic_guidance.pdf
51 U.S. Department of Defense, *Quadrennial Defense Review Report,* February 2010, p.59, available at: http://csis.org/files/publication/090809_qdrahc_revised.pdf

52 "VN, US Convene First Defense Policy Dialogue," August 18, 2010, available at: http://news.chinhphu.vn/Home/VN-US-convene-first-defense-policy-dialogue/20108/8377.vgp

53 Xin Qiang, "The Development of U.S.-Vietnam Security Cooperation and its Influencing Factors," *China International Studies*, No.6, 2014, p.62.

54 "Panetta Sends Message to China during Historic Visit to Vietnam," Foxnews, June 3, 2012, available at: http://www.foxnews.com/politics/2012/06/03/panetta-urges-for-more-us-naval-access-to-vietnam-harbor/

55 Vietnam Embassy in the U.S., "Vietnam, US hold defense dialogue," October 30, 2013, available at: http://vietnamembassy-usa.org/news/2013/10/vietnam-us-hold-defense-dialogue

56 Mark E. Manyin et al., Pivot to the Pacific? The Obama Administration's "Rebalancing" Toward Asia, CRS report, March 28, 2012, p.10.

57 The White House, Office of the Press Secretary, Barack Obama, "Remarks by President Obama to the Australian Parliament," Canberra, Australia, November 17, 2011, available at: https://www.whitehouse.gov/the-press-office/2011/11/17/remarks-president-obama-australian-parliament

58 U.S. Department of Defense (DoD): "Sustaining U.S. Global Leadership: Priorities for the 21st Century Defense," January 2012, available at: http://www.defense.gov/news/defense_strategic_guidance.pdf.

59 Zhang Ming, "An Analysis of the Obama Administration's Asia Pacific Military 'Rebalancing'," *Contemporary International Relations*, No. 4, 2013, pp.37–44.

60 United States Secretary of Defense Leon Panetta, "The US Rebalance Towards the Asia-Pacific," 2 June, 2012, Singapore, The 11th IISS Asia Security Summit The Shangri-La Dialogue, available at: http://www.iiss.org/en/events/shangri%20la%20dialogue/archive/sld12-43d9/first-plenary-session-2749/leon-panetta-d67b

61 Ashton B. Carter, Deputy Secretary of Defense, "Remarks at the Von der Heyden Fellows Program Endowment Fund Lecture Series at Duke University," Durham, N.C., November 29, 2012, available at: http://www.defense.gov/transcripts/transcript.aspx?transcriptid=5158

62 Ashton B. Carter, Deputy Secretary of Defense, "Remarks Delivered at the National Bureau of Asian Research," October 3, 2012, available at: http://www.defense.gov/transcripts/transcript.aspx?transcriptid=5130.

63 The U.S. Department of Defense, *Quadrennial Defense Review Report*, March 2014, available at: http://www.defense.gov/pubs/2014_Quadrennial_Defense_Review.pdf

64 U.S. Department of Defense, "United States and Australia Advance Space Partnership," November 14, 2012, available at: http://www.defense.gov/releases/release.aspx?releaseid=15678

65 United States Secretary of Defense Leon Panetta, "The US Rebalance Towards the Asia-Pacific," 02 June 2012, Singapore, The 11th IISS Asia Security Summit The

Shangri-La Dialogue, available at: http://www.iiss.org/en/events/shangri%20la%20dialogue/archive/sld12-43d9/first-plenary-session-2749/leon-panetta-d67b

66 Ninan Koshy, "India: Linchpin of Asia Pivot?" September 20, 2012, available at: http://fpif.org/india_linchpin_of_the_pivot/

67 Cao Xiaoyang, "U.S. 'India Pacific' Maritime Security Strategic Deployment and its Impact," *Contemporary International Relations*, No. 8, 2014, pp.30–31.

68 Bitzinger, R. A. and Raska, M, "The Air-Sea Battle Debate and the Future of Conflict in East Asia," 2013, Singapore: RSIS Policy Brief.

69 US Department of Defense, "Joint Operational Access Concept 2012," Washington, DC: US Government Printing Office.

70 Liu Peng and Zhu Yitong, "The Employment of Smart Power in the U.S. Military Strategy: A Case Study of the Airsea Battle Strategy," *Fudan American Review*, No2, 2011, pp.101–102.

71 The U.S. Department of Defense, "Defense Budget Priorities and Choices Fiscal 2014," April 2013, available at: http://www.defense.gov/pubs/DefenseBudgetPrioritiesChoicesFiscalYear2014.pdf

72 Hillary Clinton, "America's Pacific Century," *Foreign Policy*, October 11, 2011, p.57.

73 Masahiro Kawai and Ganeshan Wignaraja, "Asian FTAs: Trends, Prospects and Challenges," *Journal of Asian Economics*, Vol.22, No.1, 2011, pp.1–22.

74 The ASEAN Secretariat, ASEAN Economic Community Blueprint, January 2008, available at: http://www.aseansec.org/5187-10.pdf.

75 Article 1, clause 3 of the Trans-Pacific Strategic Economic Partnership Agreement stipulates that "The Parties seek to support the wider liberalisation process in APEC consistent with its goals of free and open trade and investment." See "Trans-Pacific Strategic Economic Partnership Agreement," 2005, available at: https://web.archive.org/web/20071020114836/http://www.mfat.govt.nz/downloads/trade-agreement/transpacific/main-agreement.pdf

76 Wu Xinbo, "American Asia Pacific Strategy," in Zhou Fangyin, ed., *Asia-Pacific Strategies of Major Powers*, Beijing: Social Sciences Academic Press, 2013, p.35.

77 Douglas Paal, remarks at Carnegie event, " 'Rebalancing' America's Ties to Asia: An Assessment of the Obama Initiative," December 6, 2011, available at: http://carnegieendowment.org/files/120611_transcript_RebalancingAsiaTies.pdf

78 Kenneth Lieberthal, "Understanding the U.S. Pivot to Asia," Washington, D. C., January 31, 2012, available at: http://www.brookings.edu/~/media/events/2012/1/31-us-asia/20120131_pivot_asia.pdf

79 "The Trans Pacific Partnership, the economic pillar of the US Asia Pacific strategy," available at: http://www.voachinese.com/content/back-to-asia-20121005/1521318.html

80 Asia Society, "Complete Transcript: Thomas Donilon at Asia Society New York," available at: http://asiasociety.org/new-york/complete-transcript-thomas-donilon-asia-society-new-york

81 Phillip C. Saunders, "China's Rising Power, the U.S. Rebalance to Asia, and Implications for U.S.-China Relations," *Issues & Studies*, Vol.50, No.3, September 2014, p.22.
82 Cui Liru, "U.S. 'Rebalancing' Strategy and Its 'Competition & Cooperation' Relations with China," *Fudan American Review*, No.2, 2013, p.26.
83 Chen Yali, "The America's Rebalancing Strategy: Practical Appraisal and China's Response," *World Economics and Politics*, No.11, 2012, p.65.
84 Tom Donilon, "America Is Back in the Pacific and Will Uphold the Rules," *Financial Times*, November 27, 2011.
85 Graham Allison, *Destined for War: Can America and China Escape Thucydides's Trap?*, Houghton Mifflin Harcourt, 2017.
86 John J. Mearsheimer, *The Tragedy of Great Power Politics*, New York: W. W. Norton, 2001.
87 Patrick M. Cronin, ed., *Cooperation from Strength: The United States, China and the SCS*, Centre for a New American Security, January 2012, p.7–8.
88 See the Report of the 18th National Congress of the Communist Party of China.
89 "Xi Jinping: Further concern for the ocean, understanding the ocean, and promoting the construction of a powerful maritime country," Xinhuanet.com, July 31, 2013, available at: http://news.xinhuanet.com/politics/2013-07/31/c_116762285.htm
90 Mark E. Manyin et al., *Pivot to the Pacific? The Obama Administration's "Rebalancing" Toward Asia*, CRS report, March 28, 2012; Evan Braden Montgomery, "Contested Primacy in the Western Pacific: China's Rise and the Future of U.S. Power Projection," *International Security*, Vol.38, No.4, Spring 2014, pp.115–149; US Department of Defense, "Annual Report to Congress: Military and Security Development Involving the People's Republic of China 2015," April 2015, pp.31–43.
91 Ben Dolven et al., *Chinese Land Reclamation in the SCS: Implications and Policy Options*, CRS report, June 18, 2015, pp.4–19.
92 Wang Chuanjian, "SCS Issue and Sino-US Relations," *Contemporary Asia-Pacific Studies*, No. 2, 2014, p.14.
93 Speech By Mr. Lee Kuan Yew, Minister Mentor of Singapore, at US-ASEAN Business Council's 25th Anniversary GALA Dinner, Washington D.C., October 27, 2009, available at: http://www.ttalk.biz/TTQ_20091028.htm
94 Javier C. Hernandez, "Benigno Aquino Says U.S. Must Act if China Moves on Reef in SCS," *The New York Times*, May 19, 2016, available at: http://www.nytimes.com/2016/05/20/world/asia/benigno-aquino-philippines-south-china-sea.html?_r=0
95 "US Fears Chinese Aggression in Pacific," *Financial Times*, May 25, 2010.
96 Wang Yiwei, "Rethinking the SCS: A Perspective of Sino-US Relations," *Fudan American Review*, 2006, p.95.
97 Patrick M. Cronin, "America's Security Role in the SCS," Testimony before Subcommittee on Asia and Pacific, House Committee on Foreign Affairs, July 23, 2015, p.6.

98 Hillary R. Clinton, "Remarks at National Convention Center," Hanoi, Vietnam, July 23, 2010, available at: http://www.state.gov/secretary/20092013clinton/rm/2010/07/145095.htm.

99 Ann Scott Tyson, "U.S. Protests Chinese Shadowing in International Waters," *The Washington Post*, March 10, 2009, available at: http://www.washingtonpost.com/wp-dyn/content/article/2009/03/09/AR2009030900956.html

100 Agence France-Presse, "China 'aggressive' on sea: US commander," March 20, 2009, available at: http://www.defencetalk.com/china-aggressive-on-sea-us-commander-16353/

101 Jim Webb, Jr., "U.S. Senate Unanimously 'Deplores' China's Use of Force in SCS," June 27, 2011, available at: http://webb.senate.gov/newsroom/pressreleases/06-27-2011.cfm

102 Patrick Ventrell, "SCS," Press Statement, Washington, DC, August 3, 2012, available at: http://www.state.gov/r/pa/prs/ps/2012/08/196022.htm

103 159 Cong. Rec. S6026-Supporting Peaceful Resolution of Disputes in The Asia-Pacific Maritime Domains, available at: https://www.gpo.gov/fdsys/pkg/CREC-2013-07-29/pdf/CREC-2013-07-29-pt1-PgS6026.pdf

104 Admiral Harry B. Harris, Jr., Commander, U.S. Pacific Fleet, Remarks to Australian Strategic Policy Institute, Canberra, Australia, March 31, 2015, in Ronald O' Rourke, *Maritime Territorial and Exclusive Economic Zone (EEZ) Disputes Involving China: Issues for Congress*, CRS report, June 1, 2015, p.62.

105 Jane Perlez, "A U.S. Admiral's Bluntness Rattles China, and Washington," *The New York Times*, May 6, 2016, available at: http://www.nytimes.com/2016/05/07/world/asia/us-admiral-harry-harris.html?_r=0

106 Xin Qiang, " 'Five No's' Policy: The U.S. Adjustment of the SCS Policy," *The Chinese Journal of American Studies*, No.6, 2014, p.57.

107 Wu Shicun, *The SCS Dispute: Origin and Development*, Beijing: Economic Press China, 2010, pp.1–2.

108 Deputy Assistant Secretary of Defense for South and Southeast Asia Robert Scher, "Maritime Disputes and Sovereignty Issues in East Asia," Hearing before the Committee on Foreign Relations, United States Senate, 111th Congress, First Session, July 15, 2009, available at: https://www.gpo.gov/fdsys/pkg/CHRG-111shrg53022/pdf/CHRG-111shrg53022.pdf

109 Joseph Yun, "Managing Tensions in the SCS-Keynote Speech," The Center for Strategic and International Studies (CSIS), June 5, 2013, available at: http://csis.org/event/managing-tensions-south-china-sea

110 Daniel R. Russel, "Maritime Disputes in East Asia," Testimony before the House Committee on Foreign Affairs Subcommittee on Asia and the Pacific, Washington DC, February 5, 2014, available at: http://www.state.gov/p/eap/rls/rm/2014/02/221293.htm.

111 "The Ministry of Foreign Affairs urgently summoned the provisional representative of the Philippine Embassy in China to make a solemn protest against the Philippine passage of the Baseline Bill," website of the Ministry of Foreign Affairs of China, 19 February 2009, available at: http://www.fmprc.gov.cn/mfa_chn/wjbxw_602253/t537943.shtml; Sam Bateman, "The SCS: When the Elephants Dance," *RSIS Commentary*, 91/ 2010, August 16, 2010.

112 "CLM/17/2009," May 7, 2009, available at: http://www.un.org/depts/los/clcs_new/submissions_files/mysvnm33_09/chn_2009re_mys_vnm_e.pdf

113 Wei Zongyou, "Interpreting Obama Administration's SCS Policy," *Pacific Journal*, No.2, 2016, p.29.

114 Daniel R. Russel, "Maritime Disputes in East Asia," Testimony before the House Committee on Foreign Affairs Subcommittee on Asia and the Pacific, Washington DC, February 5, 2014, available at: http://www.state.gov/p/eap/rls/rm/2014/02/221293.htm.

115 The Atlantic Council, "Webcast: The Future of Asian Security with Admiral Samuel J. Locklear III," March 6, 2014, from online video clip, Atlantic Council Official Website, available at: http://www.atlanticcouncil.org/events/webcasts/webcast-the-future-of-asian-security-with-admiral-samuel-j-locklear-iii

116 Barack Obama, "Remarks by President Obama and President Benigno Aquino III of the Philippines in Joint Press Conference," April 28, 2014, Manila, Philippines, available at: https://www.whitehouse.gov/the-press-office/2014/04/28/remarks-president-obama-and-presidentbenigno-aquino-iii-philippines-joi.

117 United States Department of State, Bureau of Oceans and International Environmental and Scientific Affairs, *Limits in the Seas, China: Maritime Claims in the SCS*, No.143, December 5, 2014, pp.11–24.

118 Deng Fan, "The Trend of US Policy of Interference with Issues Related to SCS," *Pacific Journal*, No.11, 2011, p.84.

119 Hillary R. Clinton, "Remarks at National Convention Center," Hanoi, Vietnam, July 23, 2010, available at: http://www.state.gov/secretary/20092013clinton/rm/2010/07/145095.htm.

120 Ju Hailong, "Research on the Obama Administration's SCSs Policy," *Contemporary Asia-Pacific Studies*, No.3, 2011, p.99.

121 "China proposes 'two-track approach' to solve the SCS issue," *People's Daily*, August 11, 2014, available at: http://world.people.com.cn/n/2014/0811/c157278-25439125.html

122 Kurt M. Campbell, "Maritime Territorial Disputes and Sovereignty Issues in Asia," Testimony Before the Senate Foreign Relations Committee Subcommittee on East Asian and Pacific Affairs, Washington, DC, September 20, 2012, available at: http://www.state.gov/p/eap/rls/rm/2012/09/197982.htm

123 Daniel R. Russel, "Maritime Disputes in East Asia," Testimony before the House Committee on Foreign Affairs Subcommittee on Asia and the Pacific, Washington

DC, February 5, 2014, available at: http://www.state.gov/p/eap/rls/rm/2014/02/221293.htm.

124 Zhou Qi, "The Evolution of U.S. SCS Policy and its Root Causes After the Cold War," *World Economic and Politics*, No. 6, 2014, pp.35–40.

125 The data is collected from Daily Press Briefings from 2010 to 2016 on the U.S. Department of State website, available at: https://2009-2017.state.gov/r/pa/prs/dpb/2016/index.htm

126 Ju Hailong, "Evolution of the International Public Opinion Environment for China to Safeguard Its Rights in the SCS," *People's Tribune*, No. 20, 2015, pp.60–69.

127 Michael Fuchs, Deputy Assistant Secretary of the State, "Remarks at the Fourth Annual SCS Conference," July 11, 2014, available at: http://www.state.gov/p/eap/rls/rm/2014/07/229129.htm.

128 Daniel R. Russel, Assistant Secretary, Bureau of East Asian and Pacific Affairs, Testimony Before the Senate Foreign Relations Committee, "Maritime Issues in East Asia," Washington DC, May 13, 2015, available at: http://www.state.gov/p/eap/rls/rm/2015/05/242262.htm.

129 John Kerry, "Remarks at Intervention at the East Asia Summit," Kuala Lumpur, Malaysia, August 6, 2015, available at: http://www.state.gov/secretary/remarks/2015/08/245758.htm.

130 Li Yan, "Freedom of navigation Issue in Sino-US Relations," *Contemporary International Relations*, No.11, 2015, pp.22–28.

131 Franckx, "American and Chinese Views on Navigational Rights of Warships," *Chinese Journal of International Law*, Vol.10, No.1, 2011, pp.187–206; Kamrul Hossain, "The UNCLOS and the US-China Hegemonic Competition over the SCS," *Journal of East Asia & International Law*, Vol.6 Issue1, 2013, pp.107–133; Raul Pedrozo, "Preserving Navigational Rights and Freedoms: The Right to Conduct Military Activities in China's Exclusive Economic Zone," *Chinese Journal of International Law*, Vol.9, Issue1, 2010, pp.9–29; James W. Houck, Nicole M. Anderson, "The United States, China, and Freedom of Navigation in the SCS," *Washington University Global Studies Law Review*, Vol.13, Issue 3, 2014, pp.441–452.

132 "Pentagon: US to equip Philippines with powerful radar," June 12, 2012, available at: http://globalnation.inquirer.net/39913/pentagon-us-to-equip-philippines-with-powerful-radar

133 John Kerry, "Remarks with Philippine Foreign Secretary Albert del Rosario," December 17, 2013, available at: http://www.state.gov/secretary/remarks/2013/12/218835.htm.

134 Michael Fuchs, Deputy Assistant Secretary of the State, "Remarks at the Fourth Annual SCS Conference," July 11, 2014, available at: http://www.state.gov/p/eap/rls/rm/2014/07/229129.htm.

135 Puneet Talwar, "The U.S.-Vietnam Relationship: Advancing Peace and Prosperity in 2015," Remarks at Diplomatic Academy of Vietnam, Hanoi, Vietnam, January 23, 2015, available at: http://www.state.gov/t/pm/rls/rm/2015/236213.htm

136 "US to partially lift Vietnam arms embargo," *BBC News*, October 2, 2014, available at: http://www.bbc.com/news/world-us-canada-29469719

137 "Obama lifts US embargo on lethal arms sales to Vietnam," *BBC News*, May 23, 2016, available at: http://www.bbc.com/news/world-asia-36356695

138 Jane Perlez, "In China's Shadow, U.S. Courts Old Foe Vietnam," *New York Times*, August 17, 2014, p.A4.

139 Chia Lin Sien and Colin Mac Andrews, eds., *Southeast Asian Seas: Frontiers for Development*, New York: McGraw-Hill International Book Company, 1981, p.226.

140 "Joint Statement from the Japan-U.S.-Australia Defense Ministers Meeting," U.S. Department of Defense News Release, Release No: NR-270–14, May 30, 2014, available at: http://www.defense.gov/releases/Release.aspx?ReleaseID=16726.

141 "U.S. Military Reaffirms US-Japan-India-Australia Naval Alliance to Conduct Military Exercises Near the SCS," *Huanqiu*, March 3, 2016, available at: http://world.huanqiu.com/exclusive/2016-03/8642144.html

142 "US, Japan and India Hold Joint Military Exercises in the Indian Ocean to Maintain 'Freedom of the Sea'," *Huanqiu*, October, 16, 2015, available at: http://world.huanqiu.com/exclusive/2015-10/7774805.html

143 "U.S. Military Reaffirms US-Japan-India-Australia Naval Alliance to Conduct Military Exercises Near the SCS," *Huanqiu*, March 3, 2016, available at: http://world.huanqiu.com/exclusive/2016-03/8642144.html

144 "Japan Urges Europe and U.S. to Support Philippines, India and Australia to Form Unified Front Against China," *Huanqiu*, June 10, 2015, available at: http://msn.huanqiu.com/world/exclusive/2015—06/6646640.html.

5

Responses of Major Neighboring Countries around China

"When elephants fight, the grass is trampled; yet, when they make love, the grass also tends to suffer."

—Lee Kuan Yew, Minister Mentor of Singapore

"Big fish eat small fish and small fish eat shrimps. For the shrimp, the little fish and even the middle-to-large sized fish of all dimensions represented here today, we face more than a Manichean choice between life and death, war and peace."

—Malcolm Turnbull, Prime Minister of Australia

Neighboring is originally a geographical concept, which refers to a border area controlled or radiated by State power. With the increasingly frequent exchanges among countries in the era of globalization, the meaning of "neighboring" has gone beyond the geographical boundaries, becoming a comprehensive research domain of geographical, political, economic, cultural, and militaristic significance, which refers to land, sea, and space adjacent to or associated with external countries or forces.[1] Thus, China's neighboring can be categorized as the neighboring in a narrow sense and the neighboring in a broad sense. The former refers to the countries and a region directly adjacent to China's territory while the latter goes beyond the geographical boundaries and involves countries or regions with strategic interests in both land and sea.[2] This book mainly discusses the neighboring in a narrow sense when studying the SCS issue. It should be noted that although some countries (such as Australia) are included into the discussion for their close relationship with the United States and their great significance to China's maritime strategy, they do not share a border with China.

Due to different interests, the neighboring countries take various attitudes to the U.S. rebalancing strategy in the Asia-Pacific region and its involvement in the SCS issue, and take different sides in the China-U.S. competition unfolding before them. Therefore, the book categorizes the neighboring countries into five units, ASEAN countries, Japan, India, Russia, and Australia, to evaluate diverse diplomatic options and figure out the underlying causes.

ASEAN: Mingled Hope and Fear

Given the outstanding role of the ASEAN in the realms of geopolitics, ASEAN occupies a very prominent position in the U.S. strategic layout in the Asia-Pacific region. In its geographical structure, ASEAN is located to the south of the juncture of the Pacific Ocean and Eurasian continent, at the crossroads of the Asian continent and the Australian continent, and is the check point on key passage between the Pacific Ocean and the Indian Ocean.[3] As a regional group, ASEAN is also a stakeholder in the SCS issue. It has interests in maintaining regional peace, settling disputes peacefully, and hoping all parties to abide by international law, especially the UNCLOS.[4] Besides, there are waterways and straits of great strategic significance, especially the Malacca Strait, which is known as the "lifeline on the sea" and is listed by the United States as one of the 16 waterways that the United States must control in the world. The ASEAN region is the only place through which the United States and its Asia Pacific allies can transport energy and resources from the Middle East into the Pacific, and the hub for Asia-Pacific countries to engage in maritime trade of commodities. Controlling the maritime threat of ASEAN and ensuring the smooth flow of commercial and military resources constitute the primary strategic interests of the United States in the region.[5] Therefore, the status of ASEAN within the U.S. Asia-Pacific strategy is inevitably vital and cannot be neglected in the SCS issue.

ASEAN's Contradictions and the Underlying Reasons

Considering ASEAN's prominent strategic position, ASEAN's responses in the SCS issue are particularly noteworthy when the Obama administration has vigorously implemented the strategy of rebalancing to the Asia-Pacific region and actively interfered in the SCS issue. In order to balance China's growing influence, some ASEAN countries hold a positive view on the U.S. military presence in the Asia-Pacific region, hoping to use the U.S. influence to balance China's rise. To some extent, some ASEAN countries have expressed their support and welcome to the U.S. rebalancing strategy towards Asia Pacific. Some U.S. officials believe that a considerable part of the impetus for the rebalancing strategy stems from the strong demands of Southeast Asian countries for the United States to play a leading role in the region.[6] But as a close neighbor of China, ASEAN does not want to see these two great powers completely engaging in confrontation. As a special regional actor sandwiched between China and the United States, ASEAN's role in the rebalancing strategy in the Asia-Pacific region is quite contradictory, and the relevant Member States have different attitudes toward the U.S. intervention in the SCS issue.

Based on multiple interests and historical considerations, ASEAN countries have always had a complex and contradictory attitude towards the U.S. policy in the region, and their positions are not consistent either. In general, ASEAN welcomes the return of the United States to Asia, in line with its expectations to establish closer economic relations with the United States, as well as hoping the United States to play an active role in the region. But ASEAN is unwilling to see the U.S. new Asia Pacific strategy "militarized," and even less willing to be kidnapped in the U.S. chariot to bring more conflicts and tensions to the region. After all, peace and stability are in line with the fundamental interests of all countries in the region. Specifically, the reasons for the abovementioned complex contradictory attitudes of ASEAN countries are as follows.

First, the "historical imprint" towards the U.S. Southeast Asian policy. The past years have seen the ASEAN's hesitation between the "over militarization" and "systematic neglect" toward the U.S. policy in the region.[7] The former believes that the U.S. policy shift in Southeast Asia is primarily focused on the military cooperation. Washington should be more proactive and creative in contacting ASEAN countries at the economic level, and should not be limited in one particular country.[8] While the latter pointed out that the relationship between ASEAN and the United States has been systematically "ignored" by Washington in the past two decades, because the strategic focus of the United States in Asia Pacific has been located in Northeast Asia, Japan and China. Despite the Obama administration's "pivot" or "rebalance" to Asia, the U.S. approach has been dismissed as more rhetoric than substantive grand strategy, its credibility under renewed scrutiny following President Obama's canceled visit to Southeast Asia in

October 2013.[9] It can be said that ASEAN countries welcome the United States to return to Southeast Asia economically, and anticipate such strategic attention is sustainable and predictable.

Second, complex attitudes towards China. ASEAN and China are close neighbors, and have established close ties in politics, culture, economy, and other aspects in history. In the face of China's rapid rise since the 20th century, ASEAN countries have a complex and contradictory understanding of China. Such theories as "China threat," "China opportunity," and "China friend" are intertwined, which leads to the diversified policy choices, such as to check and balance China, restrain and reform China.[10] Thus, ASEAN has not adopted a "one-sided" strategy toward the U.S. new Asia-Pacific strategy and its active involvement in the SCS issue, in that not all ASEAN countries regard China as an "opponent" or "enemy." Besides, although some ASEAN Member States and China have direct sovereignty disputes in the SCS, ASEAN is not a party to the SCS dispute, so it is not necessary to involve ASEAN in the vortex of confrontation with China. After the confrontation between China and the Philippines on Scarborough Shoal on April 10, 2012, the Philippines strongly urged ASEAN countries to make clear their position on this issue,[11] and the United States also called on ASEAN to play an "active" role on the SCS issue;[12] however, ASEAN did not show a tendency to "support" the United States and the Philippines as to the incident, nor did it put forward political suggestions for peaceful settlement of the incident.

Third, ASEAN's geographical identity as a "divided Southeast Asia." Geographical structure influences the foreign relations and strategic orientation. The region is not connected like the Asian continent, but is divided by numerous mountains, rivers, lakes, oceans, and forests. This broken geographical structure makes it impossible to form a unified nation in history.[13] Overall, Southeast Asian countries can be divided into two parts: continental Southeast Asia and maritime Southeast Asia. The former incorporates Thailand, Myanmar, Vietnam, Cambodia, and Laos, while the latter mainly comprises Indonesia, the Philippines, Malaysia, Singapore, and Brunei. This divided geographical identity not only makes the Southeast Asian countries form a quite different political and economic structure and religious and cultural traditions for a long time, but also directly affects their geopolitical orientation towards the great powers outside the region.[14] Generally speaking, continental Southeast Asia is closer to China, thus its response to the U.S. rebalancing toward Asia Pacific is relatively cautious and restrained. While maritime Southeast Asia tends to be close with the United States and holds a relatively supportive and cooperative attitude towards the rebalancing strategy in Asia Pacific.[15] Nonetheless, the influence of geographical condition is not a decisive factor, and there are many other complicated and changeable factors influencing the policy choices.

Fourth, ASEAN's "balanced diplomacy with great powers." After the Obama administration came to power, the United States implemented the strategy of "returning to Southeast Asia" and signed the Treaty of Amity and Cooperation in Southeast Asia established by ASEAN, which is undoubtedly welcomed by ASEAN, since the latter not only needs the security commitment of the United States, but also relies on extensive economic and technological exchanges and cooperation. As ASEAN Foreign Minister Surin Pitsuwan has stated, of all the regional powers, the United States is the only one that can provide security to Southeast Asian countries.[16] Especially in the context of China's rapid rise, some Southeast Asian countries have become even more dependent on the United States in security matters. With the United States "returning" to the Asia-Pacific region, some ASEAN countries expect that the United States can balance China in the region, but they are not willing to become a tool for the United States to contain China or make actions to irritate China in fear of bringing security risks. Simon Tay, a Singaporean scholar, once pointed out that "Many would welcome an American role. But not one that tries to be the dominant power itself or simply balances China."[17] At present, except for the Philippines' dispute with China over the SCS issue, other ASEAN countries have not shown a tendency to follow Washington. In other words, ASEAN is not willing to take a side between the two powers, instead it takes a delicate "balanced diplomacy between great powers," that is, on the premise of avoiding any great power completely dominating the regional issues, it makes use of the comparative advantages, interest conflicts, and power competition among the major powers to maintain the balance of power in Southeast Asia and realize its own interests.[18]

The Philippines and Vietnam

As a long-standing ally of the United States in Southeast Asia, the Philippines has been one of the most controversial countries with China on the SCS issue. Thus, it warmly welcomes the U.S. "return" to the Asia-Pacific region, and hopes to challenge China in the SCS issue with American support. Since Aquino III took office in June 2010, the Philippines has greatly strengthened its relations with the United States. During the year, the Philippines not only received $143 million in aid from the United States, but also a follow-up of $434 million in five-year assistance contracts,[19] and has directly participated in several U.S. military exercises in the SCS. The Philippines publicly supports the United States to intervene in the SCS issue on multilateral occasions, such as the East Asia Summit, the ARF, and the ASEAN-U.S. Leaders' Summit, trying to intensify the SCS issue at the international level without direct risk. Since U.S. statements about Washington's obligations under the 1951 Mutual Defense Treaty between the Philippines and the United States are ambiguous, Manila is actively seeking an unequivocal U.S. commitment to defend the Philippines in the event of a military confrontation with China in the SCS.[20]

The strong ties with the United States have made some of the pro-American faction in the Philippines lose their basic rational judgment, thus resulting in a radical position on the SCS issue.[21] In February 2011, Del Rosario, Foreign Minister of the Philippines, publicly labeled the United States as "the only strategic partner of the Philippines."[22] On June 7, Gazmin, Philippine Defense Minister, announced that "the stability, security and free flow of the world's second busiest maritime route (the SCS) are related to the interests of the United States." "The presence of the United States is a deterrent to some countries engaging in illegal activities in the SCS, and it is a protection of the rights and interests of the weak and small countries in the region."[23] To further strengthen the alliance, the Philippines and the United States launched a "2 + 2" consultation mechanism in 2012 for defense and foreign ministers to hold dialogues on issues including the SCS issue, regional security, and U.S. Defense Assistance to the Philippines. In July, the Aquino government reopened the military bases which had been closed to the United States since 1992. On April 28, 2014, the two sides signed *The Enhanced Defense Cooperation Agreement*, which is a 10-year pact that gives the U.S. forces greater access to selected military bases on a temporary and rotational basis.[24] It shows that the U.S.-Philippines alliance has entered a new stage. In January 2016, the Philippines planned to provide eight military bases to the United States and proposed to patrol the SCS in concert with the U.S. Navy.[25] With the U.S deepening involvement in the SCS issue, the Philippines will stir up trouble and follow suit. It is inevitable that the SCS issue will become further complicated and internationalized.

Vietnam has a special role in the U.S. rebalancing in the Asia-Pacific region. Although it has a long history of resentment with the United States, with the U.S. "pivot" to Asia Pacific, Vietnam has increasingly become the strategic fulcrum for the United States to "return" to Southeast Asia. Some scholars believe that Vietnam and the United States have made great progress in their relationship during the 21st century. A closely related Vietnam-U.S. quasi alliance is certainly not what China would like to see, but in fact, Vietnam-U.S. relations are indeed rising rapidly.[26] The close relationship between the United States and Vietnam is undoubtedly related to the SCS dispute between China and Vietnam. For Vietnam, the U.S. strong involvement in the SCS issue has made the situation beneficial to Vietnam. With the presence of the United States, Vietnam's policy on the SCS issue can "go further," while China does not dare to overreact. Vietnam's challenge to China on the SCS issue can also echo the United States' policy, and even obtain assistance from the United States.[27] As a Vietnamese diplomat said in an interview in December 2010, it was their best choice to invite the United States to intervene in the SCS issue and check and balance China's influence.[28]

Based on the above considerations, Vietnam has not only taken advantage of its ASEAN rotating presidency to convince the United States to intervene in the SCS issue and put pressure on China since 2010, but also vigorously promotes the Vietnam-U.S. Defense exchange, invites the U.S. defense minister to pay an official visit to Vietnam, and initiates the Vietnam-U.S. joint military exercise. Vietnam also actively participated in TPP negotiations, strengthened Vietnam-U.S. economic relations, and integrated into the regional economy.[29] In addition, in his speech at the Shangri-La dialogue on May 31, 2013, Vietnamese Prime Minister Nguyen Tan Dung declared that Vietnam "supports the principle of freedom of navigation," and "is willing to build strategic trust and release goodwill for countries in the region" and "welcomes countries outside the region to intervene in regional affairs with the goal of promoting peace, stability and development."[30] When the Vietnamese President Truong Tan Sang visited the United States in July he said, "we appreciate U.S. support to solve the matter by peaceful means in accordance with international law, DOC, and moving toward COC. We welcome the United States' support as well as other countries' support in the matter in order to ensure peace, stability, prosperity not only in the East Sea (namely the SCS) but also in Asia Pacific and the world at large."[31] Due to a negative historical memory of the United States that remains unresolved due to the Agent Orange and ordinance dumping issues, the controversies over human rights, and the fact that Vietnam is not willing to infuriate China while developing its relations with the United States, it remains to be seen how far Vietnam can go in "following" the United States.

Indonesia, Malaysia, and Brunei

Indonesia, Malaysia, and Brunei are all parties to the SCS issue. Thus, they are also stakeholders in the United States involvement in the SCS issue. However, unlike the radical Philippines and Vietnam, the three countries have relatively mild reactions to the U.S. intervention.

As the largest country in ASEAN with a leading role in the region, Indonesia skillfully pursues a "dynamic balance" among major powers. On the one hand, out of concerns about China's rise and the SCS issue, Indonesia has maintained a relatively supportive attitude towards the U.S. military presence in the region, regarding it as a "necessary evil."[32] For the above reasons, Indonesia has generally welcomed the Obama administration's rebalancing strategy toward Asia Pacific. As Dewi Fortuna Anwar, the political adviser to Indonesia's vice president, said, "Beijing's increasingly assertive behavior in disputed maritime areas in the South and East China seas has undermined some of the results of China's earlier charm offensive. Hence, there is an urgent need for the development of a more robust regional structure in which China's overwhelming power can be harnessed more peacefully and productively within an East Asian community."[33] In 2012, Indonesia adopted a tacit attitude in response to the U.S. deployment of military forces in northern Australia. During Indonesian President Joko Widodo's first visit to the United States in October 2015, the two countries upgraded their bilateral relations from "comprehensive partnership"[34] to "strategic partnership," and Indonesia even expressed its intention to join the TPP in this period.[35]

Yet, while welcoming the U.S. rebalancing toward Asia, it does not mean that Indonesia is fully turning to the United States and its allies. Some in Indonesia have raised concerns and complaints about the rotational basing of 2,500 U.S. marines in Darwin, Australia, and many in Indonesia still remember the United States' support for regional rebels in the late 1950s.[36] Therefore, Indonesia's support for the United States to "return to Asia Pacific" and its involvement in the SCS issue is limited, because it does not want the situation in the SCS to deteriorate, and it does not want to see its leading position in ASEAN to be undermined due to excessive intervention by a foreign power. It is still Indonesia's priority to resort to the balance of foreign relations among major powers.

As a direct dispute party over the sovereignty of the SCS, Malaysia is relatively rational and moderate as to the U.S. rebalancing toward Asia Pacific and its involvement in the SCS issue, and its relation with China is also the friendliest among countries in the SCS dispute.[37] Considering its dispute over sovereignty over the SCS with China and its concerns about China's increasingly powerful maritime strength, Malaysia has no reason to refuse the U.S. goodwill in the context of active returning to Asia Pacific.[38] Especially in the field of security, Malaysia believes that the U.S. military presence in Southeast Asia has a positive effect on regional security, and it expects to maintain the strategic balance in the SCS with the help of Washington. Since 2010, Malaysia has carried out various forms of exchanges and cooperation with the United States, including defense ministers' meeting, warship visits, joint military exercises, signing memoranda, etc.[39] In this regard, Azmi Hassan, a Malaysian geostrategic expert, comments that the most effective way for Malaysia to send signals to China is to engage in joint military exercises with the United States.[40] As the U.S. President Obama visited Malaysia for the first time in 48 years in April 2014, the U.S.-Malaysia relations reached a climax.

Malaysia does not completely take side with the United States. It remains an active member of the Non-Alignment Movement, taking a hard line against Israel and maintaining close relations with Iran, the strong enemy of the United States. Meanwhile, a strain of grassroots and party-political anti-Western sentiment is another constraint on closer security cooperation with Washington.[41] Besides, Malaysia's diplomacy has always been described as strong pan-Asia characteristics, and has long been committed to shaping the regional pattern by taking ASEAN as the center, such as the East Asia Summit, the expanded ASEAN Defense Ministers Meeting, and so on. This also determines that Malaysia will not fully follow up the U.S. strategy of rebalancing toward the Asia-Pacific region, and show a wavering attitude on some issues.[42] Therefore, Malaysia does not want to see the United States excessively intervene in the SCS dispute, avoids taking radical measures to worsen the regional situation, and advocates peaceful settlement of the SCS dispute through bilateral or multilateral cooperation.

As a small country in Southeast Asia, Brunei plays a less important role in U.S. strategic layout in the Asia-Pacific region. Although Brunei is a direct party to the SCS issue, it has done very little on the issue due to its lack of necessary political strength, and has never put forward any influential initiatives.[43] Therefore, under the circumstances that the United States returns to the Asia-Pacific region and actively intervenes in the SCS dispute, Brunei's response is relatively detached, and there is no "following," "neutral," "balanced," or "opposing." It should be pointed out that although Brunei gives access to part of its military facilities since the United States announced its "return" to Southeast Asia in 2009, it only allows the U.S. Navy to enter the port of Brunei under certain conditions.[44] At the same time, Brunei has participated in regional military exercises led by the United States for many times,[45] even acquiesced in the joint military exercises held by the United States, Japan, and Australia in its coastal waters;[46] such behaviors are basically "routine" and do not exceed the relatively mild SCS policy that Brunei has long pursued. Unlike the Philippines and Vietnam, Brunei did not drift with the tide in face of the U.S. rebalancing strategy in the Asia-Pacific region. Instead, Brunei advocated a peaceful settlement of the SCS issue, and opposed the use of force and the intervention of external forces, hoping to maintain peace and stability in the SCS region by strengthening cooperation with neighboring countries.[47]

Singapore, Thailand, Cambodia, Laos, and Myanmar

As a quasi-ally of the United States in Southeast Asia, Singapore has always played an important role as a defense partner and logistics supporter of the U.S. military. It hopes that the United States will continue to play a role in balancing China's influence. As soon as the Obama administration launched the rebalancing strategy in the Asia-Pacific region, Singapore expressed its optimistic attitude, reiterating that the presence of the United States in Asia is an indispensable part of the regional security. Singapore Prime Minister Lee Hsien Loong also said in his congratulatory message for Obama's reelection that Singapore welcomed the U.S. rebalancing strategy to reach a wide range of Asian regions, including Southeast Asia and ASEAN.[48] In September 2012, in a public speech at Chin's Central Party School, Lee denied the American decline argument, claiming that the role of the United States in Asia is irreplaceable.[49] In the view of Singapore's successive leaders, the role of the United States as a regional security protector and strategic balancer in Asia is irreplaceable. Once the United States loses this power advantage, Singapore will be put in an awkward situation.[50]

Singapore's attitude on the SCS issue can be summarized as "neutral and useful, maintain stability and peace."[51] As a non-claimant in the SCS, Singapore has become increasingly active on the issue since 2010, articulating that its critical national interests are at stake when it comes to freedom of navigation and over-flight, while urging restraint on all claimant parties and calling for ASEAN to negotiate on the COC, and advocating that the SCS dispute should be based on international law and be settled in a peaceful way. Some scholars believe that Singapore's position on freedom of navigation is as similar to that of the United States.[52] It should be noted that although Singapore welcomes the U.S. "return" to the Asia-Pacific region and hopes to maintain regional balance with the help of the United States, it does not mean that Singapore supports the U.S. policy of containing China. K. Shanmugam, former Foreign Minister of Singapore, has warned the United States against anti-China rhetoric: "The world and Asia are big enough to accommodate a rising China and a reinvigorated US."[53] Academic opinion in the region has generally been cautious on the pivot emphasizing the need for the United States to adopt a non-provocative approach that avoids signaling "containment" to China.[54]

Thailand, Cambodia, and Laos are not the parties to the SCS dispute. They have relatively little demand for U.S. security and maintain good bilateral relations with China. Therefore, their responses to the U.S. rebalancing strategy in the Asia-Pacific region are lukewarm. Thailand is a treaty ally of the United States in Southeast Asia; however, it maintains close relations with China. In face of the U.S. rebalancing strategy in the Asia-Pacific region, Thailand is more concerned about the negative impact on China-Thai relations, and avoids any entrapment in the great-power tussle between Beijing and Washington in Southeast Asia.[55] Based on the above considerations, Thailand doesn't unconditionally cooperate with the United States, but carefully maintains a delicate balance with the two great powers. The renting incident of U-Tapao military base in 2012 shows that under the background of the United States "returning" to Southeast Asia, Thailand is cautious about its interaction with the United States at military level, and is not willing to be labeled as a "follower" of the United States, let alone serving as a tool for "containing China."[56]

Cambodia has long pursued a "neutral" foreign policy and maintained close bilateral relations with China. Therefore, Cambodia's response to the U.S. rebalancing strategy is relatively mild and neutral. Especially on the SCS issue, Cambodia advocates peaceful settlement of disputes, opposes the internationalization of the SCS issue, and the involvement of foreign countries in the SCS dispute. Cambodian Prime Minister Hun Sen stressed that "the parties concerned should use existing mechanisms to solve the problem through consultation and should not try to put pressure on China allying with the United States or Japan."[57] He has urged the parties concerned to strictly abide by the COC in the SCS, warning against internationalizing the SCS issue and being interfered by the forces outside the region, while supporting the resolution of the SCS issue within the framework of ASEAN and China.[58] Cambodia's policies and responses are objective and unbiased, which are conducive to the stability in the SCS.

Laos has been pursuing a friendly policy towards China for a long time, and has listed China as its main target country for developing all-round foreign relations.[59] As an indirect dispute party to the SCS issue, Laos' position on SCS is relatively fair, and opposes internationalizing and complicating the SCS issue, and does not support ASEAN's involvement in the SCS dispute. At the informal meeting of U.S.-ASEAN leaders held in the United States on February 15, 2016, the United States and ASEAN discussed whether the statement mentioned the SCS. Due to the opposition of Laos and other countries, the statement of the U.S.-ASEAN meeting did not mention the SCS.[60] It can be seen that Laos is relatively indifferent to the U.S. rebalancing strategy in the Asia-Pacific region, and it certainly doesn't actively follow the United States in its attempts to check and balance China.

Considering the historic changes in Myanmar's political development in recent years, the Obama administration promotes the rebalancing strategy in the Asia-Pacific region at the level of values diplomacy to enhance its relations with Myanmar and to make it a "democratic model." In order to obtain political support from Washington and lift economic sanctions, the Myanmar government also shows a positive attitude towards the U.S. Southeast Asian strategy, which led to the rapid warming up of U.S.-Myanmar relations.[61] Since 2009, U.S. officials, including Barack Obama and Hillary Clinton, have visited Myanmar frequently. Myanmar's Foreign Minister, leader of the National League for Democracy, Aung San Suu Kyi, and Myanmar President, U Thein Sein, have also visited the United States. Meantime, Myanmar has witnessed a series of anti-China incidents since 2011, such as the Myitsone Dam issue, which is interpreted by some Western media as "showing a diplomatic independence posture towards China,"[62] and the Myanmar government's policy of "getting rid of China and turning to the United States."[63]

In conclusion, Myanmar's foreign policy seems to have reached a new crossroads. As U Zaw Htay, director of Myanmar's Presidential office, said in 2013, one of the most important challenges facing Myanmar is how to adjust its foreign policy, including how to actively participate in ASEAN issues, and how to formulate policies related to the SCS issue, ASEAN, the United States, and China.[64] At present, Myanmar is still in a critical period of political transformation, and its domestic and foreign trends are full of uncertainties. The relationship between Myanmar and the United States is also restricted by domestic political situations, the democratization process, and the improvement of human rights conditions in Myanmar.[65] At the same time, as Myanmar's largest neighbor, China is not only Myanmar's traditional friend, but also Myanmar's most important trade and investment partner. Therefore, regardless of Myanmar's political situation, developing friendly relations with China is in the fundamental interests of Myanmar.[66] In the future, Myanmar is less likely to take side with the United States and more likely to strike a balance between China and the United States.

Japan: Departure from Asia for America

East Asia is the priority of the United States when implementing the rebalancing strategy in the Asia-Pacific region. The United States needs to continuously cultivate its strategic partners in East Asia in order to minimize the impact of cuts to the defense budget and relative decline. As an ironclad ally and anchor of the north of the United States in the Asia-Pacific region, Japan has always been included in the post-WWII American Asia-Pacific strategic layout, and actively caters to U.S. policy.[67] Meanwhile, Japan effectively seeks great synergy with the U.S. rebalancing strategy toward Asia Pacific to strengthen the Japan-U.S. alliance, enhance its position in the U.S. strategy in the Asia-Pacific region and even in the world, as well as takes the opportunity to lift its collective self-defense right and promotes the construction of its own political and military power, so as to compete with China in the power competition in East Asia.[68]

The Strategic Motivation of Japan's Attention to the SCS Issue

As the only country in history that occupied the islands and reefs in the SCS on a large scale in modern terms, Japan is quite concerned about the changes of the situation in the SCS. Japan realizes the geostrategic importance of SCS, and continues to retain high levels of attention in this area. Up to now, Japan has become the second foreign power after the United States to interfere with the SCS issue. For one thing, Japan focuses on the strategic position of the SCS and its economic interests. For another, it takes the opportunity to compete with China for regional influence, and respond to China's policy orientation in the dispute over the Diaoyu/Senkaku Islands and the delimitation of the East China Sea.

First, the SCS is regarded as the lifeline of the sea. From the perspective of geographical structure, the SCS is a strategic transportation route connecting East Asia, Africa, and Europe, and a strategic artery connecting the Pacific Ocean and the Indian Ocean. For a country with extremely poor natural resources, Japan's oil imports from the Middle East Asia and commodity imports and exports to Europe and Southeast Asia need to pass through the SCS. Statistics show that more than 80 % of Japan's oil supply and more than 70 % of its trade traverse through the SCS,[69] while a detour east of the Philippines would increase the cost by 25 %.[70] The security situation of the SCS is extremely crucial to Japan both in wartime and peacetime, thus the SCS has always been regarded as a "maritime lifeline." With the rising of the SCS issue since the 21st century, Japan has paid more attention to maritime security. In its National Security Strategy released in December 2013, the Japanese government took "protecting maritime traffic lanes" and "ensuring freedom of navigation on the high seas" as an important agenda within Japan's maritime security, and proposed that Japan should not only strengthen its own security, but also play a leading role in maintaining an "open and stable ocean" based on the norms of international law. Therefore, Japan will take necessary measures to deal with various factors threatening maritime routes and ensure maritime traffic safety.[71]

Second, Japan has economic interests in the SCS. For an island nation with few natural resources, how the seas are managed greatly influences Japan's national prosperity and security. As a maritime State, Japan is heavily reliant on the maritime resources in the SCS for its economic survival and people's livelihood, which is a primary driving force for Japan's long-term pursuit of its foreign strategy of expanding into the ocean.[72] Historically, abundant resources such as fish, algae, and natural bird droppings in the SCS have aroused great interest in Japan. This was also an important factor in inspiring Japan's "down south" and extending the encroachment from Ryukyu and Taiwan to the Spratly Islands. After the 1950s and 1960s, with the advancement made in submarine oil and gas resource exploitation technology and the discovery of rich mineral and oil resources in the SCS, Japan's interest in resources in the SCS has increased unprecedentedly. Over the years, Japan has been involved in the development of oil and gas resources in the SCS by means of enterprise investment, which has become one of the actual beneficiaries of the joint development of resources in the SCS.

Third, Japan competes with China for regional influence. For a long time, Southeast Asia has not only been Japan's important raw materials and commodity sales market, but also the key region for Japan's investment in Asia. It is also an important steppingstone for Japan to become a political and military power. Therefore, it plays an irreplaceable role in Japan's regional strategy. With the rapid rise of China after the Cold War, however, China's influence in Southeast Asia is greatly accelerating. In 2010, China became the largest trading partner of ASEAN, and the construction of China-ASEAN free trade area (CAFTA) was officially launched, and the economic relations between China and ASEAN were further strengthened. Besides, China is not only a member of the ARF, Asia Europe Meeting (ASEM), ASEAN "10+3" (APT) cooperation mechanism, and East Asia Summit, but also a partner of the ASEAN Foreign Ministers' meeting (AMM). Within the framework of the "10+3" cooperation mechanism, the ASEAN-China Dialogue Forum has been established. With the Belt and Road Initiative put forward, the Silk Road Fund, the 21st Century Maritime Silk Road and Asian Infrastructure Investment Bank will further strengthen the interconnection between China and ASEAN countries and promote the building of a community with a shared future.[73] The increasingly close relationship between China and ASEAN and the mounting influence of China in Southeast Asia put Japan under great pressure, fearing that it would be marginalized in regional affairs. Against this background, Japan regards the SCS issue as an opportunity to drive a wedge between China and Southeast Asian countries, and compete with China for regional dominance and superiority.

Fourth, Japan's response to China's policy orientation on the Diaoyu/Senkaku Islands dispute and delimitation of the East China Sea is partly made by focusing on the SCS issue. The maritime disputes in East Asia seem to be isolated from each other, but in fact, they have internal linkages. The warming up of territorial disputes between the two countries is often an indicator for a third party to make policy adjustments.[74] China has maritime disputes with some Southeast Asian countries in the SCS, as well as the Diaoyu/Senkaku Islands and maritime delimitation disputes with Japan in the East China Sea. Japan is worried that China may apply its behavior in the SCS to the Diaoyu/Senkaku Islands dispute. As a result, China's policy toward the SCS is regarded by Japan as the policy on Diaoyu/Senkaku Islands.[75] For example, after China promulgated the Law of the PRC on the Territorial Sea and the Contiguous Zone in 1992, Japan regarded the China-Japan Diaoyu/Senkaku Islands dispute and the SCS dispute as interrelated issues, even though there are fundamental differences.[76] After the collision between Chinese fishing boat and Japanese coastal guard in the waters near the Diaoyu/Senkaku Islands in 2010 and Japan's unilateral nationalization of the Diaoyu/Senkaku Islands in 2012, the Japanese government linked the East China Sea dispute and the SCS dispute, believing that if the SCS dispute is eventually settled in a way beneficial to China, then the same approach shall be applied to the East China Sea issue, which is unfavorable to Japan's claim for sovereignty over the Diaoyu/Senkaku Islands and the EEZ in the East China Sea.[77]

Japan Welcomes the United States to Implement Its Rebalancing Strategy toward Asia Pacific

The Japan-U.S. alliance has been the cornerstone of Japan's foreign policy since WWII. Therefore, Japan warmly welcomes the United States' new Asia-Pacific strategy, and attempts to invite neighboring countries to build an anti-China unified front. Specifically, Japan's measures cover the following three aspects: first, Japan enhances relations with the Philippines, Vietnam, and other countries that have maritime sovereignty disputes with China; expands the bilateral defense cooperation; and helps those countries strengthen the construction of coastal police forces by providing flexible official assistance. Second, Japan promotes value diplomacy, actively invites India and Australia to join the U.S.-Japan alliance against China, forming the "democratic security diamond" (G4) in the

Asia-Pacific region and building a regional "democratic security network." Third, through close cooperation with the abovementioned countries, Japan tries to form a "siege outlook" encircling China, and creates a unified front with the United States and Japan as the axis and the Philippines, Vietnam, India, Australia, and other countries as the periphery.[78]

To express its support for the United States, Japan actively sought to join the TPP, which is the main economic pillar of the U.S. rebalancing strategy. Although there are many debates in Japan on whether to participate in the TPP negotiations,[79] the Japanese government ultimately displayed a positive attitude to TPP. Naoto Kan, then Prime Minister, said in October 2010 that TPP was an important part of the stability and prosperity of East Asia. It was necessary for Japan to study TPP to promote the establishment of the Asia Pacific Free Trade Zone, which revealed its intention to join the TPP.[80] Despite the opposition of domestic agricultural and other interest groups, Japanese Prime Minister Shinzo Abe officially announced that Japan would join the TPP negotiations at a press conference held on the evening of March 15, 2013.[81] On November 10, 2016, the Japanese House of Representatives approved the TPP agreement.

It is undeniable that Japan actively seeks to join the TPP negotiations for consideration of many factors, including expanding exports, boosting its economy, changing the backward situation of trade liberalization, promoting agricultural reform, striving for making rules, and playing a leading role in promoting the construction of the Asia Pacific Free Trade Area.[82] What is noteworthy is that there is a profound "China factor" behind Japan's entry into TPP. In the face of China's rapid rise in recent years and its positive role in the economic integration of East Asia, Japan is under great pressure. At the same time, the territorial disputes and historical cognitive problems between China and Japan in 2010 made bilateral relations deteriorate, which led to the rise of Japan's hostility towards China. To some extent, the TPP provides Japan with another opportunity to offset China as an external security threat. Therefore, Japanese voters are reluctant to "block" the government on this issue.[83]

In this context, Japan hopes to show its support for the U.S.-led economic cooperation in the Asia-Pacific region by joining the TPP, repair and consolidate the Japan-U.S. alliance, and realize an effective binding of their declining economies. On the other hand, it can be used to balance the rising of China and increase the counterweight with China, so as to change Japan's passive position in regional economic cooperation.[84] Although the United States did not exclude China from the TPP, it added higher environmental protection and labor standards requirements. Considering that China is often criticized on the above two standards,

Japan actively sought to join the TPP negotiations in a bid to contain China, which can be regarded as an implicit support for U.S. rebalancing towards Asia Pacific.

Cooperate with the United States in the SCS issue

In view of the maritime disputes between China and the neighboring countries in the SCS, Japan has shown inexplicable "worries." Although Japan is not a direct dispute party to the SCS issue, and so far Japanese officials have not published a complete policy document on the SCS issue, domestic public opinion, including some Japanese officials, scholars, and media circles, generally attributed the rising tension of the SCS issue to China's aggressive marine expansion.[85] In a report on April 25, 2010, Japan's Sankei Shimbun claimed that "China's control over the Spratly Islands has become a fact, and the future of Diaoyu/Senkaku Island is worrying."[86] In May, the retired Navy Admiral Sumihiko Kawamura suggested that "in response to China's aggressive maritime behavior, the United States, Japan and other allies in the region should monitor China's naval movements by holding more joint naval exercises and coordinating their actions, so as to provoke China's behavior on the high seas to meet international standards."[87]

Yomiuri Shimbun, Japan's largest newspaper, published the "China Threat Theory" on the front page of 2014's New Year's edition, highlighting that Beijing wants to become a "maritime power" with modern military strength, claiming that China's move poses a threat to the United States and Japan, and calling on the Japanese authorities to keep a close eye on China and be on full alert while revitalizing the economy.[88] In the end of May, Shinzo Abe, then Japanese Prime Minister, accused China of "violating international law and international code of conduct" on the SCS issue at a series of international conferences such as the Shangri-La Dialogue, intending to "isolate China" in the region.[89] Japan's hype of a SCS issue reflects a strong sense of crisis accumulated in Japanese society against the background of China's rapid rise in recent years, and also manifests Japan's diplomacy of "following the steps of the U.S."[90]

Meanwhile, Japan actively cooperates with the United States to promote the internationalization of the SCS issue, claiming that disputes over the SCS issue should be resolved within an international framework involving the participation of the United States and Japan. At the foreign ministers' meeting of the ARF held in July 2010, after U.S. Secretary of State Hillary Clinton accused China of taking a more offensive stance on the high seas, and claimed that "resolving the SCS sovereignty dispute is the key to regional stability and is related to the national interests of the United States,"[91] Japan has also held a press conference to reiterate its position. Okada, then Japan's Foreign Minister, declared at the press conference that the SCS was a regional transportation artery, which was crucial to the peace and development of Asian countries. Japan believed that coordination on the SCS issue should not be limited to the countries concerned, but should bring ASEAN countries, the United States, Japan, and other countries into the international framework and carry out multilateral dialogue.[92]

Nonetheless, Japan has pointed a finger at China's actions in the SCS, and has made every effort to promote the internationalization of the SCS issue. On July 8, 2011, Matsumoto, then Japanese Foreign Minister, expressed concerns about China's mounting military influence in the SCS, claiming that Japan would be committed to strengthening the construction of an international discussion mechanism on the SCS issue.[93] Besides, after the United States sent warships into the SCS in the name of defending "freedom of navigation" in October 2015, the competition between China and the United States in the SCS has escalated dramatically. In response to the provocative behavior of the United States, Japanese Chief Cabinet Secretary Suga Yoshihide expressed his firm support for the United States in defending the right to freedom of navigation on February 1, 2016. As to China's actions on the SCS, Suga Yoshihide commented that "China's unilateral act of changing the status quo and increasing tension is a common concern of the international community."[94] For the purpose of checking and balancing China, the United States frequently puts pressure on China on the SCS issue, while Japan supports the United States. for consideration of maintaining the maritime lifeline and balancing China. Thus, the common strategic goals of both sides—to check and balance China—converge on the SCS issue. In this process, Japan and the United States jointly promote the internationalization of the SCS issue, which may also maximize the strategic effect.[95]

Reform and Coordination in Defense

In order to better meet the U.S. strategic needs in security in the Asia-Pacific region, and take the opportunity to break through the restrictions of the post-war Peace Constitution and further advance to a political and military power, the Abe government has made a number of defense reforms, mainly covering the following aspects:

First, the three principles of arms export were revised. On April 1, 2014, Japanese Prime Minister Shinzo Abe scrapped the three principles on arms exports and adopted instead the three principles on the transfer of defense equipment and technology, encouraging proactive exports of defense-related devices. The new three principles include: (a) to abide by the resolutions of the UN

Security Council and the international treaties signed by Japan, and prohibit the export of weapons and equipment to the countries involved in conflict; (b) to promote international peace, international cooperation and enhance Japan's security, a transparent and strict auditing should be carried out; and (c) the exported weapons and equipment can be used for other purposes or transferred to a third country, provided that they are properly managed.[96] The three principles indicate that Japan has abandoned the "three principles of arms export," which seriously violates its claims to be a "peaceful country," and stains its national image as a "peaceful country."

Second, the right of collective self-defense was lifted. On February 28, 2013, Shinzo Abe, who had just concluded his visit to the United States, said that in order to contain China's "provocative behavior" on the Diaoyu/Senkaku Islands, Japan needed to re-discuss the prohibition of collective self-defense rights stipulated in the Constitution, which was a must for building a strong Japan.[97] The United States also publicly encouraged Japan to lift its right to collective self-defense. During his visit to Japan on April 5, 2014, Hagel, then U.S. Secretary of Defense, claimed that in order to further promote the U.S.-Japan alliance, it was particularly necessary to expand the function of the self-defense force. Therefore, the United States would "welcome and support" Japan's efforts to lift the right of collective self-defense.[98] After a period of social mobilization and public opinion preparation, the Abe government finally broke through the restrictions of Article 9 of the Peace Constitution and officially announced on July 1, 2014, that the right of collective self-defense was lifted by amending the interpretation of the Constitution.[99]

Third, the Abe government promoted the new Security Act. In mid-May 2015, Abe's Cabinet passed a security bill, revising the system framework and legal text related to the exercise of collective self-defense right, so as to improve the coordination and cooperation with the U.S. military, and to build a combat force that can be dispatched at any time. The prominent feature of the new security act is that it breaks through the geographical restrictions of the past security cooperation between the United States and Japan, and extends the cooperation to global issues. At the same time, Japan's security policy orientation has shifted from "regional factors" to "nature of events." Considering the strong subjectivity and flexibility in the "nature of events," it is favorable for Japan to participate in foreign intervention. Under the framework of the new security act, the defense targets of Japan's self-defense forces tend to be diversified, and the defense scope has become increasingly blurred. Its overseas military activities may also become more frequent with aggressive tendencies.[100]

Fourth, the Abe government has vigorously increased military investment and strengthened military buildup. After taking office at the end of 2012, Shinzo Abe increased Japan's defense spending by 0.8 % and put a stop to Japan's defense budget reduction for 10 consecutive years. Since then, Japan's defense budget has been growing. On December 24, 2013, Abe's cabinet approved the 2014 annual budget plan with a total amount of 95.88 trillion yen, in which the expenditure on defense was about 4.9 trillion yen, an increase of 131 billion yen over the previous year, with an increase of 2.8 %. About 102.1 billion yen in the military budget will be used to purchase advanced fourth generation F35 fighters and related equipment and personnel training.[101] On December 24, 2015, in the 2016 annual budget approved by the Japanese cabinet with a total amount of 96.72 trillion yen, the expenditure for defense expenditure exceeded 5 trillion yen for the first time and reached 5.05 trillion yen, an increase of about 1.5 % over last year. Besides, the military budget is mainly used for military procurement, including the purchase of advanced E-2D Early Warning Aircraft, MV-22 tilt-rotor Transport Aircraft, F-35 Stealth Fighter, and SH-60k Reconnaissance Helicopter.[102] Japan's actions are appreciated by the United States as it provides strong support for the United States to promote the rebalancing toward Asia Pacific in military, and also increases the confidence for Japan to confront China on Diaoyu/Senkaku Islands dispute while simultaneously decreasing the two countries' trade imbalance.

India: From "Look East" to "Act East"

As the overlord in South Asia, India has emerged as an important constituent of the U.S. strategy of pivoting toward the Asia-Pacific region. From the very inception of the rebalancing strategy, the Obama administration has underscored India's important role in the framework and emphasized the role that India could play in the new power dynamics. By rechristening the "Asia Pacific" as the "Indo-Pacific," the United States highlighted the strategic significance of both the Indian Ocean and India in the United States' new approach to Asia. On his visit to India in November 2010, President Obama declared that India-U.S. relations were strategic partnership in the 21st century, and welcomed India to play a leading role in the prosperity and security of the entire region.[103] India was also the only country in the Asia Pacific that was explicitly identified as a valuable strategic partner in the Pentagon report of January 2012, which states that the United States is also investing in a long-term strategic partnership with

India to support its ability to serve as a regional economic anchor and provider of security in the broader Indian Ocean region.[104] In June 2012, former Secretary of Defense Leon Panetta described the India-U.S. defense partnership as a linchpin of the United States' rebalancing strategy and requested that New Delhi play a bigger role in the security of the Asia Pacific.[105] Then what is India's attitude toward America's expectations?

Cognition of Indian Strategic Community

The Indian domestic response to U.S. "strategic rebalancing" can be divided into three categories: the welcoming, the skeptical, and the pragmatic.

Those who welcome the United States to "return" to Asia, and strengthen the presence of power in the Asia-Pacific region, generally take a positive attitude. They hope to get rewarded by Washington through cooperating with the United States to deal with the challenges brought about by China's rise, such as helping India suppress its old enemy Pakistan and consolidating New Delhi's hegemony in South Asia.[106] India has long dreamed of pursuing a great power status. Back to the days before India's independence, Nehru had a clear definition of India's international role, "India will either become a big country with a strong voice or disappear."[107] Therefore, in the context of America's "return" to the Asia-Pacific region, the welcoming faction aspires to take the strategic opportunity to achieve the national dream of being a great power. The strategic shift of the United States to Asia has an important geopolitical effect, which forces China to treat India more rationally, in that Beijing needs to focus on the challenges from the East launched by U.S. military forces. At the same time, the greater the pressure imposed by the United States in the Pacific, the more likely China will remain "silent" in its southwest border areas.

The welcoming faction also believes that India is no match for China in terms of national defense and strategic capabilities. At present, China's GDP is four times that of India, and its military expenditure is more than three times that of India. Therefore, India's capability to balance China alone has always been doubtful, and external balancing from the U.S. and its allies may be the only resort available to New Delhi.[108] The welcoming faction has the following considerations: (a) they are worried that China's rise will impact India's position as a great power in Asia; (b) they are worried that China will challenge India's dominant position in South Asia and the Indian Ocean; (c) they are worried about the border issue that exists between China and India; (d) they are worried about the close relationship between China and Pakistan; and (e) they are worried that

China's growing military capabilities threaten India.[109] For the welcoming faction, the United States and India have a convergence of interests in containing China's "expansion" in Asia. In other words, there is a common understanding between the United States and India in playing a positive role in the Asia-Pacific region and pursuing to be a global power. Thus, China acting as a common target meets the security needs of India.[110]

The skeptical group doubts the real desire of the United States to "elevate" India and the credibility of the rebalancing strategy toward Asia Pacific. They believe that India-U.S. relations have been warming up after the United States launched the rebalancing strategy, but the United States and India harbor disagreements. India is just a part in the U.S. rebalancing strategic layout. Although both sides have common interests on issues related to China, they are only in a temporary relationship for mutual benefit. India is also a target to encircle and contain. From a long-term and overall perspective, once India's power in the Indo-Pacific grows rapidly and threatens the dominant position of the United States in the region, Washington will turn its back on New Delhi mercilessly.[111] As one Indian strategic analyst points out, although India is as concerned about China's rising as the United States, India is reluctant to be a part of any grand containment strategy against China.[112]

The skeptics also believe that weak economic recovery and uncertain domestic political disputes will discount the commitment and investment of the United States to the rebalancing strategy, and raise many questions regarding the "sustainability" of the U.S. rebalancing policy. Moreover, the economic interdependence between China and the United States and the need for Beijing's support on a range of regional and global issues will put a constraint on the United States to counterweigh China's rise. What's more, the rapid power shift to China may push Washington to gradually embrace Beijing, rather than counterbalance the China's potential regional dominance.[113] Therefore, the skeptics do not reject the normal cooperation with the United States, but are more cautious to attribute the promotion of bilateral strategic relations to the influence of a "third party," namely China.

The pragmatists believe that India must keep a sober mind in face of the United States' cajoling and inducement. It should neither bandwagon the United States to balance China with rebalancing strategy nor be indifferent to it. The best policy is to keep equilibrium between the two powers and act according to the domestic and international situation, so as to maintain its strategic autonomy.[114] As highlighted in the report entitled "Nonalignment 2.0: A Foreign and Strategic Policy for India in the Twenty First Century" issued by the Centre for

Policy Studies (CPR) in New Delhi in February 2012, "India does not define its national interests on the basis of ideology, but maintains its maximum strategic autonomy to pursue its own development goals and strive for a more just and equitable global order."[115]

As far as pragmatists are concerned, India needs to face up to the following realities: First, India's domestic social and clan contradictions are complex, regional development is very uneven, and India's development needs a stable surrounding environment. Second, participating in the China-U.S. cold war initiated by the United States is bound to offend China, place India-China relations in a difficult position, and even lead India into disputes and conflicts with neighboring countries.[116] Third, both economically and diplomatically, the U.S.-China relationship is closer and cooperation is more extensive than that of the U.S.-India relations. G-2 or Chimerica has shown that India is in a relatively marginal position in the trilateral relationship.[117] Therefore, if there is a conflict between China and India, what position the United States will take is still unclear.[118] Fourth, there are also many differences of interests between India and the United States, including differences in their foreign strategic views (India advocates multi-polarization and non-alignment, and the United States advocates maintaining unipolar system through alliance), asymmetry of strategic vision and capability (India is weak and pays attention to the surrounding security environment; the United States is strong and emphasizes global strategic layout), economic competition and disputes (such as India's retail industry is open to the United States), regional security policy differences (such as India's security concerns after the withdrawal of U.S. troops from Afghanistan), etc.[119] Fifth, binding with the U.S. strategy in Asia will constrain India's strategic autonomy and weaken its ability to achieve strategic security and project power externally. This is undoubtedly a strategic "inaction" for India.[120] Based on the above cognition, the pragmatists hold that India should make rational policy choices on the basis of comprehensive and objective evaluation of its own strategic interests and the trilateral relations between India, the United States, and China and strive to achieve the goal of "seeking the best from both sides."

India's Official Response

Compared with the debate in Indian strategic community, India's official response to the U.S. rebalancing strategy in the Asia-Pacific region is more cautious with an ambiguous attitude: India does not want to be an American follower in the rebalancing strategy, even though it welcomes the United States to strengthen its presence in Asia.

As for the ambiguous attitude released by Indian officials, Nirupama Rao, former Indian Ambassador to the United States, said in a speech at Brown University during February 2013 that India welcomed in-depth U.S. participation in Indo-Pacific regional issues, as this area is vital to India's security and prosperity. India and the United States have other common interests in the region. When it comes to China, she articulated that many observers were interested in India-U.S. contacts in the region, as if this was aimed at China. Such view was neither viable nor sustainable, especially given that India and China also have a huge overlap of interests in the region. After all, China is India's biggest neighbor. Rao also called on Asian countries, including the United States, to actively build a "coordination among great powers" mechanism to promote mutual compromise. She called this mechanism an "inclusive balance," that is, the United States and all the major powers in the region, such as China, Japan, India, and Russia, are working hard together to build a multipolar order.[121] It can be perceived that India does not want to fall into a strategic competition trap between China and the United States against the background of the U.S. strategic shift to the Asia-Pacific region. Considering the strategic complexity and uncertainty brought about by the eastward shift of U.S. strategic focus, a continued non-aligned policy may be the best choice for India.

In its interaction with the United States, India has adhered to the principle of maximizing its own interests. In action, India should not only rely on the U.S. pivot strategy to the Asia-Pacific region, moderately check and balance China's rise, and obtain benefits from it, but also avoid excessively irritating China and becoming an instrument in the U.S. containment strategy against China. It is not difficult to find that India, which is sandwiched between the two powers of China and the United States, has actually adopted a hedging strategy in face of the power shift of great powers in Asia.[122] India's behavior is reflected in promoting security relations with the United States, intervening in the SCS issue, and implementing the "Act East Policy."

In the security relationship between India and the United States, although there are many doubts about the reliability of the United States, India has gained a lot of benefits from its defense cooperation with the United States, which is in line with India's pursuit of military power and nuclear power status. In April 2012, as soon as Nancy Powell, the new U.S. Ambassador to India, took office, India and the United States signed arms sales contracts totaling $8 billion.[123] With the advancement of the U.S. rebalancing strategy toward Asia Pacific at the military level, India has also upgraded the level of security cooperation with the United States. For this reason, Indian Defense Minister Antony has stressed that the future defense cooperation between the United States and India needs to go beyond the purchasing phase and shift the focus of cooperation to technology transfer, so as to enhance India's independent research and development capability of defense products.[124] Thus, in face of the U.S. pivot strategy toward Asia Pacific, India has also actively increased its arms procurement from the United States and improved its capability of independent research and development of domestically produced weapons, so as to reduce excessive dependence on Russia, its traditional military cooperation partner.

In addition, after the United States announced its "return" to the Asia-Pacific region, joint military exercises between India and the United States have been strengthened, mainly manifest in the following aspects: First, the number of exercises is up to 50 times a year, and it is still on the rise.[125] Second, the scale of these exercises has been expanding, involving more services and arms. Third, drill subjects are more diversified. Fourth, the exercise sites tend to expand from India and Thailand to Indian-Kashmir and Alaska. While carrying out security cooperation with the United States, India sometimes moderately displays scruples about China's feelings. For example, in May 2013, the United States, Japan, and India held consultations on the joint military exercise, but India believed that this might stimulate China's sensitive nerves. It should be changed to a bilateral exercise between the United States and India or between Japan and India, and in the end India decided to withdraw from the exercise in Guam.[126]

India is catering to the United States on the SCS issue as well. The outstanding geostrategic and security significance and economic value such as energy resources of SCS is the extrinsic motivation for India to take action in the region.[127] After the United States announced its "return" to the Asia-Pacific region, the United States brought in India to form a multi-party joint pressure on China on the SCS issue. For example, Hillary Clinton, then Secretary of State, appealed to India when she attended the ARF in July 2011 that "The more our countries trade and invest with each other and with other partners, the more central the Asia-Pacific region becomes to global commerce and prosperity, and the more interest we both have in maintaining stability and security. As the stakes grow higher, we should use our shared commitments to make sure that we have maritime security and freedom of navigation."[128] Accordingly, in response to China's oil exploitation in the SCS, S.M. Krishna, then foreign minister of India, declared in early April 2012 that the "SCS is the property of the world," stressing that the routes in the SCS must be free from any national interference and should be used to promote trade-related activities of neighboring countries.[129] Although it is hard to say that the United States and India have reached a certain consensus on the SCS issue based on the abovementioned remarks, such statements are "echoing from afar."

At present, the Indian government has not issued an official document on the SCS issue. However, according to the statements of Indian officials and diplomatic officials, some scholars have summarized India's attitude on the SCS dispute as follows: First, India is not a party to the SCS dispute, but is concerned about the overall development of the SCS. Second, India's freedom of navigation and commercial interests in the SCS should be respected. Third, India's activities in the SCS have no political implications.[130] Obviously, India's emphasis on "freedom of navigation" and commercial interests in the SCS coincides with the attitude of the United States on the SCS issue in recent years. In fact, Indian scholars have acknowledged that India emphasizes so-called freedom of navigation in the SCS and strengthened its maritime security relations with Southeast Asian countries. It indicates that the words and deeds of India in the SCS issue and regional affairs have tended to be consistent with those of the United States.[131]

Although India's SCS policy may be influenced by the United States, it may not necessarily be the result of the United States' endeavors. As the implementation of the U.S. rebalancing strategy toward Asia Pacific and Washington's efforts to pressurize China on the SCS issue are bound to infuriate China, it is not of great benefit to India. As Antony, India's Defense Minister, stressed in July 2012, "a confrontation with China in the SCS is not India's policy."[132] It can be seen that the reason why India makes the necessary voice on the SCS issue is that, in addition to highlighting its strategic presence in the region, India hopes to form containment on China through indirect support for other sovereign claimants, to prevent China from exerting overall dominance in the SCS. At the same time, India is aware that it is not in its fundamental interests to fall into direct confrontation with China on the SCS issue. As far as India is concerned, it hopes to stir up trouble on the SCS issue, but it is not willing to see chaos in the region, let alone start a fire.[133]

Launching the "Act East Policy"

In the early 1990s, India launched the "Look East Policy" based on the changes of domestic and international situation, so as to integrate into the dynamic Asia-Pacific region as soon as possible. In order to actively introduce India's power when implementing the rebalancing strategy in the Asia-Pacific region, the

Obama administration convinced India to further promote its Look East policy to form coordination with America's rebalancing strategy. In July 2011, when participating in the second round of India-U.S. strategic and economic dialogue, Hillary Clinton, then U.S. Secretary of State, strongly encouraged India to expand its influence beyond South Asia and particularly in East Asia, claiming that "it is time to lead," and "India's leadership has the potential to positively shape the future of Asia Pacific," therefore, the United States supports India "not only to look east, but also to move closer to the East and make a difference."[134] The U.S. deputy national security adviser Ben Rhodes also said that President Obama welcomed India's Look East policy, asserting that "just the United States, as a Pacific Ocean power, is going to be deeply engaged in the future of East Asia, so should India as an Indian Ocean power and as an Asian nation."[135] In June 2012, during the third India-U.S. strategic dialogue, Hillary Clinton once again urged India to play a more active leadership role in the Asia-Pacific region, and made it clear that the United States was willing to actively support India's Look East policy as it was growing into an Act East policy, and was committed to broader, deeper, more purposeful relations.[136]

With the continuous encouragement and support of the United States, India has also taken the opportunity to speed up the process of Act East. In August 2014, Indian Foreign Minister Sushma Swaraj, speaking on her first visit to Vietnam, claimed that it was no longer just looking east, but it was time to take practical actions.[137] In November, Indian Prime Minister Modi told at the 12th ASEAN India summit that India had turned "Look East Policy" into "Act East Policy."[138] Evidently, the Act East Policy is India's latest adjustment to its Asia-Pacific strategy, which can be described as an upgraded version of the Look East Policy (or version 2.0).[139] In view of the many appeals made by U.S. Secretary of State Hillary Clinton to India's Look East Policy, and the subtle timing of India's Act East Policy, it is natural for the outside world to think that Modi government's Act East Policy is a kind of "echo" to the United States,[140] and there is a certain correlation between them.[141] In fact, in the joint statement issued by India and the United States in September 2014, India's Act East policy has been linked with the U.S. rebalancing strategy in the Asia-Pacific region.[142]

As for the abovementioned actions between the United States and India, some scholars believe that India's Look East policy has been changed into a more assertive Act East policy. This is not only related to the encouragement of the United States, but also a reflection of the United States and India's strategic coordination in the Asia-Pacific region, and is also the result of India's efforts to serve as the regional "balancer."[143] Nonetheless, India's Act East Policy aims at in-depth integration into the economic cooperation in the Asia-Pacific region, while the U.S. rebalancing strategy in the Asia-Pacific region has prominent characteristics of being offensive, directional, and containing. Therefore, although India and the United States are gradually moving towards "strategic proximity" in the context of the United States "returning" to the Asia-Pacific region, there is still a long way to go to achieve "strategic convergence."

Russia: Double-Headed Eagle Policy

Russia's role in the U.S. rebalancing strategic layout in the Asia-Pacific region is not prominent. Neither President Obama's speech in the Australian Parliament in 2011 nor Secretary of State Hillary Clinton's famous article named *America's Pacific Century*, or the speeches made by U.S. senior officials such as Biden, Donilon, Hagel, and Kerry mention Russia. In other words, Russia seems to have been neglected deliberately or unintentionally in the U.S. strategy of rebalancing toward Asia Pacific. Still, it has a great influence on Russia's national interests and foreign policies, and cannot reduce the importance of the Asia-Pacific region in Russia's foreign strategy. From the geopolitical point of view, the eastward shift of the American strategic focus impacts the Russian strategic circumstances in both the west and east. The diplomatic battlefield of the United States and Russia also shifted from Europe to the Asia-Pacific region.[144] Therefore, no matter how American policy makers position Russia in the Asia-Pacific region, at least from the Russian side, it still pays attention to the U.S. rebalancing strategy toward Asia Pacific and makes correspondingly necessary responses.

Responses from Russian Academic Circles

The high-profile announcement of the United States' return to the Asia-Pacific region has aroused the attention of Russian scholars. Some believe that the purpose of the United States is to contain China and maintain its economic superiority. Taking TPP as an example, Alexei Fenenko, a researcher at the Institute of International Security of the Russian Academy of Sciences, believes that TPP is an American attempt to direct regional processes in a direction that would benefit it most. First, the TPP creates an economic connection between the two Pacific coasts dominated by the United States. Second, the emergence of the TPP weakens the ASEAN (trade agreement). Third, the TPP will undermine the CAFTA, dampen China's economic influence in Southeast Asia, and erode the CAFTA mechanisms in the future. Fourth, the TPP is eroding the system of political consultations under the ASEAN+3 (China, Japan, and South Korea), ASEAN+6 (China, Japan, South Korea, India, Australia, and New Zealand) formulas, and also the East Asia Summit. Fifth, the TPP is creating a new context of relations in the Pacific region as a trans-Pacific association led by the United States and based on three pillars of the U.S. presence in the Pacific: the U.S.-Japanese alliance, the revived ANZUS, and U.S.-friendly Latin American countries (Chile and Peru).[145]

Some scholars have pointed out that the purpose of implementing the rebalancing strategy in the Asia-Pacific region is to maintain American dominant position in the region by meeting the security needs of its allies and partner countries in the Asia-Pacific region. For example, Feodore Lukiyanov, a famous Russian expert on international relations and foreign policy, believes that China's rise has brought various security risks to neighboring countries. Some Asian Pacific countries expect that the United States will continue to act as the provider of public security in the Asia-Pacific region. The United States takes the opportunity to counterweight China's rise by strengthening traditional relations with Japan, Australia, the Philippines, Thailand, Singapore, and making new partnership with India and Vietnam. As a result, China has been encircled.[146] Though Russian scholars make various calculations on the purpose of the U.S. rebalancing strategy toward Asia Pacific, they reach a consensus that the rebalancing strategy is directed against China.

Additionally, Russian scholars have given suggestions on the path selection in response to the U.S. rebalancing strategy, which are generally divided into two categories, namely, "assisting the U.S. to contain China" and "making cooperation to resist America."[147] The former believes that in face of the fierce China-U.S. competition in the Asia-Pacific region, Russia is best to keep neutral, or assist the United States to check and balance China with reservations, so as to maximize Russia's national interests. The latter believes that Russia should seize the strategic opportunity and avoid being involved in a conflict with the great powers while deftly getting its benefits.[148]

For those who support containment of the United States, they learned the historical lessons from the United States' persistent squeeze on Russia's strategic space after the Cold War and the close geostrategic relation with China, Russia cannot be a bystander in any US rebalancing strategy, as it will eventually damage Russia's own interests. Therefore, Russia should cooperate with China and other emerging Asia-Pacific countries to strengthen strategic cooperation and check and balance the U.S. rebalancing in the Asia-Pacific region. Russia has important strategic interests in the Asia-Pacific region. Russia cannot turn a blind eye to the increasingly prominent position of this region in the global strategic landscape. Therefore, Russia should launch its own version of "return" to the Asia Pacific and implement Russia's "double-headed eagle" strategy. At present, most Russian scholars support Russia's seeking of cooperation to check and balance America. They advocate strengthening strategic cooperation among emerging countries, such as Russia, China and India, and balancing the influence of the United States and its allies in the Asia-Pacific region by using the cooperation mechanism such as BRICs and the Shanghai Cooperation Organization (SCO).[149]

Opportunity versus Challenge

There are two different views on the impact of the U.S. rebalancing strategy on Russia, which are "opportunity theory" and "challenge theory."[150] The former believes that the U.S. rebalancing strategy in the Asia-Pacific region is an opportunity for Russia. Russia should seize the strategic opportunity when the United States returns to the Asia-Pacific region, actively cooperate with the United States, and even form alliances to balance China's influence. The "opportunity theory" is mainly based on the following judgments:

First, the shift of U.S. strategic focus to the East can partly alleviate Russia's strategic pressure in Europe. Although the shift of U.S. strategic focus from Europe to Asia Pacific does not mean that NATO's strength will be weakened, at least the strategic pressure of the United States on Russia in Europe and the post-Soviet Union regions (such as the Caucasus and the CIS part) will be relieved to a certain extent.[151]

Second, the rebalancing strategy in the Asia-Pacific region can increase the chips in the game between Russia and China. Due to the asymmetry of China-Russian relations, especially the trade imbalance, Russia has concerns about China's rising influence in Central Asia and views itself as a source of raw materials.[152] The rebalancing strategy in the Asia-Pacific region will inevitably bring strategic pressure to China, forcing the latter to seek support from Russia, and then promote China to solve the imbalance problem in bilateral relations.

Third, Russia and the United States share a common goal of balancing China's growing influence in the region by strengthening their presence in Asia and diversifying their diplomatic relations. In the view of some analysts, promoting understanding with NATO and the United States will help Russia offset the potential risks posed by China's rising influence. Therefore, Moscow should welcome the U.S. rebalancing strategy and cooperate with the past enemy, if possible, ally with it.

Fourth, the U.S. military forces are deployed in the Asia-Pacific region, and China and the United States will engage in fierce competition around the Taiwan Strait issue, the SCS issue, the Diaoyu/Senkaku Islands dispute, and the entire western Pacific region. It means that Russia will stay away from any military pressure from the United States to a certain extent. The greater the involvement of the United States in the abovementioned issues, the less security pressure from the United States on Russia.

The "opportunity theory" is not the official position of the Kremlin, neither the mainstream in Russia. On the one hand, Russia itself has a large "trust deficit" with the United States. As some Russian scholars have said, Russia lists the United States, not China, as the biggest and most direct threat.[153] According to a 2012 poll conducted by the Levada Center in Russia, the majority of Russians think that the United States is Russia's enemy, and not China.[154] On the other hand, cooperation with the United States contradicts Russia's core foreign policy objectives towards China. In response to the potential adverse effects of China's rise on Russia's interests, Moscow has always been careful not to make any initiatives to infuriate China. President Putin even denounced "the words and deeds of foreign experts trying to intimidate Russia-China relations."[155] Lilia Shevtsova, a Russian political scholar, once pointed out that "words criticizing China in Russian official documents are prohibited."[156]

These phenomena reflect that Russia, as a neighboring country with a border of more than 4000 km with China, is vulnerable to geopolitical pressures. As a result, Moscow needs to maintain a delicate balance in its relations with Beijing, especially in the Russia-US-China trilateral relations. As a result, Russian policy makers have never publicly supported any coordination with Washington in the Asia-Pacific region, and will possibly remain in this position for the foreseeable future.

The "challenge theory" holds that the "dividend" brought to Russia by the U.S. rebalancing strategy toward Asia Pacific should not be overestimated. In fact, the strategy will accumulate potential burden and pose a challenge to Russia's new Asia policy. It will also worsen the regional security situation, which is contrary to Russia's demand for a stable surrounding environment. Therefore, Russia should take an objective and cautious attitude towards the rebalancing strategy. The main reasons are as follows:

First, the U.S. rebalancing strategy toward Asia Pacific will impact Russia's efforts to downplay the China-centric Asian policy. For a long time, Russia's Asian policy has been often criticized for its overreliance on China. Russia's partners in Asia should be more diversified. Therefore, Russia needs to strengthen its relations with Asian countries, especially Japan, India, South Korea, and Vietnam.[157] Moscow has concerns that intimate contacts between the United States and Asian countries will weaken Russia's friendly relations with traditional partners in the region, such as India, or complicate Russia's efforts to strengthen relations with other Asian countries, such as Vietnam. The arms and nuclear cooperation between Washington and New Delhi has degraded Russia-India relations. Moreover, closer relations between the United States and Asian countries will undermine Russia's influence in the region.

Second, the U.S. shift to the Asia-Pacific region will also challenge Russia's "Asian ambition," which is not in line with Russia's demand for multi-polarization in Asia. Moscow believes that the increasingly fierce competition between China and the United States caused by the U.S. pivot to the Asia-Pacific region will squeeze the geostrategic space of other countries, and further limit Russia's (already low) ability to shape the political and economic landscape in the region. In other words, the tug-of-war between the two regional influential powers in the Asia-Pacific region is not a blessing for the formation of other influential powers in the region.

Third, Russia needs a stable surrounding environment. In the long run, the Unites States' new Asia-Pacific strategy will certainly lead to tension between China and the United States, thus causing regional instability. Moscow, on the other hand, has always been very sensitive to instability around. At the same time, the geopolitical environment in the south and the west is complex enough. Therefore, the tension between China and the United States will inevitably destabilize Russia's eastern border area. What is more worrying is that the escalation of confrontation between China and the United States will also force Russia to take sides between Beijing and Washington, which will lead to the failure of its strategic ambiguity in the trilateral relations.

Russian Official Response

Compared with the heated debates in academic circles, the Russian official response to the U.S. rebalancing strategy in the Asia-Pacific region is relatively lukewarm. Russian officials have not even come up with a specific term to name the rebalancing strategy. The new version of Foreign Policy Concept released in February 2013 does not mention the rebalancing policy,[158] which is in sharp contrast to the Kremlin's harsh response to Washington's policies in Europe and Eurasia. It would be unreasonable to conclude that Russia's leaders have neglected the U.S. policy of "returning" to Asia, especially given the background, in which

Moscow is seeking to realize its own interests in the Asia-Pacific region. On the whole, the reasons why the Russian authorities are silent on the U.S. rebalancing strategy in the Asia-Pacific region are as follows:

First of all, the rebalancing strategy in the Asia-Pacific region has recently been launched, and Russia has yet to find that the policy actually hinders its own interests in the Asia-Pacific region. Second, it is generally believed that Russia is not the direct target of the U.S. rebalancing strategy, and that China is the main target of U.S. strategic containment. Although American officials and experts have denied this, it does not change Moscow's basic understanding of the rebalancing strategy. Third, it is not surprising for elites in Russian political circle and academic circles that the United States has launched the rebalancing strategy toward Asia Pacific. At the same time, it does not mean that Washington's policy in East Asia has changed overwhelmingly. The rebalancing strategy is the continuity, rather than reform, in American foreign policy. Finally, the U.S. rebalancing strategy toward Asia Pacific is still under Russia's assessment. How long the strategy can last and how much impact it will have on Russia's national interests are still unknown.[159] It can be seen that Russian officials are relatively detached and calm in examining the U.S. rebalancing strategy, and the so-called silence is just a strategic tactic. The reason why Moscow is not in a hurry to take a stand on this issue is that the power game between China and the United States in the Asia-Pacific region has not yet developed to the point where Russia must pick a side. In other words, silence in official discourse does not mean Russia's inaction in practical actions.

In fact, in face of the U.S. rebalancing strategy in the Asia-Pacific region and its strong intervention in the SCS dispute, the Kremlin has not deviated from its "double-headed eagle" foreign strategy. Furthermore, Russia has spared no effort to promote and improve its own eastward strategy in the east (also known as the Russian version of "turning to Asia Pacific/rebalancing strategy").

As a big country across Eurasia, the focus of Russia's foreign relations has long been biased towards the European or western part of its territory, rather than the eastern part. Especially in the past 10 years after the end of the Cold War, Moscow devoted more energy to dealing with NATO's eastward expansion, the Kosovo crisis, and European anti-missile defense, but only made meager efforts to deal with the North Korea nuclear crisis, the Russian-Japanese island dispute, or the U.S. anti-missile program in Asia. Such a situation has led to a large gap between Russia's Asian and European policies, which is why some Western scholars once questioned whether Russia has the ability to enhance and strengthen its influence in the East.[160] From the perspective of interactions between Russia and the United States in the new century, the main contradiction and cooperation between Russia and the United States are concentrated in Europe and the Middle East, whether on the issue of anti-missile defense, NATO's eastward expansion, or in dealing with Afghanistan affairs and the Syrian crisis. In contrast, Russia and the United States, which are only separated by the Bering Strait, have little interaction in the Pacific region. Although Russians often label themselves as "a power in Asia Pacific," Americans do not seem to agree with it.[161] Some American scholars have also pointed out that Russia's contribution to the economy and security of the Asia-Pacific region is so limited that it is far-fetched to regard Russia as a big power in the Asia-Pacific region. "Russia is at best a second rate Pacific player."[162]

In order to fix the "strategic imbalance," and also in response to the realistic consideration of the U.S. rebalancing strategy in the Asia-Pacific region, Moscow has significantly accelerated the pace of eastward expansion in recent years, and has participated in economic cooperation under the framework of APEC, strengthened cooperation with major strategic partners in the Asia-Pacific region, and safeguarded the security of Russia's eastern border.[163] At least from Russia's point of view, strengthening the relations with Asia-Pacific countries is not only conducive to the economic development of Russia's Siberia and Far East, but also can remain flexible as to strive for its strategic leeway by playing the "Asia Pacific card" with European and American countries.[164]

At the Far East social and economic development conference held in Habarovsk on July 2, 2010, then President Medvedev said that Russia must vigorously enhance its role in the Asia-Pacific region and make more active efforts in the region.[165] In September 2012, Russian President Vladimir Putin wrote an article pointing out that Russia is an organic part of the Asia-Pacific region, and this dynamic region is the most important factor influencing Russia's success. Therefore, Russia will not stand idly by on Asian affairs.[166] Since then, Russia's pivot to the Asia Pacific was further promoted since the 2013 Ukraine crisis and its break with the West. For example, at the APEC Business Leader's Summit on November 10, 2014, Putin publicly stated that Russia's priority strategic direction was to strengthen cooperation with countries in the Asia-Pacific region and that the potential of cooperation between Russia and other countries in the Asia-Pacific region was enormous and infinite.[167] Although the above remarks do not represent a tough Russian counterattack against the Western countries led by the United States, at least it shows that Russia is not indifferent to the changes of the situation in the Asia-Pacific region under the dual background of the United

States "returning" to the Asia-Pacific region and the deterioration of Russia's relations with the West.

At the same time, Russia's marine strategic focus has also begun to tilt towards the Pacific Ocean. On July 26, 2015, Russian President Vladimir Putin approved the new edition of the Russian Federation Ocean Theory, which specially emphasized the strategic value of the Pacific coast to Russia. In the view of the Kremlin, Russia's Far East contains rich natural resources, but it is not closely linked with the industrial developed areas in the central part of western Russia, and its population is sparse. The rapid development of countries in the Asia-Pacific region has had an enormous impact on the regional economy, population, and military process, and such impact is further deepening.[168] Therefore, Russia should not only vigorously develop land and sea transportation in the Far East, actively integrate into the Asia-Pacific economic space, build natural gas pipelines and a submarine communication network in the Far East, but also constantly expand the Pacific Fleet, and improve the quantity and quality of its Eastern garrisons,[169] in that the Pacific Fleet is not only the main force available to safeguard Russia's national interests and national security in the Asia-Pacific region, but its campaign area extends from the east coast of Africa to the west coast of America, occupying more than 50 % of the waters, which determines its special position in the Russian navy and even the entire Russian armed forces.[170] In this regard, Zuo Fengrong, a Chinese expert on Russian studies, has also pointed out that Russia has begun to attach importance to the Pacific, for the rich resources in the EEZ and continental shelf, as well as its need to drive the development of the Far East and respond to the U.S. strategic "return" to Asia Pacific.[171]

Attitude on Specific Issues

On the SCS issue, Russia has adopted a policy of "selective strategic cooperation" based on the principle of pragmatism, in combination with the needs of multiple interests: On the one hand, by strengthening strategic interaction with China, Russia can offset the strategic pressure exerted by the United States and NATO, and cope with the U.S. strategy of rebalancing toward Asia Pacific; on the other hand, it has strengthened its cooperation with other countries in the Asia-Pacific region to enhance regional influence and balance China's challenges to Russia in the Asia-Pacific region.[172] Undoubtedly, in order to take into account China's feelings, Russia has long maintained a restrained and cautious attitude on the SCS issue and has not stirred up troubles on the issue. However, Russia has not given up pursuing realistic interests through market means. For example, Russia has an active arms trade and energy resource trading agreements with Southeast Asian countries (Indonesia, Vietnam, Malaysia, etc.). As Russian scholar Morozov has said, although China is Russia's main partner in the Asia-Pacific region, the potential cooperation opportunities brought to Russia by some Southeast Asian countries' active investment in naval and military technology should not be neglected. In order to ensure that their own interests will not be harmed, countries around the SCS compete to invest in naval construction. Only Russia can maintain the balance of power between them.[173]

Russia also shows a wavering attitude toward TPP. On the one hand, TPP has not only economic purpose but also strong political motivation. It will cause more regional fragmentation rather than strengthening of regional unity. TPP is not a desirable cooperation approach for Russia. Russia is obviously not ready for the high standard requirements and accelerated liberalization, and Russia has other top priorities in this region.[174] Meantime, most Russia's major trading partners are in Europe. Even if the TPP negotiation is inconsequential, the impact on Russia's foreign trade will be limited in the short term.[175]

On the other hand, some scholars believe that supporting the TPP has no obvious benefits for Russia, while its negative impact lies in realities on the ground, which will at least arouse China's dissatisfaction or even antagonism. Based on the above considerations, Russia is inclined to support the "ASEAN+6" to counter the TPP, while remain ambivalent as to its position. Ivan Timofeev, project director of Russia's State Duma International Affairs Committee, says that Russia has no intention of joining any party in the China-U.S. competition, and still takes this position in the future, unless it is absolutely necessary. Moscow will not take the risk to damage China's economy and good neighborly relations to join the U.S.-Japan-ROK alliance, yet Russia will not become China's follower either.[176] Thus, Russia's attitude towards TPP is another manifestation of its "double-headed eagle" diplomacy.

Australia: Embrace of the United States

If Japan is the "anchor of the north" of the U.S. Asia-Pacific security strategy, then Australia is the "anchor of the south." As a medium-sized power and a member of the Western club, Australia has always been an indispensable member in the U.S. Asia-Pacific strategic framework.[177] This is not only because of Australia's superior geostrategic position, which straddles the Pacific Ocean and faces the Indian Ocean, bordering on Southeast Asia and a series of archipelago in the north and Antarctica in the south, occupying the pivotal position of the "Indo-Pacific Strategic Belt."[178] Moreover, Australia has been one of the most reliable allies of the United States since WWII, and relying on powerful countries has been a long-term foreign strategic tradition of Australia. As Charles Krauthammer, a Washington Post columnist, points out, "Australia understands that peace and prosperity do not come with the air we breathe but are maintained by power -- once the power of the British Empire, now the power of the United States . . . an American retreat or defeat would be catastrophic for Australia and for the world."[179] Unsurprisingly, therefore, sustaining a close security alliance with the United States is a non-partisan consensus of the Australian government, and is generally supported by both the government and the opposition,[180] which has become an unshakable key part of Australia's foreign policy and strategic planning.

Australian Official Response

Australia's diplomatic tendency of aligning itself with the U.S. position is fully reflected in its attitude towards the U.S. new Asia-Pacific strategy. After the United States announced its "return" to the Asia-Pacific region, Canberra has expressed its firm support on various occasions. In March 2011, Julia E. Gillard, then Prime Minister of Australia, publicly stated in a speech to the U.S. Congress that the United States had a decisive influence on the peace and security of the Asia-Pacific region. Australia would stand firmly with its allies and jointly safeguard the stability of the region.[181] In November, Australia warmly received the U.S. President Barack Obama, which marks Australia as a "bridgehead" to promote the new Asia-Pacific strategy. In March 2012, then Defense Secretary Stephen Smith also stressed that the U.S. presence in the Asia-Pacific region was a key force to ensure peace, security, and prosperity in the region; therefore Australia strongly supported the United States. When China is rising together with India, ASEAN, etc., Australia is desperate to develop a comprehensive partnership with China, and to maintain a military alliance with the United States. There is no contradiction between these two options.[182]

The development of close alliance and defense relations with the United States has also won strong public support in Australia. According to a 2012 poll conducted by Australia's Lowy Institute, 87 % of Australians agree to maintain alliance with the United States, of which 59 % believe it is "very important" for Australia's security and 28 % consider it "quite important," and 74 % agreed with the deployment of the U.S. Marine Air Ground Task Force (MAGTF) in

Australia.[183] According to the opinion poll launched by the agency in 2015, as many as 80 % of the respondents think that the U.S.-Australia military alliance is very important for Australia's security; 77 % of the respondents think that the United States and Australia share common values, and such values lay foundation for the alliance; and 70 % of the respondents think that without the U.S.-Australia alliance, Australia may invest more on defense.[184]

Moreover, in order to achieve effective cooperation with the United States, Australia has issued a series of strategic documents to adjust its Asia-Pacific strategy accordingly. For example, since 2012, Australia has successively issued strategic reports such as the assessment of the situation of Australian Defense Forces (ADF), the white paper of Australia in the Asian century, the national security strategy, and the national defense white paper.[185] These documents reiterate the importance of the Australia-U.S. alliance to varying degrees. They welcome the eastward shift of the U.S. strategic focus and support the United States to strengthen its presence in the region, as well as point out the direction for Australia's new Asia-Pacific strategy.

Cooperation with the United States at the Diplomatic Level

Australia's cooperation at the diplomatic level is mainly manifest in how it follows the United States and takes a position of favoring the United States and its allies. Since one of the important purposes of the U.S. rebalancing strategy in the Asia-Pacific region is to meet the challenges brought about by China's rise, the United States has frequently challenged China on a series of issues, such as accusing China of not abiding by international rules, failing to shoulder its due responsibilities, being aggressive in diplomacy, and bullying the small as a great power. Canberra basically maintains the same attitude as Washington in the diplomatic pressure and offensive posture exerted on China, which is prominent on the SCS issue.[186]

Australia has important strategic interests in the SCS, including energy and resources transportation, commercial trade channels, etc. At the same time, the region is also the forefront of northern Australia's security, and its involvement in SCS issues will help to enhance Australia's international role.[187] Objectively speaking, during the period of Rudd and Gillard administrations, Australia exercised restraint on SCS issue, regarding the issue as a sovereignty dispute between China and some Southeast Asian countries, and had no direct relationship with Australia. Based on this understanding, Australian politicians rarely got involved in specific actions when discussing the SCS issue, and only verbally promoted the COC in the SCS.[188]

In his speech at the East Asia Summit on November 20, 2012, Australian Prime Minister Gillard said, "we don't take a position on the territorial claims but we believe it is in everybody's interest that issues in the SCS are managed in a peaceful way in accordance with international law . . . And we do believe that a code of conduct would assist with making sure that any you know issues in the SCS, any conduct there, could be managed in accordance with the code. That's Australia's position. It's been one of long standing and it's one we'll continue to argue for."[189] In the official documents related to the SCS issue, Australia's 2013 National Defense White Paper stated that Australia hoped to solve the sovereignty disputes in the SCS region through peaceful means and abide by the principles of international law, avoided the use of force, and safeguarded the freedom of navigation and maritime security in the SCS.[190]

With the further implementation of the U.S. rebalancing strategy in the Asia-Pacific region, its involvement in the SCS issue has gradually shifted from "implicit" to "explicit," from "behind the scenes" to "in front of the stage." The United States not only encouraged the claimant states to fight against China, but also sent warships into the Spratly Islands, thus putting pressure on China and challenging China's bottom line on the SCS issue. In this context, Australia no longer stays out of the way and begins to show a strong posture, associating the SCS issue with its own strategic and security interests. In May 2015, Peter Jennings, a senior official of the Australian Ministry of Defense, called for Australia to be prepared to send warships and aircraft to the SCS in response to China's "expansion" in the SCS, so as to prevent China from controlling strategic key points in the region.[191] On June 1, Australian defense chief Kevin Andrew made remarks at the Shangri-La Dialogue in Singapore, saying that China reserves the right to set up an ADIZ. In any case, Australian military aircrafts have the right to continue to fly over the disputed area in the SCS, because "international transit passages whether on the sea or in the air should remain free and open for access to any country to legitimately use that, particularly for trade purposes."[192]

In conclusion, Australia and the United States have synchronized on the SCS issue. When the United States has not yet involved in the SCS issue, Australia's SCS policy appears relatively detached. When the United States intervened in the SCS dispute with a strong posture, Australia's position on the SCS issue is poised to be tough.[193] Besides, although Australia still does not hold a position on the sovereignty dispute of the SCS, nor does it give up urging the parties to the dispute to resolve their differences peacefully by relying on international law, international mechanisms, and recognized codes of conduct, it pays high attention to the freedom of navigation in the SCS and supports the United States to continue to participate in regional issues,[194] which has greatly encouraged Washington and enhanced the legitimacy of its intervention.[195]

Security Response

Australia's response at the security level is mainly reflected in reliance on the United States, persistently strengthening the Australia-U.S. alliance, increasing military investment and support for the United States. But the U.S.-Australia alliance is an asymmetric and unequal alliance, that is, Australia's dependence on the United States for security is far greater than that of the United States on Australia. On the surface, the U.S.-Australia alliance adopts a shared security and defense policy, but in fact, it is the United States that provides security to Australia. Australia only shares part of the security responsibility at the request of the United States.[196] As in many vastly unequal relationships, the power lies with the bigger party. Therefore, the United States occupies an outstanding position in the field of Australian security and defense. It can be said that without the security provided by the United States, Australia has lost a security defensive front line. As described in the first Australian National Security Strategy Report released by Gillard government in January 2013, the Australia-U.S. alliance is Australia's most important security relationship, which constitutes the cornerstone of Australia's defense and security cooperation since the end of WWII. This alliance is a key guarantee for Australia's national defense capability and an anchor for regional security and peace. The value of the Australia-U.S. alliance not only lies in the field of defense, but also promotes Australia's prosperity and security. The United States is an important part of the global economy and security, and it provides the key support for Australian people to live in a Western rules-based world order today.[197]

It is based on this recognition of security dependence and American global status that Australia has given full support and cooperation under the framework of the U.S. rebalancing strategy toward Asia Pacific, advancing the Australia-U.S. alliance to a new phase. Since 2011, Australia and the United States have not only planned a new military deployment, but also reached an agreement on the stationing and rotation of the U.S. Navy and Air Force in northern Australia, thus opening a new round of security interaction between the two sides.[198] Furthermore, Australia has unilaterally increased its military investment and armament construction to "coordinate" with the security requirements of the United States. According to Australia's 2016 National Defense White Paper, Australia's defense budget will increase to US $42.4 billion from 2020 to 2021, which is expected to account for 2 % of Australia's GDP. Meanwhile, the ADF will add another 5000 military personnel and the number of Royal Australian Navy (RAN) submarines will double to 12.[199] In addition, Australia and the United States have also strengthened and expanded military training, exercises, security mechanisms, and other fields. While the United States has increased the deployment of its air and sea forces in Australia, Australia has also adjusted its military forces, mainly by mobilizing more warships, fighters, and military personnel to the northwest region to assist in the U.S. military exercises.[200] In the joint exercise code named Talisman Sabre held by Australia and the United States in July 2013, the two sides involved up to 28,000 troops, which is the largest bilateral joint military exercise in the history of the two countries.[201]

In the meantime, Australia and the United States have also strengthened the construction of bilateral security dialogue mechanism. Since 1985, the Australia-U.S. ministerial consultation meeting (2+2 mechanism for foreign ministers and defense ministers) has become the main annual forum for the two countries to discuss and coordinate their foreign and security policies. Especially after the United States announced its "return" to the Asia-Pacific region, Australia and the United States conducted all-round dialogues and consultations on bilateral alliance relations, the security situation in India and the Pacific region, and global challenges.[202] In May 2013, the two countries signed the U.S.-Australia Defense Trade Cooperation Treaty to ensure that the two countries' armed forces can "acquire the best technology in the fastest way." In addition, Australia and the United States have also expanded their cooperation field from traditional security fields to non-traditional security fields such as space and Internet. For example, the Joint Declaration on Cyberspace signed by Australia and the United States in September 2011 clearly stated that cooperation in space early warning and cyber threats should be expanded. The statement also points out that once either side of Australia and the United States is under cyber-attack, it can also start the mechanism of Australia, New Zealand, and the United States security alliance.[203] Through the expansion and cooperation in the above fields, Australia has not only strengthened its joint combat capability with the United States, but also demonstrated its support for the rebalancing strategy in the Asia-Pacific region. In this way, Australia has increasingly become a key fulcrum for the United States to promote the new Asia-Pacific strategy.

Economic Support

Australia's economic support is mainly manifested in its active participation in TPP negotiations and its integration into the American-designed regional economic integration. It is acknowledged that one of the core measures of the United States to "return" to the Asia-Pacific region is to launch TPP negotiations, and its purpose is to weaken China's growing economic influence and maintain American dominant position in the regional economic issues. As for the TPP negotiations, Australia followed in the steps of the United States to announce its participation in the TPP negotiations, two months after the U.S. announcement in September 2008. From March 2010 to March 2012, Australia has presided over two rounds of negotiations (i.e., the first round and the eleventh round). In order to encourage more countries to join the TPP negotiations, Australian Prime Minister Abbott publicly stated in a speech delivered at the American Australian Association in June 2014 that "we support the TPP negotiations and agree with President Obama's leadership over free trade."[204] Since then, Australia has also joined the United States in welcoming the TPP negotiations in October 2015. The reasons why Australia supports and joins the TPP negotiation are as follows:

First, TPP is conducive to breaking the deadlock in multilateral trade negotiations, integrating the existing FTA network, and promoting regional economic cooperation, which is in line with Australia's regional economic cooperation strategy. Second, joining the TPP negotiation will help to maintain and consolidate the political and economic alliance with the United States and jointly promote the Asia-Pacific cooperation strategy. Third, Australia believes that TPP will help to eliminate the drawbacks of non-institutionalized cooperation in the Asia-Pacific region with APEC as the main platform, and promote the development of Asia-Pacific cooperation in a more normative and binding way. Fourth, TPP can help Australia strengthen its ties with the major economies in the Asia-Pacific region in various ways, and integrate Australia's regional and bilateral cooperation in East Asia into the overall cooperation in Asia Pacific .[205] Fifth, as a high-quality and comprehensive FTA, TPP will encourage Australian companies to improve their competitiveness and provide a series of better products and services for Australian consumers.[206] Thus, despite the criticism from some labor organizations and economic interest groups, two major political parties have expressed their support for Australia's accession to the TPP negotiations.[207]

Criticism and Controversy

Australia's policy choice on the U.S. return to the Asia-Pacific region has aroused criticism and concern in Australia. The relevant disputes mainly focus on two aspects: first, whether it is wise to follow the United States and strengthen the Australia-U.S. alliance in the context of the U.S. "return" to the Asia-Pacific region. Second, under the circumstances of China's rapid rise, how Australia can deal with these two major countries is the biggest dilemma for its foreign policy at present.[208] For example, Professor Hugh White of the Australian National University expressed his concern about Australia's cooperation in strengthening the Australia-U.S. alliance. Over the past decade, he has repeatedly warned of the risks of promoting the Australia-U.S. alliance, believing that it is in Australia's interest to convince the United States to give up its geopolitical advantages, and Canberra should encourage Washington to step forward in this direction.[209] Malcolm Fraser, a former Australian Prime Minister, notes that Canberra should avoid giving the impression that it was "too close to the United States,"[210] and even suggested that Australia cancel its alliance with the United States. At the press conference of his new book *Dangerous Allies* in 2014, Fraser urged Canberra to withdraw the U.S. air, sea, and ground forces stationed in Darwin base in Australia within one year, and to close its defense facilities in Pine Valley in four to five years, so as to get rid of strategic dependence on the United States.[211]

Some scholars and political pundits in Australia believe that the greater the U.S. military presence in Australia, the more likely Australia will fall into potential conflicts between China and the United States. In this regard, Raoul Heinrichs of the Center for Strategic and Defense Studies of the Australian National University points out that it's dangerous for Australia to facilitate the U.S. presence in Asia and increase its dependence on a declining ally, because China may target Australia in its war with the United States.[212] Andrew O'Neil, director of the Institute for Asian Studies at Griffith University, agrees that Australia is facing the risk of a more real trap as China rises and challenges America's strength.[213] In view of Australia's dilemma, Hugh White holds that with the continuous rise of China, the times that it replaces the United States as the world's top economic power is coming. The reversal of China-U.S. power balance requires Australia and the United States to gradually adapt to the rise of China and regard it as an equal member.[214] According to White, Australia should actively lobby the United States to share Asian leadership with China. If China and the United States go into confrontation, Australia will be put in a disadvantageous position in that it will be a jeopardizing and costly deal for Australia to stand with either side.[215]

To sum up, as a medium-sized power sandwiched between the two great powers of China and the United States, Australia should maintain and constantly recalibrate the Australia-U.S. alliance to safeguard its national security interests. Considering "the United States is still the world's strongest military power and Australia's most important strategic partner," it is in Australia's strategic interests to continue to expand and advance the Australia-U.S. alliance, including maintaining security and stability in the Asia-Pacific region by continuing to support the U.S. military rebalancing.[216] Furthermore, Australia should seize the "economic opportunity" of China's vigorous development, and promote economic and trade relations with China, and seek benefits from China's rise. It can be said that the interdependence will promote the further development of China-Australia bilateral relations to a certain extent.[217] For Australia, it must seek a balance between security demands and economic interests, and strive to promote China-U.S. strategic cooperation rather than to provoke tensions and conflicts, and make efforts to keep the Indo-Pacific region multilateral rather than to degenerate into bipolarity. Only in this way can Australia avoid the embarrassment of picking a side and losing in the long term.

Notes

1 Feng Shaolei and Feng Shuai, "Reconsidering China's Neighboring Security: Characteristics, Functions and Trends," *Journal of International Security Studies*, No. 2, 2013, p.35.
2 Qi Huaigao et al., *China's Peripheral Security and Its Neighboring Diplomacy against the Backdrop of Its Rising*, Beijing: Zhonghua Book Company, 2014, pp.4–5.
3 Chu Zhaofeng, "U.S.-ASEAN Relations in the Context of American Asia-Pacific Strategy," *Global Review,* No. 1, 2012, p.15.
4 Sun Guoxiang, *Perspectives on the SCS Disputes*, Hong Kong: City University of Hong Kong Press, 2017, p.189.
5 Chu Zhaofeng, "U.S.-ASEAN Relations in the Context of American Asia-Pacific Strategy," *Global Review*, No. 1, 2012, p.15.
6 Sheldon Simon, "Military Commitments and Human Rights Concerns," *Comparative Connections*, May 2013, p.55.
7 Alice Ba, "Systemic Neglect? A Reconsideration of US Southeast Asia Policy," *Contemporary Southeast Asia*, Vol.31, Number 3, December 2009, pp.368–398.
8 Barry Desker, "The Eagle and the Panda: An Owl's View from Southeast Asia," *Asia Policy*, Number 15, January 2013, p.30.
9 Euan Graham, "Southeast Asia in the US Rebalance: Perceptions from a Divided Region," *Contemporary Southeast Asia*, Vol.35, No.3, 2013, p.306.
10 See Yu Changshen, "ASEAN Views of and Policy Responses to China's Rise," *Contemporary Asia-Pacific Studies*, No. 3, 2013, pp.111–128.
11 "Manila to Asean: Take Stand Now," The Manila Times, April27, 2012, available at: http://www.manilatimes.net/in-dex.php/news/top-stories/21780-manila-to-asean-take-stand-now.

12 Victoria Nuland, "Daily Press Briefing," Washington, D.C. April 23, 2012, available at: http://www.state.gov/r/pa/prs/dpb/2012/04/188322.htm
13 Liang Zhiming, "On the Relative Unity and Diversity of Southeast Asia," *Social Scientist*, No.5, 2000, p.4.
14 Euan Graham, "Southeast Asia in the US Rebalance: Perceptions from a Divided Region," *Contemporary Southeast Asia,* Vol.35, No.3, 2013, pp.305–332.
15 Zhang Xuekun, "Divergent Perceptions of Southeast Asian Countries towards the US Rebalance Strategy," *International Forum*, No.3, 2015, p.29.
16 Surin Pitsuwan, "America's Role in Asia: Recommendations from both Sides of the Pacific," Seol, 16 Dec, 2008, available at: http://www.asiafoundation.or.kr/document/ARA%20Seoul/NEA.pdf.
17 Fareed Zakaria, "The U.S. Can Out-charm China," *Newsweek*, Dec.12, 2005.
18 Wang Sen and Yang Guanghai, "ASEAN's Diplomacy of Balancing Great Powers in the SCSs," *Contemporary Asia-Pacific Studies*, No.1, 2014, p.36.
19 Thomas Lum, "The Republic of Philippines and U.S. Interests," CRS report, Jan. 3, 2011, p.9.
20 Sheldon W. Simon, "Conflict and Diplomacy in the SCS: The View from Washington," *Asian Survey*, Vol.52, No.6, November/December 2012, p.1007.
21 Ju Hailong, "American Factors in Philippines' SCS Policy," *China International Studies*, No.3, 2013, pp.58–69.
22 Jerry E. Esplanada, "Del. Rosario Defines 3 Pillars of Foreign Policy," Philippine Daily Inquirer, March 3, 2011, available at: http://www.manilamaildc.net/2011/03/03/del-rosario-defines-3-pillars-of-foreign-policy/.
23 "US Presence in SCS Sought to Protect Rights," June 7, 2011, available at: http://maritimesecurity.asia/free-2/south-china-sea-2/us-presence-in-south-china-sea-sought-to-protect-rights/
24 Ernest Z. Bower, "Engagement in the Indo-Pacific: The Pentagon Leads by Example," Aug 22, 2013, available at: http://csis.org/publication/engagement-indo-pacific-pentagon-leads-example
25 "The Philippines Proposes to Patrol the SCS with the United States and Open Eight Military Bases to the United States," on January 15, 2015, available at: http://world.people.com.cn/n1/2016/0115/c1002-28056892.html
26 Nguyen Manh Hung, "Vietnam-US Relations: Past, Present, and Future," *Asia Pacific Bulletin*, No.69, Washington, DC: East-West Center, September 24, 2010.
27 Cao Yunhua, Ju Hailong, ed., *Report on SCS Situation From 2012 to 2013*, Beijing: Current Affairs Press, 2013, p.183.
28 "Stirring up the SCS," Asia Report, No.223, 23 April, 2012, p.7, available at: http://www.crisisgroup.org/~/media/files/asia/north-east-asia/223-stirring-up-the-south-china-sea-i.pdf

29 Li Chunxia, "From Enemy to Comprehensive Partnership: Vietnamese Strategic Considerations about Vietnam-US Relations," *International Forum*, No.4, 2014, pp.14–16.

30 Nguyen Tan Yong, "Building Strategic Trust for Peace, Cooperation and Prosperity in Asia Pacific Region," *Shangri-La Dialogue*, Beijing: World Publishing Company, 2013, pp.12–14.

31 The White House, Office of the Press Secretary, "Remarks by President Obama and President Truong Tan Sang of Vietnam after Bilateral Meeting," July 25, 2013, available at: https://www.whitehouse.gov/the-press-office/2013/07/25/remarks-president-obama-and-president-truong-tan-sang-vietnam-after-bila

32 Liselotte Odgaard, "The SCS: ASEAN's Security Concerns About China," *Security Dialogue*, Vol.34, No.1, 2003, p.1

33 Dewi Fortuna Anwar, "An Indonesian Perspective on the U.S. Rebalancing Effort toward Asia," *The National Bureau of Asia Research Commentary*, February 26, 2013, p.3.

34 For a detailed study of the comprehensive partnership between the United States and Indonesia, see Qiu Chaobing, "The U.S.-Indonesian Comprehensive Partnership: Progress and Implications," *Chinese Journal of American Studies*, No.2, 2015, pp.93–111.

35 "The Relationship Between the United States and Indonesia has been Upgraded to a 'Strategic Partnership'," *China Youth Daily*, October 28, 2015, p.A07.

36 Dewi Fortuna Anwar, "An Indonesian Perspective on the U.S. Rebalancing Effort toward Asia," *The National Bureau of Asia Research Commentary*, February 26, 2013, p.4.

37 For example, Mahathir, the former Prime Minister of Malaysia, has repeatedly denied in public the "China Threat Theory" advocated by the West. See "Mahathir: China Makes Us Feel Safe," *China Youth Daily*, November 16, 2005; "Overlapping Issues: China is Called on to be More Cautious," *Utusan Malaysia*, June 16, 2011, quoted from Gong Xiaohui, "Analysis on Malaysia's SCS Policy in 2011," *Southeast Asian Studies*, No. 6, 2011, p.28.

38 Liao Xiaojian, "Analysis on Malaysia's Relationship with US and China after US 'Returning to Asia'," *Southeast Asian Studies*, No.1, 2012, pp.47–49.

39 Cao Yunhua, Ju Hailong, ed., *Report on SCS Situation From 2012 to 2013*, Beijing: Current Affairs Press, 2012, pp.231–232; Cao Yunhua, Ju Hailong, ed., *Report on SCS Situation From 2012 to 2013*, Beijing: Current Affairs Press, 2013, pp.197–199; Stuart Grudgings, "China's Assertiveness Hardens Malaysian Stance in Sea Dispute," *Reuters*, Feb 26, 2014, available at: http://uk.reuters.com/article/uk-malaysia-china-maritime-insight-idUKBREA1P1Z020140226

40 Azmi Hassan, "disappointment with China's attempt," *Utusan Malaysia*, June 16, 2011, quoted from Gong Xiaohui, "Analysis on Malaysia's SCS Policy in 2011," *Southeast Asian Studies*, No. 6, 2011, p.26.

41 Euan Graham, "Southeast Asia in the US Rebalance: Perceptions from a Divided Region," *Contemporary Southeast Asia*, Vol.35, No.3, 2013, pp.323–324.
42 Zhang Xuekun, "Divergent Perceptions of Southeast Asian Countries towards the US Rebalance Strategy," *International Forum*, No.3, 2015, p.27.
43 Wang Sen and Yang Guanghai, "ASEAN's Diplomacy of Balancing Great Powers in the SCSs," *Contemporary Asia-Pacific Studies*, No.1, 2014, p.40.
44 Ju Hailong, "Marine Security Policy and Practice in Brunei," *Forum of World Economics & Politics*, No.5, 2011, p.63.
45 For example, Brunei participated in the joint military exercise held by the United States, the Philippines, Singapore, Thailand, and Indonesia in the Strait of Malacca and other waters from June 14 to 24, 2011.
46 Luo Yongkun, "Brunei's SCS Policy," *International Information*, No. 9, 2012, p.15.
47 Ju Hailong, ed., *Report on SCS Situation From 2013 to 2014*, Beijing: Current Affairs Press, 2015, pp.330–340.
48 Barry Desker, "The Eagle and the Panda: An Owl's View from Southeast Asia," *Asia Policy,* Number 15, January 2013, p.30.
49 Prime Minister Lee Hsien Loong, "China and the World-Prospering and Progressing Together," Speech to the Central Party School in China, 6 September 2012, available at: www.pmo.gov.sg/content/pmosite/mediacentre/speechesninterviews/primeminister/2012/September/speech_by_prime_ministerleehsienloongatcentralparty-schoolenglish.html#.UnHNbOv2MdU
50 Seng Tan, "Riding the Chinese Dragon: Singapore's Pragmatic Relationship with China," in Jun Tsunekawa, ed., *The Rise of China: Responses from South East Asia and Japan*, NIDS Joint Research Series No.4, 2009, p.36.
51 Li Mingjiang and Zhang Hongzhou, "Singapore's Policy towards the SCS: Be Neutral and Useful, Maintain Stability and Peace," *Southeast Asian Studies*, No.6, 2011, p.16.
52 Barry Desker, "The Eagle and the Panda: An Owl's View from Southeast Asia," *Asia Policy,* Number 15, January 2013, pp.26–30.
53 "Singapore warns US against anti-China election rhetoric," BBC News Online, 9 February 2012, available at: http://www.bbc.com/news/world-asia-16958611
54 Euan Graham, "Southeast Asia in the US Rebalance: Perceptions from a Divided Region," *Contemporary Southeast Asia*, Vol.35, No.3, 2013, pp.318–319.
55 Kitti Prasirtsuk: "The Implications of U.S. Strategic Rebalancing: A Perspective from Thailand," *Asia Policy,* Number 15, January 2013, p.34.
56 Kitti Prasirtsuk: "The Implications of U.S. Strategic Rebalancing: A Perspective from Thailand," *Asia Policy,* Number 15, January 2013, p.35.
57 "Cambodia opposes to internationalize issue of SCS," Chinadaily, October 28, 2010, available at: http://www.chinadaily.com.cn/world/2010-10/28/content_11473378.htm

58 "Cambodian Prime Minister Hun Sen says he opposes the internationalization of the SCS issue," *Huanqiu*, April 9, 2012, available at: http://world.huanqiu.com/hot/2012-04/2593454.html

59 Fang Yun, "Comprehensive Foreign Policy of Laos and the Relationship between China and Laos," *Southeast Asian And South Asian Studies*, No.2, 2011, pp.14–19.

60 Fan Lingzhi, "Due to the opposition of Laos and other countries, the statement of the US ASEAN meeting did not mention the SCS," *Huanqiu*, February 17, 2016, available at: http://world.huanqiu.com/exclusive/2016-02/8554175.html

61 Li Yun, "The Evolution and Trend of the Obama Administration's Myanmar Policy," *Contemporary International Relations*, No.12, 2015, p.22.

62 Associated Press, "Myanmar Said to Begin Moving Political Prisoners," November 16, 2011, available at: http://news.yahoo.com/myanmar—said—begin—moving—political—prisoners—144547401.html.

63 Chinese scholar Cai Penghong believes that the evolution of Myanmar's situation is not necessarily the result of Myanmar's implementation of the policy of "leaving China and turning to the United States," but the basic logic of Myanmar's domestic political development. See Cai Penghong, "The Changing Political Situation in Myanmar and an Analysis of China-Myanmar Relations," *Journal of International Relations*, No.4, 2015, pp.109–111.

64 "New Myanmar takes over the next year's ASEAN leader," *New York Times (Chinese version)*, October 11, 2013, available at: http://cn.nytimes.com/asia-pacific/20131011/c11asean/

65 Li Yun, "The Evolution and Trend of the Obama Administration's Myanmar Policy," *Contemporary International Relations*, No.12, 2015, pp.27–28.

66 In fact, Aung San Suu Kyi, a well-known political activist in Myanmar, attaches great importance to the relations with neighboring countries, especially with China. Her visit to Beijing in June 2015 and the restoration of the relationship between the NLD and China testifies China's status in the international community.

67 Noboru Yamaguchi, "A Japanese Perspective on U.S. Rebalancing toward the Asia-Pacific Region," *Asia Policy*, No.15, January 2013, pp.7–12.

68 For example, some scholars pointed out that under the promotion of the Obama administration and the active operation of the Japanese government, the Asia-Pacific security pattern with the United States as the "single axis" has shown an increasingly obvious change over the years, that is, it has gradually changed to the pattern of "US as axis and Japan as subordinate axis." Japan has been making itself the "subordinate axis" in the Asia-Pacific region through continuous strengthening of Japan-US alliance and promoting its military strength, strengthening bilateral and trilateral security interaction with other U.S. Asian Pacific allies, and carrying out various strategic security cooperation with the "strategic partner countries" of the United States in the Asia-Pacific region, such as India, Indonesia, Vietnam, etc. See

Xin Qiang, "'Subordinate Axis': Changing Role of Japan in the U.S. Asia-Pacific Security Structure," *World Economics and Politics*, No.4, 2014, pp.39–53.

69 Céline Pajon, "Japan and the SCS Forging Strategic Partnerships in a Divided Region," Asie.Visions, No.60, January 2013, p.7.

70 Zhang Yaohua, "Japan's Role in the SCS Issue," *China International Studies*, No.3, 2011, p.52.

71 The Government of Japan, *National Security Strategy of Japan*, December 2013, p.24.

72 Wang Chuanjian, "Japan's SCS Policy: Connotation and Extension," *Foreign Affairs Review*, No.3, 2011, p.106.

73 Zhang Xuekun and Ou Xuanxi, "An Analysis of the Causes and Approaches of Japan's Involving in the SCS Issue," *Pacific Journal*, No.4, 2016, p.37.

74 Yang Jilong, "On the Japan Factor in the SCS Dispute," *Pacific Journal*, No.12, 2013, p.95.

75 Tomotaka Shoji, "The SCS: A View from Japan," *NIDS Journal of Defense and Security*, No.15, Dec. 2014, p.131.

76 Céline Pajon, "Japan and the SCS Forging Strategic Partnerships in a Divided Region," *Asie.Visions*, No.60, January 2013, p.8.

77 Paul Midford, "Japan's Approach to Maritime Security in the SCS," *Asian Security*, Vol.55, No.3, 2015, pp.537–539.

78 Shen Yamei, "Japan's Response to the U.S. Strategic Eastward Movement and its Impact," *Contemporary World*, No. 11, 2013, pp.66–67.

79 For domestic disputes in Japan, please refer to He Ping, "The Strategic Intention and Policy Debate of Japan's Participation in TPP Negotiations," *Japanese Studies*, No. 4, 2012, pp.34–49.

80 Liu Changli, "Motivation, Constraints and Policy Measures of Japan's Participation in TPP Negotiations," *Japanese Studies*, No. 1, 2011, p.66.

81 "Japan officially announced its accession to the TPP negotiations," xinhuanet, March 15, 2013, available at: http://news.xinhuanet.com/2013-03/15/c_115045112.htm

82 Liu Changli, "Motivation, Constraints and Policy Measures of Japan's Participation in TPP Negotiations," *Japanese Studies*, No. 1, 2011, pp.67–72.

83 Liu Lingqi and Liu Haichao, "Motivation for Japan's TPP Decision and Assessment of the Status quo of Japan-US Negotiations," *Contemporary International Relations*, No. 3, 2015, p.55.

84 See Liu Changli, "Motivation, Constraints and Policy Measures of Japan's Participation in TPP Negotiations," *Japanese Studies*, No. 1, 2011, pp.70–71; Jiang Yuechun, "Japan Joins TPP Negotiation: Intention and Aftermath," *Global Review*, No.1, 2012, pp.29–30.

85 Wang Chuanjian, "Japan's SCS Policy: Connotation and Extension," *Foreign Affairs Review*, No.3, 2011, p.105.

86 "Japanese media: China's rule over Spratly Islands has become a fact, and the future of Diaoyu/Senkaku Island is worrying," *Global Times*, April 26, 2010, 3rd edition.
87 Christian Caryl, "Naval Gazing in Asia," available at: http://www.foreignpolicy.com/articles/2010/05/18/.
88 "Japanese media: China's building a maritime power threatens the United States and Japan," available at: http://www.apdnews.com/asia/neasia/7013.html
89 Michael Auslin, "Japan Steps up as Regional Counterweight," *The Wall Street Journal*, June 5, 2014.
90 Lin Xiaoguang, "Japan's Strategic Intension in Getting Actively Involved in the SCS Issue and Its Policy Trend," *Peace and Development*, No.2, 2012, p.55.
91 Hillary Clinton, "Offering to Aid Talks, U.S. Challenges China on Disputed Islands," *New York Times*, available at: http://www.nytimes.com/2010/07/24/world/asia/24diplo.html.
92 Li Zongze, "Japan once again stated that it should discuss the SCS issue within the international framework composed of the United States and Japan," *Huanqiu*, available at: http://world.huanqiu.com/roll/2010-07/964737.html
93 Yu Qing, "Japan plans to join hands with the United States to internationalize the SCS issue to check and balance China," available at: http://world.people.com.cn/GB/15115845.html
94 "The United States continues to provoke in the SCS issue, and Japan openly supports the United States' freedom of navigation," *Huanqiu*, available at: http://world.huanqiu.com/exclusive/2016-02/8487835.html
95 Hui Gengtian, "Multi-level Dynamics for Internationalization of SCS Issue," *Journal of Strategy and Decision-Making*, No.2, 2013, p.21.
96 "Japan revises the three principles of arms export and says goodbye to 'peaceful country'," xinhuanet, April 8, 2014, available at: http://news.xinhuanet.com/world/2014-04/08/c_ 1110132744.htm
97 Xin Qiang and Fu Da'an, "The Diaoyu/Senkaku Islands Dispute From the Perspective of China-US Competition in Security," *Chinese Journal of American Studies*, No. 1, 2014, p.46.
98 "Hagel Discusses US-Japan Defense Relations in Interview," April 5, 2014, available at: http://www.globalsecurity.org/military/library/news/2014/04/mil-140405-afps03.htm
99 "Abe cabinet decided to amend the constitutional interpretation to lift the right of collective self-defense," China News Network, July 1, 2014, available at: http://www.chinanews.com/gj/2014/07-01/6339585.shtml; Liu Weidong, "An Analysis of U.S. Policy toward Japan's Lifting the Ban on 'Collective Selfdefense'," *Contemporary International Relations*, No.4, 2015, pp.28–35.
100 Meng Xiaoxu and Wang Shan, "Japan's New Security Bills and Strategic Dilemma," *Contemporary International Relations*, No.8, 2015, pp.16–21.

101 "Japan raises defence spending budget," *Jagran Post*, Dec. 24, 2013, available at: http://post.jagran.com/japan-raises-defence-spending-budget-1387865459
102 "Japan's defense budget hits a record high," December 25, 2015, available at: http://world.people.com.cn/n1/2015/1225/c157278-27977457.html
103 "Obama Endorses India's Security Council Bid," CBC News, November 8, 2010, available at: http://www.cbc.ca/news/world/obama-endorses-india-s-security-council-bid-1.887948
104 US Department of Defense (DoD),"Sustaining U.S. Global Leadership: Priorities for the 21st Century Defense," January 2012, p.2, available at: http://www.defense.gov/news/defense_strategic_guidance.pdf
105 "Leno Panetta calls for closer defence ties with India," BBC, June 6, 2012, available at: http://www.bbc.com/news/world-asia-18336854
106 Wang Aijuan, "India's Measures to Cope With the US Strategy of "Rebalancing" Toward Asia Pacific," *Journal of PLA Nanjing Institute of Politics*, No. 5, 2012, p.68.
107 Jawaharlal Nehru, *Discovery of India*, Beijing: World Affairs Press, 1958, p.57.
108 C. Raja Mohan, "India: Between 'Strategic Autonomy' and 'Geopolitical Opportunity'," *Asia Policy*, Number 15, January 2013, p.23.
109 Thaliyakkattil Srikanth, "An Analysis of India's Hedging Strategy towards China," *Journal of Contemporary Asia-Pacific Studies*, No.4, 2013, pp.25–31.
110 Zhang Li, "US Pivot to Asia and India's Role Choice," *South Asian Studies Quarterly*, No.2, 2012, pp.5–6.
111 Wang Aijuan, "India's Response to the US Military Strategy of Rebalancing in the Asia Pacific Region," *Journal of PLA Nanjing Institute of Politics*, No.5, 2012, p.69.
112 Jyoti Thottam, "Six Things to Watch from Hillary Clinton's India Tour," *Time*, July 19, 2011, available at: http://world.time.com/2011/07/19/six-things-to-watch-from-hillary-clintons-india-tour/
113 C. Raja Mohan, "India: Between 'Strategic Autonomy' and 'Geopolitical Opportunity'," *Asia Policy*, Number 15, January 2013, p.25.
114 Sudesh Rani, "US Rebalancing in Asia-Pacific: Indian Response and Way Ahead," *South Asia journal*, Issue 13, Spring 2015, available at: http://southasiajournal.net/us-rebalancing-in-asia-pacific-indian-response-and-way-ahead/
115 Centre for Policy Research, "Nonalignment 2.0: A Foreign and Strategic Policy for India in the Twenty First Century," Feb. 2012, p.8, available at: http://www.cprindia.org/sites/default/files/working_papers/NonAlignment%202.0_1.pdf
116 Arun Sahgal, "India and US Rebalancing Strategy for Asia-Pacific," July 09, 2012, available at: http://www.idsa.in/idsacomments/IndiaandUSRebalancingStrategyforAsiaPacific_asahgal_090712
117 Sylvia Mishra, "India's Response to the US Pivot and Asian Geopolitics," available at: http://earp.in/en/indias-response-to-the-us-pivot-and-asian-geopolitics/
118 Sunjoy Joshi, et al., "Beyond the Plateau in U.S.–India Relations," The Heritage Foundation Special Report, No.132, April 26, 2013.

119 For details of the interest differences between India and the United States, see Thaliyakkattil Srikanth, "US Strategic Rebalancing toward Asia-Pacific: India's Policy Options," *South Asian Studies Quarterly*, No.1, 2013, pp.28–30.
120 Robert M. Hathaway, "India and the US Pivot to Asia," Yale Global, February 24, 2012, available at: http://yaleglobal.yale.edu/content/india-and-us-pivot-asia
121 Deepa M. Ollapally, "India's Response to the U.S. Rebalance," in Report of *Balancing Acts: The U.S. Rebalance and Asia-Pacific Stability*, August 2013, pp.46–47.
122 Harsh V. Pant and Yogesh Joshi, "Indian Foreign Policy Responds to the U.S. Pivot," *Asia Policy*, No. 19, January 2015, pp.89–114.
123 "U.S. and India plan to sign a $8 billion arms sales bill," cankaoxiaoxi.com, April 28, 2012, available at: http://mil.cankaoxiaoxi.com/2012/0428/33328.shtml.
124 "The United States allows India to purchase its most advanced weapon technology and jointly develop equipment," xinhua.com, June 8, 2012, available at: http://news.xinhuanet.com/mil/2012-06/08/c_123251896.htm
125 Karl F. Inderfurth, Nicholas Lombardo, "Panetta to India: Why Now? For What?," Center for Strategic & International Studies, May 31, 2012, available at: http://csis.org/publication/panetta-india-why-now-what
126 "India's withdrawal from joint naval exercises with the United States and Japan for fear of China," phoenix.com, May 23, 2013, available at: http://news.ifeng.com/world/detail_2013_05/13/25233739_0.shtml
127 Wang Chuanjian, "India's SCS Policy: Intention and Influence," *Foreign Affairs Review*, No. 3, 2010, pp.107–122; David Scott, "India's Role in the SCS: Geopolitics and Geoeconomics in Play," *India Review*, Vol.12, No.2, 2013, pp.51–69.
128 Hillary Clinton, "Remarks on India and the United States: A Vision for the 21st Century," speech in Chennai, India, July 20, 2011, available at: www.state.gov/secretary/rm/2011/07/168840.htm
129 "SCS region property of world, says Krishna," *The Hindu*, April 6, 2012, http://www.thehindu.com/news/national/article3287504.ece?homepage=true
130 Lin Minwang, "Why Does India Involve in the Dispute in the SCS?", *South Asian Studies Quarterly*, No.4, 2014, pp.16–17.
131 C. Raja Mohan, *Sino-Indian Rivalry in the Indo-Pacific*, Washington, D.C.: Carnegie Endowment for International Peace, 2012, pp.182–183.
132 "Indian defense minister says not to confront China's SCS," xinhuanet, July 23, 2012, available at: http://news.xinhuanet.com/mil/2012-07/23/c_123456690.htm
133 Lin Minwang, "Why Does India Involve in the Dispute in the SCS?", *South Asian Studies Quarterly*, No.4, 2014, p.19.
134 Sarah Parnass, "Hillary Clinton Urges India to Lead in China's Neighborhood," *ABC News*, July 20, 2011, available at: http://blogs.abcnews.com/thenote/2011/07/hillary-clinton-urges-india-to-lead-in-chinas-neighborhood.html

135 "US backs India's Look East policy, seeks greater Asia Pacific role for India," *Firstpost*, Nov.23, 2011, available at: http://www.firstpost.com/world/us-supports-indias-look-east-policy-137741.htm

136 "US wants to actively support India's Look East policy: Clinton," *India Post*, November 11, 2011, available at: http://www.indiapost.com/us-wants-to-actively-support-indias-look-east-policy-clinton/

137 "Time to Change 'Look East Policy' to 'Act East Policy': Sushma Swaraj," August 25, 2014, available at: http://www.ndtv.com/india-news/time-to-change-look-east-policy-to-act-east-policy-sushma-swaraj-653063

138 " 'Look East' policy now turned into 'Act East' policy: Modi," *The Hindu*, November 14, 2014, available at: http://www.thehindu.com/news/national/look-east-policy-now-turned-into-act-east-policy-modi/article6595186.ece

139 Jayanth Jacob, " 'Look East' Policy is now 'Act East'," *Hindustan Times*, Oct.4, 2014, available at: http://www.hindustantimes.com/india/look-east-policy-is-now-act-east/story-y8VHBxBw6LxMXSQbuMbYVN.html

140 The Brookings Institution, "India's Asia-Pacific Policy: From 'Look East' to 'Act East'," September 9, 2014, p.3

141 Wu Zhaoli, "India's Asia Pacific Strategy: Development, Objective, and Implementation," *South Asian Studies,* No.4, 2015, p.104.

142 The White House, Office of the Press Secretary, "U.S.-India Joint Statement," September 30, 2014, available at: https://www.whitehouse.gov/the-press-office/2014/09/30/us-india-joint-statemen

143 Ge Hongliang, "India's New Asia-Pacific Strategy: The Modi Administration's 'Act East Policy'," *South Asian Studies*, No.1, 2015, p.70.

144 Sun Zhe and Xu Hongfeng, "The Impact of the Eastward Shift of the Obama Administration's Strategic Focus on US-Russian Relations," *Chinese Journal of American Studies*, No. 1, 2013, p.14.

145 Alexei Fenenko, "Can Russia play an active part in the Pacific game?", February 4, 2012, available at: http://valdaiclub.com/opinion/highlights/can_russia_play_an_active_part_in_the_pacific_game/

146 Cheng Chunhua, "America's return to Asia Pacific and Russia's response--Based on the perspective of Russian academic research," *Journal of PLA Nanjing Institute of Politics,* No.4, 2012, p.66.

147 This paragraph mainly refers to Dr. Cheng Chunhua's analysis of the Russian academic community's strategic thinking in response to the "rebalancing" of the Asia-Pacific region of the United States. I would like to express my gratitude. See Cheng Chunhua, "America's 'return' to Asia Pacific and Russia's response--Based on the perspective of Russian academic research," *Journal of PLA Nanjing Institute of Politics*, No.4, 2012, pp.68–70.

148 Cheng Chunhua, "America's 'return' to Asia Pacific and Russia's response--Based on the perspective of Russian academic research," *Journal of PLA Nanjing Institute of Politics*, No.4, 2012, p.68.
149 Cheng Chunhua, "America's 'return' to Asia Pacific and Russia's response--Based on the perspective of Russian academic research," *Journal of PLA Nanjing Institute of Politics*, No.4, 2012, p.69.
150 Isabelle Facon, "Russia's Perspective on the US Pivot: Opportunities and Constraints in the Asia Pacific," in Hugo Meijer eds., *Origins and Evolution of the US Rebalance toward Asia*, New York: Palgrave Macmillan, 2015, pp.261–265.
151 This has been reflected in the Obama administration's approach to the entire post-Soviet region. Compared with the Bush Jr. administration, the Obama administration has given priority to "reset" relations with Russia and has attached a relatively limited attention to Ukraine, Georgia, and Central Asia.
152 Lilia Shevtsova, "Russia's 'Pivot' to China: Is It Real or Fake?," *Global Asia*, March 28, 2013.
153 Artyom Lukin, "Russia: Between the US and China," *East Asia Forum*, July 24, 2012.
154 Levada Analytical Center, Russian Public Opinion 2010–2011, Moscow, 2012, p.274.
155 Fiona Hill and Bobo Lo, "Putin's Pivot: Why Russia Is Looking East," *Foreign Affairs*, July 31, 2013.
156 Shevtsova, "Russia's 'Pivot' to China," *Global Asia*, March 28, 2013.
157 Isabelle Facon, "Russia's Perspective on the US Pivot: Opportunities and Constraints in the Asia Pacific," in Hugo Meijer eds., *Origins and Evolution of the US Rebalance toward Asia*, New York: Palgrave Macmillan, 2015, pp.257–258.
158 Kontseptsiya vneshney politiki Rossiyskoy Federatsii, February 12, 2013, website of the Russian Ministry of Foreign Affairs, www.mid.ru
159 Isabelle Facon, "Russia's Perspective on the US Pivot: Opportunities and Constraints in the Asia Pacific," in Hugo Meijer eds., *Origins and Evolution of the US Rebalance toward Asia*, New York: Palgrave Macmillan, 2015, pp.259–260.
160 Fiona Hill and Bobo Lo, "Putin's Pivot: Why Russia Is Looking East," *Foreign Affairs*, July 31, 2013.
161 Guo Jinyue, "Russia and the United States Asia-Pacific 'Rebalancing' Strategy," *Russian, East European & Middle Asian Studies*, No.5, 2014, p.78.
162 Richard Weitz, "As Tensions with West Rise, Moscow Looks to Asia," *The Diplomat*, July 25, 2013, available at: http://thediplomat.com/2013/07/as-tensions-with-west-rise-moscow-looks-to-asia/
163 Liu Fenghua, "Russia's Policy of Eastward Movement: Achievements, Problems and Trend," *Russian Studies*, No.1, 2013, pp.11–18.
164 Zuo Fengrong, "Russia's New Asia-Pacific Strategy and Its Impact upon China-Russia Relations," *The Journal of International Studies*, No.2, 2013, p.119.

165 "The Russian President: to strengthen Russia's role in the Asia-Pacific region," Rosatom (Chinese version), July 2, 2010, available at: http://sputniknews.cn/russia/20100702/42825210.html

166 Vladimir Putin: "An Asia-Pacific Growth Agenda," *The Wall Street Journal Asia*, September 6, 2012, available at: http://online.wsj.com/article/SB10000872396390443847404577629312716242648.html

167 "Russian President Vladimir Putin: Strengthening Asia-pacific Cooperation is a Strategic priority," China News Network, November 10, 2014, available at: http://www.chinanews.com/gn/2014/11-10/6765638.shtml

168 "New Oceanographer priorities for Crimean Black Sea Fleet," on July 29, 2015, available at: http://www.china.com.cn/haiyang/2015-07/29/content_36172145.htm

169 Ma Jianguang and Sun Qianjie, "Study on the Evolution of Russia's Maritime Strategy and Its Geopolitical Influence," *Pacific Journal*, No.11, 2015, p.24.

170 Shi Menghua and Yin Cheng, "Russian Fleet Sails for 'New Pacific Century'," *PLA Daily*, September. 19, 2001.

171 Zuo Fengrong, "Preliminary Exploration of Russia's Maritime Strategy," *Foreign Affairs Review*, No.5, 2012, p.136.

172 Liu Fei, "Russia's Policy of the SCS and Its Impact on Chinese Maritime Disputes," *Northeast Asia Forum*, No.1, 2016, pp.87–95.

173 See Li Guanqun, "The Influence of Russia on China's Maritime Geostrategy," *Contemporary World And Socialism*, No.1, 2013, p.108.

174 PIR Center and ASEAN Center in Mgimo University, "Sino-American Rivalry in Asia: Conclusions for Russia," *Security Index*, Volume 18, No.4, 2012, pp.59–60.

175 Institute of World Economics and Politics Chinese Academy of Social Sciences, "TPP Strategy of Russia, Canada and New Zealand," in Tang Guoqiang, ed., *Study on the Trans-Pacific Partnership Agreement and Economic Integration in the Asia-Pacific Region*, Beijing: World Affairs Press, 2013, p.304.

176 "Competition between China and U.S. in the Asia-Pacific Region, How Russia Positions Itself," Huanqiu, April 28, 2013, available at: http://world.huanqiu.com/depth_report/2013-04/3883852.html

177 William T. Tow, Russell Trood, "The 'Anchors': Collaborative Security Substance or Smokescreen?", in Brad Williams and Andrew Newman, eds., *Japan, Australia and Asia-Pacific security*, New York: Routledge, 2006, pp.70–71.

178 Commonwealth of Australia, *Australia in the Asian Century White Paper*, Canberra: Department of the Prime Minister and Cabinet, 2012, p.74, available at: http://asiancentury.dpmc.gov.au/white-paper.

179 Charles Krauthammer, "Why I Love Australia," *The Washington Post*, June 23, 2006, available at: http://www.washingtonpost.com/wp-dyn/content/article/2006/06/22/AR2006062201468.html

180 Bruce Vaughn, Thomas Lum, *Australia: Background and U.S. Relations*, CRS report, December 14, 2015, p.1.

181 "Julia Gillard's Speech to Congress," *The Sydney Morning Herald*, March 10, 2011.

182 "Minister for Defence–Interview with Chris Uhlmann," 28 March, 2012, available at: http://www.minister.defence.gov.au/2012/03/28/minister-for-defence-interview-with-chris-uhlmann-abc-7-30/

183 Fergus Hanson, "Australia and New Zealand in the World, Public Opinion and Foreign Policy," Lowy Institute Poll, 2012, available at: http://www.lowyinstitute.org/publications/lowy-institute-poll-2012-public-opinion-and-foreign-policy.

184 Alex Oliver, "The Lowy Institute Poll 2015: Australia and the World," June 2015, pp.9–10.

185 Allan Hawke and Ric Smith, *Australian Defence Force Posture Review*, Department of Defence: Canberra, 30 March 2012; Australian Government, *Australia in the Asian Century*, White Paper, October 2012; Australian Government, *Strong and Secure: A Strategy for Australia's National Security*, January 23, 2013; Australia Department of Defence, *Defence White Paper 2013、2014、2015、2016*.

186 Sun Junjian, "Australia's Response to U.S. Strategy of 'Return to the Asia-Pacific'," *Contemporary International Relations*, No.8, 2014, pp.36–37.

187 Wang Guanghou, "Analysis on Australia's SCS Policy," *Southeast Asian Studies*, No.6, 2011, pp.10–12.

188 Lu Peng, "Between the Middle Power Dream and the National Interests--Australia International Strategy and its SCS Policy," *Asia-Pacific Security and Maritime Affairs*, No.2, 2015, p.21.

189 Louise Yaxley, "Prime Minister rubs shoulders at East Asia Summit," *ABC News*, November 20, 2012, available at: http://www.abc.net.au/pm/content/2012/s3637015.htm

190 Department of Defence of Australia, *Defence White Paper 2013*, Canberra, May 3, 2013, p.25.

191 John Garnaut and David Wroe, "Australia urged to send military to counter China's control over sea lanes," *The Sydney Morning Herald*, May 15, 2015, available at: http://www.smh.com.au/federal-politics/political-news/australia-urged-to-send-military-to-counter-chinas-control-over-sea-lanes-20150515-gh2uks.html

192 David Wroe, "SCS: Australia will ignore Chinese air defence zone, says Kevin Andrews," *The Sydney Morning Herald*, June 1, 2015, available at: http://www.smh.com.au/federal-politics/political-news/south-china-sea-australia-will-ignore-chinese-air-defence-zone-says-kevin-andrews-20150601-ghe7o1.html

193 Lu Peng, "Between the Middle Power Dream and the National Interests--Australia International Strategy and its SCS Policy," *Asia-Pacific Security and Maritime Affairs*, No.2, 2015, p.23.

194 For Australia's official position on the SCS, see Zhuang Guotu and Lu Qiuli, "Basic Stance of Australia Official on SCS Disputes in Recent Years," *Southeast Asian Affairs*, No.3, 2013, pp.97–101.

195 Sun Junjian, "Australia's Response to U.S. Strategy of 'Return to the Asia-Pacific'," *Contemporary International Relations*, No.8, 2014, p.37.

196 Chen Hongqiao, "U.S.-Australia Cooperation and U.S.'s Asia Pacific Rebalancing Strategy," *Contemporary Asia-Pacific Studies*, No.1, 2014, p.64.

197 Australian Government, *Strong and Secure: A Strategy for Australia's National Security*, January 23, 2013, p.22.

198 Under the agreement, the United States will deploy between 200 and 250 marines at the Royal Darwin Military base in northern Australia from 2012, increasing to 2,500 over five years. So far, there have been many rotations of American troops in Darwin.

199 Australian Department of Defence, *Defence White Paper 2016*, February 25, 2016.

200 Wang Lianhe, "New Trends in U.S.-Australia Security Alliance," *Contemporary International Relations*, No.1, 2014, p.37.

201 Australian Department of Defence, "Australia's 'Fighting Felines' combine for Talisman Saber," 25 July, 2013, available at: http://www.defence.gov.au/defence-news/stories/2013/jul/0725c.htm

202 For more information, please refer to the communiqué or statement issued by the Australian and US Ministerial Consultation (AUSMIN) in recent years.

203 U.S. Department of State, "U.S.-Australia Ministerial Consultations 2011 Joint Statement on Cyberspace," Washington D.C, September 15, 2011, available at: http://www.state.gov/r/pa/prs/ps/2011/09/172490.htm

204 Tony Abbott, "Address to the American Australian Association Business Luncheon," available at: https://www.pm.gov.au/media/2014-06-10/address-american-australian-association-business-luncheon-new-york.

205 Yu Xiaoyan, "The Political Economic Analysis of Australia's Promotion of TPP Negotiation," *Asia-pacific Economic Review*, No.6, 2012, pp.12–14.

206 Group Captain Graham Edwards, "On Balance-Is the US Rebalance Good for Australia?", The Centre for Defence and Strategic Studies (CDSS), August 2015, p.4.

207 Bruce Vaughn, Thomas Lum, *Australia: Background and U.S. Relations*, CRS report, December 14, 2015, Summary.

208 Peter Jennings, "The U.S. Rebalance to the Asia-Pacific: An Australian Perspective," *Asia Policy*, Number 15, January 2013, pp.40–41; Tomohiko Satake and Yusuke Ishihara, "America's Rebalance to Asia and its Implications for Japan-US-Australia Security Cooperation," *Asia-Pacific Review*, Vol.19, No.2, 2012, pp.19–20; Vince Scappatura, "The US 'Pivot to Asia', the China Spectre and the Australian-American Alliance," *The Asia-Pacific Journal*, Volume 12, Issue 36, Number 3, September 2014, pp.14–17.

209 Hugh White, "The Limits to Optimism: Australia and the Rise of China," *Australian Journal of International Affairs*, Vol.59, No.4, December, 2005, pp.469–80; Hugh White, "Power Shift: Australia's future between Washington and Beijing," *Quarterly Essay*, Vol.39, 2010, pp.1–74; Hugh White, *The China Choice: Why America Should Share Power*, Collingwood, VIC: Black Inc, 2012.

210 Peter Jennings, "The U.S. Rebalance to the Asia-Pacific: An Australian Perspective," *Asia Policy*, Number 15, January 2013, p.40.

211 Malcolm Fraser and Cain Roberts, *Dangerous Allies*, Melbourne: Melbourne University Press, 2014, pp.276–277.

212 Raoul Heinrichs, "We're carrying the flag for the US," The Lowy Interpreter, September 14, 2011, available at: http://www.lowyinterpreter.org/post/2011/09/14/Australia-Overreliant-and-under-prepared.aspx

213 Andrew O'Neil, "Australia's Asia White Paper Review and the Dilemmas of Engagement," *Security Challenges*, 8–1, Autumn 2012, pp.13–18.

214 Hugh White, "Power shift: rethinking Australia's place in the Asian century," *Australian Journal of International Affairs*, Vol. 65, No. 1, February 2011, pp.81–93.

215 Hugh White, "Power Shift: Australia's Future between Washington and Beijing," *Quarterly Essay 39*, September 2010, p.62.

216 Australia Department of Defence, *Defence White Paper 2016*, February 25, 2016, p.15.

217 Ma Bisheng, "How Does Australia Respond to China's Rise?", *Foreign Affairs Review*, No.1, 2014, p.56.

6

The U.S. Congressional Involvement in the SCS Dispute

"The President provides leadership and commands information, expertise, secrecy, speed and efficiency. Congress represents the people's wider, more sober, more deliberate (more cautious) longer-term values and judgments."

—Louis Henkin

"(The Senate) reaffirms the strong support of the United States for the peaceful resolution of maritime territorial disputes in the SCS; deplores the use of force by naval and maritime security vessels from China in the SCS; calls on all parties to the territorial dispute to refrain from threatening force or using force to assert territorial claims; and supports the continuation of operations by the United States Armed Forces in support of freedom of navigation rights in international waters and air space in the SCS."

—The 217th Senate resolution on the 112th Congress (S.Res.217)

As the legislative branch of the "separation of the three powers" system, Congress not only plays a key role in the domestic politics, it also functions as an integral part of the American government in shaping its foreign policy. Robert Zoellick, former U.S. Deputy Secretary of State, once made a classic comment about the congressional influence on U.S. foreign policy-making, "in any event, today's reality is that Congress and the Executive need to work out a partnership--with its creative tension-- to guide US foreign policy in a new and very different era."[1] The influence of Congress in foreign affairs is also reflected incisively and vividly on the SCS dispute. Admittedly, the U.S. government is the "pioneer" to get involved in the SCS tensions after the Cold War, but Congress is the pusher behind the scenes. Especially with the intensification of the SCS issue since the beginning of the 21st century, Congress has been holding hearings and analyzing the research reports on the SCS; in the meantime, members of the Congress have frequently introduced related bills and issued statements, delivered speeches, and wrote letters to actively intervene in the SCS issues, which becomes a non-negligible factor influencing the U.S. policy and the maritime order in SCS.

The Role of Congress in the Making of U.S. Foreign Policy

The foreign policy behavior of the United States is the result of a complex multi-level interaction under the comprehensive influence of both domestic and foreign factors. From the perspective of diplomatic decision-making actors, the U.S. Constitution vests diplomatic power to the President and the Congress. Specifically, the diplomatic responsibility of the President or the Executive Branch includes: response to foreign events, proposals for legislation, negotiation of international agreements, policy statements, policy implementation, and other independent actions. While Congress formulates or influences American foreign policy in the following ways: introducing bills, making policy statements, enacting legislation, enacting legislation to restrict or deny the funding, making informal advice, exercising oversight, etc.[2] Due to an unclear power allocation, however, the two institutions have been conflicting with each other and struggling for diplomatic dominance for a long time,[3] resulting in the alternate historical period of the so-called imperial Congress and imperial Presidency.[4]

After the Cold War, with the in-depth development of globalization, the influence of public diplomacy, and the blurring of domestic and diplomatic boundaries, Congressional status in U.S. diplomatic policy-making process is significantly promoted and gradually acts as an "anchor and rudder" manipulating American diplomacy.[5] The diplomatic power of Congress has been strengthened in part, and it tends to be more "personalized" and localized, more partisan and ideological, and is more inclined to promote American values overseas.[6] Thus, Alton Frye, former vice chairman of Foreign Relations Committee, once pointed out that "as to foreign affairs, times are gone when the Congress always respects the Executive's decisions. Only when an essential and effective alliance is formed with Congress in domestic affairs can an American President succeed in foreign affairs."[7] James M. Lindsay, a congressional expert on foreign affairs, also believes that the main decision-maker of U.S. foreign policy is in the administrative system, but Congress is still an important "participant" and "judge." Congress plays an irreplaceable role in supervising the foreign policy and legalizes the mature foreign policy of the government.[8] The above facts indicate that the executive system headed by the President shall listen to the voice of Congress when formulating and implementing foreign policy initiatives.

The function of Congress in the U.S. foreign policy-making process is reflected in many ways.[9] In the field of human rights, Congress is the important driving force in the U.S. human rights diplomacy. When the discrepancies occur between Congress and the Executive, Congress is apt to put pressure on the Executive to adopt a more robust human rights policy. For example, Congress has passed legislation to impose specific sanctions on other countries' serious violations of religious freedom, and issued annual country reports on human rights practices to make unwarranted accusations of the human condition in other countries. In the field of military power, the United States maintains its global hegemony after the Cold War. With its strong military capacity, the United States often uses or threatens to use force to carry out diplomatic strategy. When it interferes in the policy-making process, Congress does its utmost to expand its power and influence, and becomes an absolutely necessary part. In the field of national security, Congress also plays a significant role in security policy-making. On issues involving major security interests of the United States, the Congress basically maintains cooperation with the Executive, but it is more "subtle" than the Executive. In most cases, Congress is more concerned with the U.S. national interests rather than other countries' responses. For example, in 1992, Congress enacted legislation to impose new sanctions and controlled measures against Iran, Iraq, and other countries that assisted in acquiring mass destruction weapons. In the field of economy and trade, Congress functions mainly according to the clear-cut authorization of the Constitution and the characteristics of trade policy. Compared with security policy, the making of trade policy and even the implementation of the trade policy, to a large degree, are areas where Congress can intervene.

Congress also has a significant impact on U.S China policy. Back to the founding of the PRC, Congress was deeply involved in U.S. China policy-making. Conservative forces in Congress, mainly Republican members, advocated offering military and economic aids to the Kuomintang regime, and demanded the defense of Taiwan, while denying the legitimacy of the PRC government.[10] After the establishment of diplomatic ties between China and the United States in

1979, the Senate and the House of Representatives passed the *Taiwan Relations Act* in a short time, seeking to express dissatisfaction with the Carter administration's secret negotiations with China on the establishment of diplomatic relations, and advocating the protection of Taiwan's interests.[11] History has proved that the *Taiwan Relations Act*, which was initiated by the U.S. Congress, has become a major impediment to the sound and steady development of China-U.S. relations.

With Congressional support, the relations between the United States and Taiwan has been strengthened since the establishment of diplomatic ties between China and the United States. For example, in The Arms Sales Communiqué of 17 August 1982, the United States officially promised to reduce arms sales to Taiwan, and promoted a gradual final settlement. Due to the support and interference of conservatives and pro-Taiwan factions in the United States, however, the issue of U.S. arms sales to Taiwan has not been solved. In fact, it has tended towards an intensified status. The Arms sales to Taiwan have become a "master card" of the United States to alienate cross-strait relations and contain China. Another example is the establishment of the "Congressional Taiwan Caucus" in April 2002, which provides a brand-new official guarantee for the further development of U.S.-Taiwan relations. After the Trump administration came to power, both houses of Congress passed the "U.S.-Taiwan Travel Act" in March 2018 to promote high-level exchanges between the United States and Taiwan. The bill grossly violates the one-China principle and the provisions of the Three China-US Joint Communiqués, and wantonly interferes with China's internal affairs, which has become a strategic tool to contain China, bringing instability and uncertainty to China-U.S. relations. As a result of its long-term intervention in the Taiwan issue, the U.S. Congress acts as a "trouble maker" in China-U.S. relations, while upholding itself as a "protector and defender" of U.S.-Taiwan relations.[12]

Moreover, Congress has frequently intervened and exerted pressure on issues concerning China, such as the Tibet issue, trade policy, human rights, technology export control, Hong Kong, and other Chinese affairs, creating turmoil in China's stable political and economic development. The hostile actions of the U.S. Congress have severely affected China-U.S. relations and even left a negative impression on the Chinese public of the Congressional backtracking on China-U.S. relations. Congress plays a vital role in U.S.-China policy to the point that some Chinese scholars emphasize "if one doesn't know Congress, he will neither understand American society, nor American federalism and what makes America, in the end he will lose the vision of China-U.S. relations."[13]

In addition to the abovementioned issues, Congress also actively engages in the SCS dispute. Especially when tensions in the SCS area have been rising sharply in recent years, Congress began to frequently involve through the introduction of bills, holding hearings, and reviewing reports, as well as Congressmen's speeches, statements, and letters.[14] Furthermore, Congress influences the policy direction of executive authorities in the SCS through legislation and oversight, acting as a "political operator" to propel the U.S. government and the military to intervene in the SCS issue. Meanwhile, the personal opinions of Congressmen on the SCS issue will be directly submitted to government officials or transmitted to news media; in this way, it places public and political pressure on the policy-making departments. As some scholars point out, if the U.S. Congress is the "engine" to drive the U.S. government's involvement in the SCS issue, then the stance of Congress and its Members is a "barometer" to demonstrate the U.S. government's SCS policy.[15] Given the importance of Congress in American foreign policy-making, China-U.S. relations, and the SCS issue, it shouldn't be overlooked when studying the SCS dispute, especially the American involvement in the SCS issue.

The Legislations

The basic and main function of Congress as the legislature is to enact legislation. There are four categories of legislation: bill, joint resolution, concurrent resolution, and resolution. If a bill introduced by the Senate or the House of Representatives is passed by both houses of Congress, then it is presented to the President for signing. The President can sign it into law, or veto it by returning it to Congress within 10 days. If the Bill is vetoed by the President, the Congress can override the President's veto by not less than two thirds of the votes, and then the Bill becomes Law. It is the same with joint resolutions. While the concurrent resolutions and the resolutions only represent the opinion and position of Congress, and do not need to be signed by the President, thus having no legal effect, they create additional pressure through the news media and other channels.

Congress begins to enact legislation concerning the SCS issue after the Cold War, and is directly involved through legislative intervention. By searching the key words "SCS" in the "legislation" section of the U.S. Congress website, beginning on March 10, 1995, Republican representative Benjamin A. Gilman first introduced a resolution on the SCS issue in the 104th Congress. As of December 31, 2020, the Congress has introduced a total of 67 bills (see Table 6.1), including

Table 6.1. Bills on the SCS issue introduced by U.S. Congress (Up till Dec.31, 2020)

No.	Number and theme	Time of first introduction	Congress	Primary proposer	Political party
1	H.Res.114, Expressing the Sense of House of Representatives that the United States should Support Peace and Stability in the SCS	Mar.10, 1995	104	Benjamin Gilman	Republican Party
2	S.Res.97, A Resolution Expressing the Sense of the Senate with Respect to Peace and Stability in the SCS	Mar.30, 1995	104	Craig Thomas	Republican Party
3	H.R.1563, To Authorize Appropriations for Foreign Assistance Programs, and for other Purposes	May.3, 1995	104	Benjamin Gilman	Republican Party
4	H.R.2053, United States-China Policy Act of 1995	July.18, 1995	104	Doug Bereuter	Republican Party
5	H.R.2058, United States-China Policy Act of 1995	July.19, 1995	104	Doug Bereuter	Republican Party
6	H.R.3684, To prohibit the importation into the United States of goods produced, manufactured, or exported by the People's Liberation Army of China or any Chinese defense industrial trading company	June.20, 1996	104	Benjamin Gilman	Republican Party
7	H.Res.461, Regarding U.S. concerns with human rights abuse, nuclear and chemical weapons proliferation, illegal weapons trading, military intimidation of Taiwan, and trade violations by the People's Republic of China and the People's Liberation Army, and directing the committees of jurisdiction to commence hearings and report appropriate legislation	June.25, 1996	104	Christopher Cox	Republican Party

No.	Number and theme	Time of first introduction	Congress	Primary proposer	Political party
8	H.R.1119, National Defense Authorization Act for Fiscal Year 1998	Mar.19, 1997	105	Floyd Spence	Republican Party
9	H.Res.103, Expressing the sense of the House of Representatives that the United States should maintain approximately 100,000 United States military personnel in the Asia and Pacific region until such time as there is a peaceful and permanent resolution to the major security and political conflicts in the region	Mar.20, 1997	105	Doug Bereuter	Republican Party
10	H.R.2188, To Ensure Commercial Activities of People's Liberation Army of China or any Communist Chinese Military Company are not Extended Normal Tariff Treatment by the United States or Treated as Normal Commercial Intercourse with the United States	July.1, 1997	105	Tillie Fowler	Republican Party
11	S. 1083, United States-People's Republic of China National Security and Freedom Protection Act of 1997	July.29, 1997	105	Connie Mack, III	Republican Party
12	H.R.2580, To Ensure Commercial Activities of People's Liberation Army of China and Communist Chinese Military Company are Under Supervision and Management of "International Emergency Economic Powers Act" Act	Sept.30, 1997	105	Tillie Fowler	Republican Party

Continued

Table 6.1. *Continued*

No.	Number and theme	Time of first introduction	Congress	Primary proposer	Political party
13	H.R.2647, To Ensure Commercial Activities of People's Liberation Army of China and Communist Chinese Military Company are Under Supervision and Management of "International Emergency Economic Powers Act" Act	Oct.9, 1997	105	Tillie Fowler	Republican Party
14	S.Res.66, A resolution expressing the sense of the Senate regarding the release of 24 United States military personnel currently being detained by the People's Republic of China.	Apr.5, 2001	107	Craig Thomas	Republican Party
15	S.Res.217, A Resolution Calling for a Peaceful and Multilateral Resolution to Maritime Territorial Disputes in Southeast Asia	June.27, 2011	112	Jim Webb	Democratic Party
16	H.Res.352, Calling for a Peaceful and Collaborative Resolution of Maritime Territorial Disputes in the SCS and its Environs and other Maritime Areas Adjacent to the East Asia Mainland	July.15, 2011	112	Ileana Ros-Lehinen	Republican Party
17	H.Res.616, Expressing the sense of the House of Representatives regarding United States relations with the People's Republic of China	Apr.16, 2012	112	Randy Forbes	Republican Party

18	S.Res.524, A Resolution Reaffirming the Strong Support of the United States for the 2002 Declaration on Conduct of Parties in the SCS Among the Member States of ASEAN and the People's Republic of China, and for other Purposes	July.23, 2012	112	John Kerry	Democratic Party
19	H.R.631, To promote peaceful and collaborative resolution of maritime territorial disputes in the SCS and its environs and other maritime areas adjacent to the East Asian mainland	Aug.2, 2012	112	Eni F. Faleomavaega	Democratic Party
20	H.R.772, To promote peaceful and collaborative resolution of the SCS dispute	Feb.5, 2013	113	Eni F. Faleomavaega	Democratic Party
21	S.Res.167, A Resolution of Reaffirming the Strong Support of the United States for the Peaceful Resolution of Territorial, Sovereignty, and Jurisdictional Disputes in the Asia-Pacific Maritime Domains	June.10, 2013	113	Robert Menendez	Democratic Party
22	H.R.3979, Carl Levin and Howard P. "Buck" McKeon National Defense Authorization Act for Fiscal Year 2015	Jan.13, 2014	113	Louis James Barletta	Republican Party

Continued

Table 6.1. *Continued*

No.	Number and theme	Time of first introduction	Congress	Primary proposer	Political party
23	S.Res.412, A resolution reaffirming the strong support of the United States government for freedom of navigation and other internationally lawful uses of sea and airspace in the Asia-Pacific region, and for the peaceful diplomatic resolution of outstanding territorial and maritime claims and disputes	Apr.7, 2014	113	Robert Menendez	Democratic Party
24	H.R.4495, Asia-Pacific Region Priority Act	Apr.28, 2014	113	Randy Forbes	Republican Party
25	H.Res.704, Reaffirming the strong support of the United States government for freedom of navigation and other internationally lawful uses of sea and airspace in the Asia-Pacific region, and for the peaceful diplomatic resolution of outstanding territorial and maritime claims and disputes	July.31, 2014	113	Randy Forbes	Republican Party
26	H.Res.714, To reaffirm the strong support of the United States government for the peaceful and collaborative resolution of maritime and jurisdictional disputes in the SCS and the East China Sea as provided for by universally recognized principles of international law, and to reaffirm the vital interest of the United States in freedom of navigation and other internationally lawful uses of sea and airspace in the Asia-Pacific region	Sept.8, 2014	113	Eni F. Faleomavaega	Democratic Party

27	S. 1356, National Defense Authorization Act for Fiscal Year 2016	May.14, 2015	114	Johnson Ron	Republican Party
28	S.Res.183, A Resolution Calling for Suspension of Construction of Artificial Land Formations on Islands, Reefs, shoals, and other Features of the Spratly Islands and for a Peaceful and Multilateral Resolution to the SCS Territorial Dispute	May.21, 2015	114	Brian Schatz	Democratic Party
29	S. 1635, Department of State Authorities Act and Embassy Security of Fiscal Year 2016	June.18, 2015	114	Bob Corker	Republican Party
30	S. 1705, Intelligence Authorization Act for Fiscal Year 2016	July.7, 2015	114	Richard Burr	Republican Party
31	H.Res.631, Calling upon the United States Senate to give its advice and consent to the ratification of the United Nations Convention on the Law of the Sea	Mar.1, 2016	114	Joe Courtney	Democratic Party
32	H.R.4909, National Defense Authorization Act for Fiscal Year 2017	Apr.12, 2016	114	Mac Thornberry	Republican Party
33	S. 2865, Asia-Pacific Maritime Security Initiative Act of 2016	Apr.27, 2016	114	Benjamin Cardin	Democratic Party
34	S. 2943, National Defense Authorization Act for Fiscal Year 2017	May.18, 2016	114	John McCain	Republican Party

Continued

Table 6.1. *Continued*

No.	Number and theme	Time of first introduction	Congress	Primary proposer	Political party
35	S.Res.526, A resolution calling for all parties to respect the arbitral tribunal ruling with regard to the SCS and to express United States policy on freedom of navigation and overflight in the East and SCSs	July.12, 2016	114	Cory Gardner	Republican Party
36	H.Res.830, Calling for all parties to respect the arbitral tribunal ruling with regard to the SCS and to express United States policy on freedom of navigation and overflight in the East and SCSs	July.13, 2016	114	Mike Pompeo	Republican Party
37	H.R.5890, Asia-Pacific Maritime Security Initiative Act of 2016	July.15, 2016	114	Matt Salmon	Republican Party
38	S. 3509, SCS and East China Sea Sanctions Act of 2016	Dec.6, 2016	114	Marco Rubio	Republican Party
39	S. 659, SCS and East China Sea Sanctions Act of 2017	Mar.15, 2017	115	Marco Rubio	Republican Party
40	H.R.2176, Asia-Pacific Defense Commission Act	Apr.26, 2017	115	Stephanie Murphy	Democratic Party
41	H.Res.311, Reaffirming the 40 years of relations between the United States and the Association of Southeast Asian Nations (ASEAN), and the shared pursuit of economic growth and regional security in Southeast Asia	May.3, 2017	115	Joaquin Castro	Democratic Party

42	S.Res.157, A resolution recognizing that for 50 years, the Association of South East Asian Nations (ASEAN) and its 10 members–Brunei, Cambodia, Indonesia, Laos, Malaysia, Myanmar, the Philippines, Singapore, Thailand, and Vietnam–have worked toward stability, prosperity, and peace in Southeast Asia	May.4, 2017	115	Benjamin Cardin	Democratic Party
43	H.Res.339, Calling upon the United States Senate to give its advice and consent to the ratification of the United Nations Convention on the Law of the Sea	May.18, 2017	115	Joe Courtney	Democratic Party
44	H.R.2621, Strengthening Security in the Indo-Asia-Pacific Act	May.24, 2017	115	Mac Thornberry	Republican Party
45	S. 1519, National Defense Authorization Act for Fiscal Year 2018	July.10, 2017	115	John McCain	Republican Party
46	H.R.5515, John S. McCain National Defense Authorization Act for Fiscal Year 2019	Apr.13, 2018	115	Mac Thornberry	Republican Party
47	S. 2736, Asia Reassurance Initiative Act of 2018	Apr.24, 2018	115	Cory Gardner	Republican Party
48	S. 2987, John S. McCain National Defense Authorization Act for Fiscal Year 2019	June.5, 2018	115	James Inhofe	Republican Party
49	H.Res.998, Resolution on U.S. Navy	July.16, 2018	115	Robert Wittman	Republican Party
50	H.R.6828, Strategy for Engagement with Southeast Asia	Sept.13, 2018	115	Ann Wagner	Republican Party

Continued

Table 6.1. *Continued*

No.	Number and theme	Time of first introduction	Congress	Primary proposer	Political party
51	H.R.6888, Asia Reassurance Initiative Act of 2018	Sept.25, 2018	115	Kevin McCarthy	Republican Party
52	H.Res.99, Expressing the sense of the House of Representatives that there is a need to rebuild the Navy and ensure that it is prepared to engage with adversaries around the world through an increased investment in the United States naval power	Feb.5, 2019	116	Jim Banks	Republican
53	H.R.1632, Southeast Asia Strategy Act	Mar.7, 2019	116	Ann Wagner	Republican
54	S. 987, U.S.-China Economic and Security Review Act of 2019	Apr.2, 2019	116	Christopher A. Coons	Democratic
55	H.R.2565, U.S.-China Economic and Security Review Act of 2019	May 7, 2019	116	Brad Sherman	Democratic
56	S. 1634, South China Sea and East China Sea Sanctions Act of 2019	May 23, 2019	116	Marco Rubio	Republican
57	H.Res.454, Calling upon the United States Senate to give its advice and consent to the ratification of the United Nations Convention on the Law of the Sea	June 20, 2019	116	Joe Courtney	Democratic
58	H.R.3508, South China Sea and East China Sea Sanctions Act of 2019	June 26, 2019	116	Mike Gallagher	Republican

59	S.Res.284, A resolution calling upon the United States Senate to give its advice and consent to the ratification of the United Nations Convention on the Law of the Sea	July 25, 2019	116	Mazie K. Hirono	Democratic
60	S.Res.406, A resolution recognizing that for 50 years, the Association of South East Asian Nations (ASEAN) and its 10 members, Brunei, Cambodia, Indonesia, Laos, Malaysia, Myanmar, the Philippines, Singapore, Thailand, and Vietnam, have worked with the United States toward stability, prosperity, and peace in Southeast Asia, and expressing the sense of the Senate that the United States will continue to remain a strong, reliable, and active partner in the ASEAN region	Nov.5, 2019	116	Robert Menendez	Democratic
61	S.Res.607, A resolution recognizing that in the 25 years since normalizing diplomatic relations, the Socialist Republic of Vietnam and the United States of America have worked toward increased stability, prosperity, and peace in Southeast Asia, and expressing the sense of the Senate that the United States will continue to remain a strong, reliable, and active partner in the Southeast Asian region	June 4, 2020	116	Cory Gardner	Republican

Continued

Table 6.1. *Continued*

No.	Number and theme	Time of first introduction	Congress	Primary proposer	Political party
62	H.Res.1018, Recognizing that in the 25 years since normalizing diplomatic relations, the Socialist Republic of Vietnam and the United States of America have worked toward increased stability, prosperity, and peace in Southeast Asia, and expressing the sense of the House of Representatives that the United States will continue to remain a strong, reliable, and active partner in the Southeast Asian region	June 24, 2020	116	Ted S. Yoho	Republican
63	H.R.7675, South China Sea Freedom of Navigation Act	July 20, 2020	116	Anthony Brindisi	Democratic
64	S. 4272, STRATEGIC Act	July 22, 2020	116	James E. Risch	Republican
65	H.R.7982, PUSHBACK Act	Aug.7, 2020	116	Scott Perry	Republican
66	S. 4629, America LEADS Act	Sep.17, 2020	116	Robert Menendez	Democratic
67	H.Con.Res.121, Recognizing the People's Republic of China as the greatest foreign threat to United States peace, security, and stability	Oct.20, 2020	116	Andy Biggs	Republican

Source: The U.S. Congress website: https://www.congress.gov/

Note: Bills introduced by the Senate are prefixed with S.; bills introduced by the House of Representatives are prefixed with H.R.; simple resolutions introduced by the Senate are prefixed with S. Res.; and simple resolutions introduced by the House of Representatives are prefixed with H.Res..

39 bills, 27 resolutions, and 1 concurrent resolution. It should be noted that some of the bills are directly related to the SCS issue, while some do not have the word "SCS" in the theme, but their contents are related to the SCS issue anyway, such as the Defense Authorization Act in some fiscal years. Therefore, such Bills are also counted as legislative activities concerning the SCS issue.

Due to the influence of the internal operation mechanism of both houses of Congress, party attributes, and external environment, some bills have been introduced repeatedly by a representative, such as the United States-China Policy Act of 1995 (H.R.2053, H.R.2058) introduced by a Republican representative Doug Bereuter in the 104th Congress, and Calling upon the United States Senate to give its advice and consent to the ratification of the UNCLOS (H.Res.631,H.Res.339) introduced by a Democratic representative Joe Courtney in the 114th and 115th Congresses. Meanwhile, some legislative proposals with the same theme and content have been introduced, respectively, by two representatives. For example, Reaffirming the strong support of the United States government for freedom of navigation and other internationally lawful uses of sea and airspace in the Asia-Pacific region, and for the peaceful diplomatic resolution of outstanding territorial and maritime claims and disputes (H.Res.704) introduced by a Democratic representative Robert Menendez in 113th Congress, was reintroduced by a Republican representative Randy Forbes. Another example is Asia Reassurance Initiative Act of 2018 (S. 2736), which is respectively proposed in the Senate and the House of Representatives at 115th Congress by two Republican representatives, Cory Gardner and Kevin McCarthy. Considering the different timing and process, the "repeated" proposals mentioned above are recorded as two legislative activities.

From the perspective of the theme and content, bills concerning the SCS issue can be classified as follows (see Table 6.2). The legislation about "China-U.S. relations" takes the largest proportion, with 16 items in total, followed by "Asia-Pacific Maritime Security" (12 items), "national defense and military authorization" (11 items), "SCS stability" (10 items), "cooperative settlement of disputes" (6 items), "freedom of navigation" (6 items), "sanctions against China" (2 items), and "others" (4 items). The table also illustrates that there are 40 items introduced by the House of Representatives and 27 items introduced by the Senate; 47 items are introduced by the Republican Party, and 20 items are introduced by the Democratic Party, and this is also consistent with the long-standing Republican value of emphasis on defense and security.

Table 6.2. U.S. Congress bills concerning the SCS issue from 1995 to 2020

Theme	Amount	Republican proposal	Democratic proposal	The Senate	The House of Representatives	Bill	Resolution	Law
China-U.S. relations	16	13	3	4	12	12	4	0
Asia- Pacific Maritime Security	12	8	4	3	9	10	2	1
National defense and military authorization	11	11	0	6	5	10	1	6
SCS stability	10	5	5	5	5	3	7	2
Cooperative settlement of disputes	6	1	5	3	3	2	4	0
Freedom of navigation	6	3	3	2	4	1	5	0
Sanctions against China	2	2	0	2	0	2	0	0
Others	4	3	1	1	3	2	2	0
Total	67	47	20	27	40	42	25	9

Source: The U.S. Congress website: https://www.congress.gov/

Holding Hearings

Hearing is a way to exercise oversight, as well as an important means for Congressional intervention in diplomatic issue. By inviting witnesses from government departments and professional fields, Congress has a better understanding of the current situation and makes its strategic position clear to the public, while the message coming from Congress is of great value to the Executive as well. In recent years, tensions are on the rise and China-U.S. interacts intensively, the SCS issue naturally becomes a "hot topic" when it comes to the Asia-Pacific region and China-U.S. relations. Thus, Congress frequently invited the witnesses from the DoS, the DoD, universities, think tanks, and other institutions to the hearings on the SCS issue, which demonstrates its concern over the issue as well as its "expectations" on the SCS Policy formulated and implemented by the executive department.

The hearings on the SCS issue are mainly held by the Committee on Foreign Affairs and the Committee on Armed Services. By searching the "hearings" on the Foreign Affairs Committee website and the Armed Services Committee website, it is found that by the end of 2020, Congress has held 63 hearings on the SCS issue, including 34 in the Senate (see Table 6.3) and 29 in the House of Representatives (see Table 6.4). It should be noted that some of the hearings directly refer to the SCS issue, and some do not refer to "SCS" on the theme, but the contents are still related to the issue, such as the Hearings on the U.S. Asia-Pacific policy, U.S.-China relations, China's rise, etc., in which witnesses delivered speeches or made inquiries on the SCS issue, thus those should also be counted as hearings related to the SCS issue.

In terms of theme and content, the hearings on the SCS issue held by both Houses of Congress mainly involve the situation evaluation in different periods, the interests of the United States in the SCS, security and challenges in the Asia-Pacific region, American Asia-Pacific policy and the SCS dispute, the relationship between the United States and ASEAN countries, the U.S. Alliance System in the Asia Pacific and the SCS dispute, the impact of the SCS issue on the United States, the SCS dispute, and U.S.-China relations. Generally, most of the hearings are specialized consultations and policy assessments on the development of the SCS and the Asia-Pacific region, and the speeches made on the hearing are mostly focused on criticizing, preventing, and boycotting China's policies and behaviors in the SCS. For example, Congress made a quick response shortly after the USNS Impeccable incident in March 2009. On July 15, the 111th Senate Committee on Foreign Affairs held a hearing on "maritime disputes and

Table 6.3. U.S. Senate Hearings on the SCS Issue (Up to Dec.31, 2020)

No.	Topic	Time	Congress	Committee	Witness
1	Maritime Disputes and Sovereignty Issues in East Asia	July.15, 2009	111	Foreign Relations	Scot Marciel, Robert Scher, Peter Dutton, Daniel Blumenthal, Richard Cronin
2	Maritime Territorial Disputes and Sovereignty Issues in Asia	Sept.20, 2012	112	Foreign Relations	Kurt Campbell
3	U.S. Pacific Command and U.S. Forces Korea	Apr.9, 2013	113	Armed Services	Samuel J. Locklear
4	Rebalance to Asia II: Security and Defense: Cooperation and Challenges	Apr.25, 2013	113	Foreign Relations	Joseph Y. Yun, David F. Helvey, Janine Davidson, Michael J. Green
5	U.S. Pacific Command and U.S. Forces Korea	Mar.25, 2014	113	Armed Services	Samuel J. Locklear
6	National Security & Foreign Policy Priorities in the FY 2015 International Affairs Budget	Apr.8, 2014	113	Foreign Relations	John F. Kerry
7	The Future of U.S.-China relations	June.25, 2014	113	Foreign Relations	Daniel R. Russel

No.	Topic	Time	Congress	Committee	Witness
8	Global Challenges and U.S. National Security Strategy	Jan.27, 2015	114	Armed Services	James N. Mattis, John M. Keane, William J. Fallon
9	Global Challenges and U.S. National Security Strategy	Feb.10, 2015	114	Armed Services	Eric S. Edelman, Michèle A. Flournoy
10	U.S. defense policy related to Asia Pacific	Apr.14, 2015	114	Armed Services	Graham T. Allison, Kurt M. Campbell, Michael J. Green, Gary Roughead
11	United States Pacific Command and United States Forces Korea	Apr.16, 2015	114	Armed Services	Samuel J. Locklear, Curtis M. Scaparrotti
12	Safeguarding American Interests in the East and SCSs	May.13, 2015	114	Foreign Relations	Daniel R. Russel, David B. Shear
13	Department of Defense Maritime Activities and Engagement in the SCS	July 8, 2015	114	Foreign Relations	Daniel R. Russel, David B. Shear
14	Maritime Security Strategy in the Asia-Pacific Region	Sept.17, 2015	114	Armed Services	Harry B. Harris, David B. Shear
15	The Changing Landscape of U.S.-China Relations: What's Next?	Sept.29, 2015	114	Foreign Relations	Christopher Johnson, Melanie Hart

Continued

Table 6.3. *Continued*

No.	Topic	Time	Congress	Committee	Witness
16	U.S. Pacific Command and U.S. Forces Korea	Feb.23, 2016	114	Armed Services	Harry B. Harris
17	U.S.-China Relations: Strategic Challenges and Opportunities	Apr.27, 2016	114	Foreign Relations	Antony J. Blinken
18	U.S. Policy Options in the SCS	July13, 2016	114	Foreign Relations	Dennis C. Blair, Kurt M. Campbell
19	American Leadership in the Asia Pacific, Part 1: Security Issues	Mar.29, 2017	115	Foreign Relations	Randy Forbes, Robert L. Gallucci
20	Policy and Strategy in the Asia Pacific	Apr.25, 2017	115	Armed Services	Aaron L. Friedberg, Kelly E. Magsamen, Ashley J. Tellis
21	United States Pacific Command and United States Forces Korea	Apr.27, 2017	115	Armed Services	Harry B. Harris
22	American Leadership in the Asia Pacific, Part 4: View from Beijing	Nov.14, 2017	115	Foreign Relations	Michael Pillsbury, Graham Allison, Max Baucus
23	Global Challenges and U.S. National Security Strategy	Jan.25, 2018	115	Armed Services	Henry A. Kissinger, George P. Shultz, Richard L. Armitage

24	American Leadership in the Asia Pacific, Part 5: "The Asia Reassurance Initiative Act"	May.15, 2018	115	Foreign Relations	Randall G. Schriver, Alex N. Wong
25	The China Challenge, Part 2: Security and Military Developments	Sept.5, 2018	115	Foreign Relations	Oriana Skylar Mastro, Abraham M. Denmark
26	Recent Chinese and Russian Naval Activities	Dec.11, 2018	115	Armed Services	Matthew J. Kohler, Lori E. Reynolds
27	U.S. Force Posture in the Indo-Pacific Region	Dec.12, 2018	115	Armed Services	James H. Anderson, Brian D. Beaudreault, Tracy King
28	China and Russia	January 29, 2019	116	Armed Services	Elbridge Colby, Ely Ratner, Damon M. Wilson
29	United States Indo-Pacific Command and United States Forces Korea	February 12, 2019	116	Armed Services	Philip S. Davidson, Robert B. Abrams
30	A New Approach for an Era of U.S.-China Competition	March 13, 2019	116	Foreign Relations	James M. Talent, Oriana Mastro, Gloria D. Steele

Continued

Table 6.3. *Continued*

No.	Topic	Time	Congress	Committee	Witness
31	ARIA In Action, Part 3: Implementation and the Indo-Pacific Strategy	October 16, 2019	116	Foreign Relations	David R. Stilwell, Randall G. Schriver
32	U.S. Policy in the Indo-Pacific Region: Hong Kong, Alliances and Partnerships, and Other Issues	September 18, 2019	116	Foreign Relations	David Stilwell
33	Advancing Effective U.S. Competition with China: Objectives, Priorities, and Next Steps	July 22, 2020	116	Foreign Relations	Stephen E. Biegun
34	Advancing U.S. Engagement and Countering China in the Indo-Pacific and Beyond	September 17, 2020	116	Foreign Relations	Julie J. Chung, Philip T. Reeker, David R. Stilwell

Source: The U.S. Senate Committee on Foreign Affairs website:
https://www.foreign.senate.gov/hearings
The U.S. Senate Committee on Armed Services website:
https://www.armed-services.senate.gov/hearings

Note: Data from the U.S. Senate Committee on Foreign Affairs website can be retrieved from 2003; data from the U.S. Senate Committee on Armed Services website can be retrieved from 2001.

Table 6.4. U.S. House of Representatives Hearings on the SCS Issue (Up to Dec.31, 2020)

No.	Topic	Time	Congress	Committee	Witness
1	Regional Overview of East Asia and the Pacific	Mar.3, 2010	111	Foreign Affairs	Kurt M. Campbell
2	The U.S.-Philippines Alliance: Deepening the Security and Trade Partnership	Feb.7, 2012	112	Foreign Affairs	Kurt Campbell, Peter Lavoy
3	Beijing as an Emerging Power in the SCS	Sept.12, 2012	112	Foreign Affairs	Toshi Yoshihara, Bonnie Glaser, Peter Brookes, Richard Cronin
4	U.S. Relations with Vietnam	June 5, 2013	113	Foreign Affairs	Joseph Y. Yun, Daniel B. Baer
5	China's Maritime and other Geographic Threats	Oct.30, 2013	113	Foreign Affairs	Perry Pickert, Rick Fisher, Steven Mosher, Peter Sandby-Thomas
6	Maritime Sovereignty in the East and SCSs	Jan.14, 2014	113	Foreign Affairs	Bonnie S. Glaser, Peter Dutton, Jeff M. Smith
7	America's Future in Asia: From Rebalancing to Managing Sovereignty Disputes	Feb.3, 2014	113	Foreign Affairs	Daniel R. Russel

Continued

Table 6.4. *Continued*

No.	Topic	Time	Congress	Committee	Witness
8	Resourcing the Pivot to Asia: East Asia and Pacific FY 2015 Budget Priorities	May 20, 2014	113	Foreign Affairs	Daniel R. Russel, Denise Rollins
9	A New Era of U.S.-China Relations?	Sept.17, 2014	113	Foreign Affairs	Christopher K. Johnson, Gordon Chang
10	Across the Other Pond: U.S. Opportunities and Challenges in the Asia Pacific	Feb.26, 2015	114	Foreign Affairs	Karl D. Jackson, Van Jackson, Matthew P. Goodman, Abraham M. Denmark, Patrick Mulloy
11	The U.S. Rebalance in East Asia: Budget Priorities for FY 2016	Apr.23, 2015	114	Foreign Affairs	Daniel R. Russel, Jonathan Stivers
12	China's Rise: The Strategic Impact of Its Economic and Military Growth	June 17, 2015	114	Foreign Affairs	Jerome A. Cohen, Han Dongfang, Adam Hersh, Alison Kaufman, Derek M. Scissors
13	U.S. Economic and Military Alliances in Asia	July 15, 2015	114	Foreign Affairs	Balbina Hwang, Walter Lohman, James L. Schoff, Randall Schriver

14	America's Security Role in the SCS	July 23, 2015	114	Foreign Affairs	Patrick M. Cronin, Andrew S. Erickson, Mira Rapp Hooper, Michael D. Swaine
15	U.S. Strategic Interests and the APEC and East Asia Summits	Dec.2, 2015	114	Foreign Affairs	Michael H. Fuchs, Bruce Hirsh
16	FY 2017 Budget Priorities for East Asia: Engagement, Integration, and Democracy	Apr.19, 2016	114	Foreign Affairs	Daniel R. Russel, Jonathan Stivers
17	SCS Maritime Disputes	July 7, 2016	114	Foreign Affairs	Abraham Denmark, Colin Willett
18	Diplomacy and Security in the SCS: After the Tribunal	Sept.22, 2016	114	Foreign Affairs	Dean Cheng, Elbridge Colby, Amitai Etzioni, Amy Searight
19	Step or Stumble: The Obama Administration's Pivot to Asia	Dec.6, 2016	114	Foreign Affairs	Kelley Currie, Richard J. Ellings, Barry C. Lynn, Derek M. Scissors
20	Checking China's Maritime Push	Feb.28, 2017	115	Foreign Affairs	Michael Auslin, Dean Cheng, Michael D. Swaine
21	Military Assessment of the Security Challenges in the Indo-Asia-Pacific Region Files	Apr.26, 2017	115	Armed Services	Harry Harris

Continued

Table 6.4. *Continued*

No.	Topic	Time	Congress	Committee	Witness
22	Revitalizing U.S.-ASEAN Relations	May17, 2017	115	Foreign Affairs	Zachary M. Abuza, Walter Lohman, Amy Searight
23	U.S. Interests in the Asia Pacific: FY 2018 Budget Hearing	July 27, 2017	115	Foreign Affairs	Gloria Steele, Susan Thornton
24	The Military and Security Challenges and Posture in the Indo-Pacific Region	Feb.14, 2018	115	Armed Services	Harry Harris
25	Asia's Diplomatic and Security Structure: Planning U.S. Engagement	May 23, 2018	115	Foreign Affairs	Aparna Pande, Amy Searight, Michael D. Swaine
26	The Fiscal Year 2020 National Defense Budget Request from the Department of Defense	March 26, 2019	116	Armed Services	Patrick M. Shanahan, Joseph F. Dunford
27	National Security Challenges and U.S. Military Activities in the Indo-Pacific	March 27, 2019	116	Armed Services	Philip S. Davidson, Robert B. Abrams, Randall G. Schriver

28	Smart Competition: Adapting U.S. Strategy Toward China at 40 Years	May 8, 2019	116	Foreign Affairs	Elizabeth Economy, Samm Sacks, Kelly Magsamen, Aaron Friedberg
29	China's Maritime Ambitions	June 30, 2020	116	Foreign Affairs	Gregory B. Poling, Oriana Skylar Mastro, Andrew S. Erickson

Source: House Committee on Foreign Affairs website:

https://foreignaffairs.house.gov/hearings

House Committee on Armed Services website:

https://armedservices.house.gov/hearings

Note: Data from the U.S. House Committee on Foreign Affairs website can be retrieved from 2006 and that of the Armed Services is from 2016.

sovereignty in East Asia" presided by Senator Jim Webb, who urged the U.S. government to help countries in the region, including Vietnam and the Philippines, to confront what he saw as China's aggressive and intimidating actions in the SCS.[16] On September 12, 2012, the 112th House of Representatives held a hearing entitled "Beijing as an Emerging Power in the SCS," Ileana Ros-Lehinen, chairman of the Committee on Foreign Affairs, stressed that the U.S. Navy shall continue to maintain peace in the waters in the Pacific, including the SCS. China's aggressive and intimidating actions in the SCS had increased the possibility of conflicts in the SCS, therefore it was necessary for the United States to respond to the threats and challenges posed by the Chinese Navy to U.S. Navy strategy.[17]

Since then, Congress has also declared its position as to China's island and reef construction in the SCS and its impact on regional order. On July 23, 2015, at the hearing entitled "America's Security Role in the SCS" held by the House Committee on Foreign Affairs presided by Scott Perry, he criticized China's construction on islands and reefs in the SCS, believing that China had deliberately concealed its real intentions, especially military purposes. China's actions threatened regional and global security, and the United States needed to respond promptly. At the hearing, Members also expressed their concern that China might establish an ADIZ on the built up islands and reefs in the SCS. The hearing concluded that the United States needs to continue to implement FONOPs in the SCS and respond to China's threat with joint efforts by strengthening the military strength of U.S. alliances.[18] On May 15, 2018, at a hearing entitled "American Leadership In the Asia Pacific, Part 5: The Asia Reassurance Initiative Act," Randall G. Schriver, Assistant Secretary of Defense for Asian and Pacific Security Affairs, also claimed that "China should and does have a voice in shaping the international system, as do all countries. However, in recent years, we have grown concerned by China's strategic intentions and trajectory, including some activities in the region that we view as destabilizing and counterproductive—in the SCS, for example. Although the United States will continue to pursue a constructive, results-oriented relationship with China, we will not accept policies or actions that threaten to undermine the international rules-based order, a system that has benefited everyone in the region, including China. We will stand up for and defend that order, and we will encourage others to do the same; and although we are committed to cooperating with China where our interests align, we will compete, vigorously, where our interests diverge."[19]

Table 6.5. The U.S. China Economic and Security Review Commission Hearings on the SCS Issue from 2002 to 2020

No.	Time	Congress	Topic	Witness
1	Jan.17, 2002	107	Impact of Military and Dual-Use Technology Exports to China	Michael Garcia, Daryl Hatano, Paul Godwin
2	Dec.4, 2003	108	China's Growth as a Regional Economic Power: Impact and Implications for the U.S.	Bates Gill, David I. Steinberg, Martha O. Blaxall
3	Feb.6, 2004	108	China's Military Modernization and the Cross-Strait Balance	Jason E. Bruzdzinski, Lyle J. Goldstein, Richard P. Lawless
4	July 21–22, 2005	109	China's Growing Global Influence: Objectives and Strategies	Charles W. McMillion, Avery Goldstein, Randall G. Schriver
5	Sept.15, 2005	109	China's Military Modernization and Cross-Strait Balance	Joan Johnson-Freese, Roger Cliff, James Keith
6	Mar.16–17, 2006	109	China's Military Modernization and U.S. Export Controls	Jim Kolbe, Mark A. Stokes, Cortez A. Cooper
7	Aug.3–4, 2006	109	China's Role in the World—Is China a Responsible Stakeholder?	Ernest J. Wilson, John Calabrese, Cynthia A. Watson
8	Feb.1–2, 2007	110	The U.S.-China Relationship: Economics and Security in Perspective	Thomas P. Ehrhard, Charles W. Hooper, Kenneth W. Allen
9	Mar.29–30, 2007	110	China's Military Modernization and Its Impact on the United States and the Asia Pacific	Tim Ryan, Cortez A. Cooper, Andrew S. Erickson

Continued

Table 6.5. *Continued*

No.	Time	Congress	Topic	Witness
10	Feb.27, 2008	110	China's Views of Sovereignty and Methods of Access Control	Robert G. Sutter, Peter A. Dutton, Allen R. Carlson
11	Mar.4, 2009	111	China's Military and Security Activities Abroad	Bernard D. Cole, Eric McVadon, Paul J. Smith
12	June 11, 2009	111	The Implications of China's Naval Modernization for the United States	Peter Dutton, Paul S. Giarra, Michael McDevitt
13	Feb.4, 2010	111	China's Activities in Southeast Asia and the Implications for U.S. Interests	Andrew Scobell, Bronson Percival, Richard P. Cronin
14	Jan.27, 2011	112	China's Active Defense Strategy and Its Regional Impact	Oriana Skylar Mastro, Roger Cliff, Cortez A. Cooper
15	Mar.10, 2011	112	China's Narratives Regarding National Security Policy	David M. Lampton, Gilbert Rozman, John S. Park
16	Apr.13, 2011	112	China's Foreign Policy: Challenges and Players	John W. Garver, Richard Weitz, Daniel J. Kritenbrink
17	Jan.26, 2012	112	China's Global Quest for Resources and Implications for the United States	Patrick Cronin, Lyle Goldstein, Tabitha Mallory
18	Feb.7, 2013	113	China's New Leadership and Implications for the United States	James Mulven, Roy D. Kamphaus, David M. Lampton

19	Apr. 4, 2013	113	China's Maritime Disputes in the East and SCSs	Michael McDevitt, Michael Swaine, Peter Dutton
20	Jan.30, 2014	113	China's Military Modernization and Its Implications for the United States	Roger Cliff, David Gompert, Mark Stokes
21	Mar.13, 2014	113	China and the Evolving Security Dynamics in East Asia	Robert Sutter, Bonnie Glaser, Ely Ratner
22	May 13, 2015	114	China's Relations with Southeast Asia	Bonnie Glaser, Mira Rapp Hooper, Patrick Cronin
23	Jan.21, 2016	114	Developments in China's Military Force Projection and Expeditionary Capabilities	David Finkelste, Thomas Bickford, Michael McDevitt
24	Mar.10, 2016	114	China-South Asia Relations	Lisa Curt, James F. Moriar, David Brewster
25	Mar.31, 2016	114	China and the U.S. Rebalance to Asia	David Lampt, Kathleen H. Hicks, Dan Blumenthal
26	Apr.13, 2017	115	Hotspots along China's Maritime Periphery	Christopher D. Yung, James E. Fanell, Robert G. Sutter
27	Jan.25, 2018	115	China's Belt and Road Initiative: Five Years Later	Ely Ratner, Daniel Kliman, Andrew Small

Continued

Table 6.5. *Continued*

No.	Time	Congress	Topic	Witness
28	Feb.15, 2018	115	China's Military Reforms and Modernization: Implications for the United States	Kathleen Hicks, Tate Nurkin, Cortez Cooper
29	Apr.5, 2018	115	China's Relations with U.S. Allies and Partners in Europe and the Asia Pacific	Ankit Pand, Russell Hsiao, Amy Searig
30	June 20, 2019	116	A "World-Class" Military: Assessing China's Global Military Ambitions	Christopher A. Ford, M. Taylor Fravel, Phillip C. Saunders,
31	Sept. 4, 2019	116	U.S.-China Relations in 2019: A Year in Review	Victor Shih, Andrew Polk, Andrew Krepinevich Jr.
32	Feb. 20, 2020	116	China's Military Power Projection and U.S. National Interests	Dennis Blair, Kevin McCauley, Greg Poling
33	June 24, 2020	116	The Chinese View of Strategic Competition with the United States	Barry Naughton, Kristine Lee, Alison Kaufman
34	Sept. 9, 2020	116	U.S.-China Relations in 2020: Enduring Problems and Emerging Challenges	Andrew Scobell, Joel Wuthnow, Bill Hayton

Source: U.S.-China Economic and Security Review Commission website: https://www.uscc.gov/

Note: Considering the large number of witnesses at hearings, only three witnesses are listed in this table.

It should be noted that Congress established the U.S.-China Economic and Security Review Commission (USCC) in October 2000, in order to monitor the impact of China-U.S. trade exchanges on the U.S. economy and security in the context of China's accession to the World Trade Organization (WTO), and held a certain number of annual hearings on economic and security issues. Since 2002, the Commission has also held a number of hearings directly or indirectly related to the SCS issue (see Table 6.5). These Hearings are the main foundation for submission of research reports to Congress, and also an important channel for Congress to intervene in the SCS issue. For example, the USCC held a hearing entitled "China's maritime disputes in the East and SCSs" on April 4, 2013, and the discussions of the hearing later became the main content of the third part of chapter II, "China's maritime disputes," in its Annual Report to Congress 2013.[20]

Requiring Reports

Congress exercises its oversight by requiring the Executive to submit reports of three kinds. The first is the report on specific issues in certain policy areas, such as the annual human rights report submitted by the DoS. The second is to inform Congress of actions that have been or will be taken, such as foreign aid, arms sales, etc. The third is that Congress requires the Executive to submit a report on a policy issue. In fact, the request for reports in itself is a signal from Congress to the Executive that Congress is paying attention to these issues, prompting the Executive to take Congressional tendencies seriously.[21] In recent years, with the aggravation of the SCS situation, Congress has also requested the Executive to submit reports on the SCS issue. These reports include: the report on the SCS issued by the U.S. CRS, the annual report issued by USCC, the annual report on China's military strength issued by the DoD, and other special reports concerning the SCS issue.

CRS Report

The CRS, a component of the Library of Congress, conducts research and analysis for Congress on a broad range of issues on American law, domestic social policy, foreign defense and trade, government and finance, and resource science and industry, with the purpose of "providing timely, objective, and authoritative research and analysis to committees and Members of both the House and Senate, regardless of political party affiliation."[22] The SCS issue among them has also been brought to the attention of CRS.

The CRS issued a research report entitled "Maritime Territorial Disputes in East Asia" on May 14, 2014, which analyzed the situation of maritime disputes in East Asia, including the SCS. It believes that Congress should push the United States to strengthen its military presence in the disputed waters, provide more resource support to Southeast Asian countries, and encourage China and ASEAN to exchange views on the COC in the SCS to reduce regional tensions.[23] In the report "Chinese Land Reclamation in the SCS: Implications and Policy Options" issued on June 18, 2015, CRS also believes that China's construction of islands and reefs in the SCS has impact on diplomacy, law, and military, complicating the diplomatic efforts and legal process to reduce regional tensions, also violating the purpose of DOC in the SCS, and endangering the U.S. Asia-Pacific security strategy.[24] The report entitled "SCS Disputes: Background and U.S. Policy," issued on February 23, 2017, also analyzes the divergence between China and the United States on the issue of freedom of navigation. According to the report, the United States and most countries admit that coastal states have the right to manage economic activities in the EEZ, but have no right to manage freedom of navigation and over flight passing through the EEZ, including warships and military aircraft, while China maintains that the UNCLOS entitles coastal states to regulate economic activities and to oversee the freedom of navigation and over flight of foreign vessels passing through its EEZ.[25]

Later, in the report entitled "Maritime Territorial and Exclusive Economic Zone (EEZ) Disputes Involving China: Issues for Congress" submitted by the CRS on May 24, 2018, it mentions that China's maritime territory and EEZ claims in the South and East China Seas bring the following potential policy and oversight problems to the Congress: whether the United States has enough strategies to respond to China's "salami slicing" strategy, whether appropriate actions have been taken to reduce the risk that the United States may fall into crisis or conflict due to territorial disputes involving China, and whether it should accede to the UNCLOS.[26] In the research report "China Naval Modernization: Implications for U.S. Navy Capabilities—Background and Issues for Congress" released on August 1, it believes that "defending territorial sovereignty in the SCS and controlling the SCS to the maximum extent" is one of the objectives of China's naval modernization. It points out that China's anti-intervention and regional rejection strategy will delay the arrival of U.S. troops and reduce the effectiveness of U.S. military intervention.[27]

On October 3, 2018, the CRS released an evaluation report entitled "The Trump administration's 'Free and Open Indo-Pacific': Issues for Congress." It further points out that the SCS dispute is one of the environment factors for Trump's India Pacific strategy, because China's continuous military modernization and its militarization on artificial islands in the SCS have changed the strategic picture of East Asia, therefore the United States must make a corresponding response.[28] On January 31, 2019, the CRS released another report entitled "China's Actions in South and East China Seas: Implications for U.S. Interests—Background and Issues for Congress." It recommends that the U.S. government should pool enough resources to counter China's "salami slicing" strategy and its behavior of advancing gradually to a dominant position in the "gray zone," hoping these acts will increase the cost of China's actions and ultimately safeguard and enhance the interests of the United States in the region.[29]

USCC Annual Report

The annual report issued by the USCC also covers the SCS issue. Since the first report of USCC was issued in 2002, almost each annual report discusses and evaluates the SCS dispute, except for an unreleased report in 2003 and the report released in 2006.[30] Generally, these reports not only analyze the situation in the SCS and the status quo of disputes, but also offer a regular evaluation on China's military growth and its impact on the situation in the SCS and the Asia-Pacific region. With the rising tension in the SCS since 2009, the U.S. China Economic and Security Review Committee pays more attention to the SCS. In response to China's rise and to meet the needs of China's propaganda, the keynote in the report is used mainly to criticize China's policies and behaviors in the SCS.

The annual report of 2010 claimed that China's assertiveness in the SCS constituted a potential threat to American interests, including the freedom of navigation.[31] In 2011, USCC repeated in its report that China continued a pattern of provocation in disputed waters of the SCS. China's policy in the region appears to be driven by a desire to intimidate rather than cooperate. Many of China's activities in the region may constitute violations of the UNCLOS and the *Declaration on the Conduct of Parties in the SCS*.[32] According to the annual report of 2012, while China's maturing naval forces underpin its confidence and capabilities in the SCS, nonmilitary Chinese actors have been the major players in the disputes. In particular, fishing vessels, civilian maritime law enforcement agencies, energy companies, and local governments in coastal provinces play important roles in establishing and strengthening China's claims.[33] According to the annual report of 2013, two key drivers shape China's approach to its maritime disputes: first, China encourages ardent popular nationalism, which it exploits to support its foreign policy aims in the East and SCSs. Second, China views sovereignty over claims in the East and SCSs as central to its national security, territorial integrity, and economic development.[34] The annual report of 2014 further criticizes that "China moved aggressively in asserting its claims in the SCS, using unilateral and destabilizing actions to advance its territorial ambitions."[35]

In the 2015 annual report, USCC summarizes U.S.-China security relations, stating that they suffered from rising tensions and growing distrust, largely due to China's cyber espionage activities against a range of U.S. government, defense, and commercial entities and its island-building campaign in the SCS. According to the report, the dramatic land reclamation and construction activities on the land features in the Spratly Islands appear to be driven by several factors: China's desire to unilaterally impose its claims and avoid arbitration or negotiation with other parties over the disputes; China's ambition to enhance its ability to project power into the SCS; and, potentially, China's intention to establish an ADIZ over part of the SCS.[36] The 2016 annual report discussed the tribunal in the case regarding China's SCS claims and activities and analyzed China's response in details, concluding that international tribunal ruled overwhelmingly in the Philippines' favor and is a blow to China's credibility.[37] The 2017 annual report claims that "through the year, China tightened its effective control over the SCS by continuing to militarize the artificial islands it occupies there and by pressuring other claimants and regional countries to accept its dominance. It has not been deterred by, and in fact has rejected, the 2016 ruling by the Permanent Court of Arbitration [actually the Tribunal housed in the PCA] in The Hague."[38]

According to the 2018 report, China took new steps to consolidate its military posture and improve its ability to project power into the SCS. Chinese forces are now capable of overpowering any other SCS claimant, challenging U.S. presence operations in the region, and presenting a significant obstacle to the U.S. military during a conflict. China deployed advanced anti-ship and surface-to-air missiles to its Spratly Island outposts for the first time, demonstrating its ability to create a military buffer around the southern reaches of the SCS.[39] The report of 2020 also pointed out that "China employs gray zone operations and paramilitary forces to coerce its neighbors, accomplishing objectives such as seizing territory or restricting maritime access in the South China Sea."[40]

Military and Security Developments Involving the PRC

Pursuant to the "National Defense Authorization Act for Fiscal Year 2000," the U.S. DoD shall submit a report on China's military development each year to provide factual, descriptive, and analytical information to Capitol Hill. The report shall make a comprehensive assessment and analysis of China's military strategy, military resources, military modernization and development trend, military exchanges, military strength situation in the Taiwan Strait, China-U.S. military relations, and China's policies on specific security issues. Since the first report was issued in 2000, it has been published every year, except for 2001. The SCS issue concerning China's sovereignty and security is undoubtedly one of the chief parts of the report.

In terms of word frequency, "the SCS" as keywords was mentioned less than 10 times before 2009, catching relatively limited political attention. Since 2010, it becomes a high-frequency word, mentioned in reports more than 50 times. It is consistent with the current situation of the SCS tension and the intensification of China-U.S. conflicts in the SCS since 2010. In terms of content, the report repeatedly mentions the geostrategic value of the SCS in the Asia-Pacific region, contending that some Asia-Pacific States and regions rely heavily on the flow of oil and commerce through SCS shipping lanes, including more than 80 % of the crude oil to Japan, South Korea, and Taiwan, indicating the role of the SCS as a strategic sea line.[41] Speaking of the geostrategic value of the SCS, the reports in recent years mainly focus on the following issues:

First, China's claim of rights and interests in the SCS. In July 2009, then State Councilor Dai Bing-guo proposed that national sovereignty and territorial integrity belong to one of China's "core interest." In September 2011, *China's Peaceful Development* issued by the State Council Information Office of the PRC clearly defined the "core interest."[42] In this context, whether the SCS belongs to China's core interests has once aroused the debate in academic circles and public discussions both at home and abroad,[43] and attracted the attention of the Pentagon. For example, the 2013 Military and Security Developments involving the PRC states that senior Chinese officials have identified protecting China's sovereignty and territorial integrity as a "core interest" and China's opposition to and willingness to respond to actions it perceives as challenging this core interest, and this was demonstrated by Chinese actions at Scarborough Reef in the SCS in 2012.[44] The reports of 2014 and 2015 reiterate the importance of the SCS as a national core interest.[45] In addition, the reports repeatedly criticize that the Chinese government maintains that its maritime rights extend to virtually the entire SCS and often illustrates its claims using a "nine-dashed line" that encompasses much of the SCS area. At the same time, China is ambiguous about the precise meaning of the nine-dashed line. To date, China has not clarified the meaning of the line or articulated its legal basis.[46]

Second, China's approach to safeguarding rights and interests in the SCS. According to the annual reports in recent years, it is not difficult to find that the United States is increasingly inclined to believe that China's approach to safeguarding sovereignty and maritime rights and interests in the SCS has transitioned from navy-dominant single defensive force in the past to a mode of "military-civilian integration." The "military" means strengthening the modernization of the Navy, which is the fundamental and guarantee to safeguard China's rights and interests in the SCS; the "civilian" refers to the continuous expansion of maritime law enforcement forces and maritime militia forces, which is an important supplement for safeguarding Chinese rights and interests in the SCS. Military-civilian integration is the main approach to protecting China's maritime rights in the new period.

For example, the Annual Report of 2011 directly points out that Beijing appears eager to strengthen its claim to the disputed region over the long term. This includes legal efforts as well as the deployment of more capable naval and civilian law enforcement ships. A more robust presence would position China for force projection, blockade, and surveillance operations.[47] According to the Annual Report of 2014, China prefers to use its civilian maritime agencies around these islands, and uses the PLA Navy in a back-up role or as an escalatory measure.[48] The Annual Report of 2015 also claims that "China has demonstrated this model at Scarborough Reef, Second Thomas Shoal, and CNOOC-981's drilling operations south of the Paracel Islands."[49] In the Reports of 2017 and 2018, the development of China's maritime surveillance force, maritime militia, and other civilian maritime forces and their role in jointly safeguarding the rights and interests of the SCS together with the Navy have also attracted great attention.[50]

Third, China's construction of islands and reefs in the SCS. In 2013, China's large-scale construction of islands and reefs in the SCS increasingly concerned the U.S. military. For this reason, the Annual Report of 2015 specially takes a chapter to analyze China's construction of islands and reefs in the SCS, and believes that China is attempting to change facts on the ground by improving its defense infrastructure in the SCS.[51] The Annual Report of 2016 further elaborates that China's actions in the SCS, particularly its land reclamation on features in the Spratly Islands, enhanced the appearance of

China's ability to exercise control over disputed areas in the SCS, raised tensions in the SCS, and caused concern over China's long-term intentions.[52] The Annual Report of 2017 also points out that although China's land reclamation and artificial islands do not strengthen China's territorial claims as a legal matter or create any new territorial sea entitlements, China will be able to use its reclaimed features as persistent civil-military bases to enhance its presence in the SCS and improve China's ability to control the features and nearby maritime space.[53]

The Report of 2018 is consistent in the keynote, saying that no substantial Chinese land reclamation occurred in the SCS in 2017, but infrastructure development on reclaimed features continued. It reiterated the claim that the United States does not take a position on sovereignty over disputed land features in the SCS, but recognizes that China's reclamation activities have far surpassed that of all other claimants. The United States opposes further militarization of disputed land features and calls for all claimants to avoid unilateral, coercive changes.[54] The report of 2019 and 2020 further claimed that "the construction of new airfields and hangars on outposts in the South China Sea extends the possible operating areas of PLA aviation forces. Future deployments of PLA combat aircraft operating from Spratly Island outposts could feature extended range and/or loiter time over the South China Sea or even reach into the Indian Ocean."[55]

Report on Asia-Pacific Maritime Security Strategy

According to the Defense Authorization Act of Fiscal Year 2015, the U.S. DoD shall submit a detailed report on the Department's handling of marine security issues in the South and East China Seas to the Senate Armed Services Committee and the House Armed Services Committee within 180 days after the Bill is passed. In August 2015, the U.S. DoD finally submitted a report entitled "Asia-Pacific Maritime Security Strategy." The report is a collection of cliché in content. After analyzing the maritime disputes and the balance of maritime power in the Asia-Pacific region, it says that the United States has a strong interest in ensuring all claimants seek to address and resolve their issues peacefully, without conflict or coercion. At the same time, the Report also accuses China of using a steady progression of small, incremental steps to increase its effective control over disputed areas, thereby avoiding escalation to military conflict.[56]

Congressmen's Direct Participation

Congressmen are the main initiators and participants of Congress in international affairs. Generally, they take a stand on some international issues through statements, speeches, and letters to government officials. According to publically available information, Congressmen directly participate in the SCS issue mainly through the abovementioned means in recent years, although Dana Rohrabacher, a Member of the House of Representatives, took a tour in the SCS to inspect Mischief Reef (Meiji Jiao) on a Philippine C-130 military cargo transport plane at the end of 1998.[57]

Statements on the SCS Issue

On May 23, 2012, John Kerry, then Chairman of the Senate Committee on Foreign Relations, made a statement at a hearing that analyzed U.S. national security and strategic imperatives for ratifying the Law of the Sea Convention. He remarked that "as American national security focus shifts towards the Asia Pacific region, it is more important than ever that the U.S. is a part of this Treaty. China and other countries are staking out illegal claims in the SCS and elsewhere. Becoming a party to the treaty would give an immediate boost to U.S. credibility as the United States pushes back against excessive maritime claims and illegal restrictions on warships or commercial vessels."[58] Representative Eliot L. Engel, the leading Democrat on the House Committee on Foreign Affairs, made a statement on the 981 drilling rig incident of May 9, 2014, condemning "Chinese drilling and intimidation of Vietnamese vessels near the Paracel islands are needless provocations that threaten peace and stability across the region. China's behavior is clearly adversarial."[59] At the same time, a bipartisan group consisting of senators Robert Menendez, Marco Rubio, Ben Cardin, Jim Risch, John McCain, and Patrick Leahy contended that "China's recent movement of an oil drilling rig escorted by military and other ships into disputed waters in the SCS off the coast of Vietnam—and the subsequent aggressive tactics used by Chinese ships, including the ramming of Vietnamese ships—is deeply troubling."[60]

Chinese President Xi Jinping visited the United States on September 25, 2015, and Senator Ben Cardin stated that "we must express directly that as an Asia-Pacific nation, we find China's building of artificial islands in the SCS provocative. These actions threaten regional stability, disrupt the free flow of commerce, and require a peaceful diplomatic resolution to disputes that is consistent with international law."[61] On October 27, Representative Eliot L. Engel made the following statement regarding U.S. Navy exercises near disputed areas in the SCS, "Freedom of navigation is a basic principle of international law followed by civilian and military mariners across the globe, and while the United States does not take a position on sovereignty claims in the SCS, we do take a position on the importance of this principle and will stand up for it on the global stage. By claiming disputed islands and marine features hundreds of miles from its shores, China undermines international law, threatens regional stability, and disrupts lawful commerce that drives growth and progress for our allies and partners in Asia."[62] On October 29, Senator Ben Cardin issued the following statement in support of unanimous finding by the International Tribunal for the Law of the Sea in a case brought by the Philippines against China regarding its claims in the SCS. Senator Cardin also repeated his call for the U.S. Senate to ratify the UNCLOS.[63]

In 2016, after the Tribunal ruled in Philippines' favor in the case regarding the SCS, Congressmen also issued statements one after another, overwhelmingly supporting the Philippines and demanding China to abide by and implement the tribunal's decision. For example, on July 12, 2016, Democratic Members of the House Committees on Foreign Affairs and Armed Services issued the following statement regarding the International Tribunal's decision in the case of The Republic of the Philippines v. The People's Republic of China, "We welcome the Tribunal's ruling today in the case of The Republic of the Philippines vs. The PRC. The ruling underscores the importance of the UNCLOS. We view it as binding on both parties involved and we hope that all parties will abide by it."[64] Senator Bob Corker, Chairman of the Senate Foreign Relations Committee, also made a statement: "this ruling is a rejection of China's aggressive attempts to control disputed areas of the SCS, and hopefully all parties will refrain from any actions that would undermine security and stability in the region." "In response, the United States should expand political, economic and securities ties with our allies and partners and continue efforts to defend freedom of navigation and over flight through routine patrols in the East and SCSs."[65] Senator Marco Rubio was pleased with the ruling as well, believing that "China has no historical title to the entire SCS and that China's actions have breached the Philippines' rights."[66]

On December 16, Senator Ben Cardin released a statement on China's seizure of an U.S. Navy unmanned scientific research submersible in waters off the SCS: "China's seizure of an U.S. Navy unmanned scientific research submersible in international waters off the SCS is a remarkably brazen violation of international law. No matter its motivation, China needs to explain its actions and immediately return the undersea drone, untampered with, to the United States.

China's increasingly aggressive behavior in the SCS—including the militarization of the artificial features that it has built in the region, in direct contradiction of a pledge made by President Xi not to do so—is deeply disturbing, and not consistent with the actions of a nation seeking to build a constructive and cooperative relationship with the United States."[67] On June 22, Senator Ben Sasse, a Member of the Senate Armed Services Committee, released a statement regarding reports that American military aircraft and pilots have been targeted by laser attacks in the SCS: "The use of lasers to target American aircraft in the SCS is yet another example of China's overt aggression in the region. I hope Secretary Mattis raises these incidents and others in his meetings with President Xi."[68]

Public Speeches on the SCS Issue

In a major speech on China's policy at the Center for American Progress in Washington, D.C. on December 7, 2010, John Kerry, Chairman of the Senate Committee on Foreign Relations, made a remark that "China shocked the region by declaring the SCS to be one of its "core interests", on par with Tibet and Taiwan, despite the fact that six different countries have long laid claims to territory and resources there."[69] On May 14, 2012, Senator McCain delivered a speech at the Center for Strategic and International Studies on the theme of defining the interests of the United States in Asia, remarking that the United States, as a Pacific power, has a vital role to play, claiming that although the United States has no claim on the dispute itself, this dispute will endanger the core interests of the United States in Asia. It is not only because the United States has 1.2 trillion U.S. dollars of trade passing through the SCS every year, but also because the Philippines, as one of the disputing parties, is an ally of the United States. The reason is that a rising Asia must avoid the dark side of real politics, namely, the powerful countries do what they want and the weak countries suffer.[70] On June 28, Senator Joe Lieberman delivered remarks entitled "The SCS and Asia-Pacific in Transition" at the Center for Strategic and International Studies, stating that China's claims of nine-dashed line is ambiguous and pushing the region in a wrong direction, which is a discouraging message. It raises questions about what kind of power China will become and how it will get along with its neighbors. In fact, the scope, nature, and basis of China's claims in the SCS are broad, which naturally fosters an atmosphere of anxiety and pushes other claimants, especially Vietnam and the Philippines, to consolidate their own claims.[71]

On June 25, 2014, Senator Robert Menendez, Chairman of the Senate Foreign Relations Committee, delivered a speech that stated "we have seen an increasingly provocative China on the seas, coercing and intimidating neighbors, in both the East China Sea and SCS, and attempting to use the threat of military force to address territorial and regional disputes." "China's provocative actions in the SCS, threaten not just regional stability but long-standing U.S. interests in the free-flow of commerce, freedom of navigation and in the peaceful diplomatic resolution of disputes consistent with international law."[72] On December 4, Representative Eliot L. Engel, the leading Democrat on the House Committee on Foreign Affairs, made remarks on the floor of the House of Representatives, condemning aggressive actions and calling for a peaceful resolution to disputes in the East and SCSs, "Not right that China thinks it can dominate and be aggressive in terms of claiming the seas as its own even though many of those seas are literally thousands of miles away from mainland China."[73]

On July 12, 2016, Senator Dan Sullivan made remarks at the 6th Annual SCS Conference held by the Center for Strategic and International Studies. He concluded by focusing on what specific actions the United States and its allies should take in response. First, America must continue to maintain a favorable military balance in the Asia-Pacific region that secures enduring national interests, upholds treaty commitments, and safeguards open seas and open commerce. Second, the United States will continue to fly, sail, and operate wherever international law allows, including regular operations by the U.S. military to challenge any excessive claim to a territorial sea around these features. Third, the United States government must clearly communicate our interests before Chinese activity begins, rather than waiting for China to initiate a "Gray Zone" maneuver that knocks the United States on heels and limits our response. Fourth, the U.S. Navy must continue to maintain a regular presence of surface combatants and rotational aviation assets inside the first-island chain to uphold the commitment to freedom of the seas and respond in a crisis. Fifth, the United States must strengthen alliances and develop new partnerships with countries like India, Vietnam, Malaysia, and Indonesia. Additionally, we must continue to invest in the capabilities of partners and allies.[74]

On March 7, 2018, Representative Rick Larsen delivered remarks at a Brookings Institution Event "The end of U.S. engagement with China?," saying that China continues in its efforts to be a development and growth model, challenging existing international rules and the international order. China's continued efforts to create and militarize artificial islands in the SCS and its unwillingness to comply with international norms there can seem to indicate that China is not interested in finding mutually beneficial solutions either.[75] On March 20, Senator Bob Menendez expressed his concerns with President Trump's

China policy, criticizing that "As China's political leadership consolidates power, and as the country expands into the SCS and pursues an aggressive economic agenda around the world, the President, for his part, praises these dictatorial moves- meanwhile, he's failed to deliver on his promises for better trade deals."[76]

Letters to the Government and Officials

If necessary, Congressmen submit letters directly to relevant Government Departments or Officials to express their concern or make corresponding requests. In recent years, to prevent China's rights protection in the SCS and safeguard U.S. maritime hegemony in the Asia-Pacific region, they have written to U.S. government departments and officials on the SCS issue for many times, demanding that the White House and the Military should take a tough stance against China.

On July 19, 2011, Senator Jim Webb wrote a letter to State Department Legal Advisor Harold Koh, requesting a legal clarification of the U.S. commitment to come to the aid of the Philippines under the *Mutual Defense Treaty between the Republic of the Philippines and the United States of America*, signed on August 30, 1951. He writes that "our transparency on this matter is of great importance to our ally, the Philippines, and to the entire Southeast Asian region."[77] On November 29, Representative Ed Royce wrote a letter to Ray Mabus, Secretary of the U.S. Navy, calling for increased U.S.-Filipino maritime security cooperation, specifically through transfer of additional decommissioned U.S. military vessels.[78] On March 19, 2015, Senators John McCain, Jack Reed, Bob Corker, and Bob Menendez sent a joint letter to Secretary of Defense Ash Carter and Secretary of State John Kerry concerning Chinese maritime strategy and the alarming scope and pace of land reclamation now being conducted by China in the SCS. They emphasized the need for a comprehensive U.S. strategy for addressing the China's broader policy and conduct to assert its sovereignty claims in the South and East China Seas, including land-reclamation and construction activities.[79]

On May 22, 2015, Senators John McCain and Jack Reed, Chairman and Ranking Member of the Senate Armed Services Committee, sent a letter to Secretary of Defense Ash Carter regarding the U.S. invitation to China to participate in the 2016 Rim of the Pacific military exercise in Hawaii. Senators McCain and Reed wrote, "Given China's behavior in the past year alone, including its disregard for the interests of our allies, international law, and established norms, we do not believe Beijing should have been invited to this prestigious U.S.-led military exercise in 2016," "China appears more intent on waging a maritime sovereignty competition and bullying its neighbors than contributing in a substantive manner to regional peace."[80] On June 22, Senator Marco Rubio urged President Obama and his administration to prioritize several areas of concern in U.S.-China bilateral relationship, including China's aggressive actions in the SCS, cyber-attacks against U.S. government networks, and increased repression of the Chinese people. Rubio wrote in a letter, "I am deeply concerned by the Chinese government's recent aggressive actions against the United States and our allies as well as its increasingly repressive posture at home," "I urge your administration to make these issues a priority during the U.S.-China Strategic and Economic Dialogue (S&ED) that begins today. After six years of your Administration's participation in this dialogue, we need more than talking points. We need to see a change in Chinese behavior or real consequences for China's increasingly egregious actions."[81]

On July 12, 2016, Representative Eliot L. Engel called on governments around the world to respect and abide by the decision of the Tribunal related to China's claims in the SCS. In a letter sent to more than 100 governments around the world, Engel underscored the importance of upholding international law and ensuring that all countries play by the same rules. "While the United States does not take a position on the claims made by various parties, we call on all countries to respect the Tribunal's decision and to uphold the integrity of international law. I urge your government to clearly state your support, along with the majority of the international community, for the Tribunal's proceedings as legitimate and binding under international law," wrote Engel.[82] On May 10, 2017, Senators Ben Cardin, Bob Corker, Cory Gardner, Ed Markey, Marco Rubio, and Brian Schatz wrote to President Trump urging his administration to take any necessary steps, including routinely exercising freedom of navigation and over flight in the SCS. They believed that exercising the American decades-long FONOPs program "is critical to U.S. national security interests and to peace and prosperity in the Asia-Pacific region."[83] On May 25, 2018, Senators Marco Rubio, Cory Gardner, and Ed Markey urged Secretary of State Mike Pompeo and Secretary of Defense Jim Mattis to "respond to Beijing's introduction of advanced weapons systems into the SCS." They expressed grave concerns about China's ongoing militarization of the SCS, which is contrary to international law and intended to undermine the rules-based international order in the Indo-Pacific region.[84]

The Characteristics and Impact of Congressional Involvement in the SCS Issue

The characteristics of tectonic evolution were generally developed with inheritance and stability since Caledonian movement in northern Ordos Basin, but structural geometry of Paleozoic strata had changed in different periods and blocks.

Congress, as a prime actor in American involvement in the SCS issue, takes various actions to interfere with the issue in different periods, but still retains its logical consistency. Especially compared with the administration's articulations and actions on the SCS dispute, the stance of Congress on this issue has its own characteristic and tendency. At the same time, the actions of Congress on the SCS issue also have an important impact on the formulation of the U.S. government's SCS policy, public opinion, policies of regional allies and perimeter states of the SCS, as well as the regional order.

Looking back on the attitude and actions of Congress on the SCS issue, it is not difficult to find that its intervention presents the following characteristics.

A Bipartisan Consensus on the South Sea Issue Has Been Reached

As the two major political parties in the United States, the Democratic Party and the Republican Party have occupied a monopoly position in American politics for a long time. These two parties compete and cooperate on issues, and the "donkey vs. Elephant" becomes a partisan ridicule. Due to different party attributes and political traditions, as well as the different demands of the interest groups they represent, their positions on some domestic and foreign issues can be different. In particular, when the President and the majority of the Congress belong to different political parties, conflicts arise between the Government and Congress on certain issues.

Using the Congressional Bills on the SCS issue as an example, during the period of 1995–1997 (104th–105th Congress), the Republicans were the majority in Congress. In order to put pressure on the Clinton administration, it was Republicans who introduced bills related to the SCS issue. Of course, the fact that the Democrats did not introduce a bill on the SCS issue during this period does not mean that they are naturally friendly to China nor overlook the SCS issue, but reflects their long-term different political stance on China's policy. During this period, Congress introduced bills such as Expressing the Sense of House of Representatives that the United States should Support Peace and Stability in the

SCS (H.Res.114), A Resolution Expressing the Sense of the Senate with Respect to Peace and Stability in the SCS (S.Res.97), United States-China Policy Act of 1995(H.R.2053, H.R.2058), and To Prohibit the Importation into the United States of Goods Produced, Manufactured, or Exported by the PLA of China or any Chinese Defense Industrial Trading Company (H.R.3684), Expressing the sense of the House of Representatives that the United States should maintain approximately 100,000 United States military personnel in the Asia and Pacific region until such time as there is a peaceful and permanent resolution to the major security and political conflicts in the region (H.Res.103), To Ensure Commercial Activities of PLA of China or any Communist Chinese Military Company are not Extended Normal Tariff Treatment by the United States or Treated as Normal Commercial Intercourse with the United States (H.R.2188), etc. Those bills embody the Republican Party's consistent tough stance towards China over the years.

However, the situation in Congress has changed significantly since 2011. During the 112th, 113th, 114th, and 115th Congresses, both Republicans and Democrats introduced the bills regarding the SCS issue. Twenty-three Bills were introduced by Republicans, which was still more than the 14 introduced by Democrats, but the increasing Bills introduced by Democratic Party, to some degree, implies that the issue has aroused the common concern of both parties, and the two parties have reached a consensus on the SCS issue. As Senator Joseph Lieberman put it in June, 2002, "there really is a bipartisan consensus on this particularly important aspect of American foreign policy."[85] In fact, judging from the contents of the Bills on the SCS introduced by Congress during this period, whether it was introduced by Republicans or Democrats, both parties required the administration to respond to China's SCS claims and actions, safeguard the freedom of navigation in the SCS, and maintain the dominant position of the United States in the Asia-Pacific region.

Additionally, judging from the hearings on the SCS issue held by the U.S. Congress from 112th to 115th Congress, both Republicans and Democrats participated in and convened the hearings, whether in the Senate or the House of Representatives. For example, Senate Committee on Foreign Relations held hearings on Safeguarding American Interests in the East and SCSs on May 13, 2015, DoD Maritime Activities and Engagement in the SCS on July 8, and U.S. Policy Options in the SCS on July 13. Senate Committee on Armed Services held a hearing on U.S. Force Posture in the Indo-Pacific Region on December 12. The House Committee on Foreign Affairs held hearings on Beijing as an Emerging Power in the SCS on Sept. 12, 2012; Maritime Sovereignty in the

East and SCSs on Jan. 14, 2014; America's Security Role in the SCS on July 23, 2015; Checking China's Maritime Push on Feb. 28, 2017; and Asia's Diplomatic and Security Structure: Planning U.S. Engagement on May 23, 2018. Moreover, Members of Congress who directly intervene in the SCS issue through statements, speeches, and letters are from both parties, such as Republicans McCain, Rubio and Democrats Kerry, Robert Menendez, and Elliot L. Engel. The above reflects reality: that the Democratic Party and the Republican Party not only pay a lot of attention to the SCS issue, but also take more consistent steps.[86]

The Degree of Congress Intervention Varies in Different Periods, and Is Closely Related to U.S.-China Strategy and the Situation in the SCS

Congressional intervention in the SCS issue is not consistent, but varies in different periods, which can be roughly divided into four periods: the "silence" period before 1995, the low-frequency intervention from 1995 to 2001, the "relatively calm" period from 2002 to 2008, and the high-frequency intervention from 2009 to 2020.

Before 1995, Congress remained silent in general on the SCS issue. The reason is that the U.S. strategic goal was to concentrate all resources and forces against the Eastern bloc led by the Soviet Union during the Cold War. Although the United States prevented and contained China's development, it was still subordinate to its strategy on the Soviet Union. Therefore, it was for the consideration of the Cold War that the United States had military presence and military surveillance against China in the SCS, instead of intervening purposefully in the SCS dispute itself. For example, when there is political need to unite with China to resist the Soviet Union, neither the U.S. Government nor Congress supported U.S. intervention in the battle of the Paracel Islands between China and Vietnam in 1974 and the battle of the Spratly Islands in 1988.[87] As the Soviet Union collapsed, the U.S.-Soviet-China triangle relationship became a part of history. Although China-U.S. relations deteriorated sharply during China's political turmoil in 1989, the United States did not look on China as a major strategic opponent before 1995. At the same time, the SCS issue did not attract the attention of the international community. That is why the U.S. Congress did not intervene in the SCS issue during the Cold War and in the early post-Cold War years.[88]

From 1995 to 2001, the Mischief Reef incident, the Taiwan Strait Crisis, and collision in the SCS took place. The tense maritime situation and changes in China-U.S. relations diverted Congressional attention to the SCS issue and began low-frequency intervention (mainly through legislative activities).

In February 1995, there was a dispute between China and the Philippines over the discovery by the Philippines of China's construction of so-called military facilities (actually civilian production facilities) in the waters of Mischief Reef in the SCS. For this reason, the Philippine military sent troops to demolish survey marks set up by China on the Spratly Islands and reefs such as Half Moon Shoal and Second Thomas Shoal, attack Chinese fishing boats, and arrest Chinese fishermen. At the same time, the Philippines also organized dozens of domestic and foreign journalists to carry out "interviews" in Mischief Reef, deliberately escalating the situation to ensure worldwide attention. After the Mischief Reef incident, in order to express their "concern" about the incident and the situation in the SCS, in March 1995, Republican Benjamin Gilman introduced a Bill on Expressing the Sense of House of Representatives that the United States should Support Peace and Stability in the SCS (H.Res.114), and Republican Craig Thomas introduced A Resolution Expressing the Sense of the Senate with Respect to Peace and Stability in the SCS (S.Res.97), which is the first time that Congress has intervened in the SCS issue by way of legislation.

From July 1995 to March 1996, the United States violated its previous commitment to China and allowed Lee Teng-hui, then leader of Taiwan, to visit the United States, which raised strong protests from Beijing. The Chinese military immediately conducted missile tests and military exercises in the Taiwan Strait, and the United States sent two aircraft carrier battle groups, which brought the Taiwan Strait into an unprecedented tense and turbulent situation. The Taiwan Strait Crisis prompts Congress to realize that the PLA poses a threat to the security of Taiwan and could affect the freedom of navigation in the SCS. After the Taiwan Strait Crisis, Congress carried out 11 legislative activities related to the SCS issue. Nevertheless, they only mentioned the SCS issue incidentally in the content, expressing the concern of the United States about the security of sea lanes and freedom of navigation in the SCS, and believed that maintaining the freedom of navigation in the SCS is a fundamental interest of the United States. It indicates that the SCS issue has gradually raised Congressional concern in this period, although it has not yet risen to the top agenda. Despite that, compared with that before 1995 when Congress hardly interfered with the SCS issue, Congress mentioned the issue in a number of bills during this period, which highlights its increasing emphasis on the SCS issue.

From November 1997 to April 1999, Congress hardly intervened in the SCS issue, which was related to the gradual improvement of China-U.S. relations and the relative stability of the SCS situation. After the previous Taiwan Strait crisis, the China-U.S. relations began to ease in 1997–1998. President Jiang Zemin and his U.S. counterpart Bill Clinton successively paid friendly official visits, and established the goal of "working together to establish a constructive strategic partnership between China and the United States." In May 1999, the bombing of the Chinese Embassy in Yugoslavia led to another setback in China-U.S. relations. After the George W. Bush administration came to power in 2001, the United States identified China as its "strategic competitor." On April 1, an aircraft collision between Chinese and the United States units took place in the SCS, which worsened China-U.S. relations. On April 5, the U.S. Congress introduced a Resolution expressing the sense of the Senate regarding the release of 24 U.S. military personnel currently being detained by the PRC (S.Res.66). As China-U.S. relations intensified, the terrorist attack on September 11, 2001, forced the United States to shift its strategic focus to counter-terrorism. In order to gain China's support in its anti-terrorism strategy, the U.S. government ceased igniting flashpoints over the SCS issue, and devoted its energy towards counter-terrorism.

During the period 2002–2008, anti-terrorism became the new focus. With the United States committed to anti-terrorism, China-U.S. relations developed steadily due to common interests in the fight against terrorism. In this context, Congress neither introduced Bills or Resolutions on the SCS issue, nor did the Committee on Foreign Affairs and Committee on Armed Services hold hearings on the issue. Members of Congress rarely made speeches, statements, and letters on the issue either. The "calm period" does not mean that the United States completely removed itself from the SCS issue. In fact, the U.S. China Economic and Security Review Committee, which is subordinate to Congress, also held a handful of hearings on the SCS issue and released its annual report involving the SCS dispute. These hearings and reports, however, are only routine, annually monitoring, investigating, and evaluating the overall economic and security relations between China and the United States. They had a relatively limited impact on the SCS issue.

From 2009 to 2020, Congressional intervention in the SCS issue reached its peak. During this period, 53 Bills were introduced in Congress on the SCS issue, accounting for 79 % of the total of 67. According to the information available on the website of the United States Congress, as of December 31, 2020, the Senate and the House held 63 hearings on the SCS issue between 2009 and 2020. Meanwhile, the USCC held 34 hearings on the SCS issue from 2002 to 2020, of which 24 were held from 2009 to 2020, accounting for 71 % of the total. In addition, research reports, statements, speeches, and letters from Congressmen on the SCS issue also showed a massive upsurge. The reason why Congress began to refocus on the SCS issue in this period is that the U.S. strategy towards China and the situation in the SCS changed significantly. First, after the Obama administration took office, the White House shifted the U.S. strategic focus from Middle East to Asia and implemented the policy of strategic "rebalancing" towards the Asia Pacific. One of the goals of the rebalancing strategy is to respond to China's rise as noted previously, thus the SCS is undoubtedly an important starting point for the United States to implement the strategy. Second, the countries around the SCS attempted to take advantage of the strategic opportunity of the United States "returning to Asia" to launch frequent provocative actions against China on the SCS issue, which triggered China's rebound and countermeasures, leading to rising tensions in the SCS. Third, the Trump administration has openly identified China as a "strategic competitor," and has increased pressure on China in the East China Sea, Taiwan Strait, and the SCS, resulting in fierce competition for maritime control between China and the United States in the Asia-Pacific region.

The Government and Congress Reach Overwhelming Consensus on Policy Making, but Congress Takes a Hard Line

Due to the way diplomatic power is shared under the Constitution, the President and Congress often clash with each other. Generally speaking, the President tends to take foreign policy as a way of seeking dominant power as the world leader, while the Congress takes it as an extension of domestic policy from the perspective of domestic political funding and the voters.[89] Therefore, the differences in political status and orientation lead to sharp divisions between the Congress and the President on diplomatic issues. For example, in April 2018, after U.S. President Trump announced military action to carry out precision attacks on suspected chemical weapons sites in Syria, many Democratic Congressmen criticized Trump's decision as "reckless" and "illegal," blasting him for not seeking Congressional approval for Syria strikes.[90]

Looking through the position that Congress and the Government take on the SCS issue, however, it is not difficult to find that there is no huge divergence between them. It can be said that, in addition to the personal opinions of a small proportion of Congressmen, the U.S. Government and Congress reached political consensus on the SCS issue, including that the United States has national interests in the SCS; all the parties should settle disputes by peaceful means;

the United States opposes the use or threat of force; the rights and interests of all parties should comply with the provisions of international law; freedom of navigation and over flight in the SCS should be guaranteed; the U.S. allies and partners should be supported; all claimant States should abide by the *Declaration on the Conduct of Parties in the SCS*; and the United States should continue to strengthen its military presence in the SCS. At the same time, in the proposals, hearings, and research reports drawn by the Congress, even in the speeches and statements made by Members, there is no obvious opposition to the official U.S. government position on the issue.

Taking the example of the Bill "To reaffirm the strong support of the United States government for the peaceful and collaborative resolution of maritime and jurisdictional disputes in the SCS and the East China Sea as provided for by universally recognized principles of international law, and to reaffirm the vital interest of the United States in freedom of navigation and other internationally lawful uses of sea and airspace in the Asia-Pacific region" (H.Res.714), introduced by Democrat Eni F. Faleomavaega on Sept. 8, 2014, the House of Representatives reaffirms U.S. support for the peaceful resolution of maritime territorial disputes in the South and East China Sea, supports for freedom of navigation and over flight and condemns coercive actions or the use of force to impede these freedoms in international maritime domains and airspace, calls on China to refrain from taking provocative actions, urges all claimants to fairly resolve the disputes through cooperation, and encourages continued U.S. efforts to strengthen the relations with the ASEAN and respect for principles of international law. It is in accordance with the policy of the Executive.

Another example is "A Resolution calling for all parties to respect the arbitral tribunal ruling with regard to the SCS and to express United States policy on freedom of navigation and over flight in the East and SCSs" (S.Res.526) introduced by Republican Cory Gardner on July 12, 2016. The Senate calls on all parties to respect the Tribunal ruling, and urges all parties to implement the *Declaration on the Conduct of Parties in the SCS* and to take steps toward early conclusion of a meaningful COC, opposes actions in the SCS to change the status quo by coercion or force, calls on China to cease all reclamation and militarization activities in the SCS and end provocative actions in the East China Sea, reaffirms Article V of the Mutual Defense Treaty Between the United States and the Philippines and Article V of the Treaty of Mutual Cooperation and Security between the United States and Japan, urges the DoS to utilize all diplomatic channels to communicate U.S. support for freedom of navigation and over flight in the SCS, and urges the DoD to enforce freedom of navigation and over flight in the East and SCSs. These instructions are also in accordance with the U.S. government's official policy.

If there is any "discordant note" between Congress and the Government on the SCS issue, it is that Congress often shows a robust posture. For example, Congress has publicly condemned China's actions in the SCS in various Bills or Resolutions. In a Resolution on July 15, 2011, the House of Representatives condemned the use of force by naval, maritime security, and fishing vessels from China in the SCS and the East China Sea as well as the use of force by China's North Korean ally in the Yellow Sea.[91] In another Resolution on Feb. 5, 2013, the House of Representatives again condemned the use of threat or force by naval, maritime security, and fishing vessels from China in the SCS and the East China Sea as well as the use of force by North Korea in the Yellow Sea that would escalate tensions or result in miscalculations.[92] In a Resolution on Sept. 8, 2014, the House of Representatives condemns coercive and threatening actions or the use of force to impede these freedoms in international maritime domains and airspace by military or civilian vessels.[93] On May 21, 2015, the Senate "condemns the government of the People's Republic of China's unilateral construction of artificial land formations in the disputed Spratly Islands."[94] Although the U.S. government also criticizes China's claims and actions in the SCS, the word "condemn" is rarely used. From this aspect, we can see Congress takes a more robust stance on the issue.

In addition, at a Hearing entitled "Maritime Sovereignty in the East and SCSs," held by the House Committee on Foreign Affairs on Jan. 14, 2014, some Representatives believe that the United States must be 100 % intolerant of China's military coercion in the SCS. Especially after China's establishment of the ADIZ in the East China Sea and the ratification of *Hainan Implementation of Fisheries Law*, the United States should maintain a robust military and strong diplomatic posture to counteract China's military coercion in the East and SCSs.[95] At the hearing "Checking China's Maritime Push," held by the House Committee on Foreign Affairs on Feb. 28, 2017, Ted Yoho, Chairman of the Subcommittee on Asia and the Pacific, believes that the United States for nearly a decade "has said much, and done little," in his words, "endlessly backing away from conflicts carries its own risks," thus the United States needs a new strategy to form and implement better policies to represent or reassert U.S. strengths in these critical areas.[96] In the Report to Congress of the USCC in November 2018, it advises Congress to consider imposing sanctions on key Chinese state-owned enterprises and individuals involved in China's ongoing militarization of the SCS.[97]

Congressmen Have Prejudiced and Unfair Attitudes towards China in the SCS Issue, Reflecting Their Concern and Wariness on China's Rapid Rise

The SCS issue is a dispute over sovereignty and maritime rights and interests between China and its neighboring countries. As an extraterritorial actor and a party that is not involved, the United States, as well as individual U.S. Congressmen, a third party, should take an objective and neutral position. The fact is, on the contrary, Congressmen are more inclined to reject China's claim, tending towards taking sides with other claimants.

The prejudice and unfairness exhibited by U.S. Congressmen are fully reflected in their attitude towards China's safeguarding rights in the SCS. In the 21st century, with the formation of an open economy and the national rejuvenation, China needs to understand and utilize the ocean more than ever before. At the same time, some neighboring countries disregard China's sovereignty over the SCS, continue to occupy islands and reefs, and accelerate the allocation of sea resources, all of which seriously violates China's sovereignty rights and interests in the SCS. Therefore, the strategy of "safeguarding national marine rights and interests, improving marine development capacity and building a maritime power" was clearly put forward at the 18th NCCPC in 2012. Driven by this strategy, China's approach to safeguarding the rights and interests of the SCS is diversified and frequent, which has aroused the concern and wariness of Congressmen. In fact, in recent years, Members of Congress have submitted and discussed Bills, held Hearings, and made statements, speeches, and written letters on the SCS issue, all of which are related to China's safeguarding of sovereign rights activities in the SCS.

For example, in view of the friction and conflicts among China, the Philippines, and Vietnam in the SCS, as well as the impact of China's rights safeguarding actions against U.S. vessels and military aircraft crossing the sea area and airspace in the SCS, since 2011, Members of Congress have repeatedly introduced bills condemning China's use of force in the SCS, claiming that "gunboat diplomacy" is not a constructive way to resolve maritime disputes, and have repeatedly expressed their support for the U.S. Navy's FONOPs in the SCS. On Apr. 7, 2014, Senator Robert Menendez introduced a Resolution, in which he called on China's government to withdraw its "981" drilling rig and associated maritime forces from their current positions, and reaffirmed the unwavering commitment and support for American allies and partners in the Asia-Pacific region, including the effectiveness of Article V of the United States-Philippines

Mutual Defense Treaty.[98] On May 21, 2015, Senator Schatz Brian introduced a resolution condemning the construction of artificial land formations on islands, reefs, shoals, and other features of the Spratly Islands, and urging China to clarify the meaning of the "nine-dashed line" claim and the maritime areas it claims within that space.[99] On July 13, 2016, Representative Mike Pompeo introduced a Resolution calling for all parties to respect the Arbitral Tribunal ruling with regard to the SCS, opposing any action to change the status quo by coercion, force, or threatening to use force, and calling on China to cease all reclamation and militarization activities in the SCS.[100] Similarly, in statements, speeches, and remarks at the hearings on the SCS issue, Members of Congress expressed their dissatisfaction with China's behavior in safeguarding its rights in the SCS, and almost all of the criticism and accusations made by U.S. government officials and politicians are targeted at China.

In contrast, Congressmen have turned a blind eye to the threats or actions taken by other claimants around the SCS. For example, on April 10, 2012, the Philippine Navy attempted to arrest Chinese fishermen in the waters off Scarborough Reef, which was stopped by Chinese maritime surveillance vessels. Congresswoman Ilena Ros-Lehtinen, Chairwoman of the powerful House Foreign Affairs Committee, said that "China's aggressive tactics of bullying and coercion in the SCS cannot be tolerated,"[101] while making no comment on the behavior of the Philippine Navy. In May 2014, Vietnam sent a large number of civilian and law enforcement vessels into the Paracel Islands and the adjacent waters for harassment on the ground that the "981" offshore oil drilling platform in the SCS violated Vietnam's sovereignty. After the "981" incident, Vietnam continued to harass the Chinese in the Paracel Islands and the adjacent waters on a regular basis,[102] whilst Congressmen called Chinese defensive actions "troubling" instead of criticizing the Vietnamese side for its aggressive activity.[103]

In another example, Congressmen constantly attack China's construction on islands and reefs in the SCS, which they claim has changed the topography, and threatened the freedom of navigation and regional security in the SCS. As a matter of fact, Vietnam and the Philippines have been constantly making moves on the occupied islands and reefs for a long time, constructing bases on islands and reefs, and vigorously strengthening their military constructions in the Spratly Islands, in an attempt to make their occupation permanent and legitimate. According to satellite photos in recent years, Vietnam has carried out upgrading activities on its occupied islands and reefs, and the Philippines has started similar work.[104] In comparison, China's livelihood facilities in the SCS were the most rudimentary in the past. Now, the construction of islands and reefs in the Spratly

Islands is to improve infrastructure, serve the economy and people's livelihood, and provide international public goods. Moreover, the expanded islands and reefs are a safe distance from the east and west shipping lanes of the SCS. There is no proof that the expansion of China's islands and reefs will hinder the normal passage of vessels transiting the SCS.[105] Congressmen turn a blind eye to the expansive actions of Vietnam and the Philippines, but keep eyes glued on China's construction in the SCS, which obviously lacks objectivity and impartiality.

It is undeniable that the concern of U.S. Congressmen on the SCS issue stems in part from its strategic importance. Like the U.S. government, members of Congress generally believe that the SCS is an important channel for the United States to conduct commercial and trade exchanges, and is a touchstone for the United States to maintain its strategic credibility, American rules, and status in the Asia-Pacific region, thus it is of important strategic and economic significance for the United States. Nevertheless, Congressmen's overwhelming rejection of China reflects their wariness and worry towards China's rapid rise. In the view of U.S. Congressmen, a rapidly rising China has challenged the dominant position of the United States in the SCS and the Asia-Pacific region. If the United States cannot stop China's behaviors in the SCS, it will be tantamount to losing its own dominant position. By contrast, although Vietnam and the Philippines and other neighboring countries in the SCS carry out unilateral actions, it is essentially impossible for them to pose any challenge to the dominant position of the United States because of their weak national strength. This is the fundamental reason behind Congressmen's attempts to suppress China's claims on the SCS issue. Although China's behavior in the SCS has generally been moderate and rational, and the actions of other claimant States around the SCS are often more offensive and aggressive, such as Vietnam's attack on Chinese fishing boats and the Philippines' shooting of Chinese fishermen, Congressmen have never uttered a word to criticize, condemn, or attempt to deescalate.

Although the U.S. Congress has repeatedly claimed that it does not hold a position on the sovereignty of the islands and reefs in the SCS, its intervention in the SCS issue in various ways is bound to have a huge impact on the SCS situation and the U.S. government's SCS policy. The lack of an objective and fair understanding of the SCS issue of the Congress, especially its rejection to China's legitimate rights protection behavior, has also made it more difficult for all parties to resolve the SCS issue, and impedes the development of China-U.S. relations.

Influencing the U.S. Government's Decision-Making and Driving the United States to Actively Participate in the SCS Affairs

Members of Congress discussed the significance of the SCS to the United States earlier than government officials, and called on the government to intervene in the SCS issue. Although government officials don't think that the government is fully acting upon congressional legislation activities, judging from the policy position and intervention behavior of the U.S. government on the SCS issue, the Congress is the actual "manipulator" to promote the government's active involvement. For example, after the Mischief Reef incident in February 1995, two Bills concerning the SCS were introduced by both Houses of the Congress in March. Shortly after that, the White House spokesman Christine Shelley issued the first statement regarding the SCS policy on May 10. The key point is that the United States takes no position on the legal merits of the competing claims to sovereignty over the various islands, reefs, atolls, and cays in the SCS. The United States, however, has an abiding interest in the maintenance of peace and stability in the SCS. Maintaining freedom of navigation is a fundamental interest of the United States. The United States strongly opposes the use or threat of force to resolve competing claims and would view with serious concern any maritime claim, or restriction on maritime activity, in the SCS that was not consistent with international law, including the 1982 UNCLOS.[106] Those points are intrinsically consistent with Congressional many Resolutions.

In order to challenge China's claims in the SCS, on September 17, 2015, at a hearing attended by senior Navy Admirals, Senator John McCain urged U.S. Navy vessels to enter the waters within 12 nautical miles of China's islands and reefs in the SCS. As he said, "the best sign of that commitment would be to conduct FONOPs within 12 nautical miles of China's reclaimed islands in the SCS." "The Administration's restriction on our Navy ships from operating within 12 nautical miles of China's reclaimed islands is a dangerous mistake that grants de facto recognition of China's man-made sovereignty claims."[107] McCain's statement is supported by a bipartisan group of 29 members of Congress. It was under the impetus of Congress that the U.S. Navy sent the "Larsen" missile destroyer to intrude within the 12 nautical miles of the Subi Reef waters in the SCS for the first time on October 27, 2015. Since then, the U.S. Navy has carried out many similar operations.

For punishing and restraining China's behavior in the SCS, in May 2015, Senators John McCain and Jack Reed sent a letter to Secretary of Defense Ash Carter opposing Chinese participation in the U.S.-led Rim of the Pacific military exercise.[108] In March 2016, at the 2017 budget hearing held by the House Committee on Armed Services, Representative Mark Takai from Hawaii also declared the United States should prohibit China's participation in the Rim of the Pacific exercise.[109] Under the "instruction" of Congress, the U.S. DoD finally decided to cancel China's participation in the Pacific Rim military exercise on May 23, 2018. Additionally, on May 10, 2017, members of Congress wrote to President Trump urging his administration to take necessary steps to routinely exercise freedom of navigation and over flight in the SCS.[110] On May 24, the U.S. Navy missile destroyer "Dewey" sailed within 12 nautical miles of Mischief Reef in the SCS, which was the first time the Trump administration carried out such an operation in the SCS. Obviously, the U.S. Congress is the driving force and plays an important role in such operations.

Worsening the Situation in the SCS and Complicating the SCS Dispute

Overlooking China's legitimate rights and interests in the SCS, Congress frequently accuses China of changing the status quo of the SCS, undermining the stability of the SCS region, violating the provisions of international law, affecting the freedom of navigation, and damaging the interests of neighboring countries in the SCS. U.S Congress resorts to all possible means to smear and slander China's rights protection behavior, saying it poses serious threats to the neighboring countries and the international community. On the one hand, American Congress creates a negative image of China by portraying it as an aggressive and intimidating country. On the other hand, by means of its great international influence, U.S. Congress exaggerates and misleads the international community to believe that China is a revisionist country that disobeys international rules, dismisses the Tribunal decision, and is dissatisfied with the current regional order. Undoubtedly, such continuous speculation will not only aggravate the tension in the SCS, but also mislead the American population and international community to believe that China's "aggressive" behavior is to blame for the deterioration of the situation in the SCS.

More importantly, the intervention of Congress will complicate the SCS issue and increase difficulty to resolve the issue peacefully. Congressmen's robust attitude against China on the SCS issue, as well as their direct or indirect "support" for Vietnam, the Philippines, and other countries, will release a wrong signal to the disputing parties in the SCS, which will make those claimants believe that the United States unswervingly supports to fight for maritime rights and interests with China, and encourages to infringe upon China's sovereignty and rights in the SCS. For example, in recent years, some Congressmen have strongly advocated supporting ASEAN's multilateral position on the SCS issue, encouraging ASEAN countries to unite and fight against China, calling on the U.S. government to provide more military and political support to Southeast Asian countries, and repeatedly emphasizing the security treaty obligations between the United States and its Asia-Pacific allies, particularly the Philippines and Japan. The move is bound to cause the abovementioned adverse consequences. In addition, some Members of Congress also called on more countries outside the region, such as Australia, to follow the steps to implement the freedom of navigation in their own way or join the U.S. in the SCS issue. All these moves will lead to the internationalization and complexity of the SCS dispute, and increase the difficulty for China and relevant countries in the region to resolve conflicts and solve problems at the regional level.

Posing a Setback on China-U.S. Relations and Worsening Peace and Stability in the Asia-Pacific Region

It is known that Congress represents populism in American politics, which is not ideologically friendly to China. Especially in the context of China's rapid rise and developing China-U.S. strategic competition, Congress has brought the SCS issue into the U.S. domestic political agenda, constantly hyped the SCS issue, and over-exaggerated China's threat, which is bound to have an impact on the development of China-U.S. relations. Congress has been driving the U.S. military to frequently carry out the FONOPs in the SCS, intruding within the 12 nautical miles of relevant islands and reefs in the SCS without Chinese permission, which seriously violated China's maritime sovereignty and rights and interests, and struck at China's political nerves. The militarization and provocative behavior of the U.S. military against China in the SCS is closely related to the instigation and pressure from Congress. It is likely to trigger military confrontation and conflict between China and the United States in the SCS in some form.

At the same time, the long-term interaction and confrontation between China and the United States on the SCS issue will also result in misunderstanding, miscalculation, and misperception about the national image and strategic intention with each other: American people believe that China is using its rapidly expanding national strength to bully smaller neighboring countries, expand its sphere of influence, infringe on the U.S. strategic interests of navigation freedom and security in the SCS, and ultimately challenge both U.S. strategic interests in the Asia-Pacific region and world leadership. While Chinese people will think that the United States is violating China's maritime sovereignty and suppressing China's legitimate maritime rights and interests under the pretext of defending the so-called freedom of navigation in the SCS, which is essentially to curb China's rise. The latent "hostility" between the Chinese and American people will easily lead the two countries to slip into Thucydides trap.[111] In view of the huge size of China and the United States and their influences in the Asia-Pacific region and even in the world, any act that undermines the steady development of China-U.S. relations, such as stirring up trouble and creating tension in the SCS, is an ominous move for peace and stability in the Asia-Pacific region.

Notes

1 Robert Zoellick, "Congress and the Making of US Foreign Policy," *Survival*, Vol.41, No.4, Winter 1999–2000, p.39.
2 Richard F. Grimmett, "Foreign Policy Roles of the President and Congress," U.S. Department of State, Diplomacy in Actions, June 1, 1999, https://www.everycrsreport.com/files/19990601_RL30193_2046177bbad4fcb65cba6f9025d53bf6479d2afd.pdf
3 Zhou Qi, ed. *Congress and U.S. Foreign Policy*. Shanghai: Shanghai Academy of Social Science Press, 2006, pp.13–16.
4 Sun Zhe. *Influencing the Future: Institutional Transformation and Policy Making of the U.S. Congress*. Shanghai: Shanghai People's Publishing House, 2012 edition, p.46.
5 Sun Zhe, "American Presidential and Congressional Diplomacy," Fudan Journal (social science), No.4, 2001, pp.50–57.
6 Liu Yongtao, "U.S. Congress, Presidency and China Policy: Changes, Debates and Agendas," *Fudan American Review,* No. 2, 2009, p.85.
7 Alton Frye, *The Misunderstood Congress and American Foreign Policy, in* Wang Xi, ed., The Role of the U.S. Congress in the American Foreign Policy Process, Shanghai: Fudan University Press, 1990, pp.34–35.
8 James M. Lindsay, *Congress and the Politics of U.S. Foreign Policy*, Baltimore, MD: The Johns Hopkins University Press, 1994, pp.vii-viii.
9 Zhou Qi, ed., *Congress and U.S. Foreign Policy*, Shanghai: Shanghai Academy of Social Sciences Press, 2006, pp.46–242.
10 Sun Zhe et al., *Congress and US-China Relations: Cases and Analyses,* Beijing: Current Affairs Press, 2003, pp.43–75.
11 Xin Qiang, *The U.S. Congress Diplomacy: "Semi-Self-Contained" Congress and Taiwan Issue,* Shanghai: Fudan University Press, 2005, p.57.

12 Sun Zhe, ed., *The U.S. Congress and Taiwan Issue*, Shanghai: Fudan University Press, 2005, p.7.
13 Sun Zhe, ed., *The Congressional Research I*, Shanghai: Fudan University Press, 2002, front page 4.
14 James M. Scott, "The Challenge of the SCS: Congressional Engagement and the U.S. Policy Response," *All Azimuth: A Journal of Foreign Policy and Peace*, Vol.7, Issue 2, 2018, pp.5–30.
15 Zhang Mingling, "The U.S. Congressional Involvement in SCS Issue: Approaches and Implications," *The Journal of SCS Studies*, No.3, 2015, p.26.
16 "Maritime Disputes and Sovereignty in East Asia," Hearing before the Subcommittee on East Asian and Pacific Affairs of the Committee on Foreign Relations, United States Senate, 111th Congress, 1st Session, July 15, 2009.
17 "Beijing as an Emerging Power in the SCS," Hearing Before the Committee on Foreign Affairs, United States House of Representatives, 112th Congress, 2ed Session, September 12, 2012.
18 "America's Security Role in the SCS," Hearing before the Committee on Foreign Affairs United States House of Representatives, 114th, 1st session, July 23, 2015.
19 "American Leadership In The Asia Pacific, Part 5: The Asia Reassurance Initiative Act," Hearing before the Committee on Foreign Affairs, United States Senate, 115th Congress, May 15, 2018.
20 US China Economic and Security Review Commission, "2013 Annual Report to Congress," November 20, 2013, https://www.uscc.gov/sites/default/files/annual_reports/Complete%202013%20Annual%20Report.PDF
21 Zhou Qi, ed., *Congress and U.S. Foreign Policy*. Shanghai: Shanghai Academy of Social Science Press, 2006, p.21.
22 See the official website of CRS: https://crsreports.congress.gov/
23 Ben Dolven, Mark E. Manyin, Shirley A. Kan, "Maritime Territorial Disputes in East Asia: Issues for Congress," CRS report, May 14, 2014.
24 Ben Dolven, Jennifer K. Elsea, Susan V. Lawrence, Ronald O'Rourke, Ian E. Rinehart, "Chinese Land Reclamation in the SCS: Implications and Policy Options," CRS report, June 18, 2015.
25 Ben Dolven, Susan V. Lawrence, Ronald O'Rourke, "SCS Disputes: Background and U.S. Policy," CRS report, February 23, 2017.
26 Ronald O'Rourke, "Maritime Territorial and Exclusive Economic Zone (EEZ) Disputes Involving China: Issues for Congress," CRS report, May 24, 2018.
27 Ronald O'Rourke, "China Naval Modernization: Implications for U.S. Navy Capabilities—Background and Issues for Congress," CRS report, August 1, 2018.
28 Bruce Vaughn, Emma Chanlett-Avery, Ben Dolven, K. Alan Kronstadt, Susan V. Lawrence, Thomas Lum, Wayne M. Morrison, Ronald O'Rourke, "The Trump Administration's 'Free and Open Indo-Pacific': Issues for Congress," CRS report, October 3, 2018.

29 Ronald O'Rourke, "China's Actions in South and East China Seas: Implications for U.S. Interests—Background and Issues for Congress," CRS report, January 31, 2019.

30 See US China Economic and Security Review Commission annual report website: https://www.uscc.gov/Annual_Reports

31 See the PDF link: https://www.uscc.gov/sites/default/files/annual_reports/2010-Report-to-Congress.pdf

32 See the PDF link: https://www.uscc.gov/sites/default/files/annual_reports/annual_report_full_11.pdf

33 See the PDF link: https://www.uscc.gov/sites/default/files/annual_reports/2012-Report-to-Congress.pdf

34 See the PDF link: https://www.uscc.gov/sites/default/files/annual_reports/Complete%202013%20Annual%20Report.PDF

35 See the PDF link: https://www.uscc.gov/sites/default/files/annual_reports/Complete%20Report.PDF

36 See the PDF link: https://www.uscc.gov/sites/default/files/annual_reports/2015%20Annual%20Report%20to%20Congress.PDF

37 See the PDF link: https://www.uscc.gov/sites/default/files/annual_reports/2016%20Annual%20Report%20to%20Congress.pdf

38 See the PDF link: https://www.uscc.gov/sites/default/files/annual_reports/2017_Annual_Report_to_Congress.pdf

39 See the PDF link: https://www.uscc.gov/sites/default/files/annual_reports/2018%20Annual%20Report%20to%20Congress.pdf

40 See the PDF link: https://www.uscc.gov/sites/default/files/2020-12/2020_Annual_Report_to_Congress.pdf

41 The geostrategic value of the SCS has been specifically discussed in Annual Report to Congress: Military and Security Developments involving the People's Republic of China from 2008 to 2014.

42 Refer to *White Paper on China's Peaceful Development,* issued by the State Council Information Office of the People's Republic of China, Sept.6, 2011.

43 For related discussions, please refer to Han Xudong, "Prudent Use of National Core Interests," *Outlook Weekly*, No. 30, 2010; Da Wei, "Why Should China Declare its Core Interests?", *Global Times*, July 27, 2010, 14th Edition; Michael D. Swaine, "China's Assertive Behavior Part One: on 'core interests'," *China Leadership Monitor*, No. 34, February 22, 2011, pp.1–25; Li Ying, "China's 'core interests' Should not be Expanded," *International Herald Guide*, issue 1, 2011, 24th edition; Guan Fei, "Why the SCS is China's Core Interest," *World View*, February 2011; Toshi Yoshihara & James R. Holmes, "Can China Defend a 'Core Interest' in the SCS?", *The Washington Quarterly*, Spring 2011, pp.45–59; Kai He and Huiyun Feng, "Debating China's Assertiveness: Taking China's Power and Interests Seriously," *International Politics*,

Vol.49, No.5, 2012, pp.633–644; Wang Sheng, Luo Xiao, "The Transformation of International System and the Change of China's Peripheral Diplomacy: from maintaining stability to safeguarding rights," *Contemporary International Relations*, No.1, 2013, pp.9–15; Nie Wenjuan, "China's Identity and Understanding of National Interests in the SCS," *Journal of Contemporary Asia-Pacific Studies*, No.1, 2017, pp.139–155; Luo Xiao, "The SCS and China's Core Interests: Debate, Review and Transend," *Journal of Contemporary Asia-Pacific Studies*, No.1, 2018, pp.122–155; Zeng Yong, "Rethink the parlance of about 'core interests in SCS'," *Southeast Asian Affairs*, issue 4, 2018, pp.1–16.

44 Office of the Secretary of Defense, Annual Report to Congress: Military and Security Developments Involving the People's Republic of China 2013.

45 Office of the Secretary of Defense, Annual Report to Congress: Military and Security Developments Involving the People's Republic of China 2014, 2015.

46 Refer to the Annual Report to Congress: Military and Security Developments involving the People's Republic of China from 2013–2018.

47 Office of the Secretary of Defense, Annual Report to Congress: Military and Security Developments Involving the People's Republic of China 2011.

48 Office of the Secretary of Defense, Annual Report to Congress: Military and Security Developments Involving the People's Republic of China 2014.

49 Office of the Secretary of Defense, Annual Report to Congress: Military and Security Developments Involving the People's Republic of China 2014, 2015.

50 Office of the Secretary of Defense, Annual Report to Congress: Military and Security Developments Involving the People's Republic of China 2017, 2018.

51 Office of the Secretary of Defense, Annual Report to Congress: Military and Security Developments Involving the People's Republic of China 2015.

52 Office of the Secretary of Defense, Annual Report to Congress: Military and Security Developments Involving the People's Republic of China 2016.

53 Office of the Secretary of Defense, Annual Report to Congress: Military and Security Developments Involving the People's Republic of China 2017.

54 Office of the Secretary of Defense, Annual Report to Congress: Military and Security Developments Involving the People's Republic of China 2018.

55 Office of the Secretary of Defense, Annual Report to Congress: Military and Security Developments Involving the People's Republic of China 2019, 2020.

56 The Department of Defense of United States, "Asia-Pacific Maritime Security Strategy," August 2018, https://dod.defense.gov/Portals/1/Documents/pubs/NDAA%20A-P_Maritime_SecuritY_Strategy-08142015-1300-FINALFORMAT.PDF

57 Rigoberto Tiglao, "This the Season," *Far Eastern Economic Review*, December 24, 1998, p.18.

58 "Kerry Statement on The Law of the Sea Convention: The U.S. National Security and Strategic Imperatives for Ratification," The United States Senate Committee on Foreign Relations, May 23, 2012, https://www.foreign.senate.gov/press/chair/release/kerry-statement_on-the-law-of-the-sea-convention-the-us-national-security-and-strategic-imperatives-for-ratification-

59 "Engel Statement on Chinese Provocations in the SCS," The U.S. House of Representatives committee on Foreign Relations, May 9, 2014, https://foreignaffairs.house.gov/2014/5/engel-statement-chinese-provocations-south-china-sea

60 "Senators Express Concerns over Maritime Dispute in SCS, Call Chinese Actions 'Troubling'," May 09, 2014, https://www.foreign.senate.gov/press/chair/release/senators-express-concerns-over-maritime-dispute-in-south-china-sea-call-chinese-actions-troubling

61 "Cardin Statement on Meeting with President Xi Jinping," September 25, 2015, https://www.foreign.senate.gov/press/ranking/release/cardin-statement-on-meeting-with-president-xi-jinping

62 "Engel Statement on U.S. Navy Exercises in the SCS," October 27, 2015 https://foreignaffairs.house.gov/2015/10/engel-statement-us-navy-exercises-south-china-sea

63 "Cardin Calls on Senate to Ratify United Nations Convention on the Law of the Sea, Reacts to Ruling by International Tribunal for the Law of the Sea," October 29, 2015, https://www.foreign.senate.gov/press/ranking/release/cardin-calls-on-senate-to-ratify-united-nations-convention-on-the-law-of-the-sea-reacts-to-ruling-by-international-tribunal-for-the-law-of-the-sea

64 "Statement from Foreign Affairs & Armed Services Democrats on SCS Decision," July 12, 2016 https://foreignaffairs.house.gov/2016/7/statement-foreign-affairs-armed-services-democrats-south-china-sea-decision

65 "Corker Statement on Ruling in SCS Maritime Dispute," July 12, 2016, https://www.foreign.senate.gov/press/chair/release/corker-statement-on-ruling-in-south-china-sea-maritime-dispute

66 "Rubio Comments On Tribunal Decision Regarding SCS," July 12, 2016, https://www.rubio.senate.gov/public/index.cfm/press-releases?ID=AE4D64B2-6227-49B8-A1B7-63601A16B8F9

67 "Cardin Statement on Chinese Seizure of U.S. Navy Submersible from International Waters," December 16, 2016, https://www.foreign.senate.gov/press/ranking/release/cardin-statement-on-chinese-seizure-of-us-navy-submersible-from-international-waters

68 "Sasse Statement on SCS Laser Attacks," June 22, 2018, https://www.sasse.senate.gov/public/index.cfm/2018/6/sasse-statement-on-south-china-sea-laser-attacks

69 "Chairman Kerry Delivers A Speech On U.S.-China Relations," December 07, 2010, https://www.foreign.senate.gov/press/chair/release/chairman-kerry-delivers-a-speech-on-us-china-relations

70 Senator John McCain, "Defining American Interests in Asia," May 14, 2012, https://csis-prod.s3.amazonaws.com/s3fs-public/event/120514_TPP_McCain_Transcript.pdf

71 "Lieberman Remarks on the SCS and Asia-Pacific in Transition," June 28, 2012, http://www.lieberman.senate.gov/index.cfm/news-events/news/2012/6/lieberman-remarks-on-the-south-china-sea-and-the-asiapacific-in-transition

72 "Chairman Menendez's Opening Remarks at Hearing on the Future of U.S.-China Relations," June 25, 2014, https://www.foreign.senate.gov/press/chair/release/chairman-menendezs-opening-remarks-at-hearing-on-the-future-of-us-china-relations

73 "Engel Remarks on the Disputes in the South and East China Sea," December 4, 2014, https://foreignaffairs.house.gov/2014/12/engel-remarks-disputes-south-and-east-china-sea

74 "U.S. Senator Dan Sullivan Remarks to The Center for Strategic and International Studies holds its 6th Annual SCS Conference," July 12, 2016, https://www.sullivan.senate.gov/imo/media/doc/Sullivan_CSIS_071216.pdf

75 "Remarks as Delivered by Congressman Rick Larsen at a Brookings Institution Event: The end of U.S. engagement with China?", March 7, 2018, https://larsen.house.gov/press-release/remarks-delivered-congressman-rick-larsen-brookings-institution-event-%E2%80%9C-end-us

76 "Menendez Leads Series of Floor Speeches Condemning Trump Administration's Foreign Policy Agenda," March 20, 2018 https://www.foreign.senate.gov/press/ranking/release/menendez-leads-series-of-floor-speeches-condemning-trump-administrations-foreign-policy-agenda

77 "Senator Webb Says China's Use of Force Against Philippines 'Especially Troubling'; Seeks Clarification of U.S.- Philippines Defense Treaty," July 20, 2011, https://pacificnewscenter.com/senator-webb-says-chinas-use-of-force-against-philippines-especially-troubling-seeks-clarification-of-us-philippines-defense-treaty/

78 "Rep. Ed Royce called for increased U.S. -Filipino maritime security cooperation," November 29, 2011, http://foreignaffairs.house.gov/press_display.asp?id=2106

79 "Senators McCain, Reed, Corker, and Menendez Send Letter on Chinese Maritime Strategy," March 19, 2015, https://www.armed-services.senate.gov/press-releases/senators-mccain-reed-corker-and-menendez-send-letter-on-chinese-maritime-strategy

80 "Senators McCain and Reed Oppose Chinese Participation in U.S.-Led Military Exercise," May 22, 2015, https://www.armed-services.senate.gov/press-releases/senators-mccain-and-reed-oppose-chinese-participation-in-us-led-military-exercise

81 "As U.S.-China Dialogue Begins, Rubio Urges Obama To Seek Change In Chinese Behavior," June 22, 2015, https://www.rubio.senate.gov/public/index.cfm/mobile/press-releases?ID=68EBB9CF-5FDC-4F65-BB91-33CF94527A96

82 "Engel Urges 100+ Governments to Publicly Support SCS Decision," July 12, 2016, https://foreignaffairs.house.gov/2016/7/engel-urges-100-governments-support-south-china-sea-decision

83 "Cardin, Corker, Colleagues Write to Trump About U.S. Navigation Operations in SCS," May 10, 2017,https://www.foreign.senate.gov/press/ranking/release/cardin-corker-colleagues-write-to-trump-about-us-navigation-operations-in-south-china-sea

84 "Rubio, Gardner, Markey Urge Administration to Respond to Ongoing Chinese Militarization of SCS," May 25, 2018, https://www.rubio.senate.gov/public/index.cfm/press-releases?ID=33148BFB-AB71-4629-B939-6C2A95C44F7D

85 Joseph Lieberman, "The SCS and Asia Pacific in Transition: Exploring Options for Managing Disputes," June 28, 2012, https://csis-prod.s3.amazonaws.com/s3fs-public/event/120628_southchinasea_lieberman_transcript.pdf

86 Harry J. Kazianis, "Can Congress Stop China in the SCS?", *The National Interest*, March 22, 2015, https://nationalinterest.org/feature/can-congress-stop-china-the-south-china-sea-12459

87 You Hongbo, "US Reaction to the Paracels Battle between PRC and South Vietnam," *Southeast Asian Affairs*, No. 3, 2011, p.23; Zhang Mingling, *America's Involvement in the SCS: Process, Drives and Implications,* Hong Kong: Hong Kong Social Science Publishing Co., Ltd., 2011, pp.227–230.

88 He Weibao, "Characteristics and Causes of the US Congress Legislation on the SCS Issue," in Zheng Bingwen, Huang Ping, ed., *Blue Book of the United State: Annual Report on Research of U.S.A. (2015): New Challenges of U.S. Rebalancing Strategy*, Beijing: Social Sciences Literature Press, 2015 edition, p.186.

89 Liu Yongtao. U.S. Congressional-Presidential Relationship, Shanghai: Shanghai People's Publishing House, 2010, p.96.

90 Rebecca Shabad, "Democrats blast Trump for not seeking congressional approval for Syria strikes," April 14, 2018, https://www.nbcnews.com/politics/congress/democrats-blast-trump-not-seeking-congressional-approval-syria-strike-n865981

91 See the text link: https://www.congress.gov/112/bills/hres352/BILLS-112hres352ih.pdf

92 See the text link: https://www.congress.gov/113/bills/hr772/BILLS-113hr772ih.pdf

93 See the text link: https://www.congress.gov/113/bills/hres714/BILLS-113hres714eh.pdf

94 See the text link: https://www.congress.gov/114/bills/sres183/BILLS-114sres183is.pdf

95 Hearing of the US House of Representatives Committee on Foreign Relations, "Maritime Sovereignty in the East and SCSs," January 14, 2014, https://www.govinfo.gov/content/pkg/CHRG-113hhrg86962/pdf/CHRG-113hhrg86962.pdf

96 "Checking China's Maritime Push," Hearing of the US House of Representatives Committee on Foreign Relations, February 28, 2017, https://docs.house.gov/meetings/FA/FA05/20170228/105614/HHRG-115-FA05-Transcript-20170228.pdf

97 See the text link: https://www.uscc.gov/sites/default/files/annual_reports/2018%20Annual%20Report%20to%20Congress.pdf

98 See the text link: https://www.congress.gov/bill/113th-congress/senate-resolution/412/text?r=3&s=6

99 See the text link: https://www.congress.gov/bill/114th-congress/senate-resolution/183/text?r=2&s=9

100 See the text link: https://www.congress.gov/bill/114th-congress/house-resolution/830/text?r=2&s=10

101 "Chinese aggression in SCS cannot be tolerated: US," September 11, 2012, https://www.thehindubusinessline.com/news/world/chinese-aggression-in-south-china-sea-cannot-be-tolerated-us/article23086809.ece?ref=relatedNews

102 Zhao Weihua, "Vietnam's SCS Policy Adjustment: Evolution and Essence," *Southeast Asian Studies*, No.1, 2019, p.22.

103 "Senators Express Concerns over Maritime Dispute in SCS, Call Chinese Actions 'Troubling'," May 09, 2014, https://www.foreign.senate.gov/press/chair/release/senators-express-concerns-over-maritime-dispute-in-south-china-sea-call-chinese-actions-troubling

104 Asia Maritime Transparency Initiative, "Vietnam Expands Another Outpost," June 13, 2018, https://amti.csis.org/vietnam-expands-another-outpost/

105 Hu Bo, "Rectifying for the Construction of Nansha (Spratly) Islands and Reefs," report of Phoenix International Think Tank, March 2016, https://pit.ifeng.com/dacankao/nanshadaojiao/1.shtml

106 "Spratlys and the SCS," Statement by Christine Shelley, U.S. Department of State, Office of the Spokesman, May 10, 1995. The statement can be found in U.S. Interests in Southeast Asia, Hearings Before the Subcommittees on International Economic Policy and Trade and Asia and the Pacific of the Committee on International Relations, House of Representatives, 104th Congress, 2nd Session, May 30 and June 19, 1996, Washington DC: U.S. Government Printing Office (GPO), 1997, p.157.

107 Chairman John McCain, "Opening Statement on Maritime Security Strategy in the Asia-Pacific," Hearing of the United States Senate Committee on Armed Services, September 17, 2015, https://www.armed-services.senate.gov/imo/media/doc/9-17-15%20Asia-Pacific.pdf

108 "Senators McCain and Reed Oppose Chinese Participation in U.S.-Led Military Exercise," May 22, 2015, https://www.armed-services.senate.gov/press-releases/senators-mccain-and-reed-oppose-chinese-participation-in-us-led-military-exercise

109 "Takai: China out of RIMPAC," March 30, 2016, http://www.hawaiifreepress.com/ArticlesMain/tabid/56/ID/17205/Takai-China-out-of-RIMPAC.aspx

110 "Cardin, Corker, Colleagues Write to Trump About U.S. Navigation Operations in SCS," May 10, 2017, https://www.foreign.senate.gov/press/ranking/release/cardin-corker-colleagues-write-to-trump-about-us-navigation-operations-in-south-china-sea

111 Graham Allison, *Destined for War: Can America and China Escape Thucydides's Trap*?, Boston: Houghton Mifflin Harcourt, 2017.

7 China-U.S. Contention over Freedom of Navigation in the SCS

"The first and most obvious light in which the sea presents itself from the political and social point of view is that of a great highway; or better, perhaps, of a wide common, over which men may pass in all directions."

—Alfred Thayer Mahan

"Absolute freedom of navigation upon the seas, outside territorial waters, alike in peace and in war, except as the seas may be closed in whole or in part by international action for the enforcement of international covenants."

—Woodrow Wilson

Entering the 21st century, with the rapid rise of China and its great investment in maritime power, U.S.-China maritime competition in the Asia-Pacific region has become increasingly fierce, especially in the SCS. In order to maintain maritime hegemony, strengthen military alliances and enhance dominance in the Asia-Pacific region, the United States has frequently challenged China's maritime sovereignty and rights and impeded China's maritime development by defending the "freedom of navigation" (FON). Looking through the maritime disputes between China and the United States in recent years, it is not difficult to find that the issue of FON in the SCS has become the contentious focus. The Obama administration has publicly stated that "the United States has a national interest in freedom of navigation in the SCS."[1] During Obama's eight years in office, the

United States carried out five FONOPs in the SCS. After Donald Trump took office in 2017, the United States significantly increased patrols in the SCS, and carried out more than 10 times the same FONOPs in just two years. It is safe to say that the United States' implementation of FON in China has become one of the most important means to intervene in the SCS issue, even though after each passage there are only media reports to mark their occurrence.

America's Maritime Freedom Doctrine

As the maritime overlord, the United States has long pursued its own form of freedom of the seas, which is closely related to the development of commercial capitalism in the North American colonies. Back to the founding of the State, the founders of the United States took the principle of freedom of the sea as an important basis for the formulation of foreign policies, and also linked it with the principle of commercial freedom. For example, John Adams, who played an important role in early American foreign policy practice, expected that all the oceans and rivers on the planet should be free and open. Benjamin Franklin also believes that the more free and unrestricted the trade is, the more prosperous the relevant States will be.[2] In 1776, the United States incorporated maritime freedom into its "treaty plan" as a diplomatic guidance at the official level for the first time. Since then, in the trade treaties signed by the United States with France, the Netherlands, Sweden, Prussia, and other countries, "freedom of cargo carried by free ships," "limited embargo," "neutral trade rights," and other specific provisions reflecting the principle of freedom of the sea have been included. Moreover, the United States successfully incorporated the principle of maritime freedom in the treaties signed with 10 Latin American countries from 1824 to 1850.[3] It can be said that the United States spared no effort in promoting the freedom of the sea despite the weak national strength and limited foreign policy objectives in the early days.

World War One provided excellent chances for the United States to outline its strategy of maritime freedom on the international stage. In his message to Congress on January 22, 1917, President Wilson stressed that the development and prosperity of a country was closely related to its right to the sea. States should not be deprived of the right of free access to world trade. "The paths of the sea must alike in law and in fact be free. The freedom of the seas is the sino qua non of peace, equality and cooperation. It need not be difficult either to define or to secure the freedom of the seas if the governments of the world sincerely desire to come to an agreement concerning it."[4] The principle of freedom of the sea also ranks among the Fourteen Points, the peace principles proposed by Wilson to promote the post-war peace. As he put, "Absolute freedom of navigation upon the seas, outside territorial waters, alike in peace and in war, except as the seas may be closed in whole or in part by international action for the enforcement of international covenants."[5] Although Wilson's Fourteen Points plan failed in the end, his maritime liberalism has undoubtedly brought a positive impact on the country, which also provides an indispensable "soft power" for the United States to play a role in the global maritime politics and intervene in international maritime disputes.[6]

After World War One, the United States took the path of isolationism, but it didn't fundamentally divert its focus on maritime liberalism. In 1929, then Senator William E. Borah pointed out that if the United States did not expand the size of its navy and safeguard maritime freedom, it would not be able to effectively safeguard its own commercial interests. In the bill submitted to the Senate on February 21, Borah called on the U.S. government to promote the convening of an international conference to discuss and improve the existing international law of the sea.[7] During WWII, President Franklin D. Roosevelt also reiterated the American concept of maritime freedom on many occasions, and made great efforts to fight against the invasion of fascist countries. In his famous fireside chats, he stressed that "Generation after generation, America has battled for the general policy of the freedom of the seas. And that policy is a very simple one—but a basic, a fundamental one. It means that no nation has the right to make the broad oceans of the world at great distances from the actual theatre of land war, unsafe for the commerce of others." "That has been our policy, proved time and time again, in all of our history. Our policy has applied from the earliest days of the Republic—and still applies—not merely to the Atlantic but to the Pacific and to all other oceans as well."[8]

The United States has become a naval power after WWII, and its naval strength is unparalleled worldwide. With this advantage, the United States is in favor of the narrowest breadth of territorial sea and expanding the freedom of navigation with the widest scope as far as possible,[9] in that it can maintain the maximum freedom of movement of the U.S. Navy and Air Force. It also conforms to the strategic interests of the United States as a maritime power, that is, the more powerful a nation's maritime strength is, the more it wishes to maintain maximum freedom of the seas.

To sum up, freedom of seas for the United States means not only the freedom of navigation, but also the freedom of commerce and trade. As Richard

J. Grunewald of U.S. Naval War College describes "United States policy on international straits is dictated by the vital importance to U.S. national security interests of unimpeded commercial and military transit through, over and under sea lines of communication."[10] Compared with other countries, the United States is a strong proponent of maritime liberalism, and it is more active in promoting and defending the principle of maritime freedom. It should be pointed out that the maritime interests of the United States after WWII are no longer confined to the territorial sea and its extended waters, but expanded to a global scale. In terms of content, it is no longer limited to traditional maritime trade, high seas fishing, and marine resources development, but contains the interests of maritime security and military activities. After WWII, the U.S. military bases have been established globally, and it launched a maritime competition with the Soviet Union to obtain maritime superiority. Therefore, although the U.S. maritime policy was still to defend the so-called freedom of sea, it was to uphold hegemony in essence.

The FON Program

Freedom of navigation is a true reflection of the principle of freedom of the sea. According to the UNCLOS, the FON means that any state, whether coastal or land-locked, has the right of free navigation in any area of the high seas. Ships on the high seas are not subject to the jurisdiction or domination of other states except the flag state.[11] It should be noted that the FON stipulated in the UNCLOS is restricted by the scope of space, and navigation within the territorial sea must be subject to the effective management of sovereign states. FON must be harmless navigation, and shall not engage in acts that threaten the security of other countries, interfere with or undermine legitimate commercial and social activities. State shall have due regard to the interests of other states in exercising the freedom of the high seas and to the rights provided for in the UNCLOS in relation to activities in the area. In other words, FON is not an absolute right, it has limitations.

With the rising awareness of maritime consciousness of coastal states in the 1960s and 1970s, they have the appeal of expanding maritime jurisdiction, which poses a great challenge to the maritime freedom of the United States. For example, in view of the traditional international practice that the breadth of territorial sea is 3 nautical miles, some Western countries put forward the territorial sea breadth of 12 nautical miles, and some Latin American countries advocate extending the breadth of territorial sea up to 200 nautical miles. It seems that coastal countries and even major maritime powers have changed their understanding of the sea in the new round of "blue enclosure movement." They began to regard the sea more for its resources rather than just a "highway" connecting the world. At the Third UN Conference on the Law of the Sea, in particular, countries engaged in fierce bargaining over a series of issues, such as "innocent passage" through territorial waters, the ownership of straits and continental shelf, the division of EEZ, archipelagic states, and island systems. In this period, the United States regarded the claim of maritime area or jurisdiction put forward by some coastal states as "excessive maritime claims," which it felt were obviously inconsistent with the customary international law of the sea. By 1978, there was a consensus reached in the United States that it should be prepared to defend its navigation rights and interests, regardless of the potential for conflict and skirmishes with other coastal states.

In this context, the Carter administration directed the U.S. Military to begin carrying out the FON program in July 1979, to preserve its national interests and demonstrate non-acquiescence to excessive maritime claims asserted by coastal states.[12] Elliot L. Richardson, then the special representative of the United States to the UNCLOS, once said that U.S. Navy should have the ability to exist and assemble anywhere it is ordered to be so that its mission of deterrence can be accomplished, which is significant to American maritime interests. And the activities of U.S. Navy should not be constrained and when navigating or stationing, no country cannot control it.[13]

Although the United States actively participated in the negotiation and formulation of the UNCLOS, it did not ratify the Convention because of its effect on national security and the obstruction of domestic conservative political partisans. Therefore, the FON Program is a realistic option for the United States to respond to the "excessive maritime claims" of other states and defend its maritime hegemony. It is essentially a strategic tool for the United States to shape the order of the oceans outside the convention system.[14]

Since then, the successive U.S. governments have launched a series of policies to improve the FON Program. The Reagan administration issued the National Security Decision Directives No. 72 (NSDD72) on December 13, 1982, which clarified "the plan of the United States to exercise the right of navigation and overflight at sea," and specifically explained the "excessive sea claim."[15] On March 10, 1983, President Reagan reiterated in his maritime policy statement that the United States would continue to implement and defend the right to freedom of navigation and overflight throughout the world, including in the EEZ, in a way that "balances interests as reflected in the Convention."[16] On March 16, 1987, the

White House issued the National Security Decision Directive 265 (NSDD265) document, namely "freedom of navigation program," which once again clarified the relevant policies of the United States and its position against the "excessive sea claim."[17] On October 12, 1990, the Senior Bush administration announced the National Security Directive 49 (NSD49), namely "freedom of navigation (U)," which further demonstrated the determination of the United States to safeguard the freedom of navigation and overflight.[18]

During the Clinton administration, the United States issued the Presidential Decision Directive/National Security Council No. 32 (PDD / NSC-32) in 1995. During Bush Junior's administration, the Joint Chiefs Convention issued "CJCSI2420.01A" document in 2003, namely the "freedom of navigation program of the United States and the report on sensitive areas."[19] On December 21, 2004, the White House issued the National Security Presidential Directive NSPD-41/Homeland Security Presidential Directive HSPD-13, which is the "maritime security policy." It once again emphasizes the importance of freedom of the sea and affirms the need to safeguard the national security and homeland security of the United States through the protection of marine interests.[20] On January 9, 2009, the United States issued the National Security Presidential Directive NSPD-66/Homeland Security Presidential Directive HSPD-25, which is the "Arctic region policy," claiming that ensuring FON and overflight in the Arctic region is an important national security interest of the United States.[21] The abovementioned documents show that the FON Program was not accomplished overnight. Instead, it has experienced a process from initial establishment to refinement and improvement. It is a collection of a series of policy documents, reflecting America's ceaseless pursuit of FON on its own terms.

The purpose of the FON Program launched by the United States is aimed at countering the "excessive maritime claims" of other coastal states that are inconsistent with U.S. reading of international law. Taking account of a series of policy documents, the "excessive ocean claims" recognized by the United States includes the following six categories:

1. Historic bay/historic water claims not recognized by the United States.
2. Territorial sea base line claims not drawn in conformance with customary international law as reflected in the LOS Convention.
3. Territorial sea claims not exceeding 12 nautical miles in breath that:
   (a) overlap straits used for international navigation and do not permit transit passage in conformance with the customary international law reflected in the LOS Convention, including submerged transit of

submarines, overflight of military aircraft, and surface transit of warships/naval auxiliaries, without prior notification or authorization, and including transit in a manner of deployment consistent with the security of the forces involved; or

(b) contain requirements for advance notification or authorization for innocence passage of all vessels, including warships/naval auxiliaries, or apply discriminatory requirements to such vessels; or

(c) apply special requirements, not recognized by international law, for innocent passage based on means of propulsion, armament, or cargo.

4. Territorial sea claims in excess of 12 nautical miles.
5. Other claims to jurisdiction over maritime areas in excess of 12 nautical miles, such as security zones, that purport to restrict non-resource-related high seas freedoms.
6. Archipelagic claims that either:

(a) do not permit archipelagic sea lanes passage in conformance with customary international law reflected in the LOS Convention, including submerged passage of submarines, overflight of military aircraft, and surface transit of warships/naval auxiliaries, without prior notification or authorization, and including transit in a manner of deployment consistent with the security of the forces involved; or

(b) are otherwise not in conformance with customary international law reflected in the LOS Convention.[22]

On an operational level, the FON Program is a joint effort of the DoS and DoD. It operates on three levels: operational assertions, or FON operations, by military units; diplomatic protests of excessive claims or other diplomatic representations by the DoS; and DoS/DoD consultations with representatives of other States in an effort to promote stability and consistency in the law of the sea. Among them, FONOPs are the most effective and substantial. As Dennis Mandsager of the U.S. Naval War College points out, "protests without operations give the coastal state exactly what it wants—restrictions on our mobility and a change in our behavior consistent with the illegal claim . . . Of course, operational assertions send an even stronger signal than diplomatic protests, for protests alone seldom provide a sufficient incentive to impel relinquishment of the claim."[23] According to a study released by the Bureau of Oceanographic and International Environmental and Scientific Affairs of U.S. DoS on March 9, 1992, since the implementation of the FON Program through fiscal year 1991, the United States has operationally and diplomatically protested a 110 claims made by 35 States at the rate of approximately 30–40 per year.[24]

Since 1992, U.S. DoD issued Annual FON Reports: Operational Assertions, listing all coastal states making excessive maritime claims over the last fiscal year, as well as the reason those claims were operationally protested by U.S. forces under the FON Program.[25] It can be inferred from the reports that the target countries of the U.S. military operations include not only opponent countries, but also its allies and partners, which shows that the primary goal of the FON Program is to maintain the maritime order in favor of the United States, instead of depending on bilateral relations. The data also shows that the United States challenges the claims of its allies through FONOPs less often than that of non-allies or hostile countries. From a legal point of view, U.S. allies are more likely to take similar positions on maritime affairs.[26]

The U.S. FONOPs against China

During the Cold War, the United States relied on China to counter the strategic pressure from the Soviet Union. Plus, China's military defense focused primarily on land warfare at that time, therefore maritime issues were not as prominent as today in China-U.S. relations, and the two countries did not have serious friction on the issue of FON. According to existing records, FON first appeared on the agenda of China-U.S. relations with the dispute over the rules of innocent passage in territorial waters.

The territorial sea forms part of national sovereignty and is under a State's jurisdiction, but based on the traditional principle of "freedom of the sea," the UNCLOS adopted in 1982 clearly stipulates that foreign ships enjoy the right of innocent passage in the territorial waters of coastal states, and "passage is innocent so long as it is not prejudicial to peace, good order or security of the coastal state."[27] The coastal state may adopt laws and regulations, in conformity with the provisions of this Convention and other rules of international law, relating to innocent passage through the territorial sea. Foreign ships exercising the right of innocent passage through the territorial sea shall comply with such regulations and laws.[28] Since foreign warships' passing through the territorial sea involves the national security of coastal countries, most countries have adopted different policies and practices on the issue of warships passing through the territorial sea. Like most coastal states, China has imposed necessary restrictions on the passage of foreign warships through China's territorial waters out of concern for national security. China maintains that all foreign military ships passing through China's territorial waters need to obtain the consent of the Chinese government in advance.[29] In response to China's statement, the U.S. Navy penetrated into China's territorial waters within 12 nautical miles without prior consent and launched a FON operation to protest against China's so-called excessive maritime claim in 1986.

After the Cold War, the strategic ties established by China and the United States in response to the threat of the Soviet Union disintegrated, and contradictions between the two sides developed on many issues, including FON at sea. In February 1992, China promulgated the Law of the PRC on the Territorial Sea and the Contiguous Zone, which clearly stipulates that "foreign non-military ships shall enjoy the right of innocent passage through the territorial sea of the PRC in accordance with the law. Entry of foreign military vessels into the territorial waters of the PRC shall obtain the approval of the Central People's Government."[30] Seeing it as an "excessive maritime claim," the United States not only issued diplomatic protests against this legislation, but also sent warships to sail into China's territorial waters, thereby implementing FON operations against China. Among them, the confrontation in the Yellow Sea that occurred during this period is a typical example of the United States intruding into China's sovereign territory and negatively affecting its national security under the pretext of "freedom of navigation." In October 1994, without prior notification to China, the U.S. Navy dispatched the aircraft carrier "Kitty Hawk" to patrol along the border of China's territorial waters and intrude into China's territorial waters without permission to track a Chinese Navy Han-class nuclear-powered attack submarine that had just completed its offshore training, which led to an aerial standoff when China reacted. The United States defended its operation by asserting that warships enjoyed the "right of innocent passage" in China's territorial waters, which was in line with the provisions of international law and did not necessarily obtain China's consent in advance.[31] The Yellow Sea confrontation made both China and the United States realize the importance and urgency of establishing a maritime conflict prevention mechanism, thus promoting the signing of Agreement Between the Ministry of National Defense of the PRC and the DoD of the USA on Establishing a Consultation Mechanism to Strengthen Military Maritime Safety in January 1998.[32]

With China's rise and its moderate expansion of sea power, the divergence between China and the United States expanded from the right of innocent passage of warships in territorial waters to the right of FON in the EEZ. In order to constrain the rise of China, the United States has prominently augmented its military activities in the surrounding waters of China. One of the important means was to strengthen the implementation of the FON operation. The United States insists that, according to the Article 58 of the UNCLOS, "in the exclusive zone, all States, whether coastal or land-locked, enjoy, subject to the relevant provisions of this Convention, the FON and overflight . . . and other internationally lawful uses of the sea related to these freedoms."[33] According to the interpretation of the United States, the EEZ is a part of the high seas and belongs to international waters, where countries enjoy the highest degree of FON and overflight, while "other internationally lawful uses" including military activities carried out in the EEZ should not be restricted by coastal states. China believes that the Convention does not explicitly prohibit the navigation activities of military vessels in the EEZ. However, it stipulates that the relevant acts should be reserved for peaceful purposes.[34] In addition, States shall have due regard to the rights and duties of the coastal state and shall comply with the laws and regulations adopted by the coastal state in accordance with the provisions of this Convention and other rules of international law.[35] In other words, FON in the EEZ has a premise that it takes into account the rights of other States and conforms to the laws and regulations of coastal states, thus its scope is obviously less than that of the FON on the high seas.[36]

In response to China's claim, the United States has frequently engaged in military reconnaissance, oceanographic survey, and intelligence collection activities in the EEZ of the Yellow Sea, the East China Sea, and the SCS in the name of safeguarding FON, which has triggered maritime friction and crises.[37] In April 2001, the U.S. EP-3 reconnaissance plane conducted reconnaissance in the airspace near Hainan Island of China, and collided with a Chinese fighter plane. As a result, the Chinese fighter crashed, while the U.S. aircraft was forced to land at Lingshui Airport of Hainan Island without permission. The incident led to a diplomatic crisis between China and the United States. From 2002 to 2005, the United States repeatedly sent military survey vessels and electronic intelligence reconnaissance ships into China's EEZ in the Yellow Sea, the East China Sea, and the SCS for illegal survey and intelligence collection, posing a serious threat to China's national security. In March 2009, the U.S. Navy survey vessel Impeccable entered the waters of the EEZ of the SCS to conduct seabed topographic mapping and underwater monitoring, and encountered with Chinese ships. Afterwards, the United States protested to China, arguing that the operation of the Impeccable was on the high seas and that it enjoyed the right of FON and was not subject to the rule of international law or China's domestic law on the EEZ.[38]

In 2011, after the Obama administration proposed to "pivot to Asia" and implement the "rebalancing" strategy in the Asia-Pacific region, the implementation of the FONOPs against China has become a routine for the United States as a useful means to restrain China. During his eight years in power, U.S. warships sailed within 12 nautical miles of islands and reefs in the SCS on five occasions. In October 2015, the USS Larsen warship sailed within 12 nautical miles of Subi Reef in the Spratly Islands. In January 2016, the destroyer Curtis Wilbur sailed within 12 nautical miles of the Paracel waters, passing through the middle of the archipelago in a manner dangerous to its navigation. After Donald Trump came to power in 2017, the United States' navy patrols in the SCS, both in intensity and frequency, have far exceeded that of the Obama administration, and the situation in the SCS has become even more intense. During this period, the United States has sent aircraft carrier battle groups into the SCS for so-called routine patrols. Its warships have also repeatedly intruded within 12 nautical miles of relevant islands and reefs in the SCS without the permission of Beijing, violating China's sovereign rights and interests.

Overall, since the United States announced the FON Program, China has become a reoccurring target. According to information disclosed in the report on FON issued by the U.S. DoD since 1992, the implementation of the FONOP by the United States against China can be summarized as in Table 7.1. It should be pointed out that the annual report only publicizes the names of the claimants, and indicates whether it has carried out several FONOPs against the claimant in the year, while the information such as specific time, general geological location, and the specific times of FONOPs for a certain claimant is still confidential. The information disclosed in the report is quite limited, although it does offer a view of the current FONOPs situation, as conducted by the United States.

The Characteristics of the U.S. FONOPs Concerning China

One of the important functions of the U.S. FONOPs is to send political signals to coastal states that are considered to have "excessive maritime claims" through a variety of military operations. In most cases, FONOPs are not carried out with great fanfare, but with levels of confidentiality in a low-key manner. Since gaps exist in marine capabilities, some FONOPs conducted in EEZs and even territorial waters have not been uncovered until the release of annual FON reports.[39] For key countries and sea areas, however, the United States is extremely high-profile

Table 7.1. Overview of FONOPs conducted by the United States in China from 1991 to 2020

Oper ation / Year	Excessive straight baselines	Security jurisdiction in the contiguous zone	Jurisdiction over airspace above the EEZ	Domestic law criminalizing survey activity by foreign entities in the EEZ	Prior permission required for innocent passage of foreign military ships through territorial sea	Restrictions on foreign aircraft flying through an ADIZ
1991 (no record)						
1992					•	
1993*					•	
1994*					•	
1995 (no record)						
1996					•	
1997–2006 (no record)						
2007*		•	•	•		
2008*			•	•		

2009*			•	•		
2010*			•	•		
2011*	•		•	•	•	
2012*			•	•	•	
2013*	•	•	•	•	•	
2014*			•	•		•
2015*	•		•	•	•	•
2016*	•		•	•	•	•
2017*	•		•	•	•	•
2018*	•	•	•	•	•	•
2019*	•	•	•	•	•	•
2020*	•	•	•	•	•	•

Source: The data is based on the "FON report" issued by the U.S. DoD over years. Among them, the year 1993–1994 marked with * indicated that similar operations has been carried out in the past year; in 2007 and later years, the symbol * indicated that many operations were carried out in that year.

in implementing FONOPs. For example, the FONOPs carried out in the SCS in recent years have earned widely public attention aimed at heating up the SCS issue. Although it is difficult to analyze the relevant data comprehensively and accurately due to the lack of comprehensive information, the implementation of FONOPs towards China presents the following characteristics.

Territorial Sea and EEZ Are the Targeted Areas

In terms of the protest target, the United States has mainly focused on the territorial sea and EEZ when implementing FONOPs against China in the past two decades, which is consistent with United States' operations on a global scale. It shows that there is a huge cognitive discord between China and the United States on the right of innocent passage through the territorial sea and the military activities in the EEZ under the international law. Furthermore, the focus of FONOPs shifted from the territorial sea to the EEZ, although the territorial sea and EEZ have been equally valued in recent years.

Specifically, the United States had protested against China's maritime claims before 1997 on the grounds that the prior permission for the innocent passage through territorial sea did not comply with FON provisions under international law. This was actually a policy response to China's promulgation of the Law of the PRC on the Territorial Sea and the Contiguous Zone in 1992 and the Declaration on the Baseline of the Territorial Sea of the PRC in 1996. With the rising numbers of maritime disputes around China after 2007, protests against China began to shift to jurisdiction over the EEZ and the reconnaissance, measurement, and exercise activities of foreign ships and aircraft in the EEZ. After more than a decade of silence, the issue of innocent passage through the territorial sea has risen again since 2010. Together with the EEZ, it has become an important target for the U.S. FON operations. This is undoubtedly the true reflection of the frequent "patrols" of the U.S. warships in the EEZ of the SCS in the new period and repeatedly breaking into the 12 nautical miles of the relevant islands and reefs.

The Operation Frequency and Scope Are Expanding

Although the annual FON report issued by the U.S. DoD does not list the specific times of FONOPs, it makes a special note on whether the year is one of "multiple challenges." As can be seen from Table 7.1, except for "no record" years and certain years, the United States basically implements "multiple" FONOPs against China on an annual basis. Especially since 2007, with the deepening of U.S. involvement in maritime disputes around China and the increasingly violent contests between China and the United States in the SCS and the East China Sea, the frequency and intensity of FONOPs against China has also increased. As U.S. military autonomy has been improved and is well prepared for combat, the FONOPs conducted by the United States in the disputed areas of the SCS are more provocative and targeted, showing the United States is more determined to deter the growth of China's maritime forces and as well as muscle into the militarization of the SCS issue, which should arouse China's vigilance.[40]

Accordingly, the U.S. military before 2010 mainly challenged the following three claims of China: prior permission in innocent passage through territorial waters, jurisdiction of the airspace of the EEZ, and criminalization of foreign surveying activities in the EEZ. Moreover, only one or two of them are challenged every year. After 2011, the scope of U.S. FONOPs against China has been significantly expanded, including "excessive straight baselines," "excessive jurisdiction over contiguous areas," and "restrictions on foreign aircraft flying over the ADIZ" as the targets of new challenges, declaring actions against 4–5 of them every year. Overall, FONOPs carried out by the United States towards China are dynamic, and the relevant response objectives are not fixed. It will be adjusted accordingly with the changes of regional situation.

The United States Maintains Double Standards towards China and a Strong Intention to Contain China

According to the United States, the purpose of the FON Program is not only to safeguard legitimate rights of freedom of action in international waters, but also to enable other countries to recognize and respect what the United States sees as legitimate rights and interests of FON in territorial waters, international waters, international Straits, and archipelagic waters, which it claims are provided by the Convention. At the same time, efforts should be made to minimize the efforts of the countries concerned to derogate from these rights through "excessive maritime claims."[41] Based on this, the target countries of the U.S. military declaration include not only the so-called opponent countries (such as China, Iran, etc.), but also some allies (such as Japan, South Korea, Philippines, etc.). It seems that the United States has adopted an unbiased standard without taking sides. In practice, however, the United States does not get rid of the influence of realistic political factors, but pursues a double standard of differential treatment, which is quite obvious in the policy response to the establishment of ADIZ in China and Japan.

Japan expanded its ADIZ towards China in May 2013. In response, China also announced the establishment of the East China Sea ADIZ on November 23.[42] The attitude of the United States towards China and Japan is quite opposite. Specifically, the United States showed strong resistance to China's behavior, and identified it as an "excessive maritime proposition." Shortly after China announced the establishment of the East China Sea ADIZ, Secretary of State Kerry responded that "the United States does not recognize efforts by any State to apply its ADIZ procedures to foreign aircraft not intending to enter national airspace."[43] The Pentagon immediately dispatched two B-52 bombers to fly over the East China Sea ADIZ, challenging China's claims with practical actions. By comparison, the United States neither objects to Japan's ADIZ nor labels it as "excessive maritime claim." Such contrast is also reflected in the FON report released by the United States. According to the report, the United States has carried out FON operations each year in China's ADIZ since its establishment in 2013, while the United States has never carried out the same operations against Japan in the same period. It manifests that the United States has two faces in its policy towards China, and such double standard in its China policy aims to restrain China's development.

The Focus of FONOPs Is in the SCS

Geographically, the SCS is a high-incidence area for the United States to implement FON operations against China in recent years. In 2012, the Obama administration officially launched the "rebalancing" strategy in the Asia-Pacific region and actively intervened in the SCS issues. The SCS neighboring countries, led by Vietnam and the Philippines, also hope to realize and legitimize their vested interests in the SCS with U.S. assistance. It is under the joint agitation of countries inside and outside the region that the situation in the SCS has exacerbated sharply. In order to improve the working and living conditions of the personnel stationed on the islands and provide the international community with public goods for navigation and safety in the SCS, and also for necessary military defense needs to safeguard China's sovereignty and interests in the area, China has launched a large-scale and phased construction project of islands and reefs in the SCS's "Dangerous Ground." It is the legitimate right of the Chinese government to build on and manage the relevant islands and reefs in the SCS within its territory, and other countries have no right to interfere. In the eyes of the United States, however, China's construction projects pose a threat to the FON in the region, while Vietnam and other countries' more expanded construction is somehow harmless. Apart from criticism at the diplomatic level, the United States frequently carries out FON operations in the SCS.

In the annual FON report for fiscal year 2017 released by the U.S. DoD, it identifies the coastal states' excessive maritime claims that were challenged by U.S. Military Forces, and lists the general geographic locations where the U.S. military implements the FON operations. Among them, most of the operations against China occur in the SCS, and the number of operations is "multiple times," which reflects the current fierce competition between China and the United States in the SCS. Specifically, the United States lists the following as excessive maritime claims: the excessive straight baseline in the Paracel Islands; the jurisdiction over airspace above the EEZ in SCS and East China Sea; the restriction on foreign aircraft flying through the ADIZ without the intent to enter national airspace in East China Sea; domestic law criminalizing survey activity by foreign entities in the EEZ in SCS; prior permission required for innocent passage of foreign military ships through the TTS in the Paracel Islands; and actions or statements that indicate a claim to a TTS around features not so entitled in the Spratly Islands.[44] In the foreseeable future, the SCS will continue to be the main place for the United States to implement FON operations against China.

The FONOPs Are Being Held from "Unilateral Action" to "Multilateral Linkage"

The United States has not only stepped into the battle on its own, but also actively engaged other countries (mainly U.S. allies) to follow up and conduct joint operations in the SCS recently. For the sake of upholding alliance interests and balancing China's rise, U.S. allies such as Australia, Japan, and even Britain and France have followed suit, intending to contain China via the excuse of FON in the SCS. In response to the provocative act of the U.S. Navy missile destroyer Larsen sailing within 12 nautical miles of Subi Reef and Mischief Reef in SCS on October 27, 2015, Australian Defense Minister Marise Payne expressed his support for the United States at the first time, claiming that "all states have a right under international law to FON and freedom of overflight, including in the SCS. Australia strongly supports these rights ... and continues to cooperate closely with the United States and other regional partners on maritime security."[45] On December 15, Australia also sent warships and aircraft into the SCS to carry out a so-called routine maritime patrol in the region.[46]

As a staunch ally of the United States in the Asia-Pacific region, Japan supports the United States' FONOPs in the SCS as well. On September 15, 2016,

Japanese Defense Minister Ponmi Inada announced during his visit to the United States that Japan's self-defense forces would jointly patrol in the SCS together with the U.S. military, hold bilateral or multilateral joint military exercises with navies in the region, and provide assistance to some countries to strengthen Japan's presence in SCS.[47] In September 2018, the U.S. Reagan aircraft carrier fleet and Japan's Kaga helicopter carrier carried out joint navigation and joint exercises in the SCS.[48]

Britain and France also show up on the SCS issue, taking the FON issue in the SCS as a chance to involve themselves in Asia-Pacific affairs. The two countries made remarks at the Shangri-La Dialogue held in Singapore on June 1 that they would sail warships to the contested SCS to carry out FONOPs to challenge China's unreasonable claims.[49] Shortly afterwards, the United Kingdom dispatched Albion-class landing platform dock on August 31st to exercise FONOPs in the territorial sea of China's Paracel Islands without obtaining prior permission.[50] Nonetheless, the United States, Britain, France, and other countries work hard to win over Australia, expecting the latter to conduct its own freedom-of-navigation patrols in the SCS, or carry out joint patrols in the region. It shows that the United States' FONOPs in the SCS have transformed from "unilateral action" to "multilateral linkage."

The Essence of China-U.S. Contest on FON in the SCS

To be sure, the United States is a strong proponent of FON in international waters. Its FON assertions in the SCS reflect not only America's commitment to the general principle of maritime liberty as it perceives it to be, but also a continuation of the FON program. There should be no doubt that the United States as a maritime power attaches great importance to the FON, and its rights in accordance with international law cannot be deprived. However, FON is not absolute, and FON in the SCS has never actually been interfered with. As Hua Chunying, spokeswoman of China's Foreign Ministry, said at a regular press conference on November 16, 2018, "we have asked the U.S. or those who claim that there is a problem with the FON in the SCS many times to prove that ships and aircraft of any state have encountered problems in sailing or flying over the SCS. But so far, no one has given a clear answer. It can be seen that the so-called FON and overflight in the SCS is a false proposition that does not exist virtually."[51]

The China-U.S. contest over FON in the SCS is not truly based on the preservation of the international law, instead, it is just an excuse to curb China's rise and maintain American hegemony in the Asia-Pacific region. It is also the fundamental reason for confrontation to exist between the two sides in the SCS. At the same time, due to the ambiguous provisions of the Convention, China and the United States have made different interpretations. Specifically, the two countries hold different views on the relevant provisions of the international law of the sea, as well as the history and legal status of the intermittent line in the SCS. Consequently, the SCS seems to be evolving from "a territorial and maritime dispute" between China and the U.S. to "a show of force" primarily featuring the United States (as a strong maritime power and a user State of the SCS), and China (as a growing regional maritime power struggling to pursue its maritime interests as a coastal state).

The United States and China Dissent over the Relevant Provisions of UNCLOS

In the premises of international law, both Washington and Beijing hold different views of what FON entails under UNCLOS, especially on the right of innocent passage through territorial sea and the right of FON of warships in the EEZ. With regard to the right of innocent passage through the territorial sea, Article 17 of Section 3 of Part II in UNCLOS stipulates that "all States, whether coastal or land locked, shall enjoy the right of innocent passage through the territorial sea,"[52] and "passage should continue uninterrupted and rapid,"[53] "without prejudice to the peace, good order or security of the coastal state," and 12 harmful behaviors are listed.[54] In the view of the United States, the Convention does not stipulate that warships need to obtain the consent of coastal states in advance to pass through a state's territorial sea. As long as the warships pass innocuously, they can enjoy the right of FON. In China's view, although there is no prior consultation clause in the Convention, it stipulates that "coastal states may, in accordance with the provisions of this Convention and other rules of international law, formulate laws and regulations on innocent passage through the territorial sea for eight acts."[55] In 1992, China promulgated the *Law of the PRC on the Territorial Sea and Contiguous Zone*, which stipulates in legislation that foreign ships must obtain prior permission from Beijing before passing through China's territorial sea.

As one of the most controversial issues in the UNCLOS, the issue of EEZ is also the crux of China-U.S. maritime competition. There are salient contradictions between China and the United States on whether FON includes military activities in the EEZ, whether hydrographic survey can be distinguished from marine scientific research, and whether military intelligence collection is allowed in the EEZ.[56] According to the U.S. interpretation of the FON in Article 58 of the UNCLOS, all States enjoy freedom of overflight and navigation in the high seas, including EEZ, and are entitled to be engaged in military activities such as intelligence collection and investigation.[57] Therefore, the U.S. military has the right to freely navigate and fly over China's EEZ without obtaining China's permission. While China has wildly different interpretations of the UNCLOS, and it holds that in exercising these rights, ships of other countries "shall take due account of the rights and obligations of coastal states, and shall abide by the laws and regulations formulated by coastal states in accordance with the UNCLOS and other rules of international law, which are not inconsistent with this part."[58] Moreover, the threat or use of force and the abuse of rights must be prohibited, and the marine scientific research conducted by other countries in the EEZ and on the continental shelf should be approved by the coastal states.[59] Therefore, China's restrictions on other countries' ships in China's EEZ are totally in line with the spirit of UNCLOS.

The United States and China Dissent over the Historical and Legal Status of the Intermittent Line in the SCS

According to the United States, the SCS is directly related to its national interests, and China's U-Shaped Lines in the SCS poses a threat to freedom of commerce and navigation in the SCS. Especially since 2010, the United States has repeatedly required China to expound the intermittent line in the SCS and its legal basis. In 2014, the United States rebuked China's intermittent line in the SCS, and directly denied its historical and legal basis. In February 2014, assistant Secretary of State for Asia Pacific Affairs of the U.S. DoS reinforced at a Congressional hearing that, under the international law, maritime claims in the SCS must be derived from land features. Any use of nine-dashed line by China to claim maritime fights not based on claimed land features would be inconsistent with international law. China's ambiguity in its nine-dashed line and its SCS claims has created uncertainty, insecurity, and instability in the region.[60] On December 5, 2014, United States Department of State Bureau of Oceans and International Environmental and Scientific Affairs published a research report entitled "Limits in the Sea" No. 143, which comprehensively analyzed China's maritime claims, especially the nine-dashed line in the SCS and arising challenges. The report interprets and questions the nine-dashed line in the SCS as the line of islands and reefs, national boundaries, and historical waters/rights. It holds that China's nine-dashed line in the SCS has no legal support unless China can clarify that the ownership of islands, reefs, and related waters within the nine-dashed line conforms to the UNCLOS.[61]

As an ambiguous strategy, the Chinese government has not yet given an authoritative explanation of the nine-dashed line in the SCS. At present, the relatively authoritative interpretation is *The Nine-Dash Line in the SCS: History, Status and Implications* co-authored by Gao Zhiguo, former director of the National Institute of Marine Strategy of China, and Professor Jia Bingbing of Tsinghua University.[62] The article defines the nine-dashed line in the SCS as the boundary which defends its territorial sovereignty and historic rights. This line has three meanings: First, the nine-dashed line includes the ownership of all the islands in the SCS that lie within it. In other words, China enjoys sovereignty over the islands in the SCS and other geographical structures within the nine-dashed line. In accordance with the UNCLOS, China enjoys sovereignty, sovereign rights, and jurisdiction over the waters surrounding these islands, their seabed, and subsoil. Second, the nine-dashed line represents China's historic rights to fisheries, navigation, oil and gas development, and other marine activities in the waters and continental shelf. Third, the nine-dashed line functions as a boundary line when delimiting maritime boundaries with neighboring countries in the future.[63] Comparing the understanding of China and the United States on the nine-dashed line in the SCS, it can be said that the focus of the contest is the legal basis of the nine-dashed line in the SCS. The United States believes that international law should prevail. China's nine-dashed line in the SCS does not conform to international law, thus China cannot make sovereignty claims over the SCS on a historical basis. Conversely, China believes that historical facts and historical ownership are the important basis for China's claims in the SCS. As to the nine-dashed line in the SCS, both historical factors and principles of international law should be taken into account.[64]

The United States versus China: Competition between Existing Maritime Hegemon and Emerging Maritime Power

The United States is a non-traditional maritime power with a tenet of maritime freedom. Since its founding, the United States has regarded the sea as a crucial factor influencing its development and determining its international status. Especially after Alfred Thayer Mahan put forward the strategic theories of sea power, the United States slowly added military presences into the principle of freedom of the seas, emphasizing the management of critical sea areas and sea passages, and stressing the importance of maritime control in wartime, although it was not able to achieve this aim until World War One. After WWII, the United States established its maritime hegemony, thereafter, FON has become an important issue concerning the global mobility of U.S. military forces, the right of access to global waters, and the reliability of security commitments to allies. The U.S. FON claim originates from its maritime hegemony, global mobility of military forces, and protection of and commitment to allies.[65] As the existing maritime hegemon, the United States maintains the maritime order and rules-based system it built to safeguard the vested interests. Therefore, on the SCS issue, the United States is neither willing to share major facets of sea power in the Western Pacific with China, nor allow its strategic interests to be squeezed by the expansion of China's maritime rights and interests, nor can it accept that its right to FON in the SCS is infringed by China's claims over the SCS, though such concerns are superfluous.

China is a sea-land compound State, and is also an emerging maritime power, and its expansion on sea and pursuit of maritime interests are in the initial stage. Over the next few years, China aims to build itself into a modern maritime power, as it outlined at the 18th NCCPC, by continuing to coordinate land and sea development and accelerate the building of a strong Navy, as it proposed at the 19th National Congress. The policies and resources China has devoted to the development of maritime undertakings and the protection of maritime rights and interests are a true reflection of China's efforts to transform itself back into to a country with both maritime power and land power. Different from the offensive marine strategy of the United States, China's marine strategy embodies an enterprising nature, which is a necessary response to China's growing comprehensive national strength, increasing marine economy, and overseas interests. At present, China is mainly concentrated on the offshore or surrounding areas. The maritime issues around China, represented by the SCS dispute, involve China's core interests and important interests such as national sovereignty, national security, and national image. The so-called FON operations carried out by the United States in China's territory undoubtedly seriously infringes on China's interests, which represses the rise of emerging maritime countries and their legitimate rights and interests. Therefore, the contest between China and the United States on the FON in the SCS reflects the competition between the existing maritime hegemon and the emerging maritime power.

The Evaluation of China-U.S. Rivalry in the SCS

The China-U.S. competition on the FON in the SCS has impacted negatively in several areas. First, the United States constantly promotes Chinese militarization of the SCS with the pretext of maintaining FON, which will undoubtedly worsen the situation and jeopardize stability in the SCS. Second, the United States conducts high-intensity maritime and air reconnaissance of China in the SCS and elsewhere in the pretext of FON operations, which is likely to cause military friction and diplomatic disputes, thus exacerbating the existing disputes between China and the United States. Third, the strategic competition between the two countries in the SCS is easily hyped by the media and public opinion, which in turn magnifies disputes and takes them out of context.[66] Finally, if the United States continues to make waves and challenges China's legitimate rights in the SCS, the possibility of a greater political and military crisis between China and the United States cannot be ruled out in the future.

In fact, the United States' claim for FON in the SCS and its pressure on China are untenable both in theory and in practice. In theory, one of the main reasons for the United States to launch FONOPs in the SCS is to oppose and counter China's excessive maritime claims. However, the so-called excessive maritime claim is neither an international consensus nor a matter explicitly stipulated in the UNCLOS. It is only a unilateral interpretation of the UNCLOS by the United States. Its theoretical basis, content, and application only reflect the position of the United States, a non-party to the UNCLOS.[67] For example, the United States has repeatedly claimed that the navigation and overflight space in the SCS belong to international waters and airspace. In fact, these two concepts are neither found nor implied in the UNCLOS. They are typical interpretations created by the United States and lack the rationality of international law.

In practice, China does not interfere with international navigation in the SCS, and the FON was not in jeopardy in the region. The SCS is the most important international shipping channel in the world, with more than 40,000 ships passing every year. The SCS route is the lifeline connecting East Asia to Europe, Africa, and other regions of the world. So far, no other State has claimed that the SCS routes are under threat, and in fact, no one has imposed restrictions on navigation in the SCS. Therefore, there is no actual threat to FON in the SCS.[68] Plus, FON for civilian vessels is not at issue. China and the United States mainly differ on the specific right of the military vessels. For the United States, military vessels can conduct any activity in the EEZ, including military exercises and surveillance. Yet, the United States has not received any verbal or practical support from many coastal states.

In recent years, China has gradually emerged as a regional power and even a global power. Consequently, the Unites States views China as a threat to its global hegemony and so has a policy of containment. The China-U.S. different interpretations on FON in the SCS shows that America's moves are made to contain China's rise, rather to defend FON in SCS as it declares. Based on its strategic interests, the United States considers it a nationalistic and revisionist act for coastal states to bolster their control over their EEZ. But isn't it the same as the American nationalism when the United States declares that maintaining maritime supremacy and global engagement is its core objective?[69]

Notes

1 Hillary Rodham Clinton, "Remarks at Press Availability," National Convention Center, Hanoi, Vietnam, July 23, 2010, available at: https://2009-2017.state.gov/secretary/20092013clinton/rm/2010/07/145095.htm
2 Armin Rappaport and William Earl Weeks, "Freedom of the Seas," in Alexander Deconde, Richard Dean Burns, and Fredrik Logevall eds., *Encyclopedia of American Foreign Policy*, New York: Charles Scribner's Sons Gale Group, 2002, 2nd edition, Vol.1, p.111.
3 Qu Sheng, "A Preliminary Study of the 'Freedom of Navigation Program' in the United States," *Chinese Journal of American Studies*, No.1, 2013, pp.103–104.
4 "The President's Address to the Senate, January 21, 1917," in United States Department of the State, ed., Papers Relating to the Foreign Relations of the United States, 1917, Supplement 1, The World War (1917), pp.27–28, http://images.library.wisc.edu/FRUS/EFacs/1917Supp01v01/reference/frus.frus1917supp01v01.i0008.pdf
5 "Address of the President of the United States Delivered at a Joint Session of the Two Houses of Congress, January 8, 1918," United States Department of State, Papers relating to the foreign relations of the United States, 1918. Supplement 1, The World War (1918), p.15, available at: http://digicoll.library.wisc.edu/cgi-bin/FRUS/FRUS-idx?type=goto&id=FRUS.FRUS1918Supp01v01&isize=M&submit=Go+to+page&page=15
6 Qu Sheng, "From Maritime Freedom to Maritime Hegemony: The Transformation of Wilson's Maritime Policy Vision," *World History*, No. 3, 2017, p.16.
7 "Senator Borah on Freedom of the Seas," *The Congressional Digest*, January 1930, pp.31–32.
8 Franklin Roosevelt, "On Maintaining Freedom of the Seas," in Fireside Chats, September 11, 1941.

9 Scott G. Borgerson, "The National Interest and the Law of the Sea," Council on Foreign Relations Inc., Council Special Report No.46, 2009, pp.22–23.

10 Richard J. Grunawalt, "United States policy on international straits," *Ocean Development & International Law*, Vol.18, No.4, 1987, pp.445–446.

11 See relevant articles of the United Nations Convention on the Law of the Sea.

12 U.S. Department of Defense, "Freedom of Navigation Program: Fact sheet," March 2015, p.1, http://policy.defense.gov/Portals/11/Documents/gsa/cwmd/DoD%20FON%20Program%20--%20Fact%20Sheet%20(March%202015).pdf

13 Elliot L. Richardson, "National Security, The Law of the Sea," Vital Speeches of the Day, delivered at the launching of the USS Samuel E. Morrison, Bath, Maine, July 14, 1979 (New York: City News Publishing Co.), pp.702–704.

14 Mou Wenfu, "U.S. Strategy for Shaping Maritime Order Beyond UNCLOS," *China Review of Marine Law*, No. 2, 2014, pp.200–201.

15 The White House, *National Security Decision Directive 72*, December 13,1982, available at: http://www.fas.org/irp/offdocs/nsdd/nsdd-072.htm

16 "United States ocean policy," statement by the President, March 10, 1983, http://www.state.gov/documents/organization/143224.pdf

17 The White House, "National Security Decision Directive 265," March 16,1987, http://www.fas.org/irp/offdocs/nsdd/nsdd-265.htm

18 The White House, "National Security Directive 49," October12,1990, http://fas.org/irp/offdocs/nsd/nsd49.pdf

19 Unfortunately, these reports have not yet been declassified. Please refer to Qu Sheng, "A Preliminary Study of the US 'Freedom of Navigation Program'," *The Chinese Journal of American Studies*, No. 1, 2013, p.110.

20 The White House, "National Security Presidential Directive NSPD-41/Homeland Security Presidential Directive HSPD-13," December 21, 2004, http://fas.org/irp/offdocs/nspd/index.html

21 The White House, "NSPD-66/HSPD-25," January 9, 2009, http://fas.org/irp/offdocs/nspd/index.html

22 The White House, "National Security Directive 49," October 12,1990, http://fas.org/irp/offdocs/nsd/nsd49.pdf

23 Dennis Mandsager, "The U.S. Freedom of Navigation Program: Policy, Procedure, and Future," *International Law Studies*, Vol.72, 1998, p.121.

24 United States Department of State, Bureau of Oceans and International Environmental and Scientific Affairs, *Limits in the Seas: United States Responses to Excessive National Maritime Claims*, No.112, 1992, p.6, http://www.state.gov/e/oes/ocns/opa/c16065.htm

25 See the Annual Freedom of Navigation Report issued by U.S. Department of Defense. http://policy.defense.gov/OUSDP-Offices/FON/

26 Qi Haotian, "Unilateral implementation and conflict management--parsing America's freedom of navigation operation," *Asia-Pacific Security and Maritime Affairs*, No. 1, 2016, pp.20–21.
27 See Articles 17 and 19 of the United Nations Convention on the Law of the Sea.
28 See Articles 21 of the United Nations Convention on the Law of the Sea.
29 In fact, as early as September 4, 1958, the Chinese government issued a statement on the territorial waters, which clearly stated this position.
30 See article 6 of the Law of the People's Republic of China on the Territorial Sea and the Contiguous Zone.
31 Li Yan, "The 'Freedom of Navigation' Issue in China-U.S. Relations," *Contemporary International Relations*, No.11, 2015, pp.22–23.
32 Qian Chuntai, "Analysis on Sino-U.S. consultation mechanism for military maritime safety," *Contemporary International Relations,* No. 4, 2002, pp.8–11; Cai Penghong, "Maritime Conflicts Between China and the United States and the Construction of Mutual Trust Mechanism," *Foreign Affairs Review*, No. 2, 2010, pp.30–37; Zhang Yuan and Hu Dekun, "Sino-US Maritime Incident Prevention and Military Confidence Building," *China International Studies*, No. 2, 2014, pp.96–108.
33 See the Article 58 of the United Nations Convention on the Law of the Sea.
34 See the Article 88 of the United Nations Convention on the Law of the Sea.
35 See the Article 58 of the United Nations Convention on the Law of the Sea.
36 Yang Xianbin, "On the Freedom of Navigation in the Exclusive Economic Zone," *Studies in Law and Business*, No. 3, 2017, p.175.
37 James Kraska, Raul Pedrozo, *The Free Sea: the American Fight for Freedom of Navigation*, Annapolis: Naval Institute Press, 2018, pp.247–271.
38 Captain Raul Pedrozo, "Close Encounters at Sea: The USNS Impeccable Incident," *Naval War College Review*, Vol.62, No. 3, Summer 2009, pp.100–111.
39 William J. Aceves, "The Freedom of Navigation Program: A Study of the Relationship between Law and Politics," *Hastings International & Comparative Law Review*, Vol.19, 1995/96, pp.259–326
40 Zhang Ye, "Analysis of US Freedom of Navigation Operation in SCS under the Trump Administration," *Pacific Journal,* Vol.26, No. 9, 2018, pp.94–100.
41 J. Ashley Roach, Robert W. Smith, *Excessive Maritime Claims*, Boston: Martinus Nijhoff Publishers, 2012, p.8.
42 Li Xuanliang and Wang Jingguo, "China announced the establishment of the East China Sea Air Defense Identification Zone," *People's Daily*, November 24, 2013, p.1.
43 Ben Dolven, Mark E. Manyin, Shirley A. Kan, "Maritime Territorial Disputes in East Asia: Issues for Congress," CRS report, May 14, 2014, p.21.
44 See U.S. Department of Defense: freedom of navigation report for fiscal year 2017, https://policy.defense.gov/Portals/11/FY17%20DOD%20FON%20Report.pdf?ver=2018-01-19-163418-053

45 "Minister for Defence-Statement-Freedom of Navigation in the SCS," Department of Defence, Australia, October 27, 2015, https://www.minister.defence.gov.au/minister/marise-payne/statements/minister-defence-statement-freedom-navigation-south-china-sea

46 Frances Mangosing, "Australia conducts air patrol in SCS, says it is 'routine'," December 15, 2015, https://globalnation.inquirer.net/133858/australia-conducts-air-patrol-in-south-china-sea-says-it-is-routine

47 Li Bingbing, "Re-mention 'joint patrol', Japan has not given up on the SCS," Beijing News, September 19, 2016, A03.

48 "Japanese Warships Train with U.S. Carrier in Disputed SCS," September. 2, 2018, https://www.military.com/daily-news/2018/09/02/japanese-warship-trains-us-aircraft-carrier-disputed-south-china-sea.html

49 "France, Britain to sail warships in contested SCS to challenge Beijing," The South China Morning Post, June 4, 2018, https://www.scmp.com/news/china/diplomacy-defence/article/2149062/france-britain-sail-warships-contested-south-china-sea

50 "British navy's HMS Albion warned over SCS 'provocation'," BBC, September 6, 2018, https://www.bbc.com/news/uk-45433153

51 "Foreign ministry spokesperson Hua Chun Ying hosted a regular press conference on November 16, 2018," on November 16, 2018, https://www.fmprc.gov.cn/web/fyrbt_ 673021/jzhsl_ 673025/t1613819.shtml

52 See article 17 of Part II of the United Nations Convention on the Law of the Sea.

53 See article 18 of Part II of the United Nations Convention on the Law of the Sea.

54 The 12 categories of actions include: (a) any threat or use of force against the sovereignty, territorial integrity or political independence of the coastal state, or in any other manner contrary to the principles of international law embodied in the Charter of the United Nations; (b) any exercise or exercise with any kind of weapon; and (c) any purpose of gathering information for the coastal area, the act of impairing the defense or security of a coastal state; (d) any propaganda aimed at influencing the defense or security of the coastal state; (e) landing or landing on board any aircraft; (f) launching, landing, or loading on board any military device; (g) boarding or disembarking any commodity, currency, or person in violation of the customs, fiscal, immigration, or health laws and regulations of the coastal state; (h) violation of any intentional and serious act of pollution under this Convention; (i) any fishing activity; (j) the conduct of research or surveying activities; (k) any act intended to interfere with any communication system or any other facility or equipment of the coastal state; and (l) any other activity not directly related to passage. See article 19 of Part II of the United Nations Convention on the law of the sea.

55 The eight acts include: (a) navigation safety and maritime traffic management; (b) protection of navigational aids and facilities and other facilities or equipment; (c) protection of cables and pipelines; (d) conservation of marine living resources;

(e) prevention of violation of fishery laws and regulations of coastal states; (f) preservation of the coastal state's environment and prevention, reduction, and control of pollution; (g) marine science; and (h) prevention of violations of customs, finance, immigration, or health laws and regulations of coastal states.

56 Aris-Georges Marghelis, "American Vision of the EEZ under the Prism of Activities of Military Interest: A Critical Analysis in the Context of Sino-American Strategic Rivalry," *Asia-Pacific Security and Maritime Affairs*, No.2, 2017, pp.29–48.

57 Erik Franckx, "American and Chinese Views on Navigational Rights of Warships," *Chinese Journal of International Law*, 2011, p.203.

58 See Article 58 of the United Nations Convention on the Law of the Sea.

59 Article 246 of the United Nations Convention on the Law of the Sea.

60 Daniel R. Russel, "Maritime Disputes in East Asia," Testimony before the House Committee on Foreign Affairs Subcommittee on Asia and the Pacific, Washington DC, February 5, 2014, http://www.state.gov/p/eap/rls/rm/2014/02/221293.htm.

61 United States Department of State Bureau of Oceans and International Environmental and Scientific Affairs, "Limits in the Sea," Report, No.143, December 5, 2014.

62 Zhiguo Gao and Bingbing Jia, "The Nine-Dashed Line in the SCS: History, Status and Implications," *The American Journal of International Law*, Vol. 107, No. 1, January 2013, pp.98–124.

63 Zhiguo Gao and Bingbing Jia, "The Nine-Dashed Line in the SCS: History, Status and Implications," *The American Journal of International Law*, Vol.107, No.1, January 2013, pp.123–124.

64 Zhang Jie, "The Perception Gap on the 'U-Shaped Line' in the SCS and China's Strategic Choices," *The Journal of International Studies,* No.2, 2014, pp.55–56.

65 Li Yan, "The 'Freedom of Navigation' Issue in China-U.S. Relations," *Contemporary International Relations*, No.11, 2015, pp.24–25.

66 Li Yan, "The 'Freedom of Navigation' Issue in China-U.S. Relations," *Contemporary International Relations*, No.11, 2015, p.27.

67 Bao Yinan, "The US Theory of 'Excessive Maritime Claims' and Its Practice: A Critical Analysis," *China International Studies,* No.5, 2017, pp.111–116.

68 Yu Minyou and Lei Xiaolu, "On the Irrationality of the United States Accusing China of Impeding the Freedom of Navigation in the SCS," *Jiangxi Social Sciences*, No. 9, 2011, pp.15–16.

69 Aris-Georges Marghelis, "American Vision of the EEZ under the Prism of Activities of Military Interest—A Critical Analysis in the Context of Sino-American Strategic Rivalry," *Asia-Pacific Security and Maritime Affairs*, No.2, 2017, pp.40–44.

8

The U.S. Understanding on China's Maritime Militia

"The maritime militia should strive to learn modern equipment knowledge, improve their operational ability, and actively collect ocean information and support the construction of islands while helping fishermen raise income."

—President Xi Jinping

"In the SCS, the People's Armed Forces Maritime Militia plays a major role in coercive activities to achieve China's political goals without fighting, part of broader PRC military doctrine stating confrontational operations short of war can be an effective means of accomplishing political objectives."

—The Military and Security Developments Involving the People's Republic of China 2018

To accelerate China's maritime strategy implementation and effectively safeguard its national maritime rights and interests, China has not only strengthened its traditional naval and air forces, but also integrated and upgraded non-traditional maritime forces such as its maritime law enforcement institutions and historically less formal maritime militia in recent years. In particular, the Chinese government attaches great importance to the development of maritime militia. When President Xi Jinping visited Tanmen, Qionghai City, Hainan Province in April 2013, to visit the local marine militia composed of fishermen, he encouraged relevant personnel not only to carry out fishing activities, but also to "actively collect ocean-going information and support island construction."[1] In other words, to be the eyes and ears, and operate in a support capacity, a role they are uniquely qualified to fulfill.

Under the current situation of heated competition between China and the United States over the SCS issue, the development of China's maritime militia has attracted close attention within academic circles, politicians, think tanks, and the media in the United States. For example, in its 2016 annual report to Congress, the USCC devoted much attention to China's maritime militia, stating that the "maritime militia plays a key role in China's strategy in the SCS."[2] In June 2017, the Pentagon's 2017 Report on China's Military also declared that China was using "coercive" methods, such as using law enforcement ships and maritime militia, to pursue its maritime claims and interests in a conflict-free manner, which is the first time the United States had publicly mentioned China's maritime militia strategy at an official level.[3] Although the United States has conducted comprehensive and in-depth studies on China's maritime militia, there are still some misunderstandings and deviations in the relevant cognition, and the assessments published are far from being fair. For this reason, it is necessary to correct the erroneous perception and offer a rational and objective perspective to the development of China's maritime militia and its maritime rights protection activities.

Maritime Militia: China's Third Maritime Force?

The militia is a generally civilian armed organization that engaged in production and acts as an auxiliary and reserve force of the National Standing Army.[4] As an important part of the maritime defense force of a country, the maritime militia is fully armed and plays an irreplaceable role in maritime rights protection operations.[5] Since most of the maritime militia is made up of fishermen with fishing vessels as their main tools, the mariners and their fleets constitute the main body of the maritime militia. Maritime militia has a long history, and it is common for a country to use civilian fishing boats to assist the Navy in achieving its goals. During the Vietnam War, for example, the North Vietnamese government used civilian vessels to scout and locate U.S. warships. During the Cold War, the Soviet Union frequently utilized fishing boats as a platform for intelligence collecting. Russia, the main successor to the Soviet Union, still maintains a large fleet of commercial vessels after the Cold War, part of which is used for collecting and reporting maritime intelligence.[6]

At present, many countries have built maritime militia forces, which play an important role in assisting maritime law enforcement, rescue and relief, local security, and other affairs. In fact, the United States also maintains a modest maritime militia to assist with emergencies in undisputed coastal waters, as well as reservists for other U.S. military programs. To American observers, however, China's maritime militia is unusual for its paramilitary and covert nature. For example, Andrew S. Erickson and Conor M. Kennedy of the China Maritime Studies Institute (CMSI) of the U.S. Naval War College have long tracked China's maritime militia issues, claiming that China has the largest maritime militia in the world, and these irregular forces have always been an important part of the Chinese armed forces, so they can be referred to as the People's Armed Forces Maritime Militia (PAFMM). "China is employing not one but three major sea forces--a potent three-pronged trident." In addition to the Navy and Coast Guard, "Beijing wields the world's largest maritime militia."[7] In Congressional Hearings and media interviews, Erickson compared China's maritime militia to "Little Blue Men," and repeatedly called on U.S. officials to publicize and respond to China's use of these "Little Blue Men" in the SCS.[8]

In addition, Erickson and Kennedy published a series of articles on the theme of "Hainan Maritime Militia" on the websites of CIMSE and National Interest that were based on a large survey of Chinese literature and extensive research.[9] The advantages and characteristics of the maritime militia in Danzhou, Tanmen, Sanya, and Sansha of Hainan province are being analyzed in depth, which can be summarized into the following aspects.

First, it takes a long time to develop a modern naval force, especially a defensive one that is in step with China's maritime security needs. In the early days of the founding of the PRC, armed fishing militias were set up by the new government to resist the blockade and intrusion of the Nationalist troops in the coastal areas of the mainland. Since then, the Chinese Navy has commandeered fishing boats to recapture islands seized by the Nationalists, for naval raids against their forces and for the 1974 Battle of the Paracel Islands.[10] Second, the unit composition and system varies, but the distribution is widespread, and the organization is tight. China has a long coastline, with militia on the sea spread over a wide area. Although they vary in size and are relatively independent, they have a tight military organization structure, and are directly organized and controlled by the local military command organs of the PLA. It must be emphasized that maritime militia command authority resides within multiple entities, including both the local military organs and their government/party counterparts. Such militia is subject to the "dual-leadership" system by the local military and government's principal leaders. Since both military and government leaders are involved in local armed forces building, the National Defense Mobilization Committee (NDMC) system established at each corresponding level plays the critical role in binding them into one decision-making body.[11] Third, they are flexible and have the dual roles of being both "soldiers" and "civilians." When they wear military uniforms, they can be soldiers; when they take off military uniforms, they are civilians, just as the reservists of Western Navies do. Therefore, China's maritime militia can be coordinated with the navy, coast guard, and other maritime forces to achieve joint military-law enforcement-civilian defense.[12] Fourth, veterans are hired into the maritime militia system for their high military literacy and rich combat experience, thus strengthening the professionalization of the maritime militia.[13] Fifth, the maritime militia is in line with the Chinese strategic thinking of "People's War," which connotes the combined use of formal and informal forces to defeat a powerful enemy or multiple opponents through flexible strategies and tactics in peacetime and necessary war. In the face of the new maritime security situation, the PLA has applied this idea to the maritime field, that is, to explore the strategies and tactics of "Maritime People's War," and to make use of various forces to safeguard the country's maritime rights and interests.[14]

In the view of the United States, there are many driving factors behind the rapid development of China's maritime militia force in recent years. Among them, the important task of safeguarding maritime rights and interests, especially in the SCS, is the most direct motivation for China to strengthen its maritime militia construction. As Franz-Stefan Gady, a senior fellow at the East-West Center, puts it, in face of competing claims in the SCS, "China is trying to use these government-controlled fishermen below the radar to get the bonus without the onus to support its SCS claims."[15] At the same time, Michael McDevitt, a retired Rear Admiral, argues that it is a necessity to develop the maritime militia, for it is an essential part in China's path to achieve the dream of becoming a maritime power.[16] In addition, a report by *The Washington Post* in April 2016 pointed out that economic issue is a major driving force for the Chinese fishermen to participate in maritime rights protection activities, as the fishing resources in China's offshore waters were nearly exhausted. On the other hand, it is the simple-mannered patriotism of the fishermen.[17] It is also worth mentioning that the "incentives" injected by the Chinese government into the maritime militia system are also important for the rapid growth of the latter. Local governments, for example, have been spurred by high-level Chinese attention to invest to maritime militias. Local municipal authorities in China also offer a generous annual subsistence allowance to marine militiamen if they are injured on duty, which removes many of the militia's physical concerns.[18]

U.S. Understanding of the Role and Function of China's Maritime Militia

As a branch of the militia, the maritime militia will undoubtedly play its due role in China's maritime affairs. The role of China's maritime militia has been fully interpreted in the United States through public articles on China's grass-roots level naval commanders, coastal local government announcements, and media reports. In general, they believe that China's maritime militia bears both "outward-looking" and "inward-looking" responsibilities. The so-called outward-looking means that China regards maritime militia as a political tool to safeguard maritime rights and interests in order to realize its maritime claims. "Inward-looking" means that China takes maritime militia as a means to deal with and respond to domestic maritime management problems. Erickson and his associates in the U.S. Naval War College have pointed out that "the primary role of China's militia is to be an external defense force; its secondary role, to be a domestic security force. Domestic security roles take the form of conducting marine rescue operations and assisting maritime law enforcement (MLE) forces, while external defense roles entail performing a variety of operations to assist the PLA Navy (PLAN) as well as conducting independent operations."[19] The maritime militia combines the above two roles to serve China's maritime strategy.

Although some U.S. scholars acknowledge that China is not "unique" in using maritime militia to assist in maritime law enforcement, evacuation, disaster recovery, counter-terrorism, and defense of undisputed territory and port facilities, they firmly believe that China's maritime militia doesn't stop there and reaches far beyond that role. In July 2016, an article in *The National Interest* pointed out that China's maritime militia also played an unknown role in advancing contested island or maritime claims by harassing foreign vessels and conducting other assertive activities, such as ramming.[20] Meanwhile, a study by the Center for Naval Analysis asserts that China's maritime militia plays an underappreciated role as China's first line of defense in the maritime arena. It has allowed China to harass foreign fishermen and defy other Coast Guards without obviously implicating the Chinese State.[21] Based on all kinds of analyses in the United States, China's maritime militia force has three main functions.

First, support the front. In "support the front" missions, the Maritime Militia is to support the battlefront with human and material resources. The militia taking part in any war is the highest form of the People's participation, and is the concentrated embodiment of the militia's military attribute, as well as a military activity by itself.[22] Since the maritime militia is an important reserve force for the Chinese Navy, it can play a corresponding supporting and coordinating role in times of war. According to U.S. assessments, the Maritime Militia has roles in assisting the PLA and PLAN. It augments transport capacity through the loading and delivery of troops, vehicles, equipment, and materials; acts in a medical support role and aids in the retrieval of casualties; provides navigational assistance; conducts emergency repairs or refitting of vessels, docks, and other infrastructure; provides fuel and material replenishment at sea; and conducts other various logistical functions. It also prepares for engagement in cover and concealment operations for Army and Naval units by using smoke, corner reflectors, and chaff grenades. The maritime militia also trains to conduct mine warfare and assist in blockade operations. As in many modern militia units, the areas of construction, information, and electronic warfare are becoming increasingly emphasized.[23]

Second, rights protection. In recent years, under the worsening situation in its maritime disputes around China, the function of promoting the maritime militia to participate in national maritime rights and interests protection has been reactivated. Michael Green and his associates of the Center for Strategic and International Studies (CSIS) have pointed out that the maritime militia is the "vanguard" of maritime rights protection in the new era and the first line of defense in China's "gray zone."[24] In the SCS, in particular, China's fishing industry and the fleet that it wields has been an important foreign policy tool in Beijing's repertoire since much of China's historic claim on the SCS and current presence therein hinges on fishing activities. The fishing fleet's political and strategic role has been given special significance and potential by China's widespread employment of a relatively unknown paramilitary organization: the maritime militia.[25] The U.S. Depart of Defense's 2017 paper "Military and Security Developments Involving the PRC" also stresses that, as low-intensity coercion, the China maritime militia plays a major role in coercive activities to achieve China's political goals without fighting in the SCS.[26] In addition, American scholars believe that China's maritime militia has played significant roles in a number of military campaigns and coercive incidents over the years, including the 2009 Impeccable incident, the 2011 harassment of Vietnamese survey vessels, the 2012 Scarborough Reef standoff, and the 2014 HYSY-981 drilling rig standoff.[27] Chinese fishing boats have also been involved in dredging and reclamation in the SCS by transporting construction materials.[28] After the SCS Arbitration in 2016, China continued to deploy maritime militia to strengthen its presence in disputed waters in the SCS.

According to the analysis conducted in the United States, China is actively promoting the maritime militia in marine rights protection activities. The main reasons include: first, the use of quasi-civilian forces is a tactic to avoid direct military confrontations, allowing the Chinese government some degree of deniability.[29] Second, the maritime militia can give China an asymmetric advantage in maritime disputes. On one hand, it can deal with foreign vessels and interfere with their operations at sea. On the other hand, it can take the opportunity to reconnoiter and collect information on the location and movement of foreign vessels, and transmit messages to the Chinese military in a timely manner. Third, the use of maritime militia to safeguard maritime rights and interests can be beneficial to China's domestic image. Images of Chinese fishermen being roughed up by foreign vessels in maritime clashes are highly likely to provoke anger and protests on the internet, and have certainly won the opinion of "netizens" in China, furthering public support for Beijing's tough stance on maritime disputes.[30]

Third, emergency response, including dealing with natural disasters, accidents, public health incidents, and social security incidents.[31] The Emergency Response Law of the PRC, passed by the National People's Congress in 2007, includes provisions for militia participation in emergency response and disaster relief. Both Article 14 and 28 stipulate, respectively, that "the militia organizations shall participate in the emergency response rescue and operations in accordance with the provisions of this Law and other relevant laws, administrative regulations and military regulations as well as orders of the State Council and the Central Military Commission." "The militia organizations shall organize and carry out specialized emergency response exercise as planned."[32] According to the provisions, China's maritime militia is also responsible for assisting and responding to maritime emergencies. Although most of the maritime militia's emergency actions take place in peacetime, it can also play a role in wartime. As the marine militia is familiar with the marine environment and geographically closer to various maritime emergencies, it can be the ideal first responder to carry out emergency rescue work in time. American scholars also believe that China's maritime militia's emergency rescue work has achieved remarkable results. For example, in 2014, the Taizhou Maritime Militia Emergency Response Company in Zhejiang province carried out 136 search-and-rescue missions on its own, successfully rescuing 18 ships and 286 people.[33]

U.S. Assessment on the Influence of China's Maritime Militia

There is no doubt that Chinese fishermen and their fleet have a civilian identity, and their activities in the disputed waters are normal economic activities. In a state of war or emergency, however, these actions become strategic. James Kraska, a professor at the U.S. Naval War College, believes that "the sheer seize size and scope of the vast network of China's maritime militia complicates the battlespace, degrades any opponent's decision-making process and exposes adversaries to political dilemmas that will make them more cautious to act against China during a maritime crisis or naval war."[34] As a reserve force and supplement to the PLA, China's maritime militia has posed legal, political, and operational challenges to its rivals. For this reason, the United States has kept a close eye on the functions of China's maritime militia forces, as well as conducting an in-depth assessment of their potential impact on an opposing force's operations.

First of all, from the perspective of international law, China's maritime militia force has brought an impact on some principles. In the view of some U.S. scholars on international law, a key principle of international humanitarian law is to protect fishermen and civilian installations, such as fishing boats, from armed attacks and to discriminate between combatants and non-combatants. However, the very nature of China's maritime militia, which is mainly composed of fishermen, means that the line between civilian vessels and the Chinese Navy is blurred. Furthermore, such "civil-military integration" between China's maritime militia and naval forces means that the principle of discrimination between warships and civilian vessels, long enshrined in the laws of maritime war, is being eroded. Although the law of war at sea allows warships to engage civilian fishing vessels supporting the enemy, it is practically difficult to distinguish the legitimate civilian fishing vessels from those incorporated into the Chinese Navy as auxiliary naval forces. Thus, whether or not Chinese maritime militias play a decisive role in combat, their presence in a battlefield poses legal and operational challenges for adversaries. Moreover, in the event of a maritime tragedy, any fishing boat destroyed in a naval battle could become the centerpiece of China's political and public diplomacy efforts, a propaganda poster for weakening the will of its rivals and winning the sympathy of the international community.[35] In short, the 400 years of custom and State practice embedded in the law of naval warfare may be upended by China's unorthodox approach to maritime power with a combination of maritime militias and formal armed forces to advance China's strategic goals in the South and East China Seas.

Second, for the United States and its allies, the main challenges posed by China's maritime militia include:

1. impeding the FON at sea. It's widely known that FON at sea is a principle of maritime values vigorously defended by the United States, as well as an important excuse to intervene in the SCS dispute. In the view of the United States, the "unregulated" activities of tens of thousands of Chinese fishing boats in the SCS and other waters as well as the harassment of foreign vessels, including U.S. warships and military survey vessels, undermine the principle of FON at sea and cause serious disruption to the efforts of U.S. ships to patrol the SCS to proclaim FON.[36]
2. weakening America's maritime superiority. The United States believes that, as an auxiliary force, the maritime militia can act as the "eyes and ears" of the PLA in peacetime and support frontline forces in wartime by means of intelligence collecting, surveillance, and reconnaissance. Such a Navy-Civil combination would almost certainly cancel out some of America's maritime superiority, forcing America and its allies to polish its strategy, tactics, technology, and procedures.[37] In addition, according to Peter Brooke, a former U.S. Assistant Secretary of Defenses, while the quality of the U.S. naval forces is currently superior to those of the Chinese, it is inferior when it comes to the sheer numbers of Chinese military militia, in that "it is critical to remember that though quality is an incredibly important asset in battle, there's also a certain quality in quantity, which is something that we need to think about when we look broadly at China's naval forces, policies and strategy."[38]
3. bringing legal and operational problems for the U.S. Military. As mentioned above, in a naval battle or maritime crisis involving Chinese fishing boats, the U.S. Military will face a confusing scenario: How to identify and distinguish the civil or military activities of Chinese maritime militia according to international law? Does the military structure of the United States and its allies need to be expanded to deal with the threat posed by China's maritime militia?

Finally, China's maritime militia has a negative impact on regional security. According to experts in the United States, the maritime militia is actually a "double-edged sword" for China. By using maritime militia to safeguard maritime rights and interests, China can gain some initiative and leeway to avoid a head-on collision with foreign military forces. However, this policy carries huge security risks and will only further militarize the SCS, as China's use of its huge fishing fleet as a spearhead of its territorial claims in the SCS puts fishermen at the forefront of the dispute, which could lead to escalation in fishing disputes in the region. A small fishing friction could be a trigger for greater diplomatic and security tensions between China and regional countries. "As you urge them on with assertions of rights, nationalism and claims, fishing Masters know they can take greater risks, because they know they are going to be bailed out. So they know they can push the limits fairly strongly," said Rodger Baker of the global intelligence firm Stratfor, "that is, more crises in the disputed waters are almost inevitable."[39] Should China and its neighbors—mainly Vietnam, the Philippines, and Japan—break out in local conflicts over fishing, the United States, an ally of the countries involved, would inevitably be drawn into the conflict, and the security consequences would be incalculable.

U.S. Policy Response to China's Maritime Militia

Based on a comprehensive assessment of the potential impact of China's maritime militia, there are also intense debates in the United States about how to address such challenges. Some scholars have called on the U.S. government to publicly discuss and respond to China's maritime militia issues, putting it to the spotlight of the international community. Others have suggested that the military should take a hard line, treating China's maritime militia as part of the PLA naval force instead of as civilian vessels. If Chinese fishing boats "harass" U.S. vessels and disrupt FON in the SCS, they will face the risk of being attacked. Some experts believe that the outside world should not worry too much about China's maritime militia forces. Instead, they advocate negotiating with China through diplomacy and using existing international mechanisms to restrain China's maritime militia and force it to abide by relevant international maritime rules. Specifically, the options for the United States are as follows:

First, the United States publicizes the "misdeeds" and "criminal evidence" of China's maritime militia, pressuring China in international community. The United States argues that China's maritime militia is an important part of its military force, a Navy disguised as "civilians." Therefore, China's maritime militia should not receive civilian protection in wartime. Moreover, since China's maritime militia forces are deceptive to a certain extent, the best way to deal with them is to expose and put them on trial by international public opinion. As Erickson says, "sunlight is the best disinfectant."[40] It is necessary for the U.S. government to make public the actions of China's maritime militia, including bullying its neighbors and threatening openness and stability in the East and South China Seas. Scott Swift, a former Commander of the United States Pacific Fleet, also points out that China's maritime militia should not be viewed simply as a group of fishermen, but rather as well-organized and under clear leadership and control. China must explain to the outside world its motives and objectives for developing maritime militias, or the United States has an obligation to treat them like any other military forces under command and control.[41]

Second, U.S. political and military leaders engage the PRC/PLAN directly and publicly on China's maritime militia. On June 15, 2017, Blake Herzinger, a former U.S. Navy Officer, made a speech in the Center for International Maritime Security. He suggested that U.S. political and military leaders engage the PRC/PLAN directly and publicly on the existence and operational scope of China's maritime militia, and insist upon adherence to internationally accepted legal identification of vessels and personnel, and convey what costs will be imposed on the PRC/PLAN if they do not change their behavior. He claims that this would be an excellent opportunity for the United States to underline its commitment to good order at sea and a rules-based maritime order. By encouraging the PRC to acknowledge the Maritime Militia and its associated command structure, the United States can cut through the ambiguity and civilian camouflage under which the Maritime Militia has operated unchallenged. In the event that the PRC declines to engage, conveying the possible imposition of costs may serve as a warning that behavior negatively affecting good order at sea will not be tolerated indefinitely.[42] Erickson and others have suggested that the U.S. officials make it clear to the Chinese that maritime militias cannot prevent the United States from legally entering the SCS. The clear signaling can increase transparency in crisis-prone areas and help create "clear ramps" to avoid a continuing escalation of the crisis in the event of a danger. Even if Chinese officials refuse to discuss maritime militia issue with their American counterparts, according to Erickson, Washington's message will resonate in Beijing. In addition, if China does not cooperate, the United States could consider revoking some of the U.S.-backed "privileges" that the Chinese Navy currently enjoys, such as disqualification from participating in U.S.-sponsored Rim of the Pacific military exercises.[43]

Third, it is necessary to draw China's maritime militia into existing maritime security mechanisms to constrain their behavior through preexisting rules. The Code for Unplanned Encounters at Sea (CUES) was adopted during the 2014

Western Pacific Naval Symposium (WPNS) and provides a basis for communications, maritime safety, and maneuvering guidelines for use by ships and aircraft in unplanned encounters at sea. It is of significance in the reduction of misunderstandings and misjudgment, avoiding accidents in the air, and safeguarding regional security and stability in peacetime.[44] In September 2016, China and ASEAN reaffirmed the application of the Code of Unplanned Encounters at Sea in the SCS through a joint statement.[45] For the United States, although China is a signatory to the CUES, the agreement only covers the Chinese Navy, while the Coast Guard and maritime militia are not included. To that end, the United States holds to involve the latter two as well. As Erickson stresses, "there is a potential problem whereby China's Navy is bear hugging the U.S. Navy to learn more about our best practices," while "the Coast Guard and maritime militia are doing the dirty work in the East China Sea and the SCS." For this reason, "our approach to China's maritime forces and our interaction with them is incomplete."[46] They firmly believe that Washington should call on the Chinese Coast Guard and Maritime Militia to abide by the same code of conduct as the People's Liberation Army Navy (PLAN) and let the rules govern all irregular military forces in the region.[47]

Fourth, it is high time to work closely with regional allies and partners to jointly tackle the challenges posed by China's Maritime Militia. Since maritime militia are being employed by China to advance its strategic objectives in the East and South China Seas, a joint regional response to this challenge by relevant allies and partners will naturally be a priority for the United States in its policy response. Blake Herzinger, for example, argues in his policy recommendations that, on the one hand, the United States assists ASEAN in developing and implementing an organic maritime domain awareness (MDA) capacity with domestic, and international, interagency sharing and response capacity. MDA will be understood to be a host-nation's ability to collect, fuse, analyze, and disseminate maritime data, information, and intelligence relating to potential threats to its security, safety, economy, or environment. On the other hand, the United States should utilize U.S. Coast Guard (USCG) vessels to provide maritime law enforcement and maritime security training support to States bordering the East and SCSs that are interested in creating their own maritime militias.[48] It is clear that by joining hands with relevant countries, the United States can not only strengthen its ability to counter China's maritime militia and limit China's maritime "expansion," but also strengthen its relations with allies and partners and consolidate its leadership in the Asia-Pacific region.

An Assessment of U.S. Cognition and Response

Overall, the United States has conducted a comprehensive and in-depth study on China's maritime militia, and made a detailed assessment and analysis of its possible impact as well as U.S. response measures. Scholars, represented by Erickson of U.S. Naval War College, study China with first-hand data for their proficiency in Chinese, and have published a large number of research results. Their conclusions on China's maritime militia and broader issues of China's maritime strategy, as well as their potential implications for U.S. policy, should arouse the attention of China. Due to their inexplicable concerns over the rise of China's maritime power in the new period, as well as the relatively limited communications and understanding with China, there are quite a few defects in some researches. Plus, some researchers themselves have misunderstandings and are prejudiced against China, so there is a lack of objective evaluation on the development of China's Maritime Militia. Surely, some of the conclusions are speculative and even exaggerated, yet they are given publicity by the media and politicians as if they are factual.

First, there is a lack of objectivity and impartiality in assessing China's maritime militia strength and its development. It is widely acknowledged that enhancing and utilizing the maritime militia to safeguard maritime rights and interests is not China's foremost and exclusive initiative. Indeed, countries such as Vietnam and the Philippines have also been beefing up their maritime militias to compete for so-called maritime rights in the SCS. For example, as early as November 2009, the Vietnamese National Assembly passed the Militia and Self-defense Forces Act with an approval rating as high as 89 %. It requires that Vietnamese fishing fleets be accompanied by a group of militiamen carrying out self-defense tasks to "escort" when they go out to sea. Vietnam also sent fishing boats to support the HYSY-981 drilling rig confrontation. Vietnam's maritime militia is now ubiquitous: There are 13 marine militia platoons in Danang to assist more than 3,000 fishermen operating in China's Paracel Islands (Xisha) waters. More than 10,000 fishermen and nearly 2,000 fishing boats are employed in Khanh Hoa, and its maritime militia are equipped with long-range walkie-talkie, infrared night vision scopes, and guns.[49]

Meanwhile, armed Philippine fishing boats have been operating in the disputed waters of the SCS for years, and they constantly harass Chinese fishermen. Thomas Cloma, the first Filipino to lay claim to some of the Spratly Islands, did not hesitate in using lethal force when his armed group engaged with KMT Marines. More recently, in April 2006, armed Philippine fishing boats attacked a

Chinese fishing boat in disputed waters of the SCS without provocation, resulting in the death of four Chinese fishermen and serious injury of three.[50] In May 2014, the Philippine Coast Guard, disguised as fishermen, illegally seized a Chinese fishing boat operating in the waters off Half Moon Shoal of Spratly Islands.[51] Although China has about 90,000 fishing vessels in the SCS, far more than that of Vietnam or the Philippines, most of these vessels operate in China's offshore waters. Such concrete facts illustrate that the development of maritime militia in countries around the SCS is probably the product of a "action-response" cycle. China's efforts to strengthen its Maritime Militia, for example, have been driven in part by Vietnam's actions. The Philippines' policy option in the SCS can be stimulated by the actions of other countries in the region.[52] Therefore, on the issue of maritime militia and their rights protection, the United States should not single out China for speculation and pressure, which is obviously subjective and unfair.

Second, building a maritime militia force neither equals to nor leads to militarization of the SCS, let alone overstating its strategic role. Some American analysts believe that the maritime militia strategy is in line with Chinese strategic thinking of "People's war," and speculate that the maritime militia will become a new force, and even arbitrarily conclude that China is utilizing this new military force in the SCS dispute, thus exacerbating the militarization of the SCS.

The above cognition and conjecture is undoubtedly a distortion of the idea of "People's war." Although the concept of "People's war" has been one of the important pillars of China's military strategic thinking, as time goes on, the connotation of the concept also evolved from the traditional "People's war" to "People's war in modern times," and then to the current "People's war in the 21st century." The key change is that guerrilla warfare is no longer included in the strategic thought of militia. In contrast, the main function of militia has shifted to providing logistical and transport assistance to traditional military forces when necessary.[53] Therefore, it is of no value to mechanically and narrowly interpret the idea of "People's war." It is wrong to conclude that China's buildup of maritime militia is to implement the "People's war at sea," which will even exacerbate the militarization of the SCS issue.

History has repeatedly shown that it is a must to build a powerful naval force if a country aims to truly and effectively safeguard its maritime sovereignty, rights, and interests. In face of the severe maritime security situation in recent years, China's national defense strategic planning has a new trend, that is, putting more emphasis on building a robust Navy. For example, the White Paper on China's Military Strategy released by the Chinese Government in May 2015 shows that China will give more prominence to the construction of its Navy, strengthen its strategic deterrence and counterattack capabilities, and implement a more aggressive defense strategy.[54] China is working to build its Navy into one of the largest and most advanced in the region, and is building a strong maritime law enforcement force, while China's Maritime Militia is only an auxiliary organization. Whether China can effectively achieve its maritime strategic objectives depends crucially on a powerful naval force. In addition, there exist certain confinement factors in the development of China's Maritime Militia. For example, young people are less motivated to engage in marine fishing, leading to an aging population in fishermen. The construction of a Maritime Militia involves different interest departments, and the conflicts of interest among departments will also affect its development prospects. To sum up, the development of China's Maritime Militia has its limits, and is not as crucial in China's maritime strategy as the United States exaggerates.

Finally, the United States has made excuses for its involvement in the SCS dispute by hyping up the threat of China's Maritime Militia. The United States is neither a littoral state nor a claimant to the SCS. Therefore, the SCS dispute has nothing to do with the United States at a practical level and should not become an obstacle in China-U.S relations. However, in order to cope with the rise of China and limit the reasonable expansion of China's maritime rights, the United States is always looking for various reasons to intervene in the SCS dispute and suppress China's legitimate claims to sovereignty. Among them, hyping up the issue of China's maritime militia is the latest development of the U.S. involvement in the SCS. To be specific, the United States has hyped up the issue of maritime militia and created the threat theory of China's maritime militia for the following two purposes:

One is to seek legitimacy for the U.S. FON in the SCS. The main crux of the SCS issue lies in the sovereignty disputes among neighboring countries and the competition for resources, while the FON in this region has never been damaged or interrupted. Nevertheless, the United States has deliberately confused the sovereignty disputes in SCS with FON, repeatedly accusing China's maritime militia of violating the principle of FON and acting dangerously in violation of international law. It can be predicted that with the continuous competition between China and the United States in the SCS, the issue of maritime militia may become another excuse for the United States to forcefully push forward the FON in the SCS after the island construction issue.

The other is to seek justification for the United States to expand its military presence in the SCS. Since the United States considers China's maritime militia to be a threat to its maritime superiority and regional security, expanding its military presence in the region is clearly a policy priority. As Kraska of Naval War College puts it, "as a force multiplier, the military maritime militia poses an operational challenge that will require an expansion in U.S. and allied force structure, including warships, submarines and, especially unmanned drones and unmanned subsurface, to manage the threat."[55] To expand the U.S. military presence in the SCS by hyping up the threat of China's maritime militia also exposes Washington as the real driving force behind the increased militarization of the SCS, thus the latest U.S. intervention in the SCS dispute warrants close attention.

Notes

1 "Xi Jinping visited the marine militia in Hainan," *Beijing News*, April 11, 2013, A06.
2 U.S.-China Economic and Security Review Commission, 2016 Report to Congress, November 2016, https://www.uscc.gov/sites/default/files/annual_reports/2016%20Annual%20Report%20to%20Congress.pdf
3 The US Department of Defense, Military and Security Developments Involving the People's Republic of China 2017, May 15, 2017, https://www.defense.gov/Portals/1/Documents/pubs/2017_China_Military_Power_Report.PDF?ver=2017-06-06-141328-770
4 See Article 38 of Part 6 on militia in Law of the People's Republic of China on Military Service.
5 Zeng Pengxiang, Fu Zhigang and Lian Ronghua, "Scientific Construction of Marine Militia Management and Control System," *National Defense*, Vol.12, 2014, p.68.
6 James Kraska and Michael Monti, "The Law of Naval Warfare and China's Maritime Militia," *International Law Studies*, Vol.91, No.1, 2015, pp.456–457.
7 Andrew S. Erickson and Conor M. Kennedy, "Countering China's Third Sea Force: Unmask Maritime Militia before They're Used Again," *The National Interest*, 6 July 2016, http://nationalinterest.org/feature/countering-chinas-third-sea-force-unmask-maritime-militia-16860; Conor M. Kennedy and Andrew S. Erickson, "China's Third Sea Force, The People's Armed Forces Maritime Militia: Tethered to the PLA," China Maritime Report, China Maritime Studies Institute, U.S. Naval War College, No.1, March 2017.
8 Andrew S. Erickson, "The SCS's Third Force: Understanding and Countering China's Maritime Militia," Hearing on Seapower and Projection Forces in the SCS, 21 September, 2016; Christopher P. Cavas, "China's 'Little Blue Men' Take Navy's Place in Disputes," November 2, 2015, http://www.defensenews.com/naval/2015/11/03/chinas-little-blue-men-take-navys-place-in-disputes/; Christopher P. Cavas,

"China's Maritime Militia–Time to Call them Out?", September 18, 2016, http://www.defensenews.com/2016/09/19/chinas-maritime-militia-time-to-call-them-out

9 For a list of relevant research results, please refer to Professor Ericsson's personal website: http://www.andrewerickson.com/2017/09/understanding-chinas-third-sea-force-the-maritime-militia/

10 Andrew S. Erickson and Conor M. Kennedy, "Trailblazers in Warfighting: The Maritime Militia of Danzhou," Center for International Maritime Security (CIMSEC), February 1, 2016, http://cimsec.org/trailblazers-warfighting-maritime-militia-danzhou/21475

11 Andrew S. Erickson and Conor Kennedy, "Directing China's 'Little Blue Men': Uncovering the Maritime Militia Command Structure," September 11, 2015, https://amti.csis.org/directing-chinas-little-blue-men-uncovering-the-maritime-militia-command-structure/

12 Conor M. Kennedy and Andrew S. Erickson, "Hainan's Maritime Militia: China Builds A Standing Vanguard, Pt. 1," Center for International Maritime Security (CIMSEC), March 26, 2017, http://cimsec.org/hainans-maritime-militia-china-builds-standing-vanguard-pt-1/31556

13 Conor M. Kennedy and Andrew S. Erickson, "Riding A New Wave of Professionalization and Militarization: Sansha City's Maritime Militia," Center for International Maritime Security (CIMSEC), September 1, 2016, http://cimsec.org/riding-new-wave-professionalization-militarization-sansha-citys-maritime-militia/27689

14 Dennis J. Blasko, "Chinese Strategic Thinking: People's War in the 21st Century," *China Brief*, Vol.10, No.6, Mar.18, 2010, pp.5–8.

15 Franz-Stefan Gady, "'Little Blue Men': Doing China's Dirty Work in the SCS," *The Diplomat*, November 5, 2015, http://thediplomat.com/2015/11/little-blue-men-doing-chinas-dirty-work-in-the-south-china-sea/

16 Michael McDevitt, "Becoming a Great 'Maritime Power': A Chinese Dream," report of Center for Naval Analysis, June 2016.

17 Simon Denyer, "How China's fishermen are fighting a covert war in the SCS," *The Washington Post*, April 12, 2016, https://www.washingtonpost.com/world/asia_pacific/fishing-fleet-puts-china-on-collision-course-with-neighbors-in-south-china-sea/2016/04/12/8a6a9e3c-fff3-11e5-8bb1-f124a43f84dc_story.html?postshare=451460511139565&tid=ss_tw&utm_term=.84a1d5a3e0d4

18 Andrew S. Erickson and Conor M. Kennedy, "China's Maritime Militia: What It Is and How to Deal With It," *Foreign Affairs*, June 23, 2016, https://www.foreignaffairs.com/articles/china/2016-06-23/chinas-maritime-militia

19 Andrew S. Erickson and Conor M. Kennedy, "China's Maritime Militia," CNA Corporation, March 7, 2016, p.5, https://www.cna.org/cna_files/pdf/Chinas-Maritime-Militia.pdf

20 Andrew S. Erickson and Conor M. Kennedy, "Countering China's Third Sea Force: Unmask Maritime Militia before They're Used Again," *The National Interest*, July 6, 2016, http://nationalinterest.org/feature/countering-chinas-third-sea-force-unmask-maritime-militia-16860

21 Michael McDevitt, "Becoming a Great 'Maritime Power': A Chinese Dream," report of Center for Naval Analysis, June 2016, p.vii.

22 Zhang Yu, "The Basic Connotation of the Militia's Support to the Front in Wartime," *National Defense*, No. 6, 2002, pp.36–38.

23 Andrew S. Erickson and Conor M. Kennedy, "China's Maritime Militia," CNA Corporation, March 7, 2016, https://www.cna.org/cna_files/pdf/Chinas-Maritime-Militia.pdf

24 Michael Green, Kathleen Hicks, Zack Cooper, John Schaus, Jake Douglas, "Countering Coercion in Maritime Asia: The Theory and Practice of Gray Zone Deterrence," Report of CSIS, May 9, 2017, p.12, https://csis-prod.s3.amazonaws.com/s3fs-public/publication/170505_GreenM_CounteringCoercionAsia_Web.pdf?OnoJXfWb4A5gw_n6G.8azgEd8zRIM4wq

25 Andrew S. Erickson, Conor M. Kennedy, "Tanmen Militia: China's Maritime Rights Protection Vanguard," *National Interest*, May 6, 2015, http://www.nationalinterest.org/feature/tanmen-militia-china%E2%80%99s-maritime-rights-protection-vanguard-12816?page=show

26 The US Department of Defense, "Military and Security Developments Involving the People's Republic of China 2017," May 15, 2017, p.56, https://www.defense.gov/Portals/1/Documents/pubs/2017_China_Military_Power_Report.PDF?ver=2017-06-06-141328-770

27 Conor M. Kennedy, Andrew S. Erickson, "Model Maritime Militia: Tanmen's Leading Role in the April 2012 Scarborough Shoal Incident," Center for International Maritime Security (CIMSEC), April 21, 2016, http://cimsec.org/model-maritime-militia-tanmens-leading-role-april-2012-scarborough-shoal-incident/24573
"From Frontier to Frontline: Tanmen Maritime Militia's Leading Role Pt. 2," Center for International Maritime Security (CIMSEC), May 17, 2016, http://cimsec.org/frontier-frontline-tanmen-maritime-militias-leading-role-pt-2/25260

28 Simon Denyer, "How China's fishermen are fighting a covert war in the SCS," *The Washington Post*, April 12, 2016, https://www.washingtonpost.com/world/asia_pacific/fishing-fleet-puts-china-on-collision-course-with-neighbors-in-south-china-sea/2016/04/12/8a6a9e3c-fff3-11e5-8bb1-f124a43f84dc_story.html?postshare=4514605111395656&tid=ss_tw&utm_term=.84a1d5a3e0d4

29 Florence Looi, "Looking for China's maritime militia," *Al Jazeera*, 17 June 2016, http://www.aljazeera.com/blogs/asia/2016/06/chinas-maritime-militia-160603205135196.html

30 Andrew S. Erickson and Conor M. Kennedy, "China's Maritime Militia: What It Is and How to Deal With It," *Foreign Affairs*, June 23, 2016, https://www.foreignaffairs.com/articles/china/2016-06-23/chinas-maritime-militia

31 Refer to Article 3 of Emergency Response Law of the People's Republic of China.

32 See article 14 and Article 28 of Emergency Response Law of the People's Republic of China.

33 Andrew S. Erickson and Conor M. Kennedy, "Meet the Chinese Maritime Militia Waging a 'People's War at Sea'," *The Wall street Journal*, Mar. 31, 2015, https://blogs.wsj.com/chinarealtime/2015/03/31/meet-the-chinese-maritime-militia-waging-a-peoples-war-at-sea/

34 James Kraska, "China's Maritime Militia Upends Rules on Naval Warfare," The Diplomat, August 10, 2015, http://thediplomat.com/2015/08/chinas-maritime-militia-upends-rules-on-naval-warfare/

35 James Kraska and Michael Monti, "The Law of Naval Warfare and China's Maritime Militia," *International Law Studies*, Vol.91, No.1, 2015, pp.450–467.

36 Ryan Pickrell, "How the US Should Respond to China's 'Secret' Weapon," The Daily Caller, September 24, 2016, http://dailycaller.com/2016/09/24/how-the-us-should-respond-to-chinas-secret-weapon/

37 James Kraska and Michael Monti, "The Law of Naval Warfare and China's Maritime Militia," *International Law Studies*, Vol.91, No.1, 2015, p.466.

38 Peter Brookes, "Take note of China's non-Navy maritime forces," *The Hill*, December 13, 2016, http://thehill.com/blogs/congress-blog/foreign-policy/310077-take-note-of-chinas-non-navy-maritime-forces

39 Simon Denyer, "How China's fishermen are fighting a covert war in the SCS," *The Washington Post*, April 12, 2016, https://www.washingtonpost.com/world/asia_pacific/fishing-fleet-puts-china-on-collision-course-with-neighbors-in-south-china-sea/2016/04/12/8a6a9e3c-fff3-11e5-8bb1-f124a43f84dc_story.html?postshare=451460511139565&tid=ss_tw&utm_term=.84a1d5a3e0d4

40 Andrew S. Erickson and Conor M. Kennedy, "Countering China's Third Sea Force: Unmask Maritime Militia before They're Used Again," *The National Interest*, July 6, 2016, http://nationalinterest.org/feature/countering-chinas-third-sea-force-unmask-maritime-militia-16860

41 Christopher P. Cavas, "China's Maritime Militia a Growing Concern," Defense News, November 21, 2016, http://www.defensenews.com/naval/2016/11/22/chinas-maritime-militia-a-growing-concern/

42 Blake Herzinger, "U.S. Options for the People's Republic of China's Maritime Militias," Center for International Maritime Security, June 15, 2017, http://cimsec.org/u-s-options-peoples-republic-chinas-maritime-militias/32883

43 Andrew S. Erickson and Conor M. Kennedy, "China's Maritime Militia: What It Is and How to Deal With It," *Foreign Affairs*, June 23, 2016, https://www.foreignaffairs.com/articles/china/2016-06-23/chinas-maritime-militia

44 "The Code for Unplanned Encounters at Sea (CUES) was adopted during the 2014 Western Pacific Naval Symposium(WPNS) held in Qingdao," *People's Daily*, April 23, 2014, p.3.

45 "Strengthen confidence, carry forward our cause into the future, and promote a more comprehensive and in-depth development of China-ASEAN Relations," *People's Daily*, September 8, 2016, p.1.

46 Christopher P. Cavas, "China's 'Little Blue Men' Take Navy's Place in Disputes," November 2, 2015, http://www.defensenews.com/naval/2015/11/03/chinas-little-blue-men-take-navys-place-in-disputes/

47 Andrew S. Erickson and Conor M. Kennedy, "China's Maritime Militia: What It Is and How to Deal With It," *Foreign Affairs*, June 23, 2016, https://www.foreignaffairs.com/articles/china/2016-06-23/chinas-maritime-militia

48 Blake Herzinger, "U.S. Options for the People's Republic of China's Maritime Militias," Center for International Maritime Security, June 15, 2017, http://cimsec.org/u-s-options-peoples-republic-chinas-maritime-militias/32883

49 Dong Yu and Sha Wen, "Be Aware of Guns on Vietnamese Fishing Boats," China Military Online, April 14, 2016, http://english.chinamil.com.cn/news-channels/pla-daily-commentary/2016-04/14/content_7006595.htm

50 State Council, PRC, "Full Text: China Adheres to the Position of Settling Through Negotiation the Relevant Disputes Between China and the Philippines in the SCS," 13 July, 2016, http://english.gov.cn/state_council/ministries/2016/07/13/content_281475392503075.htm

51 "Returning Chinese fishermen say Philippine soldiers and police act as fishermen and seize people with guns," People's Daily Online, May 17, 2014, http://world.people.com.cn/n/2014/0517/c1002-25029647.html

52 Hongzhou Zhang and Sam Bateman, "Fishing Militia, the Securitization of Fishery and the SCS Dispute," *Contemporary Southeast Asia*, Vol.39, No.2, 2017, p.292.

53 Zhang Hongzhou, "Chinese Fishermen in Disputed Waters: Not Quite a 'People's War'," *Marine Policy*, Vol.68, June 2016, pp.65–73.

54 The State Council Information Office of the People's Republic of China: China's Military Strategy (White Paper), May 26, 2015, http://www.mod.gov.cn/auth/2015-05/26/content_4586723.htm

55 James Kraska and Michael Monti, "The Law of Naval Warfare and China's Maritime Militia," *International Law Studies*, Vol.91, No.1, 2015, p.466.

9

The Trump Administration's Policy on the SCS

"China seeks to displace the United States in the Indo-Pacific region, expand the reaches of its state-driven economic model, and reorder the region in its favor." "Its efforts to build and militarize outposts in the SCS endanger the free flow of trade, threaten the sovereignty of other nations, and undermine regional stability."

—National Security Strategy of the United States of America, December 2017

"We are making clear: Beijing's claims to offshore resources across most of the SCS are completely unlawful, as is its campaign of bullying to control them." "As Beijing has failed to put forth a lawful, coherent maritime claim in the SCS, the United States rejects any PRC claim to waters beyond a 12-nautical mile territorial sea derived from islands it claims in the Spratly Islands (without prejudice to other states' sovereignty claims over such islands)."

—U.S. Position on Maritime Claims in the SCS, July 13, 2020

The so-called SCS dispute is an issue between China and littoral countries of the SCS. The United States is neither a direct party to the SCS issue nor does it have any disputes with China over maritime sovereignty and maritime interests. Therefore, the SCS is not and should not be an issue between the two countries, and territorial disputes over the SCS should not hinder China-U.S. ties. However, since the end of the Cold War, the United States has increasingly attached importance to the SCS in the Western Pacific strategic chain, and tried to make it a strategic frontier to curb the expansion of China's maritime rights, to contain China's rising sphere of influence, and to maintain the American maritime hegemony. Especially since the beginning of the new century, with the increasingly rising maritime disputes between China and some Southeast Asian countries disputing the SCS, the SCS has become the best entry point for the United States and its partners to achieve common interests and thus jointly counterbalance China.

Given the important role played by the United States on the SCS issue, what kind of SCS policy Trump, who is non-traditional and anti-establishment, adopts after taking office will naturally attract great attention from all circles. Since taking office in 2017, Trump's "America First" principle and unconventional behaviors in foreign policy, coupled with his aggressive, defiant personality and sometimes outrageous and extreme rhetoric, have clouded the new administration's many Asia-Pacific policy options, including over the SCS. What is the status of the SCS issue in the Trump administration's policy on Asia Pacific and China? Has the Trump administration's SCS policy taken shape so far? What policy initiatives has it taken? Where will the future go? This chapter analyzes Trump administration's SCS policy from two aspects: policy discourse and policy practice. Through discussing U.S. academic debates about the Trump administration's SCS policy and interpreting the underlying strategic motivation behind American involvement in the SCS issue, this chapter discusses the prospects of U.S. policy on SCS in the Trump era and gives a preliminary explanation to the above questions.

The Debates over the Trump Administration's SCS Policy in the Early Days

In 2017, Donald Trump, who came up with the electoral slogan "Make America Great Again" and highlighted an "America First" mantra, set out to adjust the strategies and carried out a series of volatile foreign policies with the primary characteristic of de-Obamanization, including the termination of the "rebalancing" strategy in the Asia-Pacific region, which lead to the renewal of nationalism. During the Obama administration, the SCS issue, as a key tool for the United States to implement the "rebalancing" strategy in the Asia-Pacific region, was an important means for the United States to expand its military presence in the Asia-Pacific region, strengthen alliances, and check and balance China. Naturally, the SCS issue became a hot topic in the China-U.S. strategic competition. Since Trump took office, heated debates revolve on whether the new administration has inherited the SCS policy of the previous administrations and continued to engage in a fierce game with China, or whether it reaches some compromise or interest exchange with China in exchange for more important interest concerns of the United States. On the whole, the debate on the Trump administration's SCS policy can be divided into two arguments: the "neglect theory" and the "emphasis theory."

The "neglect theory" holders believe that Trump is super focused on the Korean Peninsula nuclear issue and economic and trade issues so that the United States does not make a valid response when China's military behavior in the SCS demands a U.S. response. The SCS issue occupies a very marginal position on the agenda of the new U.S. administration's Asia-Pacific strategy and China policy, and has been virtually neglected by the early Trump administration, either deliberately or unintentionally. For example, some media outlets reported that the Trump administration remained unclear and uncoordinated on SCS territorial disputes, which leaves U.S. allies "perplexed and anxious."[1] Trump's Asia-Pacific policy focuses on North Korea and one major issue has largely been forgotten: curtailing the Chinese military from assuming total control over the strategic SCS,[2] which enables Beijing to sail ahead in the SCS.[3] Analysts have pointed out that the Trump administration's quiet approach to the SCS has given China a "free pass," ceding ground at a critical time. Once China completes its planning, "they won't be pulling back."[4] Some scholars have even warned Washington that the borders in the SCS are vanishing and the United States must do more to stop China's encroachments, if not, its international prestige and the established regional order will suffer.[5] Moreover, the inaction of the United States will "send a dangerous signal about the strength of the U.S. alliance system and lessen the appeal of the United States as a security partner."[6]

To sum up, the Trump administration has been regarded by some media and observers as being apathetic and detached to the SCS issue, mainly due to the following factors:

First, as a "political outsider," Trump is not familiar with the SCS dispute and other international affairs, so he is unlikely to form a clear policy on the SCS in the short term. Second, North Korean nuclear issue is a very pressing threat that could have produced a great "political win." Safeguarding national security is one of the core demands of the Trump administration's "America First" policy. The new round of North Korean nuclear crisis that erupted since February 2017 was considered to be the most urgent security threat facing the United States. The Trump administration has repeated that U.S. policy of "strategic patience" with North Korea is over and that the United States doesn't have many good options left.[7] It is safe to say that the North Korean nuclear crisis captured the Trump administration's imagination. The SCS issue, by contrast, is much dimmer. Third, economic and trade issues are the focus of U.S.-China relations. To Trump administration, China poses a real economic threat to the United States, and protecting U.S. intellectual property rights and reversing unequal economic ties with China were the new administration's priorities. Fourth, since the second half of 2016, the improvement of China-Philippines relations and the positive progress made in the negotiations between China and ASEAN countries on the COC in the SCS have greatly eased the situation in the SCS, and China's ability to control the situation in the SCS has also been enhanced, which has greatly squeezed the space for the U.S. involvement. Fifth, in face of China's island-building activities in the SCS, the Trump administration has failed to come up with a set of effective measures in time, which will undoubtedly disappoint those who support the United States to be tough with China on the SCS issue.[8]

The emphasis theorists hold that the SCS issue does not rank high among the Asia-Pacific policy agenda of the Trump administration, though, the United States has never neglected the SCS issue and it still raises the concern of the U.S. political and military circles. As Colin Willet from Center for Strategic and International Studies (CSIS) puts, despite the sharp focus on the North Korea and trade relations in Asia, the administration made substantial efforts to continue building strategic relationships in Southeast Asia. The year 2017 was a relatively quiet one on the SCS itself, though, Washington continues to deepen defense and security partnerships, particularly with Vietnam, improved political relations with the Philippines and continues support for the Enhanced Defense Cooperation Agreement, and maintained consistent engagement with Southeast Asian Leaders to hear their voices.[9] Some Chinese scholars have also pointed out that the Trump administration has frequently mentioned the concept of Indo-Pacific and has been obsessed with maintaining the so-called free and open Indo-Pacific since October 2017, which means that the SCS issue as an important part of the Indo-Pacific region was not truly ignored by the Trump administration.[10] Under the Trump administration, the United States remained suspicious of China's moves in the SCS and continues to intervene in the SCS issue and takes the opportunity to increase its military deployments in the Asia-Pacific region.[11]

According to emphasis theorists, the strategic importance of the SCS determines that the Trump administration cannot ignore the SCS issue. First of all, the SCS has outstanding geostrategic value. As one of the most important commercial passageways and an important channel connecting the Pacific and Indian oceans, it is the only way for Navies and merchant vessels of Asia-Pacific countries to communicate and trade. Currently, about 30 % of seagoing trade and 50 % of oil trade pass through the area each year, including more than $1 trillion in U.S.-related trade.[12] Although the United States has no claim to territorial sovereignty over the SCS, it has interests in the SCS, mainly including the so-called free access and stability. In the view of the United States, China's claims of maritime rights and its maritime expansion in the SCS pose a major threat to free access and peace and stability in the SCS,[13] while the Trump administration clearly could not afford to turn a blind eye. Since the SCS dispute involving U.S. allies and partners in the Asia-Pacific region, if China changes the existing regional order of the SCS or even makes the SCS an inner lake, it will not only discourage bilateral relations between the United States and the SCS surrounding countries, but endanger the reliability and credibility of the U.S. alliance system, thereby undermining credibility in the strategy of the United States in the global system. Furthermore, the United States has deliberately played the "SCS card" towards China. With the surge in China's economic power in recent years, the strategic all-round competition between China and the United States was inevitable. In this situation, the United States was obliged to suppress and counter China via various means, and it is unlikely to give up any of the opportunities, let alone the SCS issue.

From the performance of the Trump administration, the SCS dispute was not its top diplomatic priority. However, it is underestimated and highly misleading to say that the United States has neglected the SCS issue. In fact, the United States is the main extraterritorial force that has complicated and accentuated the SCS issue, which has not been essentially transformed when Trump took office. Due to its focus, the Trump administration is faced a more emergent and trickier North Korean nuclear issue and trade issues threatening the national security and economic interests. It is merely a tactical prioritization based on national security and economic interests and changing regional situations, rather than strategic abandonment. In terms of both policy discourse and policy practice, the Trump administration has never ceased interfering in the SCS issue. Based on the above judgment, it can be concluded that while the Trump administration did not issue a specific strategic document on the SCS issue, the outline had already emerged, showing an obvious "two-pronged" logic: On the one hand, the SCS issue has been frequently mentioned in policy discourse, and signals and pressure have been sent to China through various occasions and channels; on the other hand, the United States stepped up its involvement in the SCS issue at the policy and practice level, and the involvement is targeted and riskier.

The Trump Administration's Attitudes toward the SCS Issue

In terms of political discourse, the statements made by senior U.S. Officials on the SCS issue convey vital message as to the Trump administration's policy on the SCS. The SCS issue is frequently mentioned in the unilateral official statements of the United States; high-level bilateral talks with Japan, India, Vietnam, and Australia; and is discussed at the Foreign Ministers' Summit between the United States and ASEAN, the Trilateral Strategic Dialogue among the United States, Japan, Australia, and India, the Quartet Strategic Dialogue among the United States, Japan, Australia, and India. The issue is being mentioned by the United States on various occasions such as the China-U.S. Diplomatic and Security Dialogue, as well as on major international occasions such as the Shangri-La Dialogue and the APEC Summit. Thus, the writer will explore the Trump administration's attitude on the SCS issue from the perspective of the representative statements of the United States on unilateral, bilateral, and multilateral occasions, providing a study that will be a useful guide as the new Biden administration passes its current "honeymoon" period.

First of all, Trump himself and his diplomatic team repeatedly and unilaterally declared the U.S. position on the SCS issue. As early as the electoral campaign, Trump sent strong signals on the SCS issue. On December 5, 2016, Donald Trump blasted China on social media for its military buildup in the SCS without U.S. consent.[14] In his Senate confirmation hearing on January 11, 2017, Secretary of State Tillerson compared China's artificial island building in the SCS to Russia's annexation of Crimea, and warned China that it must stop island-building and stop setting foot on the islands.[15] Since then, in a letter to Ben Cardin, the senior Senator on the Senate Foreign Relations Committee, Tillerson has expanded on U.S. positions, including not recognizing China's excessive claims in the SCS, nor allowing China to use artificial islands to intimidate neighboring countries or restrict FON in the SCS.[16] On January 20, when asked if President Trump agreed with Tillerson's remarks on the SCS, then White House Spokesman Spicer responded that "the United States wants to protect our interests in the SCS, and if those islands are in international waters and not part of China, we will defend international territory from any one country."[17]

At a news conference on August 2, 2017, when asked about whether the SCS issue has dropped off as a major issue in the Trump administration, Susan A. Thornton, the Acting Assistant Secretary of State for East Asian and Pacific

Affairs, not only explicitly denied the Trump administration's neglect of the SCS issue, but stressed that the United States was dedicated to protecting and defending FON and overflight in the SCS. "We also have had a number of conversations with allies and partners in the region about their concerns over latent tensions and continued concerns about maritime disputes in the SCS, and we'll press for due regard for legal processes, dispute resolution mechanisms, and upholding, certainly, international law and the UN Convention on the Law of the Sea."[18] On August 2, 2018, the U.S. Senate passed the National Defense Authorization Act for fiscal year 2019, which also made excessive accusations against the militarization of China's construction activities on islands and reefs in the SCS, claiming that China's actions in the SCS have harmed the security of U.S. allies and partners and posed a threat to U.S. core interests. To this end, the U.S. Congress required the Secretary of Defense, in conjunction with the Secretary of State, to promptly submit to Congress and make public information about China's military and intimidation activities in the SCS.[19]

On October 4, 2018, Vice President Pence publicly claimed in a speech delivered by the Hudson Institute that "today, Beijing has deployed advanced anti-ship and anti-air missiles atop an archipelago of military bases constructed on artificial islands." As a response, "the United States Navy will continue to fly, sail, and operate wherever international law allows and our national interests demand. We will not be intimidated and we will not stand down."[20] On June 1, 2019, the Indo-Pacific Strategy Report issued by the U.S. Department of Defense stated that "China has continued to militarize the South China Sea by placing anti-ship cruise missiles and long-range surface-to-air missiles on the disputed Spratly Islands and employing paramilitary forces in maritime disputes vis-à-vis other claimants." "Today, in places like the South China Sea, excessive maritime claims are attempts by coastal states to unlawfully restrict the exercise of freedoms afforded to all seafaring nations to operate in waters beyond territorial limits. The United States will continue to fly, sail, and operate wherever international law allows, and encourage our allies and partners to do the same."[21]

What is more serious is that, Secretary of State Pompeo issued a South China Sea policy statement on July 13, 2020, which claimed that "Beijing's claims to offshore resources across most of the South China Sea are completely unlawful, as is its campaign of bullying to control them." "As Beijing has failed to put forth a lawful, coherent maritime claim in the South China Sea, the United States rejects any PRC claim to waters beyond a 12-nautical mile territorial sea derived from islands it claims in the Spratly Islands (without prejudice to other states' sovereignty claims over such islands)."[22] The U.S. new SCS policy statement not only publicly denies China's sovereignty over the SCS, but also emphasizes its support for the "SCS Arbitration Case" (in favor of the Philippines) in 2016, which indicates that the United States has completely changed the basic SCS policy pursued by previous administrations and started to adopt the attitude of "taking sides." The essence of this SCS policy statement is the Trump administration's need to suppress and contain China from the political, diplomatic, and strategic aspects by taking advantage of the COVID-19 epidemic. It projects the strategic meaning that the United States will strengthen and expand its military presence in the SCS area, try to enhance its deterrence and combat effectiveness in the region, and even seek to reopen conventional military bases in the SCS in the future.

Second, concerns about the SCS issue have been frequently expressed in bilateral meetings with foreign dignitaries. In a meeting with Australian Prime Minister Turnbull on April 22, 2017, then Vice President Pence said "in the SCS and throughout the region, we will defend the fundamental freedoms of navigation and overflight, and ensure the unimpeded flow of lawful commerce, and promote peaceful diplomatic dialogue to address issues of regional and global concern."[23] On May 31, Trump again raised the SCS issue in a joint statement issued after his meeting with visiting Vietnamese Prime Minister Nguyen Xuan Phu. President Trump and Prime Minister Nguyen Xuan Phuc affirmed that the SCS is a waterway of strategic significance to the international community. The two leaders underscored the importance of FON and overflight and other lawful uses of the seas, and noted with concern the destabilizing impact that unlawful restrictions to the freedom of the seas have on peace and prosperity in the Asia-Pacific region. The two sides also affirmed full support for the peaceful resolution of disputes without the threat or use of force or coercion, in accordance with international law, including full respect for diplomatic and legal processes, and called upon all parties concerned to implement their international legal obligations in good faith in any resolution to these disputes. They highlighted the importance that parties refrain from actions that would escalate tensions, such as the militarization of disputed features. President Trump stressed that the United States will continue to fly, sail, and operate anywhere international law allows.[24] At the "2+2" talks between their defense ministers and foreign ministers on August 17 in Washington, the United States and Japan jointly expressed their opposition to militarization activities in the SCS, and advocated that "maritime disputes should be resolved through peaceful means and FON based on UNCLOS should be upheld".[25] At the "2+2" talks between the United States and Australian Foreign Ministers and Defense Ministers on July 24, 2018, U.S. Secretary of Defense Mattis also criticized China's so-called militarization in the

SCS when talking about the SCS issue, saying that in a free and open Indo-Pacific region, all countries, big or small, should respect each other's territorial integrity, sovereignty, and sovereign right to decide.[26]

During his visit to the Philippines in March 2019, Secretary of State Pompeo reaffirmed the U.S. commitment to the Mutual Defense Treaty, providing assurances that "as the South China Sea is part of the Pacific, any armed attack on Philippine forces, aircraft, or public vessels in the South China Sea will trigger mutual defense obligations under Article IV of our Mutual Defense Treaty."[27] In the official two-day visit to Vietnam in October 2020, Pompeo also stressed in a statement that "in recent years, we have strengthened and expanded our comprehensive partnership, based on a shared vision of a stable and peaceful Indo-Pacific region as well as respect for each other's independence, sovereignty, territorial integrity and political systems."[28]

It is worth pointing out that in the bilateral meetings between Chinese and American politicians, the United States has raised the SCS issue on various occasions with direct pressure on China. For example, at the first China-U.S. Diplomatic and Security Dialogue held on June 21, 2017, the United States expressed that it opposes any attempt to change the status quo in the SCS through the construction of militarized outposts, opposes excessive maritime claims that are not supported by international law, and adheres to the proposition of FON and overflight.[29] During President Trump's visit to China from November 9 to 10, the two sides candidly discussed regional and maritime security. President Trump underscored the critical importance of the peaceful resolution of disputes, unimpeded lawful commerce, and respect for international law in the East and SCS, including FON and overflight and other lawful uses of the sea, and raised concerns about militarization of outposts in the SCS.[30] Tillerson, the then Secretary of State, reiterated that the U.S. position on maritime security issues and the SCS remains unchanged. "We insist on upholding FON that claims to be consistent with international law, and that claimants should stop construction and militarization of outposts in order to maximize prospects for successful diplomacy."[31] When Secretary of State Pompeo met with visiting Chinese Foreign Minister Wang Yi in Washington on May 23, 2018, he also expressed to China the United States' continued concern about militarization in the SCS.[32] In his visit to Beijing on June 14, Pompeo reiterated U.S. concerns about China's militarization of outposts in the SCS, claiming that China's actions threatened the free flow of trade in the region and the sovereignty of other countries and undermined regional stability. He urged China to resolve the relevant disputes by peaceful means without resorting to threats, coercion, or intimidation.[33]

Finally, the United States made full use of multilateral occasions to jointly make its position clear to China and to heat up the SCS issue. At the U.S.-ASEAN Foreign Ministers' Summit in Washington on May 4, 2017, Tillerson stressed that all parties should respect international law, resolve disputes through peaceful means, and stop militarization, island building, sand reclamation, and other activities in the SCS. He also stressed that ASEAN and China should fully and efficiently implement the Declaration on the Conduct of Parties in the SCS (DOC) and reach a binding COC as soon as possible.[34] Defense Secretary Mattis also took aim at China at the Shangri-La Dialogue on June 3, saying that the 2016 ruling by the Arbitral Tribunal on the case brought by the Philippines on the SCS is binding, and called on all claimants to use this as a starting point to peacefully manage their disputes in the SCS. The scope and effect of China's construction activities in the SCS differ from those in other countries in several key ways. This includes the nature of its militarization, China's disregard for international law, its contempt for other nations' interests, and its efforts to dismiss non-adversarial resolution of issues. The United States opposes countries militarizing artificial islands and enforcing excessive maritime claims unsupported by international law. "We cannot and will not accept unilateral coercive changes to the status quo."[35] In a joint statement issued at the seventh Trilateral Strategic Dialogue between the United States, Japan, and Australia on August 6, the three Foreign Ministers expressed serious concern over the SCS dispute and strongly opposed coercive unilateral actions to change the status quo and escalate tensions. The three countries urged the claimants in the SCS to stop construction on islands and reefs, construction of guard posts, militarization in disputed waters, and unilateral changes in the inherent geomorphic pattern of the SCS. It calls on all claimants to clarify their maritime claims in accordance with the provisions of UNCLOS, to settle disputes by peaceful means in accordance with international law, and to formulate as soon as possible a binding COC in the SCS consistent with international law.[36] At the second U.S.-Japan-India Trilateral Foreign Ministers' Meeting in Washington on September 18, the three countries stressed the importance of maintaining a free and open Indo-Pacific region and reiterated the importance of FON and flight and lawful free flow of commerce in global and regional oceans, including in the SCS.[37]

At the 17th Shangri-La Dialogue held in Singapore on June 2, 2018, Defense Secretary Mattis not only promoted the Indo-Pacific strategy, but also mentioned the SCS issue, condemning that China's policy in the SCS stands in stark contrast to the openness of the U.S. Indo-Pacific strategy.[38] During the dialogue, the United States, Japan, and the ROK also held the 10th Trilateral

Defense Ministerial Meeting and discussed the security situation in the SCS. The ministers underscored their shared respect for international law as well as their shared commitment to upholding FON and overflight and other lawful uses of the sea, including in the SCS. They emphasized the importance of the peaceful resolution of conflict in accordance with international law, including the UNCLOS, and expressed strong opposition to the use of force or coercion as well as unilateral action to alter the status quo, and to the use of disputed features for military purposes in the SCS.[39] From August 1 to 5, 2018, Secretary of State Mike Pompeo kicked off his Southeast Asia tour, during which he discussed the SCS issue at important multilateral forums such as the ARF, the East Asia Summit Ministerial Meeting, the U.S.-ASEAN Ministerial Meeting, and the Lower Mekong Initiative Ministerial Meeting. Pompeo has repeatedly vowed to strengthen U.S. security and trade relations with ASEAN countries and support ASEAN centrality in regional affairs, and he also stressed the importance of maintaining a rules-based order in the SCS.[40]

At the East Asia Summit held in November 2018, Vice President Pence once again stated that "Our partnership also includes our commitment to uphold the freedom of the seas and skies, where we stand shoulder to shoulder with you for freedom of navigation; and our determination to ensure that your nations are secure in your sovereign borders on land, at sea, and in the digital world. All of these are examples of our commitment to partnership, and in each case we believe that we've made significant progress and will continue to make significant progress together."[41] On February 15, 2020, Secretary of State Pompeo and Defense Minister Esper presented China as the biggest threat in the SCS at the Munich Security Conference and accused China of "infringing" the Exclusive Economic Zones of Vietnam and the Philippines.[42] The United States hypes the SCS issue so frequently on multilateral occasions to raise the outside world's attention to the SCS issue, so as to continue to use the SCS issue to bash China.

The Trump Administration's Concrete Steps to Intervene in the SCS Issue

In bringing up the SCS issue, the Trump administration emphasized the peaceful settlement of relevant disputes through international law and multilateral means, and continues to promote multilateralization and internationalization of the SCS issue. Meanwhile, it opposed China's construction on islands and reefs in the SCS, and opposed unilateral change of the status quo by force or threat.

Such policies were basically inherited from and continuation of the SCS policy of the Obama administration. It can be said that the Trump administration did not give up the opportunity to pressure China on the SCS issue while urging China to cooperate in resolving the Korean nuclear issue and brandishing the "trade stick" to China. From the perspective of policy and practice, the Trump administration, like the Obama administration, has sent warships and military aircraft to the waters and airspace of the SCS many times to demonstrate the FON and overflight, and continues to challenge China's claims of sovereignty and rights and interests in the SCS. However, the Trump administration's intervention in the SCS issue is more targeted and riskier, and it has made necessary adjustments and innovations in the following aspects.

Increase the Intensity of Patrol in the SCS and Adjust Its Approval Process

The FON assertion is an important means for the United States to maintain its maritime freedom and the maritime hegemony, as well as an instrument to challenge the excessive maritime claims by coastal countries.[43] In recent years, with the rapid rise of China and the moderate expansion of its maritime power, the maritime competition between China and the United States in the Asia-Pacific region has become increasingly fierce. Therefore, China has become an important target for the United States to carry out FONOPs, and the SCS area is the key area for FON assertions. In Obama's times, the United States took a "case-by-case" approach, in which the Pentagon presented plans to the White House and the National Security Council for approval before taking action. During Obama's eight years in office, the United States conducted five operations in the SCS. Out of concern for upsetting China and harming China-U.S. relations, the Obama administration put a stop to operations from 2012 to September 2015, which was later restored due to pressure from Congress. In contrast, the Trump administration significantly increased its patrols in the SCS. In the four years from 2017 to 2020, the U.S. military conducted more than 25 times of FONOPs in the SCS, not to mention the additional covert operations that aren't reported in Western media.

The direct consequence of the Trump administration's intensified cruise in the SCS is that the confrontation between the Chinese and American armed forces in the SCS is almost normal. In the first half of 2020, the United States conducted more than 3,000 air military operations and more than 60 warship operations in the SCS. In July 2020, the U.S. aircraft carrier battle group Nimitz and the aircraft carrier battle group Reagan conducted exercises in the SCS. This is the first time since 2014 that the U.S. military dispatched two aircraft carriers for training in the SCS. The United States has also sent B-1B strategic bombers and E-8C reconnaissance planes to the SCS for many times, and even approached the offshore areas of Guangdong and Hainan Island in China for many times. The risk of accidental fire between the two armies increased sharply.

In July 2017, the Trump administration launched a new plan to challenge Chinese claims over SCS and adjusted existing approval procedures. Under the new plan, the White House will already be aware of the planned operations for they will be approved on a yearly basis, which will allow the operations to be conducted on a "very routine, very regular" basis, with the benefit of making each operation part of a regular program to keep the waters open, versus a "one-off event." Plus, under the plan, FONOP requests will begin with the U.S. Navy's 7th Fleet, go up to Pacific Fleet, to Pacific Command, to the Pentagon, and then to the National Security Council. The Pentagon will also send requests to the State Department the same time they are sent to the NSC, to make sure they do not undermine any concurrent diplomatic initiatives.[44] In contrast to the Obama administration, which had a policy of publicizing FONOPs, the Trump administration will not officially announce these operations. Rather, the administration will revert to the past practice of logging all FONOPs in the Navy's Annual Report.[45] These changes mean that the White House has delegated the decision-making power of patrolling the SCS, and the military has been given more flexibility and autonomy.

The "Linkage" and "Spoiling" Strategies Are Intertwined

Under the current background that the U.S. international strategic position is relatively declining and domestic political polarization is becoming increasingly intense, the Trump administration has gradually returned to rationality after taking office, and has adopted a more pragmatic linkage strategy in China policy, despite Trump's harsh words to China during his election campaign before. Central to this approach was engagement in comprehensive coordination and cooperation with China on strategic issues that related to core American interests, and to create overall linkage across various issue areas thereby enabling the United States to constrain China's behavior while safeguarding American interests.[46] The linkage strategy was also reflected in the Trump administration's handling of the SCS and North Korea nuclear issues. Shortly after the Trump administration came to power, the North Korean nuclear issue becomes the number one threat in the field of national security of the United States. The resolution to the North Korean nuclear issue will certainly require China's support and cooperation, although Trump's demonization of China did not encourage a united effort in this area. To this end, the Trump administration linked the SCS issue with the North Korean nuclear issue, and China's performance on the North Korean nuclear issue determined the U.S. attitude towards China on the SCS issue. Thus, the linkage strategy reflected the fact that President Trump preferred deal making to strategic thinking.

While adopting the linkage strategy, the Trump administration was also a "spoiler" in the SCS. Under the Trump administration, the United States made use of the territorial dispute to defend its hegemony in the region as well as to implement the linkage strategy. Whenever the situation in the SCS eases, the United States will take measures to intensify tension. For example, at a time when China and ASEAN reached a draft framework for the COC in the SCS in May 2017 and make advances on the bilateral consultations on the SCS issue, the U.S. Navy sent the Dewey missile destroyer within 12 nautical miles of Mischief Reef in the SCS to defend the FON. The purpose of the U.S. move was to show its military presence to its Asia-Pacific allies and partners, and to coerce China to cooperate with the United States on the North Korean nuclear issue. When China and ASEAN countries announced in early 2018 that they would accelerate consultations on the text of COC in the SCS, the United States sent its guided-missile destroyer USS Hopper in January 2018 into the waters within 12 nautical miles of Scarborough Shoal. In late February, the United States sent its aircraft carrier strike group Carl Vinson into the SCS on patrol. It clearly intended to stir up trouble again.

The United States Relies Heavily on Military Power, Accelerating Militarization of the SCS

The United States constantly accuses China of militarizing the SCS. In fact, the United States is the initiator and pusher of the militarization of the SCS. The United States is not a claimant to the SCS, let alone a littoral state of the SCS. However, in the name of safeguarding FON and regional security in the SCS, the United States has significantly increased its military deployment in the SCS and its surrounding areas, attempting to intervene in the development of the situation in the SCS with military. Since the Trump administration came into office, the United States increased its efforts to militarize the SCS issue, mainly in the following ways:

One was a sustained increase in military investment in the Western Pacific. At the 16th Shangri-La Dialogue in Singapore in June 2017, then Secretary of Defense Mattis emphasized that "currently 60 percent of all U.S. Navy ships, 55 percent of Army Forces, about two-thirds of the fleet Marine forces are assigned to the U.S. Pacific Command area of responsibility. Soon, 60 percent of our overseas tactical aviation assets will also be assigned to this theater."[47] Moreover, the United States has strengthened the deployment of sophisticated strategic weapons in the SCS for deterrence and reconnaissance. U.S. air force bombers such as B-1B Lancer, B-52 Stratofortress, and B-2 Spirit have been continuously rotated to Guam. Bomber rotation has provided Pacific Air Force and U.S. Pacific Command commanders with global strike and expanded deterrence capabilities to confront any potential opponents, and provided opportunities to strengthen regional alliances and long-term military partnerships in the whole region.[48]

Second, the United States accelerated steps to strengthen security cooperation with countries in the SCS. Since Trump took office, there were frequent interactions between the two countries and their militaries. The United States not only provided a large amount of military equipment to the Vietnamese Navy and Coast Guard, but also made a breakthrough by sailing an aircraft carrier to Vietnam for the first time since the end of Vietnam War in March 2018. The relationship is based on common interests, including FON, respect for international law, and recognition of national sovereignty, and both are committed to enhance defense cooperation with a focus on maritime security, humanitarian assistance and disaster relief, and peacekeeping operations.[49] In September 2019, Admiral Philip Davidson, commander of the US Indo-Pacific Command, said after the meeting of the Common Defense Committee held in Manila, "Today, we work together as friends, allies and partners to meet regional security challenges." The United States and the Philippines plan to carry out more than 300 security cooperation activities by 2020, up from 281 in 2019, because the two countries have pledged to strengthen cooperation in anti-terrorism, maritime security, cyber security, humanitarian assistance, and disaster relief.[50]

Third, the United States deepened military ties with non-regional powers in the SCS and sought to build an Asia-Pacific security network targeting China. In order to draw relevant countries into the SCS issue, the Trump administration significantly strengthened military interactions with Japan, Australia, India, and other countries. The United States revived the Quadrilateral Security Dialogue (QUAD) mechanism among the United States, Japan, Australia and India, and stressed that the four countries share common interests on the issue of FON and overflight in the SCS. On January 16, 2017, Senator John McCain and others launched the Asia-Pacific Stability Initiative, calling for the U.S. military to strengthen military cooperation with relevant countries, increase military exercises in the Asia-Pacific region, and expand the size of its Navy, an initiative strongly supported by the Pentagon and U.S. Pacific Command.[51] On April 26, Representative Stephanie Murphy and others also proposed the Asia-Pacific Defense Commission Act, advocating that the United States should enhance defense cooperation with its Asia-Pacific allies and realize the normalization of FON operations in the SCS and other places.[52] On July 28, 2020, the United States and Australia reached the Joint Statement of Ministerial Consultation between the United States and Australia in 2020, claiming that the cooperation between the two countries will focus on issues such as security in the Indian Ocean and the Pacific, bilateral defense, regional coordination, and the South China Sea.[53]

Utilize the American Order to Impose Soft Constraints on China

While increasing its military input in the SCS region, the Trump administration has employed soft power such as the so-called rules and order to pressure China. Mattis used the phrase "rules-based order" frequently at the 2017 Shangri-La Dialogue, insinuating criticism of China's island-building activities in the SCS and asserting that such an order is in the interests of the United States and all countries in the Asia-Pacific region. He further stresses that "we oppose countries militarizing artificial islands and enforcing excessive maritime claims unsupported by international law. We cannot and will not accept unilateral coercive changes to the status quo. We will continue to fly, sail and operate wherever international law allows, and demonstrate resolve through operational presence in the SCS and beyond."[54] On May 23, 2018, the United States withdrew its invitation to the Chinese Navy to participate in the 2018 annual Rim PAC exercise in response to China's militarization and disruption of regional order in the disputed waters of the SCS. Subsequently, at a meeting of senior officials of the four countries held in Singapore on June 7, the parties stressed their shared interest in strengthening a rules-based order in the Indo-Pacific region and noted their respective important roles in maintaining an open, transparent, inclusive, and rules-based regional order.[55]

Accordingly, in order to maintain the American order in the SCS, the United States also waved the stick of sanctions against China. On July 14, 2020, the U.S. Assistant Secretary of State David Stilwell said that he would not rule out any means of imposing sanctions on China, and referred to Chinese state-owned enterprises in the SCS as the "modern-day equivalents of the East India Company" during the British colonial period.[56] On August 27th, the U.S. Department of Commerce also added 24 Chinese state-owned enterprises to an Entity List overseen by the Bureau of Industry and Security, including several subsidiaries of China Communications Construction Company (CCCC). The Entity List restricts sales of U.S. goods shipped to companies on the list along with certain items made abroad with U.S. equipment or technology.[57] Secretary of State Pompeo alleged that "the PRC must not be allowed to use CCCC and other state-owned enterprises as weapons to impose an expansionist agenda."[58]

The "rules-based order" advocated by the Trump administration is essentially a regional security order dominated by the United States, or the "American order." This "US-style order" is corresponding to the regional security order that China and ASEAN countries are building through peaceful negotiations under the guidance of the "dual-track approach." Although both are in the process of establishing and practicing rule-based international order, the former is the "American norm" imposed by the United States on the countries around the SCS, which is closed and exclusive. The latter is a consensus reached through consultation and negotiation on an equal footing and is inherently open and inclusive. As a result, the United States has repeatedly accused China of SCS behaviors that violated the "rules-based order." In fact, the United States is using the discourse hegemony of "American rules" to exclude China's claims in the SCS. It intends to label China as a "destroyer" of rules and order in the SCS, and to impose soft constraints on China in terms of international public opinion and morality.

The Trump Administration's Strategic Motivations for Intervening in the SCS Issue

Facing various domestic and foreign issues and challenges, the Trump administration continued to intervene in the SCS issue from two aspects, namely policy discourse and policy practice. The prominent geostrategic value of the SCS is certainly one of the reasons for the Trump administration to attach importance to the SCS issue, but there were many deep-seated strategic motivations behind it. To be specific, the Trump administration's continuous involvement in the SCS issue was not only a reflection of the United States' growing strategic anxiety over China's rapid rise, but also a realistic need for it to actively promote its

Indo-Pacific strategy. At the same time, the Trump administration's continuous intervention in the SCS was also due to strategic considerations; reassuring America's Asia-Pacific allies and ensuring its credibility, as well as maintaining America's maritime hegemony and countering China's expansion of maritime rights.

Strategic Concern about China's Rapid Rise

With China's rapid rise in recent years, Beijing has not only failed to evolve and act as the United States had anticipated it would during 'Reform and Opening-up' but also has not reacted to events as the US strategic community wished. Through the implementation of the "Belt and Road" strategy, the establishment of the Asian infrastructure investment bank and the BRICs Bank, and the acceleration of military expansion, China has posed a strong challenge to the existing international order dominated by the United States. As a result, there has even been a round of "Who lost China?" debates, similar to those of the 1950s.[59] Testifying before the House Armed Services Committee on February 14, 2018, General Harry Harris, a Japanese-American who was nominated to be the new United States Ambassador to Australia, made claims that China's military modernization has made great progress and will soon be able to compete with the United States military, saying "the United States will be defeated by China if it does not change."[60] In March, Ely Ratner and Kurt M. Campbell, a former senior diplomat, wrote that China's international behavior is becoming "assertive." China's encroachment on U.S. dominance in geopolitical matters such as the SCS and the Taiwan Strait and its estrangement between Washington and its allies have undermined the U.S.-led security order in Asia. In particular, after the SCS arbitration case in 2016, China has maintained a tough stance, which shows that Beijing is not an institutionalized, law-abiding good country.[61] In fact, in the National Security Strategy of the United States of America[62] and Summary of the 2018 National Defense Strategy of the United States of America[63] released by the Trump administration, China was positioned as a strategic opponent and revisionist country that is challenging the leadership of the United States. The United States has played up China's threats, accusing China of building islands and reefs in the SCS as a dangerous "militarization" that endangers regional security, other countries' sovereignty, and trade freedom. It can be said that the Trump administration continued to play the "SCS card" against China, which to some extent reflects the U.S. strategic concerns about China's rise.

Practical Need of Indo-Pacific Strategy

"Indo-Pacific" is the abbreviation of the Indian Asia Pacific region. During the Obama administration, then Secretary of State Hillary Clinton used the word "Indo-Pacific" many times to summarize the strategic interests of the United States in the region.[64] In November 2017, during his trip to Asia, Trump frequently proposed to build the so-called free and open Indian Pacific region, reactivating the Indo-Pacific strategy.[65] Since then, the concept of Indo-Pacific has been repeatedly mentioned in various strategic documents issued by the United States, or in speeches made by Trump and his team.

Japan, India, and Australia are the most important strategic fulcrum countries in the Trump administration's Indo-Pacific strategy. In fact, the Indo-Pacific strategy has also received positive responses from the three countries to varying degrees. On November 12, 2017, the United States, Japan, India, and Australia held a quadrilateral meeting at the ministerial or leaders level, on the sidelines of the Association of Southeast Asian Nations (ASEAN) and East Asia Summits, to discuss common interests in Indo-Pacific region.[66] On January 18, 2018, at the third Raisina Dialogue held in New Delhi, India, senior naval officials of the United States, Japan, India, and Australia discussed issues of maritime safety and free navigation, which enabled the United States to continue placing incalculable pressure on China. The four countries have talked about establishing a joint regional infrastructure scheme as an alternative to China's multibillion-dollar Belt and Road Initiative.[67] To some extent, the Indo-Pacific strategy is an extension of the U.S. "pivot to the Asia Pacific." It is still aimed at restricting China, in this instance by hedging against China's BRI. From the perspective of geographical structure, the SCS is not only the pilot area of BRI, especially the 21st century Maritime Silk Road, but also the core area of the Indo-Pacific strategic arc. This "double-zone overlap" determines that the SCS will inevitably become the primary focus for the implementation of the Indo-Pacific strategy by the United States. Therefore, the Trump administration needed to demonstrate to the outside world the American determination and will to promote the Indo-Pacific strategy through its intervention in the SCS issues. In addition, it showed that Trump was "tough on China" in the domestic U.S. discourse.

It is worth mentioning that, on January 5, 2021, the Trump administration declassified in advance a *U.S. Strategic Framework for Indo-Pacific* (henceforth, the *Framework*) formulated by the National Security Council (NSC) in 2018, which aims to stipulate the strategic objectives and action guidelines of the United States in the Indo-Pacific region.[68] In order to deter China from using military force against the United States and U.S. allies and partners, and develop the capabilities and concepts to defeat Chinese actions across the spectrum of conflict, the *Framework* argues that the United States should do the following actions: enhance combat-credible U.S. military presence and posture in the Indo-Pacific region to uphold U.S. interests and security commitments; devise and implement a defense strategy capable of, but not limited to: (1) denying China sustained air and sea dominance inside the "first island chain" in a conflict; (2) defending the first-island-chain nations, including Taiwan; and (3) dominating all domains outside the first-island chain. Help our allies and partners improve their security posture, including military capabilities and interoperability, to ensure strategic independence and freedom from Chinese coercion. Expand partnerships and capabilities that limit China's ability to coerce allies and partners. Obviously, intervening in the SCS affairs is a necessary path for the United States to promote the above-mentioned India-Pacific strategic goals and actions.

Reassure Asia-Pacific Allies and Ensure the U.S. Strategic Credibility

The disputes over sovereignty in the SCS not only involve the Philippines, the United States' regional Allies and security partners, but also make Japan, India, Australia, and other countries outside the region pay close attention to the situation in the region. To some extent, the SCS issue is related to the credibility of the United States' Asia-Pacific treaty and alliance system, and it is also a litmus test for the effectiveness of the entire Asia-Pacific security strategy of the United States. Previously, Trump's non-establishment belief and "America First" strategy made the outside world once again believe that the United States would retreat in regional affairs and move towards neo-isolationism, as it did after World War One and the Vietnam War. Some analysts have pointed out that "America First" is essentially an isolationist foreign policy, arguing that the United States should not waste resources in participating in international affairs when it has so many domestic issues to contend with.[69] After taking office, the Trump administration pulled out of the TPP, the Paris Climate Agreement, UNESCO, the Iran Nuclear Agreement, and the United Nations Human Rights Council, which reinforced the above perception on a practical level.

Against this backdrop, the U.S. Asia-Pacific allies are generally skeptical and worried about whether the Trump administration could shoulder its constructed responsibility on the SCS issue. Take Australia as an example, in response to China's assertive actions in the SCS and the Trump administration's withdrawal from TPP, a report in the *New York Times* on December 4, 2017, raised doubts about whether Australia could continue to rely on the United States in the face of China's rise.[70] At about the same time, Hugh White, a prominent Australian scholar, wrote that the United States is fading, and China will soon be the dominant power in our region. White notes that Australia has got out of the habit of seeing the world through Washington's eyes.[71] In order to reassure the Asia-Pacific allies and partners, the Trump administration stepped up its patrols in the SCS, strengthened maritime security cooperation with Vietnam and other countries, and pushed forward the quadrilateral cooperation mechanism among the United States, Japan, India, and Australia. The United States aimed to demonstrate America's presence in the SCS, ease allied abandonment fears, and maintain its international credibility as a supplier of regional security. In other words, the U.S. activity in the SCS was designed to reassure allies and partners, make Trump look "tough on China," and keep elements within his own party happy.

Maintain American Maritime Hegemony and Contain China's Maritime Expansion

Maritime hegemony is an important cornerstone underpinning American global hegemony. Maintaining a strong Navy, establishing bases worldwide, controlling vital sea routes and strategic chokepoints, and dominating global ocean discourse and rules constitute the pillars of U.S. maritime hegemony. In January 2017, the report "Surface Force Strategy: Return to Sea Control" issued by the U.S. Navy reiterated that, as a maritime nation, the prosperity of the United States is inseparable from the freedom of the sea maintained by its Navy, and the United States cannot afford to lose its maritime superiority as a naval power.[72]

The United States believes that China's ongoing construction on islands and reefs in the SCS has seriously disrupted the regional order in the SCS and directly challenged its control over the seas in the region. In testimony before the USCC, Mira Rapp-Hooper, a research fellow at the Center for New American Security Studies (CNAS), warned that "If the United States allows a leadership vacuum to emerge around this vital waterway, however, it will come with tangible and enduring costs. China's last few years of activity in the SCS should remind us that it is increasingly capable of advancing its strategic aims near its shores. If the United States fails to prioritize the SCS, it all but guarantees that Beijing will fill this space."[73] Patrick M. Cronin has pointed out that the rapid emergence of an increasingly global PLAN suggests that American maritime superiority era will soon come to a close. "The PLAN is looking beyond the *San hai*- the Yellow Sea, SCS, and East China Sea- and out toward the Pacific and Indian Oceans.

Competition potentially could spread from China's near seas into the Indian Ocean."[74] Therefore, in order to defend the maritime hegemony of the United States, the Trump administration was bound to take various measures to encircle China in the SCS and deter China's maritime expansion, thereby reacting to domestic pressures.

The Orientation of U.S. SCS Policy

Since reform and opening-up, China has achieved leapfrog development across all facets of society, and seen a continued rise of its comprehensive national strength. With the rapid rise of China, the military superiority and deterrence of the United States, the overall advantage of economic development, and the leading ability of regional and international economic order, the diplomatic alliance system and the ability to set international discourse and issues that the United States has long enjoyed have all been greatly diminished.[75] Although it will still take a long time for China to surpass the United States, the rapid merging of the strength of the two countries has led to a sharp decline in the strategic confidence of the United States, and it is urgently attempting to find means that allow it to contain the continuous rise of China. As a result, the political circle in Washington is filled with an atmosphere that has created an opinion hostile to and hatred of China. The United States keeps hyping up the threat from China in various fields, and the momentum of preventing and even confronting China has been significantly increased. As a result, strategic competition between China and the United States in various fields has intensified significantly. For future administrations, this foundation of opposition to China will be tough to overcome, or even to reach a broad consensus on.

In the era of strategic competition between China and the United States, the SCS issue has become a new hot spot in the game between China and the United States after the Taiwan issue, human rights, and economic and trade issues. It has become a new area for the United States to restrict the rise of China. In this regard, some scholars believe that the SCS issue has gone far beyond the dispute of territorial sovereignty and maritime rights and interests, and evolved into the collision of two powers, that is, "the unparalleled maritime and aerial superiority enjoyed by the United States for a long time after WWII in the Western Pacific" and "China's strategic process of becoming a maritime power."[76] In the future, with the sharp strategic competition between China and the United States, the

U.S. policy stance in the SCS may become more assertive and it may take some new and even radical measures to counter China.

First, the United States will not soften its stance on the SCS policy, and its "taking sides" strategy will be further highlighted. Although the United States does not want any country to control the SCS alone, and supposedly remains a neutral position in the SCS sovereignty, the United States shows a biased and partial attitude for the need to deter China's rise. In order to contain China in the SCS, the United States will take a tough stance and targeted aim to China in the SCS. Ultimately, China-U.S. contradictions on the SCS issue will be even more intense in the future.

Second, the U.S will issue new SCS strategic documents to draw red lines for China to observe. To ensure the effectiveness of the U.S. SCS policy, it is not ruled out that the United States will issue relevant SCS strategic documents to "draw a red line" for China's behavior in the SCS. If China violates them, the United States may take radical measures to punish. It may change the policy of not holding a position on the sovereignty of the SCS, or openly deny China's sovereignty over the SCS, or even adopt the same measures as it takes in handling the Diaoyu/Senkaku Island issue by recognizing the administrative power of Vietnam and the Philippines over the occupied islands and reefs, and deny China's sovereignty. Furthermore, while denying China's sovereignty over the SCS, the United States may support the military construction of islands and reefs of other claiming countries through arms sales, island seizing drills, and equipment assistance, so as to enhance their ability to confront China.

Third, the United States will further strengthen the military presence in the SCS and promote the militarization of disputes in the SCS so as to maintain an effective deterrent to China. In response to China's military buildup in the SCS, the United States may adopt a "two-pronged approach." On the one hand, it will avoid direct armed conflict with China, but on the other hand, it will opt to military actions to force China not to make rash moves in the SCS issue. In the future, the United States will not rule out the possibility of acquiring new permanent military bases in countries around the SCS, such as Vietnam, to increase support for its Asia-Pacific allies and partners in maritime security. In addition, the United States is likely to be more flexible in dealing with "gray area" security issues such as China's increasingly powerful Coast Guard and maritime surveillance. For example, to counter China's maritime surveillance force, the United States Coast Guard is sent to the countries surrounding the SCS or are jointly engaged in law enforcement with the Coast Guard of China's neighboring countries.

Fourth, the United States will encourage and unite with countries outside the region to patrol in the SCS and embark on a mode of collective operations for FON. At present, the most important way for the United States to intervene in the SCS is to implement the FON. In fact, in the National Defense Authorization Act for Fiscal Year 2019, the U.S. Congress required the administration to execute the FON and overflight to the maximum extent practicable with regional partner countries and allies of the United States.[77] Under the instigation and solicitation of the United States, Japan, India, Australia, and even Britain and France in recent years have also taken an aggressive attitude on the issue and made provocations in the SCS by sending warships to transit the SCS. In the future, it is not ruled out that the abovementioned countries will routinely join the U.S. maritime patrol in the SCS for personal gain. With the joint pressure on China, the United States can achieve the goal of compromising China's interests in the SCS and even in other fields.

Fifth, the United States will supervise the implementation of the COC in the SCS or formulate the America-version COC. At present, China and ASEAN countries are conducting intensive consultations on the text of the COC in the SCS. Despite the emergence of many complex and sensitive issues, the final text of the COC is still full of optimism and expectations.[78] It is foreseeable that once the parties reach an agreement on the final text of the COC, the security cooperation mechanism, crisis management mechanism, and rules of conduct system in the SCS will be established, which means that the space for countries outside the region to intervene in the SCS issue will be further squeezed. For this reason, the United States will turn to interfering in the implementation of the relevant provisions of the post-COC era, whether the resulting COC is a political document or a legally binding document. By acting as an uninvited "watchdog," the United States will use the COC as a framework to restrain China, and even apply soft checks on China by applying double standards in the name of upholding the COC while in practice discriminating between China's behavior and that of other disputed countries in the SCS. More importantly, even if the China-ASEAN COC is issued, the United States can bypass it in the future and formulate its version of the COC to set rules and draw red lines for neighboring countries in the SCS in a hegemonic posture.

Sixth, the United States will cultivate new agents to continue to stir up the SCS issues. One of the important reasons why the SCS issue has been intensified repeatedly during the Obama administration is that the countries surrounding the SCS, such as the Philippines and Vietnam, rely heavily on the support of the United States to compete with China on the SCS issue. In particular, the

Philippine government under the leadership of Aquino III was willing to act as the agent of the United States in the SCS and unilaterally launched the SCS arbitration case against China, bringing a negative influence and setting bad precedent. After taking office, the new government of Duterte in the Philippines adjusted its China policy based on pragmatic considerations and sought to shelve the dispute over the SCS. Under the circumstances that the new Philippine government no longer acts as the "pawn" of the United States to check and balance China, the United States is bound to find and cultivate new agents for a new round of SCS strategic acts. In recent years, the United States attaches great importance to Vietnam and undertakes frequent security interactions. From this aspect, Vietnam may become the new agent of the United States.

Seventh, the United States will build the Indo-Pacific alliance system to unite against China. In its National Security Strategy Report, the Trump administration has devoted a section under the Regional Strategy to discuss the Indo-Pacific strategy, emphasizing the maritime freedom of the region and the importance of peaceful settlement of territorial and maritime disputes in accordance with international law, which shows the importance it attaches to the region. The Indo-Pacific concept itself has the intention of restricting China, aiming to network the vast forces in the Indian Pacific region to jointly respond to China's rise and maintain the regional power balance under the leadership of the United States. Although the four countries are still in the stage of establishing dialogue mechanism and building momentum, the Trump administration actively promoted the construction of "a free and open Indo-Pacific."[79] The institutionalization and operationalization of the Indo-Pacific strategy mean that it is possible to form an Indo-Pacific alliance system around the SCS in the future to counter China, which will have a hedging effect on China's BRI. In the future, there will be more intense competition among all disputing parties regarding the militarization and demilitarization of the SCS, the control and counter-control of the sea area, and the formulation and competition of rules. In this regard, China needs to pay close attention and coordinate its response correspondingly.

Eighth, the U.S. Congress will play a more active role in the SCS issue. As stated above, the U.S. administration, military, and other departments are the main institutions involved in the SCS issue; however, the U.S. Congress is the driving force behind the scene. Moreover, the attitude of members of Congress on the SCS issue is also a barometer influencing the position of U.S. politicians. The way the U.S. Congress gets involved in the SCS issue includes proposing bills, holding hearings, issuing statements, sending letters to relevant government departments and officials, making public speeches, and suggesting military vessels or aircraft to inspect the waters and airspace of the SCS. At present, the U.S. Congress is deeply involved in the SCS issue, from the previous discussion on FON involving American interests, calling for peaceful settlement of disputes, and opposing the use of force to challenging China on substantive issues such as the ADIZ and China's claim of nine-dashed line in the SCS.[80] In the foreseeable future, the U.S. Congress will continue to actively intervene in the SCS issues in such ways.

Ninth, the United States will adopt the "Navy + Coast Guard" mode in the SCS. In recent years, the United States has increasingly emphasized the role of its Coast Guard in the SCS, and has sent Coast Guard vessels to accompany naval vessels into the SCS. Such action shows that the United States has begun to attach importance to the Coast Guard forces in maritime issues in the Western Pacific, and the paramilitary vessels (rather than warships) in pursuing maritime competition is steadily expanding. It indicates that the United States may adopt a new mode of "Navy + Coast Guard" joint intervention in SCS issues in the future. In this mode, the Coast Guard forms a supplementary cooperation with the Navy to make up for the lack of naval power, and reduces the militarism specter of its naval operations, highlights the legal significance of operations, and thus reduces the risk of unnecessary military conflicts. This new mode of intervention by the United States is bound to aggravate the disputes over sovereignty in the SCS, add new confrontational factors to China-U.S. relations, and further complicate the fishery disputes between China and neighboring countries in the SCS. Therefore, China should take precautions to accelerate the reform pace of China's Coast Guard (CCG), and enhance its combat capability. Plus, China should formulate and implement the China Coast Guard Law as soon as possible, and bring the coast guard forces of China and the United States into the existing maritime security mechanisms and conclude the Code of Conduct for the Safety of Maritime Encounters between China and the United States Coast Guard at an early date. It is a must to strengthen the cooperation between CCG and maritime militia forces, and promote China-U.S. cooperation in coast guard affairs.

Tenth, the United States will double efforts to suppress China economically. It is believed that the SCS has rich oil and gas reserves and is also an important trade route. Therefore, the United States believes that the SCS dispute has bearing on its major economic interests. If the shipping routes in the SCS are destroyed or blocked, it is bound to have a major impact on the international energy and economic and trade relations, and even endanger the economic lifeline of some countries. In addition, China has used its growing economic power to launch a "charm offensive" in Southeast Asia in order to advance its objectives in the

SCS.[81] Especially since China put forward the 21st-Century Maritime Silk Road Initiative, some American scholars believe that the most important consideration of the initiative is to appease neighboring countries and eliminate their concern of China's threat as its aggressive territorial claims in the SCS.[82] Other U.S. analysts have called for a multi-pronged economic investment as well, given that China is using economic leverage such as the New Silk Road Fund and the Asian Infrastructure Investment Bank to woo Southeast Asian countries politically.[83] Considering the full-blown "trade war" with China since 2018, the United States will suppress China in economy, science, and technology, and is likely to take a series of new steps to compete with China in trade, investment, and development assistance. Consequently, the United States will achieve its intention to reverse the situation where Southeast Asian countries rely on the United States for security but China for economic growth.

Notes

1 J. Berkshire Miller, "Trump's SCS Policy Leaves U.S. Allies Perplexed and Anxious," *World Politics Review*, June 26, 2017, https://www.worldpoliticsreview.com/articles/22547/trump-s-south-china-sea-policy-leaves-u-s-allies-perplexed-and-anxious
2 Les Neuhaus, "Focusing on North Korea, Trump Neglects Strategic SCS," *Observer*, November 10, 2017, http://observer.com/2017/11/trump-neglects-strategic-south-china-sea-focuses-on-north-korea/
3 Dan De Luce, "With Trump Focused on North Korea, Beijing Sails Ahead in SCS," *Foreign Policy*, November 16, 2017, http://foreignpolicy.com/2017/11/16/with-trump-focused-on-north-korea-beijing-sails-ahead-in-south-china-sea/
4 Emily Rauhala, "The SCS fell off Trump's radar last year. He may have to pay attention in 2018," *The Washington Post*, January 1, 2018, https://www.washingtonpost.com/world/asia_pacific/the-south-china-sea-fell-off-trumps-radar-this-year-he-may-have-to-pay-attention-in-2018/2018/01/01/b7c9a27a-eb1e-11e7-956e-baea358f9725_story.html?utm_term=.62635977d5de
5 Bonnie S. Glaser and Gregory Poling, "Vanishing Borders in the SCS," *Foreign Affairs*, June 5, 2018, https://www.foreignaffairs.com/articles/china/2018-06-05/vanishing-borders-south-china-sea
6 Amy Searight Geoffrey Hartman, "Donald Trump's Huge SCS Problem (And What To Do About It)," *The National Interest*, February 8, 2017, https://nationalinterest.org/blog/the-buzz/donald-trumps-huge-south-china-sea-problem-what-do-about-it-19361
7 "US Policy of 'Strategic Patience' with North Korea over: Tillerson," http://www.cnbc.com/2017/03/17/uspolicyofstrategicpatiencewithnorthkoreaovertillerson.html;

Ken Thomas, "Pence Warns N Korea 'Era of Strategic Patience Is over'," *The Washington Times,* http://www.washingtontimes.com/news/2017/apr/16/pence-lands-in-south-korea-after-norths-failed-lau/; Krishnadev Calamur, "Tillerson Backs Policy of 'Peaceful Pressure' on North Korea," *The Atlantic*, https://www.the-atlantic.com/news/archive/2017/07/north-korea-tillerson/532989/

8 Weston S. Konishi, "China's Maritime Challenge in the SCS: Options for US Responses," Report of the Chicago Council on Global Affairs, January 2018, p.2.

9 Colin Willet, "U.S. Perspective on the SCS Order: Strategy Under the Trump Administration," *The Maritime Issues*, March 22, 2018, p.4–5.

10 Wei Zongyou, "A Preliminary Study of Trump's Government SCS Policy," *Southeast Asian Studies*, No.2, 2018, pp.125–130.

11 Su Xiaohui, "Study on Developments of the SCS Policies under the New U.S. Administration," *Pacific Journal*, No.7, 2017, pp.36–43.

12 Bonnie S. Glaser, *Armed Clash in the SCS*, New York: Council on Foreign Relations, 2012, p.4.

13 M.Taylor Fravel, "American Policy Towards the Disputes in the SCS: 1995–2017," translated by Qi Hao, *Contemporary American Review*, No.1, 2017, pp.43–45.

14 Donald J. Trump Facebook; December 5, 2016, https://www.facebook.com/DonaldTrump/posts/1015822964270572

15 "Secretary of State Designate Rex Tillerson Senate Confirmation Hearing Opening Statement," January 11, 2017, https://www.foreign.senate.gov/imo/media/doc/011117_Tillerson_Opening_Statement.pdf

16 "Rex Tillerson's written responses to questions from 'Senator Ben Cardin, Ranking Member'," undated, https://www.desmogblog.com/sites/beta.desmogblog.com/files/Ben%20Cardin%20Questions%20Tillerson.pdf

17 Demetri Sevastopulo, "US pledges to protect its interests in SCS," Financial Times, January 24, 2017, https://www.ft.com/content/161d4040-e1c8-11e6-8405-9e5580d6e5fb

18 Susan A. Thornton, "Briefing on Secretary Tillerson's Travel to the Philippines, Thailand, and Malaysia," August 2, 2017, https://www.state.gov/r/pa/prs/ps/2017/08/272998.htm

19 "H.R.5515-John S. McCain National Defense Authorization Act for Fiscal Year 2019," June 19, 2018, https://www.congress.gov/115/bills/hr5515/BILLS-115hr5515pap.pdf, pp.614–629.

20 "Remarks by Vice President Pence on the Administration's Policy Toward China," the White House, 4 October 2018, https://www.whitehouse.gov/briefings-statements/remarks-vice-president-pence-administrations-policy-toward-china/.

21 The U.S. Department of Defense, *Indo-Pacific Strategy Report: Preparedness, Partnerships, and Promoting a Networked Region*, June 1, 2019.

22 "U.S. Position on Maritime Claims in the South China Sea," 13 July, 2020, https://china.usembassy-china.org.cn/u-s-position-on-maritime-claims-in-the-south-china-sea/

23 The White House, "Remarks by the Vice President and Australian Prime Minister Turnbull at a Press Conference," April 22, 2017, https://www.whitehouse.gov/briefings-statements/remarks-vice-president-australian-prime-minister-turnbull-press-conference/

24 The White House, "Joint Statement for Enhancing the Comprehensive Partnership between the United States of America and the Socialist Republic of Vietnam," May 31, 2017, https://www.whitehouse.gov/briefings-statements/joint-statement-enhancing-comprehensive-partnership-united-states-america-socialist-republic-viet-nam/

25 The U.S. Department of State, "Remarks With Secretary of Defense James Mattis, Japanese Foreign Minister Taro Kono, and Japanese Defense Minister Itsunori Onodera at a Press Availability," August 17, 2017, https://www.state.gov/secretary/20172018tillerson/remarks/2017/08/273513.htm

26 The U.S. Department of State, "Press Availability With Secretary of Defense James Mattis, Australian Foreign Minister Julie Bishop, and Australian Defense Minister Marise Payne," July 24, 2018, https://www.state.gov/secretary/remarks/2018/07/284471.htm

27 Regine Cabato and Shibani MahtaniBio, "Pompeo promises intervention if Philippines is attacked in South China Sea amid rising Chinese militarization," *The Washington Post*, March 1, 2019, https://www.washingtonpost.com/world/pompeo-promises-intervention-if-philippines-is-attacked-in-south-china-sea-amid-rising-chinese-militarization/2019/02/28/5288768a-3b53-11e9-b10b-f05a22e75865_story.html

28 "U.S. Secretary of State Mike Pompeo visits Vietnam," https://vietnamnet.vn/en/politics/u-s-secretary-of-state-mike-pompeo-visits-vietnam-685002.html?vnn_source=trangchu&vnn_medium=box-english4

29 The U.S. Department of State, "Secretary of State Rex Tillerson and Secretary of Defense Jim Mattis at a Joint Press Availability," June 21, 2017, https://www.state.gov/secretary/20172018tillerson/remarks/2017/06/272103.htm

30 The White House, "President Donald J. Trump's State Visit to China," November 10, 2017, https://www.whitehouse.gov/briefings-statements/president-donald-j-trumps-state-visit-china/

31 The White House, "Press Briefing by Secretary of State Rex Tillerson, Beijing, China," November 9, 2017, https://www.whitehouse.gov/briefings-statements/press-briefing-secretary-state-rex-tillerson-110917/

32 The U.S. Department of State, "Remarks With Chinese Foreign Minister and State Councilor Wang Yi at a Press Availability," Washington, DC, May 23, 2018, https://www.state.gov/secretary/remarks/2018/05/282469.htm

33 Mike Pompeo, "Press Availability With Chinese State Councilor and Foreign Minister Wang Yi," Beijing, China, June 14, 2018, https://www.state.gov/secretary/remarks/2018/06/283225.htm

34 The U.S. Department of State, "Secretary Tillerson Meets With the Foreign Ministers of the Association of Southeast Asian Nations," May 4, 2017, https://www.state.gov/r/pa/prs/ps/2017/05/270657.htm
35 The U.S. Department of Defense, "Remarks by Secretary Mattis at Shangri-La Dialogue," June 3, 2017, https://www.defense.gov/News/Transcripts/Transcript-View/Article/1201780/remarks-by-secretary-mattis-at-shangri-la-dialogue/.
36 The U.S. Department of State, "Australia-Japan-United States Trilateral Strategic Dialogue Ministerial Joint Statement," August 6, 2017, https://www.state.gov/r/pa/prs/ps/2017/08/273216.htm
37 The U.S. Department of State, "Secretary of State Tillerson's Participation in the Second U.S.-India-Japan Ministerial-level Trilateral Dialogue," September 18, 2017, https://www.state.gov/r/pa/prs/ps/2017/09/274224.htm
38 The U.S. Department of Defense, "Alliances, Partnerships Critical to U.S. Indo-Pacific Strategy, Mattis Says," June 2, 2018, https://www.defense.gov/News/Article/Article/1538620/alliances-partnerships-critical-to-us-indo-pacific-strategy-mattis-says/
39 The U.S. Department of Defense, "Mattis, Indo-Pacific Partners Discuss Security Issues at Singapore Summit," June 3, 2018, https://www.defense.gov/News/Article/Article/1538895/mattis-indo-pacific-partners-discuss-security-issues-at-singapore-summit/
40 The U.S. Department of State, "Secretary Pompeo's Travel to Kuala Lumpur, Singapore, and Jakarta," July 30, 2018, https://www.state.gov/r/pa/prs/ps/2018/07/284694.htm
41 "Remarks by Vice President Pence at the 6th U.S.-ASEAN Summit," Singapore, 16 November, 2018, https://asean.usmission.gov/remarks-by-vice-president-pence-at-the-6th-u-s-asean-summit/
42 "Secretary Pompeo and Secretary Esper Speak at Munich Security Conference 2020," https://lu.usembassy.gov/secre-tary-pompeo-and-secretary-esper-speak-at-munich-security-conference-2020/
43 Dennis Mandsager, "The U.S. Freedom of Navigation Program: Policy, Procedure, and Future," *International Law Studies*, Volume 72, 1998, pp.113–127.
44 Kristina Wong, "Exclusive: Trump's Pentagon Plans to Challenge Chinese Claims in SCS," *The breitbart*, July 20, 2017, http://www.breitbart.com/national-security/2017/07/20/trump-pentagon-south-china-sea-plan/
45 The ICAS Team, "Trump Administration's SCS Policy," Institute for China-America Studies, the US, June 30, 2017, http://chinaus-icas.org/wp-content/uploads/2017/06/ABSOLUTE-FINAL-SCS-Trump-Primer.pdf
46 Wang Hao, "The Trump Administration's Policy of Linkage towards China: An Analysis," *Contemporary Asia-Pacific Studies*, No.4, 2017, p.65.
47 The U.S. Department of Defense, "Remarks by Secretary Mattis at Shangri-La Dialogue," June 3, 2017, https://www.defense.gov/News/Transcripts/Transcript-View/Article/1201780/remarks-by-secretary-mattis-at-shangri-la-dialogue/.
48 "Continuous Bomber Presence Mission," https://www.andersen.af.mil/CBP/.

49 The US Department of Defense, "Readout of Secretary Mattis' Meeting With Vietnam Minister of National Defense," Jan. 25, 2018, https://www.defense.gov/News/News-Releases/News-Release-View/Article/1423285/readout-of-secretary-mattis-meeting-with-vietnam-minister-of-national-defense/

50 Cecilia Yap, "U.S., Philippines Boost Military Pact With More Drills Planned," Bloomberg, Sept 13, 2019, https://www.bloomberg.com/news/articles/2019-09-13/u-s-philippines-boosts-military-pact-with-more-drills-planned.

51 John McCain, "Restoring American Power: Recommendations for the FY 2018-FY2022 Defense Budget," Senate Armed Services Committee, January 16, 2017, https://www.mccain.senate.gov/public/_cache/files/25bff0ec-481e-466a-843f-68ba5619e6d8/restoring-american-power-7.pdf

52 "H.R.2176-To authorize the establishment of an Asia-Pacific Defense Commission to enhance defense cooperation between the United States and allies in the Asia-Pacific region, and for other purposes," April 26, 2017, https://www.congress.gov/115/bills/hr2176/BILLS-115hr2176ih.pdf

53 "Joint Statement on Australia -U. S. Ministerial Consultations (AUSMIN) 2020," https://www.defense.gov/Newsroom/Releases/Release/Article/2290911/joint-statement-on-australia-us-ministerial-consultations-ausmin-2020/

54 The U.S. Department of Defense, "Remarks by Secretary Mattis at Shangri-La Dialogue," June 3, 2017, https://www.defense.gov/News/Transcripts/Transcript-View/Article/1201780/remarks-by-secretary-mattis-at-shangri-la-dialogue/.

55 The U.S. Department of State, "U.S.-Australia-India-Japan Consultations," June 7, 2018, https://www.state.gov/r/pa/prs/ps/2018/06/283013.htm

56 "The South China Sea, Southeast Asia's Patrimony, and Everybody's Own Backyard," https://www.state.gov/the-south-china-sea-southeast-asias-patrimony-and-everybodys-own-backyard/

57 "Commerce Department Adds 24 Chinese Companies to the EntityList for Helping Build Military Islands in the South China Sea", https://www.commerce.gov/news/press-releases/2020/08/commerce-department-adds-24-chinese-companies-entity-list-helping-build

58 "US Imposes Restrictions on Certain PRC State-Owned Enterprises and Executives for Malign Activities in the South China Sea," https://www.state.gov/u-s-imposes-restrictions-on-certain-prc-state-owned-enterprises-and-executives-for-malign-activities-in-the-south-china-sea/

59 Robert D. Atkinson, "Who Lost China?", *National Review*, July 26, 2018, https://www.nationalreview.com/magazine/2018/08/13/us-china-relations-who-lost-them/

60 "Hearing: The Military Posture and Security Challenges in the Indo-Asia-Pacific Region," Admiral Harry Harris Jr. Commander, U.S. Pacific Command Witness Statement, February 14, 2018, http://docs.house.gov/meetings/AS/AS00/20180214/106847/HHRG-115-AS00-Wstate-HarrisJrH-20180214.pdf

61 Kurt M. Campbell, Ely Ratner, "The China Reckoning: How Beijing Defied American Expectations," *Foreign Affairs*, Vol.97, No.2, March/April 2018, pp.60–70.

62 The White House, "National Security Strategy of the United States of America," December 2017, https://www.whitehouse.gov/wp-content/uploads/2017/12/NSS-Final-12-18-2017-0905-2.pdf

63 The Pentagon, "Summary of the 2018 National Defense Strategy of the United States of America," https://www.defense.gov/Portals/1/Documents/pubs/2018-National-Defense-Strategy-Summary.pdf

64 Hillary Clinton, "American's Pacific Century," *Foreign Policy*, November 2011.

65 The White House, "Statement from the Press Secretary on President Donald J. Trump's Upcoming Travel to Asia," October 16, 2017, https://www.whitehouse.gov/briefings-statements/statement-press-secretary-president-donald-j-trumps-upcoming-travel-asia/

66 Ankit Panda, "US, Japan, India, and Australia Hold Working-Level Quadrilateral Meeting on Regional Cooperation," The Diplomat, November 13, 2017, https://thediplomat.com/2017/11/us-japan-india-and-australia-hold-working-level-quadrilateral-meeting-on-regional-cooperation/

67 "Australia, U.S., India and Japan in talks to establish Belt and Road alternative: report," *The Reuters*, Feb. 19, 2018, https://www.reuters.com/article/us-china-beltandroad-quad/australia-u-s-india-and-japan-in-talks-to-establish-belt-and-road-alternative-report-idUSKCN1G20WG

68 See the PDF link, https://trumpwhitehouse.archives.gov/wp-content/uploads/2021/01/IPS-Final-Declass.pdf

69 Charles Krauthammer, "Trump's Foreign Policy Revolution," *The Washington Post*, Jan. 26, 2017, https://www.washingtonpost.com/opinions/global-opinions/trumps-foreign-policy-revolution/2017/01/26/c69268a6-e402-11e6-ba11-63c4b4fb5a63_story.html?utm_term=.8af89c419bae

70 Jane Perlez and Damien Cave, "As China Rises, Australia Asks Itself: Can It Rely on America?", *The New York Times*, Dec. 3, 2017, https://www.nytimes.com/2017/12/03/world/australia/australia-us-china-alliances.html

71 Hugh White, "Without America, Australia in the New Asia," *Quarterly Essay*, 2017, https://www.quarterlyessay.com.au/essay/2017/11/without-america

72 The U.S. Department of Defense, "Surface Force Strategy: Return to Sea Control," Jan. 9, 2017, http://www.navy.mil/strategic/SurfaceForceStrategy-ReturntoSeaControl.pdf

73 Mira Rapp-Hooper, "Hotspots along China's Maritime Periphery," Testimony before the U.S.-China Economic and Security Review Commission, April 13, 2017, https://www.uscc.gov/sites/default/files/transcripts/April%20Hearing%20Transcript.pdf

74 Dr. Patrick M. Cronin, Dr. Mira Rapp-Hooper, Harry Krejsa, Alex Sullivan, and Rush Doshi, "Beyond the San Hai: The Challenge of China's Blue-Water Navy,"

Report of CNAS, May 15, 2017, https://www.cnas.org/publications/reports/beyond-the-san-hai

75 Max Fisher, Audrey Carlsen, "How China Is Challenging American Dominance in Asia," *The New York Times*, March 9, 2018, https://www.nytimes.com/interactive/2018/03/09/world/asia/china-us-asia-rivalry.html

76 Wang Lin, "An exclusive interview with Zhu Feng: what is the nature of the SCS issue?", *Yi Cai,* May 23, 2016, http://www.yicai.com/news/5017457.html

77 "H.R.5515-John S. McCain National Defense Authorization Act for Fiscal Year 2019," June 19, 2018, https://www.congress.gov/115/bills/hr5515/BILLS-115hr5515pap.pdf, p.513.

78 Foreign Ministry of People's Republic of China: Foreign Ministry spokesman Geng Shuang presided over a regular press conference, February 5, 2018, http://www.fmprc.gov.cn/web/wjdt_674879/fyrbt_674889/t1531947.shtml

79 The White House, "President Donald J. Trump's Administration is Advancing a Free and Open Indo-Pacific," July 30, 2018, https://www.whitehouse.gov/briefings-statements/president-donald-j-trumps-administration-advancing-free-open-indo-pacific/

80 Zhao Yang and Gong Honglie, "The Reaction of the U.S. Congress to China's Land Reclamation in the Nansha Islands," *Pacific Journal*, Vol.24, No.5, 2016, pp.41–51.

81 Gregory Poling, "China's Charm Offensive Isn't Defusing Tensions in the SCS," *The World Politics Review*, December 14, 2015.

82 William Yale, "China's Maritime Silk Road Gamble," *The Diplomat*, April 22, 2015; Ma Jianying, "The U.S. Perception of and Response to China's "the Belt and Road" Initiative," *World Economics and Politics*, Vol.10, 2015, pp.104–132.

83 Patrick M. Cronin and Alexander Sullivan, *Preserving the Rules: Countering Coercion in Maritime Asia*, Center for New American Security, March 2015, p.17.

Conclusion

China's historic presence and development activities in the SCS well prove that it has indisputable sovereignty over the SCS. China is the first country to discover, name, and manage the islands and reefs of SCS and their affiliated waters. Plus, China has an irrefutable legal support to justify its sovereignty in the SCS based on the principles of international law, the international conventions, and treaties.

Shortly after the end of WWII, the then government of the Republic of China completed the task of taking over the sovereignty and jurisdiction of the SCS, and the SCS returned to the embrace of China. However, with the changing international situation during the Cold War, coupled with the domestic political instability and the weak national strength of the People's Republic of China, the situation in the SCS has changed in a way that is unfavorable to China. During this period, countries around the SCS have won national independence, rich oil and gas resources in the SCS have been discovered, and new progress has been made in the international law of the sea. To this end, countries around the SCS have put forward their claims of sovereignty and maritime rights in the SCS in accordance with the new provisions of international law of the sea, regardless of the fact that the sovereignty of the SCS is China's. This has led to the territorial disputes over the SCS.

In the process of the emergence and evolution of the SCS dispute, the United States, as an outsider and non-party, has become a key player in existing territorial disputes, which further complicates and internationalizes the SCS issue. The United States should be held accountable for destabilizing the SCS region and aggravating maritime disputes. Especially since the end of the Cold War, the United States has become a major driving force behind the SCS issue. Retrospectively, since the end of the 18th century, the United States has had different understandings of the SCS in different historical periods, and the value of the SCS to the United States has always changed with times. To sum up, there are three pairs of "positive correlation" between the United States and the SCS issue.

First, in light of historical development, U.S. policies on SCS are volatile and have gone through different stages over time. Suffice it to say that American understanding of the SCS has experienced substantial changes and has undergone a process of paying increasingly closer attention to the strategic value of the SCS. Moreover, American concern and involvement in the SCS issue are positively correlated with its overall strategic layout in the Asia-Pacific region.

In the early times, the SCS was only a sea lane for commerce and trade for the United States, and its strategic value was not considered to be outstanding. During WWII, Japan occupied some islands and reefs in the SCS and used them as war sites, which prompted the United States to reexamine the strategic value of the SCS. In the early stage of the Cold War, the United States took the SCS as a front line in its bid to contain China and the Soviet bloc. In the middle and late stages of the Cold War, the United States exercised great restraint in the SCS in order to unite with China and jointly resist the Soviet Union. After the end of the Cold War, America's conservative behavior in the SCS in the context of the strategic layout of the Asia-Pacific region has caused controversy. After the Mischief Reef Incident in 1995, the SCS was placed in the preeminent position in the U.S. Asia-Pacific strategy. With the rapid rise of China in the 21st century, the SCS has become the frontier for the United States to contain China, as well as a wrestling ground for China and the United States to play strategic games in the Asia-Pacific region.

Second, in terms of the specific policy stance of the United States on the SCS issue, the U.S. position is not invariable, but skillful, opportunistic, and targeted. In particular, when it comes to China's sovereignty and maritime rights in the SCS, the relevant policies of the United States show an obvious intention to suppress and exclude China, which is also positively related to its overall strategy towards China.

For instance, on the issue of sovereignty, the United States has breached its long-standing commitment of not taking sides, and has deliberately denied and suppressed China's sovereign rights and interests in the SCS. In particular, the U.S. position on the SCS issue since 2010 has shown a posture of targeting China and taking side with other claimants. On how to resolve the SCS dispute, in addition to advocating peaceful means, respecting the norms of international law, and opposing the use of force or coercion of force, the United States reiterates the importance of multilateral rather than bilateral negotiations, opposes unilateral changes to the status quo, denies the intermittent line in the SCS, and opposes claims of sovereignty in the SCS based on historical rights. American rivalrous intention and tit-for-tat strategies are obviously aimed at China. Furthermore, despite the fact that the international shipping routes in the SCS have never been interrupted, the United States has frequently sent warships and warplanes across the SCS and provocatively sailed within 12 nautical miles of China's islands and reefs in the SCS under the guise of safeguarding FON, which directly challenges China's so-called excessive maritime claims in the SCS. American adventuristic and assertive behaviors escalate the situation in the SCS. It not only undermines China-U.S. strategic and security relations, but also worsens the situation in the SCS and leads to further militarization of regional issues.

Third, in terms of China-U.S. rivalry in the SCS, it must be acknowledged that although there are rooms for the two sides to cooperate on maritime affairs, the China-U.S. sea power relationship is dominated by competition in strategy and security under the background of China's rapid rise. It can be said that China's rise is positively correlated with China-U.S. power competition in the SCS.

China and the United States are not doomed to war in the SCS, but can work together to cooperate in various fields such as maritime rescue, maritime environmental protection, maintenance of maritime routes, development of oil and gas resources, maritime smuggling, and crime control. Due to the U.S. maritime hegemonism in recent years, the dispute between China and the United States over maritime power in the Western Pacific has become even more prominent. In the SCS, American concern and anxiety grows along with China's rise. It gets anxious and perplexed when it comes to China-related issues and eventually steps up its involvement in the SCS dispute. In consequence, China-U.S. competition in the SCS becomes increasingly intense. In other words, American concerns about China are situated in a larger context: China has emerged as an influential player in Asia and on the global stage. American involvement in the SCS issue, to a certain extent, can reflect its anxieties over China's rapid growth and the intensity of the China-U.S. sea power competition. After Trump took office in 2017, the United States militarized disputed areas and frequently carried out FONOPs against China in the SCS, and the military competition and frictions are real and serious between China and the United States in the SCS.

Given the function of the SCS as international shipping sea lanes, it would be unrealistic to completely expel the United States from regional affairs in the SCS. The crux issue is how the United States properly takes part in the SCS issue according to regional rules and how the international community regulates the role of the United States in the SCS, especially how to restrain its illegal acts that infringe on the maritime sovereignty and rights of countries surrounding the SCS.

Bibliography

Books

Alfredo Robles Jr., *The South China Sea Arbitration: Understanding the Awards and Debating with China*, Brighton: Sussex Academic Press, 2019.

An Yingmin et al., *Security Strategy in the South China Sea and Marine Administration Strengthening*, Beijing: China Economic Press, 2011.

Anders Corr, *Great Powers, Grand Strategies: The New Game in the South China Sea*, Maryland: Naval Institute Press, 2018.

Ashley Roach J., and Robert W. Smith, *Excessive Maritime Claims*, Boston: Martinus Nijhoff Publishers, 2012.

Bob Catley and Makmur Keliat, *Spratlys: The Dispute in the South China Sea*, England: Ashgate Publishing Limited, 1997.

Cao Yunhua and Ju Hailong, ed., *South China Sea Situation Report (2011–2012)*, Beijing: Current Affairs Press, 2012.

Cao Yunhua and Ju Hailong, ed., *South China Sea Situation Report (2012–2013)*, Beijing: Current Affairs Press, 2013.

Chang Jiu and Shi Lujia, ed., *Two Hundred Years of Sino-US Relations*, Beijing: Xinhua Publishing House, 1984.

Chen Fengjun, ed., *An Analysis of Asia Pacific Security*, Beijing: China International Broadcasting Press, 2004.

Chen Hongyu, *The Territorial Sovereignty of Taiwan and its Neighboring Islands*, Taipei: Taiwan Student Book Publishing House, 2018.

Chen Tianxi, *Compilation of the Cases of Pratas Islands and Paracel Islands*, Beijing: Commercial Press, 1982.

Chia Lin Sien and Colin Mac Andrews, eds., *Southeast Asian Seas: Frontiers for Development*, New York: Mc Graw-Hill International Book Company, 1981.

Chi-Kin Lo, *China's Policy towards Territorial Disputes: The Case of the South China Sea Islands*, London and New York: Routledge, 1989.

China Frontier Literature Research Center of the National Library of China, ed., *Atlas and Records of the South China Sea Islands (Modern Volume)*, Beijing: National Library Press, 2016.

China Society of International Law, *China Annual Review of International Law: Special Issue on Jurisdiction in the South China Sea Arbitration*, Beijing: Law Press, 2016.

China Society of International Law, *Criticism of the Award of the South China Sea Arbitration*, Beijing: Foreign Languages Press, 2018.

Coral Bell, *Survey of International Affairs 1954*, translated by Yunting et al., Shanghai: Shanghai Translation Publishing House, 1984.Department of Boundary and Maritime Affairs of the Ministry of Foreign Affairs of the People's Republic of China, ed., *Compilation of Documents Responding to the South China Sea Arbitration Case*, Beijing: World Affairs Press, 2016.

Dwight D. Eisenhower, *The White House Years: Mandate for Change (1953–1956)*, New York: Doubleday & Company, Inc., 1963.

Enrico Fels, Truong-Minh Vu, *Power Politics in Asia's Contested Waters: Territorial Disputes in the South China Sea*, New York: Springer, 2016.

Eric S. Edelman, *Understanding America's Contested Primacy*, Washington, D.C.: Center for Strategic and Budgetary Assessments, 2010.

Evelyn Goh and Sheldon W. Simon, *China, the United States, and South-East Asia: Contending Perspectives on Politics, Security, and Economics,* New York: Routledge, 2008.

Fareed Zakaria, *The Post-American World: And the Rise of the Rest*, W.W. Norton & Company Incorporated, 2008.

Feng Aiqun, *Collection of the Islands of the South China Sea 10*, Taipei: Taiwan Student Book Publishing House, 1974.

Fifield R. H., *Southeast Asia in American Policy*, translated by Qun Li, Beijing: World Affairs Press, 1965.

Foreign Relations Documents of the People's Republic of China (Volume IV), Beijing: World Affairs, 1958.

Foreign Relations Documents of the People's Republic of China (Volume V), Beijing: World Affairs, 1959.

Gao Zhiguo, Jia Bingbing, *The Nine-Dash Line in the South China Sea: History, Status and Implications*, Beijing: China Ocean Press, 2014.

Graham Allison, *Destined for War: Can America and China Escape Thucydides's Trap?*, Houghton Mifflin Harcourt, 2017.

Guo Ming, ed., *The Evolution of Sino-Vietnam Relations in the Past 40 Years*, Nanning: Guangxi People's Publishing House, 1992.

Guo Yuan, *Geopolitical Study of the South China Sea*, Harbin: Heilongjiang University Press, 2007.

Guo Yuan, *Geopolitics and the South China Sea Dispute*, Beijing: China Social Sciences Press, 2011.
Halt D. G. E., *A History of Southeast Asia*, translated by Institute of Southeast Asian History of Sun Yat-Sen University, Beijing: Commercial Press, 1982.
Han Zhenhua, ed., *Compilation of Historical Materials of the South China Sea Islands*, Beijing: The Oriental Publishing House, 1988.
Hans Morgenthau, *Politics Among Nations: The Struggle for Power and Peace*, New York: Alfred A. Knopf, Inc., 1948.
Harry Harding, *A Fragile Relationship: The United States and China Since 1972*, Washington D.C.: The Brookings Institution, 1992.
Henry Alfred Kissinger, *Diplomacy*, New York: Simon & Schuster, 1994.
Huang Yao and Huang Jingwen, *The South China Sea Arbitration Case by the Philippines: Legal Analysis of the Core Issues*, Hong Kong: Joint Publishing (HK) Co. Ltd., 2019.
Hugh White, *The China Choice: Why America Should Share Power*, Collingwood, VIC: Black Inc, 2012.
Huiyun Feng, Kai He, *US-China Competition and the South China Sea Disputes*, Routledge, 2018.
International treaties (1950–1952), Beijing: World Affairs Press, 1959.
James C Hsiung, *The South China Sea Disputes and the US-China Contest: International Law and Geopolitics*, Singapore: World Scientific Publishing, 2018.
James Kraska and Raul Pedrozo, *The Free Sea: The American Fight for Freedom of Navigation*, Annapolis: Naval Institute Press, 2018.
James M. Fones, *China, United States and Its Allies: How the United States and Its Allies are Losing the South China Sea*, CreateSpace Independent Publishing Platform, 2016.
James M. Lindsay, *Congress and the Politics of U.S. Foreign Policy*, Baltimore, MD: The Johns Hopkins University Press, 1994.
Jawaharlal Nehru, *Discovery of India*, Beijing: World Affairs Press, 1958.
Jayakumar S., Tommy Koh, Robert Beckman, Tara Davenport, and Hao Duy Phan, *The South China Sea Arbitration: The Legal Dimension*, Cheltenham: Edward Elgar Pub, 2018.
John J. Mearsheimer, *The Tragedy of Great Power Politics*, New York: W. W. Norton, 2001.
Joseph S. Nye Jr., *The Future of Power*, New York: Perseus, 2011, chap. 6.
Ju Hailong, ed., *South China Sea Situation Report (2013–2014)*, Beijing: Current Affairs Press, 2015.
Ju Hailong, *China's Maritime Power and Strategy*, Beijing: Current Affairs Press, 2009.
Jurgen Schwarz, Wilfried A. Herrmann, and Hanns-Frank Seller, ed., *Maritime Strategies in Asia*, translated by Ju Hailong and Wu Yan, Beijing: People's Publishing House, 2014.
Kent G. and Valencia M. J., *Marine Policy in Southeast Asia*, University of California Press, May, 1985.
Kimie Hara, *Cold War Frontiers in the Asia-Pacific: Divided Territories in the San Francisco System*, London and New York: Routledge, 2007.
Laurence H. Shoup and William Minter, *Imperial Brain Trust: The Council Foreign Relations and United States Foreign Policy*, translated by Yi Li, Wei Liang et al., Shanghai: Shanghai Translation Publishing House, 1981.
Li Caixia, *The Historical Events Chronicle of the South China Sea Islands*, Beijing: Social Sciences Academic Press, 2017.

Li Dingyi, *Early Sino-American Diplomatic History*, Beijing: Peking University Press, 1997.

Li Guoqiang, *Studies on South China Sea: History and Current Situation*, Harbin: Heilongjiang Education Press, 2003.

Li Jinming, *South China Sea Waves: Southeast Asian Countries and the South China Sea Issue*, Nanchang: Jiangxi Universities and Colleges Press, 2005.

Li Jinming, *Research on the South China Sea Territory*, Harbin: Heilongjiang Education Press, 2014.Li Woteng, *From Map Drawing to Artificial Islands Building: Centennial History of Disputes in the South China Sea*, Taipei: Wu-Nan Culture Enterprise, 2017.

Liu Feng, *South China Sea Development and National Security*, Beijing: Xue Xi Publishing House, Hainan Publishing House, 2013.

Liu Huaqing, *Memoirs of Liu Huaqing*, Beijing: Chinese People's Liberation Army Publishing House, 2004.

Liu Liandi and Wang Dawei, *The Track of Sino-US Relations: An Overview of Major Events Since the Establishment of Diplomatic Relations*, Beijing: Current Affairs Press, 1995.

Liu Yongtao, *U.S. Congressional-Presidential Relationship*, Shanghai: Shanghai People's Publishing House, 2010.

Liu Zhongmin, *World Maritime Politics and Ocean Development Strategy of China*, Beijing: Current Affairs Press, 2010.

Lu Yiran, *The South China Sea Islands: Geography, History, Sovereignty*, Harbin: Heilongjiang Education Press, 2012.

Malcolm Fraser and Cain Roberts, *Dangerous Allies*, Melbourne: Melbourne University Press, 2014.

Mark J. Valencia, *Sharing the Resources of the South China Sea*, London: Martinus Nijhoff Publishers, 1997.

Marwyn S. Samuels, *Contest for the South China Sea*, New York and London: Methuen, 1982.

Maxwell D. Taylor, *Swords and Plowshares*, New York: Da Capo Press, 1972.

Michael Fabey, *Crashback: The Power Clash Between the U.S. and China in the Pacific*, New York: Scribner, 2017.

National Intelligence Council (NIC), *Global Trends 2025: A Transformed World*, Washington, D.C.: NIC, 2008;

Philip Joseph, *Foreign Diplomacy in China, 1894–1900: A Study in Political and Economic Relations with China*, New York: Routledge, 2019.

Policy Research Office of the State Oceanic Administration, *A Collection of International Maritime Delimitation Treaties*, Beijing: Ocean Press, 1989.

Qi Huaigao et al., *China's Peripheral Security and Its Neighboring Diplomacy against the Backdrop of Its Rising*, Beijing: Zhonghua Book Company, 2014.

Research and Design Committee of the Ministry of Foreign Affairs of the Republic of China (Taiwan), *Compilation of Archives of South China Sea Islands of Ministry of Foreign Affairs*, Vol. II (1), 1995, p. 097.

Robert D. Kaplan, *Asia's Cauldron: The South China Sea and the End of a Stable Pacific*, New York: Random House, 2014.

Robert G. Sutter, Michael E. Brown, and Timothy J. A. Adamson, with Mike M. Mochizuki and Deepa Ollapally, *Balancing Acts: The U.S. Rebalance and Asia-Pacific Stability*, August 2013.

Robert J. Mcmahon, *The Limits of Empire: The USA and the Southeast Asia since the World WarII*, New York: Columbia University Press, 1999.

Shen Keqin, *A Review of the Disputes Over the Sovereignty of the South China Sea Islands*, Taipei: Taiwan Student Book Publishing House, 2009.

Shen Wenzhou, *China's Coastal Waters: Space and Geography*, Beijing: China Ocean Press, 2006.

Shicun Wu, Keyuan Zou, eds., *Arbitration Concerning the South China Sea: Philippines versus China*, New York: Ashgate Publishing, 2016.

Smith, Philip Chadwick Foster, *The Empress of China*, Philadelphia, PA.: Philadelphia Maritime Museum, 1984.

Song Yanhui, *The United States and the South China Sea Dispute*, Taipei: Angle Publishing Co., Ltd., 2016.

Stefan Talmon and Bing Bing Jia, *The South China Sea Arbitration: A Chinese Perspective*, Oxford: Hart Publishing Ltd., 2014.

Sun Guoxiang, *Perspectives on the South China Sea Disputes*, Hong Kong: City University of Hong Kong Press, 2017.

Sun Zhe, ed., *The Congressional Research I*, Shanghai: Fudan University Press, 2002.

Sun Zhe, ed., *The U.S. Congress and Taiwan Issue*, Shanghai: Fudan University Press, 2005.

Sun Zhe et al., *Congress and US-China Relations: Cases and Analyses*, Beijing: Current Affairs Press, 2003.

Sun Zhe, *Influencing the Future: Institutional Transformation and Policy Making of the U.S. Congress*, Shanghai: Shanghai People's Publishing House, 2012 edition.

Tao Wenzhao, *U.S. China Policy in the post-Cold War Era*, Chongqing: Chongqing Press, 2006.

Tatsuo Urano, *International Conflict over the South China Sea: the History, Analysis and Documents*, Tokyo: Tosui Shobo Publishers, 1997.

The U. S. Department of State, *Foreign Relations of the United States Diplomatic Papers*, 1939, The Far East, Vol.III.

Timo Kivimaki, ed., *War or Peace in the South China Sea*, Copenhagen: NIAS Press, 2002.

Wadsworth, L. W. *A Supplementary Key to Accompany the V.K. Ting Atlas of China* (edition of 1934), Washington, the Library of Congress Reference Department Division of Maps, 1949.

Wang Wei, ed. *Evolution of U.S. Asia Pacific Policy (1776–1995)*, Jinan: Shandong People's Publishing House, 1995.

World Affairs Press, ed., *International Treaties Collection (1945–1947)*, Beijing: World Affairs Press, 1959.

World Affairs Press, ed., *A Collection of Materials on Sino-US Relations (Part 2)*, Beijing: World Affairs Press, 1960.

Wu Shicun, ed., *A Collection of Documents on the South China Sea Issue*, Haikou: Hainan Publishing House, 2001.

Wu Shicun, *The South China Sea Dispute: Origin and Development*, Beijing: China Economic Press, 2010.

Wu Xinbo, *Turbulent Water: U.S. Asia-Pacific Security Strategy in the post-Cold War Era*, Shanghai: Fudan University Press, 2006.

Wu Yi et al., *Economic Impact Assessment of South China Sea*, Beijing: Economic Science Press, 2013.

Xin Qiang, The *U.S. Congress Diplomacy: "Semi-Self-Contained" Congress and Taiwan Issue*, Shanghai: Fudan University Press, 2005.

Yonosuke Nagai and Akira Iriye, *The Origins of the Cold War in Asia*, New York: Columbia University Press, 1977.

Zalmay Khalilzad et al., *The United States and Asia: Toward a New U.S. Strategy and Force Posture*, Washington D.C.: Rand, 2001.

Zbigniew Brzezinski, *Out of Control: Global Turmoil on the Eve of the 21st Century*, New York: Collier Books, 1993.

Zbigniwe Brzezinski, *The Grand Chessboard: American Primacy and Its Geostrategic Imperatives*, New York: Basic Books, 1997.

Zhang Liangfu, *Let History Tell the Future: A Centennial Record of China's Jurisdiction of the South China Sea Islands*, Beijing: China Ocean Press, 2011.

Zhang Mingliang, *America's Involvement in the South China Sea: Process, Drives, and Implications*, Hong Kong: Hong Kong Press for Social Sciences LTD., 2011.

Zhang Shiping, *China's Sea Power*, Beijing: People Daily Press, 2009.

Zheng Zemin, *Great Powers in the South China Sea Issue*, Beijing: World Affairs Press, 2010.

Zheng Ziyue, *A Brief Geographic Record of the Islands in the South China Sea*, Beijing: Commercial Press, 1947.

Zhou Qi, ed., *Congress and U.S. Foreign Policy*, Shanghai: Shanghai Academy of Social Science Press, 2006.

Zhu Feng and Yu Mingcai, ed., *The Philippines' South China Sea Arbitration Case: Perspective*, Beijing: World Affairs Press, 2018.

Zi Zhongyun and He Di, ed., *Forty Years of US-Taiwan Relations: 1949–1989*, Beijing: People's Publishing House, 1991.

Journal Articles and Book Chapters

Acheson, "Crisis in Asia: An Examination of U.S. Policy," *The Department of State Bulletin*, Vol. XXII, No. 551, January 23, 1950, pp.111–118.

Aileen S. P. Baviera, "Security Challenges of the Philippine Archipelago," *Southeast Asian Affairs*, ISEAS - Yusof Ishak Institute, 1998, pp.213–226.

Alastair Iain Johnston, "How New and Assertive is China's New Assertiveness?" *International Security*, Vol. 37, No. 4, Spring 2013, pp.7–48.

Alice Ba, "Systemic Neglect? A Reconsideration of US Southeast Asia Policy," *Contemporary Southeast Asia*, Vol. 31, No. 3, December 2009, pp.369–398.

Alton Frye, "The Misunderstood Congress and American Foreign Policy," in Wang Xi, ed., *The Role of the U.S. Congress in the American Foreign Policy Process*, Shanghai: Fudan University Press, 1990, pp.25–35.

Ang Cheng Guan, "The South China Sea Dispute Re-visited," *Australian Journal of International Affairs*, Vol. 54, No. 2, 2000, pp.201–215.

Aris-Georges Marghelis, “American Vision of the EEZ under the Prism of Activities of Military Interest: A Critical Analysis in the Context of Sino-American Strategic Rivalry,” *Asia-Pacific Security and Maritime Affairs*, Vol. 24, No. 2, 2017, pp.29–48.

Armin Rappaport and William Earl Weeks, “Freedom of the Seas”, in Alexander Deconde, Richard Dean Burns, and Fredrik Logevall eds., *Encyclopedia of American Foreign Policy*, New York: Charles Scribner’s Sons Gale Group, 2002, Second Edition, pp.111–122.

Bao Yinan, “The US Theory of ‘Excessive Maritime Claims’ and Its Practice: A Critical Analysis,” *China International Studies*, Vol. 181, No. 5, 2017, pp.106–128.

Barry Desker, “The Eagle and the Panda: An Owl’s View from Southeast Asia,” *Asia Policy*, Vol. 8, No. 15, January 2013, pp.26–30

Bonnie S. Glaser, “Armed Clash in the South China Sea,” Report of Council on Foreign Relations, No.14, 2012, pp.1–9.

Cai Penghong, “Maritime Conflicts Between China and the United States and the Construction of Mutual Trust Mechanism,” *Foreign Affairs Review*, Vol. 27, No. 2, 2010, pp.30–37.

Cai Penghong, “The Changing Political Situation in Myanmar and an Analysis of China-Myanmar Relations,” *Journal of International Relations*, Vol. 3, No. 4, 2015, pp.102–113.

Cao Xiaoyang, “The US Military Presence in Southeast Asia After the 9/11 Incident and its Influence,” *Contemporary Asia Pacific Studies*, Vol. 15, No. 3, 2006, pp.23–30.

Cao Xiaoyang, “U.S. Indo-Pacific Maritime Security Strategic Deployment and its Impact,” *Contemporary International Relations*, Vol. 34, No. 8, 2014, pp.27–35.

Céline Pajon, “Japan and the South China Sea Forging Strategic Partnerships in a Divided Region,” *Asie Visions*, Center for Asian Studies, IFRI, No. 60, January 2013, pp.1–42.

Chalmers Johnson and E. B. Keehn, “The Pentagon’s Ossified Strategy,” *Foreign Affairs*, July/August, Vol. 74, No. 4, July/August 1995, pp.103–114.

Chang Shu, “Evolution of Indonesia’s South China Sea Policy,” *International Data Information*, Vol. 25, No. 10, 2011, pp.25–28.

Chen Fengjun, “The Global Significance of the Rise of the Asia Pacific Region—A Challenge to the ‘Four Centers Theory’,” *Journal of Contemporary Asia-Pacific Studies*, Vol. 3, No. 1, 1994, pp.12–32.

Chen Hongqiao, “U.S.-Australia Cooperation and U.S.’s Asia Pacific Rebalancing Strategy,” *Contemporary Asia-Pacific Studies*, Vol. 23, No. 1, 2014, pp.58–73.

Chen Hongyu, “The Decision-making Process and Implications of the “Republic of China” Government’s Drawing the Boundary Line of the South China Sea Islands,” *Bulletin of Academia Historica*, Vol. 30, No. 47, 2016, pp.91–118.

Chen Hongyu, “The Review of Vietnamese Official Historic Arguments on the Paracel and Spratly Islands,” *Prospect and Exploration*, Vol. 12, No. 10, 2014, pp.42–75.

Chen Xinzhi, “ROC-PRC Relations and the South China Sea Dispute,” *Issues and Studies*, Vol. 38, No. 7, July 1999, pp.23–41.

Chen Yali, “The America’s Rebalancing Strategy: Practical Appraisal and China’s Response,” *World Economics and Politics*, Vol. 26, No. 11, 2012, pp.64–82.

Cheng Chunhua, “America’s ‘return’ to Asia Pacific and Russia’s response—Based on the perspective of Russian academic research,” *Journal of PLA Nanjing Institute of Politics*, Vol. 34, No. 4, 2012, pp.65–71.

Chu Zhaofeng, "U.S.-ASEAN Relations in the Context of American Asia-Pacific Strategy," *Global Review*, Vol. 26, No. 1, 2012, pp.14–25.

Chung, Chris P. C., "Drawing the U-Shaped Line," *Modern China: An International Journal of History and Social Science*, Vol. 42, Issue 1, Jan. 2016, pp.38–72.

Colin Willet, "U.S. Perspective on the South China Sea Order: Strategy Under the Trump Administration," *The Maritime Issues*, March 22, 2018, pp.1–7.

Condoleezza Rice, "Promoting the National Interests," *Foreign Affairs*, Vol. 79, No 1, January/February 2000, pp.45–62.

Cui Liru, "The Era of Globalization and a Multipolar World," *Contemporary International Relations*, Vol. 30, the celebration special issue, 2010, pp.1–4.

Cui Liru, "U.S. 'Rebalancing' Strategy and Its 'Competition & Cooperation' Relations with China," *Fudan American Review*, Vol. 12, No. 2, 2013, pp.25–33.

David Scott, "India's Role in the South China Sea: Geopolitics and Geoeconomics in Play," *India Review*, Vol. 12, No. 2, 2013, pp.51–69.

Deng Fan, "The Trend of US Policy of Interference with Issues Related to South China Sea," *Pacific Journal*, Vol. 19, No. 11, 2011, pp.82–91.

Deng Yingwen, "On Vietnam's Measures to Internationalize the South China Sea Issue," *Southeast Asian Studies*, Vol. 42, No. 6, 2010, pp.29–36.

Dennis J. Blasko, "Chinese Strategic Thinking: People's War in the 21st Century," *China Brief*, Vol. 10, No. 6, Mar.18, 2010, pp.5–9.

Dennis Mandsager, "The U.S. Freedom of Navigation Program: Policy, Procedure, and Future," *International Law Studies*, Vol. 72, No. 6, 1998, pp.113–127.

Derek Da Cunha, "The 5th Colum, US Navy Politics," *Far Eastern Economic Review*, 3 May, 1990, p.25.

Dewi Fortuna Anwar, "An Indonesian Perspective on the U.S. Rebalancing Effort toward Asia," *Commentary*, The National Bureau of Asia Research, February 26, 2013.

Dingding Chen, Xiaoyu Pu, and Alastair Iain Johnston, "Debating China's Assertiveness," *International Security*, Vol. 38, No. 3, Winter 2013/2014, pp.176–183.

Donald S. Zagoria, "The Changing U.S. Role in Asian Security in the 1990s," in Sheldon Simon, ed., *East Asian Security in the Post-Cold War Era*, New York: M. E. Sharpe Inc., 1993, pp.42–56.

Edward Luttwak, "The Declinists, Wrong Again," *The American Interest*, Vol. 4, No. 2, November/December 2008, pp.7–13.

Edward N. Luttwak, "From Geopolitics to Geo-Economics: Logic of Conflict, Grammar of Commerce," *The National Interest*, Vol. 20, No. 2, Summer 1990, pp.17–23.

Emery K. O. et al., "Geological Structure and Some Water Characteristics of East China Sea and Yellow Sea," *UNECAFE/CCOP Technical Bulletin*, Vol. 2, 1969, pp.3–43.

Erik Franckx, "American and Chinese Views on Navigational Rights of Warships," *Chinese Journal of International Law*, Vol. 10, Issue 1, March 2011, pp.187–206.

Euan Graham, "Southeast Asia in the US Rebalance: Perceptions from a Divided Region," *Contemporary Southeast Asia*, Vol. 35, No. 3, 2013, pp.305–332.

Evan Braden Montgomery, "Contested Primacy in the Western Pacific: China's Rise and the Future of U.S. Power Projection," *International Security*, Vol. 38, No. 4, Spring 2014, pp.115–149.

Evelyn Goh, "Meeting the China Challenge: The U.S.in South east Asian Regional Security Strategies," *Policy Studies Monograph*, No. 16, Washington, D. C., East-West Center, 2005, pp.1–60.

Fang Yun, "Comprehensive Foreign Policy of Laos and the Relationship between China and Laos," *Southeast Asian and South Asian Studies*, Vol. 29, No. 2, 2011, pp.14–19.

Feng Shaolei and Feng Shuai, "Reconsidering China's Neighboring Security: Characteristics, Functions and Trends," *Journal of International Security Studies*, Vol. 31, No. 2, 2013, pp.34–57.

Feng Wenke and Bao Caiwang, "Topographic and Geomorphological Characteristics of South China Sea," *Marine Geological Research*, Vol. 2, No. 4, 1982, pp.80–92.

Franklin Roosevelt, "On Maintaining Freedom of the Seas," in *Fireside Chats*, September 11, 1941.

Fred Bergsten C, "A Partnership of Equals: How Washington Should Respond to China's Economic Challenge," *Foreign Affairs*, Vol. 97, No 4, July/August 2008, pp.57–69.

Ge Hongliang, "America's South China Sea Policy in the Post-Cold War and Its Influence on Sino-U.S. Relations", *Southeast Asia & South Asian Studies*, Vol. 30, No. 2, 2012, pp.16–21.

Ge Hongliang, "India's New Asia-Pacific Strategy: The Modi Administration's 'Act East Policy' ", *South Asian Studies*, Vol. 27, No. 1, 2015, pp.62–79.

Gideon Rachman, "American Decline: This Time It's for Real," *Foreign Policy*, No. 184, January/February 2011, pp.59–65.

Gong Jianhua, "The Causes, Current Situation and Internal Characteristics of the South China Sea Issue," *Theory and Reform*, Vol. 23, No. 2, 2010, pp.144–147.

Gong Xiaohui, "Analysis on Malaysia's South China Sea Policy in 2011," *Southeast Asian Studies*, Vol. 53, No. 6, 2011, pp.23–28.

Gregory Poling, "China's Charm Offensive Isn't Defusing Tensions in the South China Sea," *The World Politics Review*, December 14, 2015.

Guan Fei, "Why the South China Sea is China's Core Interest," *World View*, February 2011, pp.41–42.

Guan Jianqiang, "A Study on the Legal Status of the Nine-Dashed Line in the South China Sea," *International Review*, Vol. 33, No. 4, 2012, pp.15–22.

Guo Jinyue, "Russia and the United States Asia-Pacific 'Rebalancing' Strategy," *Russian, East European & Middle Asian Studies*, Vol. 34, No. 5, 2014, pp.77–81.Guo Yonghu, "Historical Investigation on the U. S. Policy to Sino-Philippine Nansha Islands Disputes: Interpretation based on the U. S. Recent Declassified Diplomatic Files," *Contemporary China History Studies*, Vol. 20, Issue 2, 2013, pp.104–111.

Guo Yonghu and Song Jianxin, "US Congress Legislation on Maritime Disputes Involving China and its Implications," *China International Studies*, Vol. 60, No. 5, 2018, pp.103–114.Guo Yuan, "The US Policies of South China Sea after the Cold War," *Academic Exploration*, Vol. 16, No. 1, 2008, pp.54–58.

Guo Yuan, "U.S. Policy on the South China Sea and Its Impact in the Early Cold War," *Pacific Journal*, Vol. 20, No. 7, 2012, pp.35–43.

Guo Yuan, "The Spratly Islands Affairs and the Negotiations among China, France and Japan," *World History*, Vol. 38, No. 3, 2015, pp.87–97.

Han Xudong, "Prudent Use of National Core Interests," *Outlook Weekly*, No. 30, 2010, p.64.

Harsh V. Pant and Yogesh Joshi, "Indian Foreign Policy Responds to the U.S. Pivot," *Asia Policy*, Vol. 10, No. 19, January 2015, pp.89–114.

He Ping, "The Strategic Intention and Policy Debate of Japan's Participation in TPP Negotiations," *Japanese Studies*, Vol. 28, No. 4, 2012, pp.34–49.He Weibao, "New Arguments on the Arrangement of the Xisha (Paracel) and Nansha (Spratly) Islands in the Treaty of Peace with Japan and Its Impact," *The Chinese Journal of American Studies*, Vol. 28, No. 4, 2014, pp.68–89.

He Weibao, "Characteristics and Causes of Legislation on the South China Sea Issue in the US Congress," in Zheng Bingwen and Huang Ping, ed., *American Studies Report (2015)*, Beijing: China Social Sciences Academic Press, 2015, pp.179–195.

He Zhigong and An Xiaoping, "The American Factor and its Influence in the Disputes in South China Sea," *Journal of Contemporary Asia-Pacific Studies*, Vol. 19, No. 1, 2010, pp.132–145.

Hillary Clinton, "America's Pacific Century," *Foreign Policy*, October 11, 2011, pp.56–63.

Hossain, Kamrul, "The UNCLOS and the US-China Hegemonic Competition over the South China Sea," *Journal of East Asia & International Law*, Vol. 6, Issue 1, Spring 2013, pp.107–133

Hu Bo, "Peaceful Power Shift Between China and the U.S. on the Seas of East Asia: Risks, Opportunities and Strategies," *World Economics and Politics*, Vol. 25, No. 3, 2013, pp.27–44.

Huang Fengzhi and Liu Boran, "The Strengthening of U.S.-ROK Alliance and China's Strategic Response," *International Forum*, Vol. 15, No. 2, 2013, pp.28–34.

Huang Yao, Huang Jingwen, "A Commentary and Refutation of the US State Department's report on China's Dashed-Line in the South China Sea," *Chinese Review of International Law*, Vol. 10, No. 3, 2015, pp.3–17.

Hugh White, "The Limits to Optimism: Australia and the Rise of China," *Australian Journal of International Affairs*, Vol. 59, No. 4, December 2005, pp.469–480.

Hugh White, "Power Shift: Australia's future between Washington and Beijing," *Quarterly Essay*, Vol. 39, 2010, pp.1–74.

Hugh White, "Power Shift: Rethinking Australia's Place in the Asian Century," *Australian Journal of International Affairs*, Vol. 65, No. 1, February 2011, pp.81–93.Hui Gengtian, "Multi-level Dynamics for Internationalization of South China Sea Issue," *Journal of Strategy and Decision-Making*, Vol. 14, No. 2, 2013, pp.16–26.

Hui Ming, "Retracing the Sovereignty of the South China Sea Islands Through Modern American Documents," *Journal of Chinese Humanities*, Vol. 66, No. 4, 2016, pp.5–22.

Ian Townsend-Gault, "Preventive Diplomacy and Proactivity in the South China Sea," *Contemporary Southeast Asia*, Vol. 20, No. 2, 1998, pp.171–190.

James A. Baker, III, "America in Asia: Emerging Architecture for a Pacific Community," *Foreign Affairs*, Vol. 70, No. 5, 1992, pp.1–18.

James Kraska and Michael Monti, "The Law of Naval Warfare and China's Maritime Militia," *International Law Studies*, Vol. 91, No. 1, 2015, pp.450–467.

James M. Scott, "The Challenge of the South China Sea: Congressional Engagement and the U.S. Policy Response," *All Azimuth: A Journal of Foreign Policy and Peace*, Vol. 7, Issue 2, 2018, pp.5–30.

James W. Houck and Nicole M. Anderson, "The United States, China, and Freedom of Navigation in the South China Sea," *Washington University Global Studies Law Review*, Vol. 13, Issue 3, 2014, pp.441–452.

Jia Qingguo, "New Understanding of China-US Relations," *The Chinese Journal of American Studies*, Vol. 9, No. 1, 1995, pp.29–49.Jia Yu, "On the Law Status of Duanxuxian (nine-segmented line) of South China Sea," *China's Borderland History and Geography Studies*, Vol. 15, No. 2, 2005, pp.112–120.

Jia Yu, "International Law Theory of South China Sea Issues," *China Legal Science*, Vol. 29, No. 6, 2012, pp.26–35.

Jia Yu, "The Historical Right in the South China Sea," *China Legal Science*, Vol. 32, No. 3, 2015, pp.179–203.

Jia Yu, "The Jurisprudential Meaning of the Nine-Dashed Line in the South China Sea," *Social Science Front*, Vol. 38, No. 4, 2015, pp.207–213.

Jiang Yang and Wang Yiwei, "South China Sea in US Asia-Pacific Security Strategy," *Southeast Asian Studies*, Vol. 40, No. 5, 1998, pp.33–37.

Jiang Yuechun, "Japan Joins TPP Negotiation: Intention and Aftermath," *Global Review*, Vol. 32, No. 1, 2012, pp.26–33.

Jianming Shen, "International Law Rules and Historical Evidence Supporting China's Title to the South China Sea Islands," *HASTINGS INT'L&COMP.L.REV*, Vol. 21, No. 1, Fall 1997, pp.1–75.

Jin Yongming, "Nature of the Dashed Line and Legal Status of Internal Water Areas in South China Sea," *China Legal Science*, Vol. 29, No. 6, 2012, pp.36–48.

Jinming L. and Dexia L., "The Dotted Line on the Chinese Map of the South China Sea: A Note," *Ocean Development & International Law*, Vol. 34, 2003, pp.287–295.

Joel Wuthnow, "Beyond Imposing Costs: Recalibrating U.S. Strategy in the South China Sea," *Asia Policy*, Vol. 12, No. 24, July 2017, pp.123–138.

John Ikenberry G., "The Future of the Liberal World Order: Internationalism after America," *Foreign Affairs*, Vol. 90, No. 3, May /June 2011, pp.56–68.

John W. Swift, P. Hodgkinson, Samuel W. Woodhouse, "The Voyage of the Empress of China," *The Pennsylvania Magazine of History and Biography*, Vol. 63, No. 1, Jan. 1939, pp.24–36.

Josef Joffe, "The Default Power: The False Prophecy of America's Decline," *Foreign Affairs*, Vol. 88, No. 5, September/October 2009, pp.21–35.

Ju Hailong, "Marine Security Policy and Practice in Brunei," *Forum of World Economics & Politics*, Vol. 31, No. 5, 2011, pp.55–64.

Ju Hailong, "Research on the Obama Administration's South China Seas Policy," *Contemporary Asia-Pacific Studies*, Vol. 20, No. 3, 2011, pp.97–112.

Ju Hailong, "American Factors in Philippines' South China Sea Policy," *China International Studies*, Vol. 55, No. 3, 2013, pp.58–69.

Ju Hailong, "A Historical Analysis on the SCS Policies of the USA: Based on the Declassified Documents of FRUS, DDRS, and DNSA," *Academic Exploration*, Vol. 58, No. 6, 2015, pp.106–115.

Kai He and Huiyun Feng, "Debating China's Assertiveness: Taking China's Power and Interests Seriously," *International Politics*, Vol. 49, No. 5, 2012, pp.633–644.

Kamrul Hossain, "The UNCLOS and the US-China Hegemonic Competition over the South China Sea," *Journal of East Asia & International Law*, Vol. 6, Issue 1, 2013, pp.107–133.

Keyuan, Zou, "China's U-Shaped Line in the South China Sea Revisited," *Ocean Development & International Law*, Vol. 43 Issue 1, Jan–Mar 2012, pp.18–34.

Kimie Hara, "The San Francisco Peace Treaty and Frontier Problems in The Regional Order in East Asia, A Sixty Year Perspective," *The Asia-Pacific Journal*, Vol. 10, Issue 17, No. 1, April 23, 2012, pp.1–17.

Kitti Prasirtsuk: "The Implications of U.S. Strategic Rebalancing: A Perspective from Thailand," *Asia Policy*, Vol. 8, No. 15, January 2013, pp.31–37.

Kurt M. Campbell, Ely Ratner, "The China Reckoning: How Beijing Defied American Expectations," *Foreign Affairs*, Vol. 97, No. 2, March/April, 2018, pp.60–70.

Lee Lai To, "China, the USA and the South China Sea Conflicts," *Security Dialogue*, Vol. 34, No. 1, March 2003, pp.25–39.

Li Chunxia, "From Enemy to Comprehensive Partnership: Vietnamese Strategic Considerations about Vietnam-US Relations," *International Forum*, Vol. 16, No. 4, 2014, pp.13–18.

Li Guanqun, "The Influence of Russia on China's Maritime Geostrategy," *Contemporary World and Socialism*, Vol. 34, No. 1, 2013, pp.104–110.

Li Guizhou, "America's Attitude towards the South China Sea: A Perspective based on American Congressional Acts," *Contemporary Asia-Pacific Studies*, Vol. 25, No. 5, 2016, pp.112–134.

Li Guoqiang, "Prospecting and Developing South China Sea Oil and Gas Resources," *China International Studies*, Vol. 56, No. 6, 2014, pp.104–115.Li Jinming, "Records of the South China Sea Territory in China's Historical Writings," *China Borderland History and Geography Studies*, Vol. 9, No. 3, 1996, pp.28–36.

Li Jinming, "Overview on the Mischief Reef Incident," *Southeast Asian Affairs*, Vol. 27, No. 1, 2000, pp.66–75.

Li Jinming, "The Legal Status of the U-shaped Line in the South China Sea: Historic Waters, Maritime Boundary or A Line of Islands Ownership?", *Southeast Asian Affairs*, Vol. 37, No. 4, 2010, pp.22–29.

Li Jinming, "The Chinese U-shaped Line in the South China Sea: Its Background and Effectiveness," *Southeast Asian Studies*, Vol. 53, No. 1, 2011, pp.41–47.

Li Jinming, "The Status quo of South China Sea Disputes and the Intervention of Major Powers Outside the Region," *Contemporary International Relations*, Vol. 31, No. 7, 2011, pp.1–8.

Li Jinming, "An Overview of Reviews on the Legal Status of the U-shaped Line in the South China Sea," *Southeast Asian Affairs*, Vol. 38, No. 2, 2011, pp.54–62.

Li Jinming, "The U-Shaped Line in the South China Sea: Background and Legal Status," *Contemporary International Relations*, Vol. 32, No. 9, 2012, pp.7–14.

Li Li, "Reflections on 'Asia Pacific Rebalancing Strategy' in American Academia," *Issus of Contemporary World Socialism*, Vol. 30, No. 3, 2013, pp.89–100.

Li Mingjiang and Zhang Hongzhou, "Singapore's Policy towards the South China Sea: Be Neutral and Useful, Maintain Stability and Peace," *Southeast Asian Studies*, Vol. 53, No. 6, 2011, pp.16–22.

Li Yan, "The 'Freedom of Navigation' Issue in China-U.S. Relations," *Contemporary International Relations*, Vol. 35, No. 11, 2015, pp.22–28.

Liang Zhiming, "On the Relative Unity and Diversity of Southeast Asia," *Social Scientist*, Vol. 15, No. 5, 2000, pp.4–8.

Liao Xiaojian, "Analysis on Malaysia's Relationship with US and China after US 'Returning to Asia'," *Southeast Asian Studies*, Vol. 54, No. 1, 2012, pp.47–52.

Lin Minwang, "Why Does India Involve in the Dispute in the South China Sea?", *South Asian Studies Quarterly*, Vol. 30, No. 4, 2014, pp.16–22.

Lin Ronggui and Li Guoqiang, "Comprehensive Study of the History and Geography of Spratly Islands," edited by Lu Yiran, *The South China Sea Islands: Geography, History, Sovereignty*, Harbin: Heilongjiang Education Press, 2012, pp.103–122.

Lin Xiaoguang, "American Asia Pacific Strategy: From Bush to Clinton," *Foreign Social Sciences Studies*, Vol. 15, No. 2, 1994, pp.17–24.

Lin Xiaoguang, "Japan's Strategic Intension in Getting Actively Involved in the South China Sea Issue and Its Policy Trend," *Peace and Development*, Vol. 29, No. 2, 2012, pp.54–59.

Ling Shengli, "A Strategic Analysis of Sino-U.S. Maritime Competition in the Asia Pacific Region," *Journal of Contemporary Asia-Pacific Studies*, Vol. 24, No. 2, 2015, pp.61–81.

Liselotte Odgaard, "The South China Sea: ASEAN's Security Concerns About China," *Security Dialogue*, Vol. 34, No. 1, 2003, pp.11–24.

Liu Changli, "Motivation, Constraints and Policy Measures of Japan's Participation in TPP Negotiations," *Japanese Studies*, Vol. 27, No. 1, 2011, pp.65–78.

Liu Chang, "Unsolved Delimitation of Indonesia's Maritime Boundaries: Current Situation, Characteristic and Outlook," *Southeast Asian Studies*, Vol. 57, No. 5, 2015, pp.35–40.Liu Fei, "Russia's Policy of the South China Sea and Its Impact on Chinese Maritime Disputes," *Northeast Asia Forum*, Vol. 25, No. 1, 2016, pp.87–95.

Liu Fenghua, "Russia's Policy of Eastward Movement: Achievements, Problems and Trend," *Russian Studies*, Vol. 3, No. 1, 2013, pp.11–18.

Liu Jianfei, "The Situation in the South China Sea and Sino-US Relations Under the Background of the US Strategic Focus Shifting Eastward," *Journal of University of International Relations*, Vol. 30, No. 4, 2012, pp.93–98.

Liu Lingqi and Liu Haichao, "Motivation for Japan's TPP Decision and Assessment of the Status quo of Japan-US Negotiations," *Contemporary International Relations*, Vol. 35, No. 3, 2015, pp.46–55.

Liu Peng and Zhu Yitong, "The Employment of Smart Power in the U.S. Military Strategy: A Case Study of the Airsea Battle Strategy," *Fudan American Review*, Vol. 11, No. 2, 2011, pp.100–121.

Liu Weidong, "An Analysis of U.S. Policy toward Japan's Lifting the Ban on 'Collective Self-defense'," *Contemporary International Relations*, Vol. 35, No. 4, 2015, pp.28–35.

Liu Yongtao, "U.S. Congress, Presidency and China Policy: Changes, Debates and Agendas," *Fudan American Review*, Vol. 9, No. 2, 2009, pp.82–98.

Liu Zhongmin, "Sea- power Issues and Post- cold- war Sino- US relations: Contradictory Perceptions and Difficult Options," *Foreign Affairs Review*, Vol. 22, No. 6, 2005, pp.55–60.

Long Xinggang and Liang Dongxing, "The U.S. Factor in South China Sea Issue," *Around Southeast Asia*, Vol. 31, No. 9, 2010, pp.16–19.

Lu Fanghua, "The US Factor in South China Sea," *Southeast Asia & South Asian Studies*, Vol. 27, No. 4, 2009, pp.6–10.

Lu Peng, "Between the Middle Power Dream and the National Interests—Australia International Strategy and its South China Sea Policy," *Asia-Pacific Security and Maritime Affairs*, Vol. 1, No. 2, 2015, pp.11–26.

Luo Rongqu, "Modern Historical Significance of the Rise of East Asia and its Prospects in the 21st Century," *Tianjin Social Sciences*, Vol. 12, No. 2, 1992, pp.4–8.

Luo Xiao, "The South China Sea and China's Core Interests: Debate, Review and Transend," *Journal of Contemporary Asia-Pacific Studies*, Vol. 27, No. 1, 2018, pp.122–155.

Luo Yongkun, "Brunei's South China Sea Policy," *International Information*, Vol. 26, No. 9, 2012, pp.13–15.

Ma Bisheng, "How Does Australia Respond to China's Rise?", *Foreign Affairs Review*, Vol. 31, No. 1, 2014, pp.56–69.

Ma Jianguang and Sun Qianjie, "Study on the Evolution of Russia's Maritime Strategy and Its Geopolitical Influence," *Pacific Journal*, Vol. 23, No. 11, 2015, pp.20–30.

Ma Jianying, "The U.S. Perception of and Response to China's 'the Belt and Road' Initiative," *World Economics and Politics*, Vol. 29, No. 10, 2015, pp.104–132.

Ma Jianying and Jiang Bin, "The Trump Administration's South China Sea Policy: Initiatives, Motivations and Prospects," *The Journal of South China Sea Studies*, Vol. 4, No. 2, 2018, pp.36–44.Ma Junping, "The Asia-Pacific Security Strategy of Bush Administration: Adjustments and Trends," *Journal of PLA University of Foreign Languages*, Vol. 28, No. 5, 2005, pp.114–118.

Malek, Melda, "A Legal Assessment of China's Historic Claims in the South China Sea," *Australian Journal of Maritime & Ocean Affairs*, Vol. 5, Issue 1, March 2013, pp.28–36.

Mao Junxiang, "Political and Legal Analysis of Philippines' Submission of South China Sea Dispute to International Arbitration," *Law Review*, Vol. 35, No. 2, 2014, pp.107–116.

Mark J. Valencia, "The Spratly Islands: Dangerous ground in the South China Sea," *The Pacific Review*, Vol. 1, Issue 4, 1988, pp.438–443.

Masahiro Kawai and Ganeshan Wignaraja, "Asian FTAs: Trends, Prospects and Challenges," *Journal of Asian Economics*, Vol. 22, No. 1, 2011, pp.1–22.

Mcdorman, Tedl, "The South China Sea: The U-Shaped Line, Islands and the Philippine-China Arbitration," *German Yearbook of International Law*, Vol. 56, 2013, pp.33–62.

Men Honghua, "Critical Moment: China, the United States and the World in the Eyes of American Elites," *Social Sciences in China*, Vol. 33, No. 7, 2012, pp.182–202.

Meng Xiaoxu and Wang Shan, "Japan's New Security Bills and Strategic Dilemma," *Contemporary International Relations*, Vol. 35, No. 8, 2015, pp.16–21.

Michael A. Glosny and Phillip C. Saunders, Robert S. Ross, "Debating China's Naval Nationalism," *International Security*, Vol. 35, No. 2, Fall 2010, pp.161–175.

Michael Beckley, "China's Century? Why America's Edge Will Endure," *International Security*, Vol. 36, No. 3, Winter 2011/12, pp.41–78.

Michael D. Swaine, "China's Assertive Behavior Part One: on 'core interests'," *China Leadership Monitor*, No. 34, February 22, 2011, pp.1–25.

Michael D. Swaine, "Perceptions of an Assertive China," *China Leadership Monitor*, No. 32, 2010, pp.1–19.

Michael D. Swaine, M. Taylor Fravel, "China's Assertive Behavior-Part Two: The Maritime Periphery," *China Leadership Monitor*, No. 35, Summer 2011, pp.16–17.

Michael Sheng-Ti Gau, "The U-Shaped Line and a Categorization of the Ocean Disputes in the South China Sea," *Ocean Development & International Law*, Vol. 43, Issue 1, Jan–Mar 2012, pp.57–69.

Michael Yahuda, "China's New Assertiveness in the South China Sea," *Journal of Contemporary China*, Vol. 22, No. 81, May 2013, pp.446–459.

Miyoshi, Masahiro, "China's 'U-Shaped Line' Claim in the South China Sea: Any Validity Under International Law?", *Ocean Development & International Law*, Vol. 43, Issue 1, Jan–Mar 2012, pp.1–17.

Mou Wenfu, "U.S. Strategy for Shaping Maritime Order Beyond UNCLOS," *China Review of Marine Law*, Vol. 10, No. 2, 2014, pp.183–217.

Nayan Chanda, "Territorial Imperative," *Far Eastern Economic Review*, February 23, 1995, p.15.

Nguyen Manh Hung, "Vietnam-US Relations: Past, Present, and Future," *Asia Pacific Bulletin*, No. 69, Washington, DC: East-West Center, September 24, 2010, pp.1–2.

Nguyen Tan Yong, "Building Strategic Trust for Peace, Cooperation and Prosperity in Asia Pacific Region," *Shangri-La Dialogue*, Beijing: World Publishing Company, 2013, pp.12–14.

Nicholas J. Spykman, "Geography and Foreign Policy," *American Political Science Review*, Vol. 32, No. 1, February 1938, pp.28–50.

Nie Wenjuan, "How Does ASEAN Assert 'Counter-Leadership' over China in the South China Sea?", *Contemporary Asia-Pacific Studies*, Vol. 22, No. 4, 2013, pp.85–106.

Nie Wenjuan, "China's Identity and Understanding of National Interests in the South China Sea," *Journal of Contemporary Asia-Pacific Studies*, Vol. 26, No. 1, 2017, pp.139–155.Nigel Holloway, "Jolt from the Blue: U.S. Prodded to Firm up its Policy on Spratlys," *Far Eastern Economic Review*, August 3, 1995, pp.22–23.

Noboru Yamaguchi, "A Japanese Perspective on U.S. Rebalancing toward the Asia-Pacific Region," *Asia Policy*, Vol. 8, No. 15, January 2013, pp.7–12.

Paul Midford, "Japan's Approach to Maritime Security in the South China Sea," *Asian Security*, Vol. 55, No. 3, 2015, pp.525–547.

Peter Jennings, "The U.S. Rebalance to the Asia-Pacific: An Australian Perspective," *Asia Policy*, Vol. 8, No. 15, January 2013, pp.38–44.

Peter Kien-Hong Yu, "The Chinese (Broken) U-Shaped Line in the South China Sea: Points, Lines, and Zones," *Contemporary Southeast Asia*, Vol. 25, No. 3, 2003, pp.405–430.

Phillip C. Saunders, "China's Rising Power, the U.S. Rebalance to Asia, and Implications for U.S.-China Relations," *Issues & Studies*, Vol. 50, No. 3, September 2014, pp.19–55.

PIR Center and ASEAN Center in Mgimo University, "Sino-American Rivalry in Asia: Conclusions for Russia," *Security Index*, Volume 18, No. 4, 2012, pp.45–62.

Qi Haotian, "Unilateral implementation and conflict management: parsing America's freedom of navigation operation," *Asia-Pacific Security and Maritime Affairs*, Vol. 2, No. 1, 2016, pp.15–30.

Qi Wenying, "On the Issue of the 'Empress of China'", edited by the editorial board of the series of books on the history of Sino-US Relations, *A Collection of Essays on the History of Sino-US Relations (Volume I)*, Chongqing: Chongqing Press, 1985, pp.63–75.

Qi Wenying, "A Preliminary Analysis of the Reasons for the Success of the First Voyage of the 'Empress of China'", edited by the editorial board of the series on the history of Sino-US Relations, *Essays on the History of Sino-US Relations (Volume II)*, Chongqing: Chongqing Press, 1988, pp.19–32.

Qian Chuntai, "Analysis on Sino-U.S. Consultation Mechanism for Military Maritime Safety," *Contemporary International Relations*, Vol. 22, No. 4, 2002, pp.8–11.

Qiu Chaobing, "The U.S.-Indonesian Comprehensive Partnership: Progress and Implications," *Chinese Journal of American Studies*, Vol. 29, No. 2, 2015, pp.93–111.

Qu Sheng, "A Preliminary Study of the 'Freedom of Navigation Program' in the United States," *Chinese Journal of American Studies*, Vol. 27, No. 1, 2013, pp.102–116.

Qu Sheng, "From Maritime Freedom to Maritime Hegemony: The Transformation of Wilson's Maritime Policy Vision," *World History*, Vol. 40, No. 3, 2017, pp.-4–16.

Raja Mohan C., "India: Between 'Strategic Autonomy' and 'Geopolitical Opportunity'," *Asia Policy*, Vol. 8, No. 15, January 2013, pp.21–25.

Raul Pedrozo, "Close Encounters at Sea: The USNS Impeccable Incident," *Naval War College Review*, Vol. 62, No. 3, Summer 2009, pp.101–111.

Raul Pedrozo, "Preserving Navigational Rights and Freedoms: The Right to Conduct Military Activities in China's Exclusive Economic Zone," *Chinese Journal of International Law*, Vol. 9, Issue 1, 2010, pp.9–29.

Richard Haass, "The Age of Non-polarity," *Foreign Affairs*, Vol. 87, No. 3, May/June, 2008, pp.44–56.

Richard J. Ellings and Edward A. Olsen, "Asia's Challenge to American Strategy," *NBR Analysis*, The National Bureau of Asian Research, Vol. 3, No. 2, 1992, pp.1–23.

Richard J. Grunawalt, "United States Policy on International Straits," *Ocean Development & International Law*, Vol. 18, No. 4, 2009, pp.445–458.

Rigoberto Tiglao, "This the Season," *Far Eastern Economic Review*, December 24, 1998.

Robert A. Pape, "Empire Falls," *National Interest*, No. 99, January/February 2009, pp.18–20.

Robert A. Scalapino, "The United States and Asia: Future Prospects," *Foreign Affairs*, Vol. 70, No. 5, Winter 1991, pp.19–40.

Robert D. Kaplan, "The South China Sea Is the Future of Conflict," *Foreign Policy*, Issue 188, Sept/Oct 2011, pp.1–8.

Robert S. Ross, "Balance of Power Politics and the Rise of China: Accommodation and Balancing in East Asia," *Security Studies*, Vol. 15, No. 3, 2006, pp.355–395.

Robert S. Ross, "China's Naval Nationalism: Source, Prospects, and the U.S. Response," *International Security*, Vol. 34, No. 2, Fall 2009, pp.46–81.

Robert S. Ross, "China's Rise, Regional Power Transfer and East Asian Security: from 1949 to the 21st century," translated by Shen Peng, *World Economics and Politics*, Vol. 23, No. 11, 2009, pp.36–43.

Robert Zoellick, "Congress and the Making of US Foreign Policy," *Survival*, Vol. 41, No. 4, Winter 1999–2000, pp.20–41.

See Seng Tan, "Riding the Chinese Dragon: Singapore's Pragmatic Relationship with China," in Jun Tsunekawa, ed., *The Rise of China: Responses from South East Asia and Japan*, NIDS Joint Research Series, No. 4, 2009, pp.21–45.

Shao Xiao: "Looking at the US–South Vietnam Alliance in the Nixon Administration from the Signing of the Paris Agreement," *History Research and Teaching*, Vol. 54, No. 1, 2010, pp.99–104.

Shao Xiao, "The Battle of the Paracel Islands and Nixon's Policy in the South China Sea," *Southeast Asian Studies*, Vol. 54, Issue 3, 2012, pp.25–31.

Sheldon Simon, "US-Southeast Asia Relations: Military Commitments and Human Rights Concerns," *Comparative Connectives, A Triannual E-Journal on East Asia Relations*, Vol.15, No.1, 2013, pp.55–65.

Sheldon W. Simon, "Conflict and Diplomacy in the South China Sea: The View from Washington," *Asian Survey*, Vol. 52, No. 6, November/December 2012, pp.995–1018.

Shen Yamei, "Japan's Response to the U.S. Strategic Eastward Movement and its Impact," *Contemporary World*, Vol. 33, No. 11, 2013, pp.65–67.

Sheng-Ti Gau M., "The U-Shaped Line and a Categorization of the Ocean Disputes in the South China Sea," *Ocean Development & International Law*, Vol. 43, No. 1, 2012, pp.57–69.

Shi Bin, "Exploring the Source of 'Militarism' in the United States," *Foreign Affairs Review*, Vol. 31, No. 4, 2014, pp.78–106.

Shi Yongming, "The U.S. Policy in the South China Sea: Target and Strategy," *Southeast Asian Affairs*, Vol. 47, No. 1, 2015, pp.1–10.

Sourabh Gupta and Leonardo Bernard, "Comments of Foreign Scholars on U. S. State Department Nine-Dashed Line Report," *Asia-Pacific Security and Maritime Affairs*, Vol. 1, No. 6, 2015, pp.97–103.

Su Xiaohui, "Study on Developments of the South China Sea Policies under the New U.S. Administration," *Pacific Journal*, Vol. 25, No. 7, 2017, pp.36–43.

Sun Junjian, "Australia's Response to U.S. Strategy of 'Return to the Asia-Pacific'," *Contemporary International Relations*, Vol. 34, No. 8, 2014, pp.36–43.

Sun Xiaoling, "The U.S. Factor in the South China Sea Dispute between China and Vietnam," *Southeast Asian Studies*, Vol. 54, No. 3, 2012, pp.32–37.

Sun Zhe, "American Presidential and Congressional Diplomacy," *Fudan Journal (social science)*, Vol. 67, No. 4, 2001, pp.50–57.

Sun Zhe and Xu Hongfeng, "The Impact of the Eastward Shift of the Obama Administration's Strategic Focus on US-Russian Relations," *Chinese Journal of American Studies*, Vol. 27, No. 1, 2013, pp.9–21.Susumu Awanohara, "Washington's Priorities: US Emphasizes Freedom of Navigation," *Far Eastern Economic Review*, Vol. 155, No. 32, August 13, 1992, pp.18–19.

Tang Shiping and Joey S. R. Long, "America's Military Interventionism: A Social Evolutionary Interpretation," *World Economics and Politics*, Vol. 25, No. 9, 2011, pp.19–38.

Taylor Fravel M., "China's Strategy in the South China Sea," *Contemporary Southeast Asia*, Vol. 33, No. 3, 2011, pp.292–319.

Taylor Fravel M., "American Policy Towards the Disputes in the South China Sea: 1995–2017," translated by Qi Hao, *Contemporary American Review*, Vol. 1, No. 1, 2017, pp.41–56.

Thaliyakkattil Srikanth, "An Analysis of India's Hedging Strategy towards China," *Journal of Contemporary Asia-Pacific Studies*, Vol. 22, No. 4, 2013, pp.25–31.

Thaliyakkattil Srikanth, "US Strategic Rebalancing toward Asia-Pacific: India's Policy Options," *South Asian Studies Quarterly*, Vol. 22, No. 1, 2013, pp.27–30.

Thomas J. Christensen, "The Advantages of an Assertive China: Responding to Beijing's Abrasive Diplomacy," *Foreign Affairs*, Vol. 90, No. 2, March/April 2011, pp.54–67.

Tomohiko Satake and Yusuke Ishihara, "America's Rebalance to Asia and its Implications for Japan-US-Australia Security Cooperation," *Asia-Pacific Review*, Vol. 19, No. 2, 2012, pp.19–20.

Tomotaka Shoji, "The South China Sea: A View from Japan," *NIDS Journal of Defense and Security*, No. 15, Dec. 2014, pp.127–141.

Toshi Yoshihara & James R. Holmes, "Can China Defend a 'Core Interest' in the South China Sea?", *The Washington Quarterly*, Spring 2011, pp.45–59.

United States Department of State, Bureau of Oceans and International Environmental and Scientific Affairs, "Limits in the Seas, China: Maritime Claims in the South China Sea," No. 143, December 5, 2014, pp.1–24.

Wang Aijuan, "India's Measures to Cope With the US Strategy of 'Rebalancing' Toward Asia Pacific," *Journal of PLA Nanjing Institute of Politics*, Vol. 34, No. 5, 2012, pp.68–72.

Wang Chuanjian, "American Policy in the South China Sea: History and Reality," *Foreign Affairs Review*, Vol. 26, No. 6, 2009, pp.87–100.

Wang Chuanjian, "India's South China Sea Policy: Intention and Influence," *Foreign Affairs Review*, Vol. 27, No. 3, 2010, pp.107–122.

Wang Chuanjian, "Japan's South China Sea Policy: Connotation and Extension," *Foreign Affairs Review*, Vol. 28, No. 3, 2011, pp.100–110.

Wang Chuanjian, "South China Sea Issue and Sino-US Relations," *Contemporary Asia-Pacific Studies*, Vol. 20, No. 2, 2014, pp.4–26.

Wang Chuanjun, "The infiltration and influence of Extra-regional Powers to the South China Sea," *Journal of Contemporary Asia-Pacific Studies*, Vol. 10, No. 11, 2001, pp.14–18.

Wang Gonglong, "The Adjustment of US Policy toward the South China Sea and the Room for Cooperation across the Taiwan Straits on This Issue," *International Forum*, Vol. 11, No. 6, 2011, pp.1–5.

Wang Guanghou, "Analysis on Australia's South China Sea Policy," *Southeast Asian Studies*, Vol. 54, No. 6, 2011, pp.10–15.

Wang Hao, "The Trump Administration's Policy of Linkage towards China: An Analysis," *Contemporary Asia-Pacific Studies*, Vol. 26, No. 4, 2017, pp.65–85.

Wang Hui, "The 'Hegemony Anxiety' and Strategic Eastward Movement of the United States," *Contemporary International Relations*, Vol. 32, No. 6, 2012, pp.32–36.Wang Jisi, "The 'Strategic Triangle' in US Policy Towards China," *The Chinese Journal of American Studies*, Vol. 6, No. 2,1992, pp.7–35.

Wang Jisi, "US China Policy From 1945 to 1955 and its Consequences," *The Chinese Journal of American Studies*, Vol. 1, No.1, 1987, pp.40–68.

Wang Jisi, "China's Search for a Grand Strategy: A Rising Great Power Finds Its Way," *Foreign Affairs*, Vol. 90, No. 2, Mar/Apr 2011, pp.72–77.

Wang K-H., "The ROC's Maritime Claims and Practices with Special Reference to the South China Sea," *Ocean Development & International Law*, Vol. 41, 2010, pp.237–252.

Wang Lianhe, "New Changes in the US-Australia Security Alliance," *Contemporary International Relations*, Vol. 34, No. 1, 2014, pp.36–42.

Wang Sen and Yang Guanghai, "ASEAN's Diplomacy of Balancing Great Powers in the South China Seas," *Contemporary Asia-Pacific Studies*, Vol. 23, No. 1, 2014, pp.35–37.

Wang Sheng, Luo Xiao, "The Transformation of International System and the Change of China's Peripheral Diplomacy: From Maintaining Stability to Safeguarding Rights," *Contemporary International Relations*, Vol. 33, No. 1, 2013, pp.9–15.

Wang Xiangyu and Li Wenlong, "The Analysis of American Element in the Dispute of South China Sea," *Journal of Guizhou Normal University (Social Science Edition)*, Vol. 42, No. 3, 2001, pp.25–28.

Wang Yiwei, "Rethinking of South China Sea Issue: A Perspective of Sino-U.S. Relations," *Fudan American Review*, Vol.6, No. 1, 2006, pp.81–103.

Wang Zheng, "Chinese Discourse on the 'Nine-Dashed Line' Rights, Interests, and Nationalism," *Asian Survey*, Vol. 55, No. 3, 2015, pp.502–524.

Wei Hongxia, "A Close Review on Obama's Rebalancing Asia Policy," *Fudan American Review*, Vol. 13, No. 1, 2013, pp.32–59.

Wei Zongyou, "A Preliminary Study of Trump administration's South China Sea Policy," *Southeast Asian Studies*, Vol. 60, No. 2, 2018, pp.123–136.

William J. Aceves, "The Freedom of Navigation Program: A Study of the Relationship between Law and Politics," *Hastings International & Comparative Law Review*, Vol. 19, 1995/96, pp.259–326.

William T. Tow, Russell Trood, "The 'Anchors': Collaborative Security Substance or Smokescreen?", in Brad Williams and Andrew Newman, eds., *Japan, Australia and Asia-Pacific security*, New York: Routledge, 2006, pp.70–88.

Wu Guifu, "The Trend of US Asia Pacific Strategic Adjustment," *Contemporary Asia-Pacific Studies*, Vol. 1, No. 5, 1992, pp.56–65.

Wu Shicun, "Thinking on Challenges and Countermeasures of the South China Sea Issue," *Administration Reform*, Vol. 4, No. 7, 2012, pp.15–19.

Wu Xinbo, "The Re-internationalization of Sino-American Relations," *World Economics and Politics*, Vol. 23, No. 8, 2009, pp.21–29.

Wu Xinbo, "On Obama Administration's Asia Pacific Strategy," *China International Studies*, Vol. 54, No. 2, 2012, pp.62–77.

Wu Xinbo, "American Asia Pacific Strategy," in Zhou Fangyin, ed., *Asia-Pacific Strategies of Major Powers*, Beijing: Social Sciences Academic Press, 2013, pp.16–49.Wu Yan, "Brunei's South China Sea Policy", in Ju Hailong, ed., The *South China Sea Situation Report (2013–2014)*, Beijing: Current Affairs Press, 2015, pp.330–340.

Wu Zhaoli, "India's Asia Pacific Strategy: Development, Objective, and Implementation," *South Asian Studies*, No. 4, 2015, pp.98–121.

Xin Benjian, "The Asia Pacific Region: The First Focus of the U.S. Global Strategy in the 21st Century—Examples, Reasons and China's Foreign Policy," *World Economics and Politics*, Vol. 15, No. 8, 2001, pp.26–31.Xin Qiang, "'Five No's' Policy: The U.S. Adjustment of the South China Sea Policy," *The Chinese Journal of American Studies*, Vol. 28, No. 6, 2014, pp.51–68.

Xin Qiang, "'Subordinate Axis': Changing Role of Japan in the U.S. Asia-Pacific Security Structure," *World Economics and Politics*, Vol. 28, No. 4, 2014, pp.39–53.

Xin Qiang, "The Development of U.S.-Vietnam Security Cooperation and its Influencing Factors," *China International Studies*, Vol. 56, No. 6, 2014, pp.61–71.

Xin Qiang, "On the 'Duality' of Sea Power Game between China and the U.S.," *Conmilit*, Vol. 42, No. 6, 2016, pp.32–40.

Xin Qiang and Fu Da'an, "The Diaoyu/Senkaku Islands Dispute From the Perspective of China-US Competition in Security," *Chinese Journal of American Studies*, Vol. 14, No. 1, 2014, pp.33–55.

Xu Gongsu, "The French Occupation of Nine Islets," *China' Frontier Issues*, Taiwan Student Book Publishing House, 1975, pp.149–160.

Xu Zhiliang, Li Lixin, Pan Hong, and Zhou Xin, "Self-evident State Boundary Implication of 'Nine-Dashed Line' in Historical Maps of China," *Pacific Journal*, Vol. 21, No. 2, 2013, pp.79–84.

Yang Jilong, "On the Japan Factor in the South China Sea Dispute," *Pacific Journal*, Vol. 21, No. 12, 2013, pp.92–101.

Yang Xianbin, "On the Freedom of Navigation in the Exclusive Economic Zone," *Studies in Law and Business*, No. 3, 2017, pp.171–180.

Yang Yi, "Peripheral Environmental Dilemma and Security Policy Paradox," *World Affairs*, Vol. 69, No.1, 2012, p.30.

Yang Zhen and Zhou Yunheng, "On the Contradiction of Sea Power between China and America," *Contemporary International Relations*, Vol. 31, No. 2, 2011, pp.6–11.

Yann-Huei S., "The Overall Situation in the South China Sea in the New Millennium: Before and After the 9/11 Terrorist Attacks," *Ocean Development & International Law*, Vol. 34 (3–4), 2003, pp.229–277.

You Hongbo, "US Reaction to the Paracels Battle between PRC and South Vietnam," *Southeast Asian Affairs*, Vol. 38, No. 3, 2011, pp.20–28.

Yu Changshen, "ASEAN Views of and Policy Responses to China's Rise," *Contemporary Asia-Pacific Studies*, Vol. 22, No. 3, 2013, pp.111–128.

Yu Minyou and Lei Xiaolu, "On the Irrationality of the United States Accusing China of Impeding the Freedom of Navigation in the South China Sea," *Jiangxi Social Sciences*, Vol. 32, No. 9, 2011, pp.13–19.

Yu Xiaoyan, "The Political Economic Analysis of Australia's Promotion of TPP Negotiation," *Asia-pacific Economic Review*, Vol. 29, No. 6, 2012, pp.9–15.

Yu Xintian, "The Prospect of East Asian Modernization and its Impact on the World," *Pacific Journal*, Vol. 2, No. 2, 1994, pp.66–74.

Yuen Foong Khong, "Primacy or World Order? The United States and China's Rise—A Review Essay," *International Security*, Vol. 38, No. 3, Winter 2013/14, pp.153–175.

Zeng Pengxiang, Fu Zhigang, and Lian Ronghua, "Scientific Construction of Marine Militia Management and Control System," *National Defense*, Vol. 12, 2014, pp.68–70.

Zeng Yong, "Rethink the Parlance of about 'core interests in South China Sea'," *Southeast Asian Affairs*, Vol. 45, Issue 4, 2018, pp.1–16.

Zeng Zhaoxuan, "A Preliminary Analysis of the Ancient Documents of the South China Sea Islands," *Collections of Essays On Chinese Historical Geography*, Vol. 7, No. 1, 1991, pp.133–160.

Zhang Hongzhou, "Chinese Fishermen in Disputed Waters: Not Quite a 'People's War'," *Marine Policy*, Vol. 68, June, 2016, pp.65–73.

Zhang Hongzhou and Sam Bateman, "Fishing Militia, the Securitization of Fishery and the South China Sea Dispute," *Contemporary Southeast Asia*, Vol. 39, No. 2, 2017, pp. 288–314. Zhang Jie, "The Perception Gap on the 'U-Shaped Line' in the South China Sea and China's Strategic Choices," *The Journal of International Studies*, Vol. 35, No. 2, 2014, pp.45–60.

Zhang Jingquan, "American Asia Rebalance Strategy and the Function of U.S.-SK Alliance," *Teaching and Research*, Vol. 61, No. 9, 2013, pp.64–71.

Zhang Jingquan, "The Reinforcement of America-Philippine Alliance and Its Function in America Rebalance Strategy to Asia-Pacific," *Southeast Asian Affairs*, Vol. 41, No. 1, 2014, pp.1–8.Zhang Lei, "The Possibility of the United States to Intervene by Military Means in the Island Disputes between China and Japan and between China and the Philippines: A Comparison from the Perspective of the Military Alliances Treaties," *Fudan American Review*, Vol. 12, No. 1, 2012, pp.47–68.

Zhang Lei, "Rethinking the Ways to Solve the Dispute about Nine-dashed Line," *Pacific Journal*, Vol. 21, No. 12, 2013, pp.50–62.

Zhang Li, "US Pivot to Asia and India's Role Choice," *South Asian Studies Quarterly*, Vol. 28, No. 2, 2012, pp.1–7.

Zhang Ming, "An Analysis of the Obama Administration's Asia Pacific Military Rebalancing," *Contemporary International Relations*, Vol. 33, No. 4, 2013, pp.37–44.

Zhang Mingliang, "The U.S. Congressional Involvement in South China Sea Issue: Approaches and Implications," *The Journal of South China Sea Studies*, Vol. 1, No. 3, 2015, pp.26–34.

Zhang Mingliang, "ASEAN's Approaches for South China Sea Issue: Process, Background and Implications," *Southeast Asian Affairs*, Vol. 43, No. 1, 2016, pp.1–12.

Zhang Mingliang, "The United States and Robert Island Affairs," *Southeast Asian Studies*, Vol. 47, No. 2, 2005, pp.60–64.

Zhang Qingmin, "US-Taiwan Military Relations in Bush's First Term: Seen from the Implementation of Bush's Decision of Arms Sale to Taiwan," *American Studies Quarterly*, Vol. 18, No. 4, 2004, pp.15–38.

Zhang Wenmu, "Paradise Is Faraway, But China Is Nearby: A Study on Geopolitics between China and Its Neighboring Countries and Regions and the Law of their Interaction," *World Economics and Politics*, Vol. 27, No. 1, 2013, pp.5–39.

Zhang Xiaoming, "U.S. South China Sea Policy: Origin and Evolution," American Studies Quarterly, Vol. 30, No. 1, 2016, pp.34–51.

Zhang Xuekun, "Divergent Perceptions of Southeast Asian Countries towards the US Rebalance Strategy," *International Forum*, Vol. 17, No. 3, 2015, pp.25–30.

Zhang Xuekun and Ou Xuanxi, "An Analysis of the Causes and Approaches of Japan's Involving in the South China Sea Issue," *Pacific Journal*, Vol. 24, No. 4, 2016, pp.33–42.Zhang Yaohua, "Japan's Role in the South China Sea Issue," *China International Studies*, Vol. 53, No. 3, 2011, pp.51–57.

Zhang Ye, "Analysis of US Freedom of Navigation Operation in South China Sea under the Trump Administration," *Pacific Journal*, Vol. 26, No. 9, 2018, pp.94–100.

Zhang Yu, "The Basic Connotation of the Militia's Support to the Front in Wartime," *National Defense*, No. 6, 2002, pp.36–38.

Zhang Yuan and Hu Dekun, "Sino-US Maritime Incident Prevention and Military Confidence Building," *China International Studies*, Vol. 56, No. 2, 2014, pp.96–108.

Zhao Suisheng, "Obama Administration's Asia Pacific Strategic Rebalancing and Sino-US Relations," *Fudan American Review*, Vol. 13, No. 1, 2013, pp.1–17.

Zhao Weihua, "Vietnam's South China Sea Policy Adjustment: Evolution and Essence," *Southeast Asian Studies*, Vol. 61, No.1, 2019, pp.16–32.

Zhao Yang and Gong Honglie, "The Reaction of the U.S Congress to China's Land Reclamation in the Nansha Islands," *Pacific Journal*, Vol. 24, No. 5, 2016, pp.41–51.

Zheng Yingping, "The Thought of Bush Administration's New Alliances Strategy," *Contemporary International Relations*, Vol. 22, No. 11, 2002, pp.43–47.

Zheng Yingping, "On New Advantages of American's Asian and Pacific Security Strategy and its Effects on Surrounding Countries of China," *Pacific Journal*, Vol. 12, No. 2, 2004, pp.56–63.Zheng Zemin, "American Policies towards South China Sea during the Cold War," *Southeast Asian Affairs*, Vol. 32, No. 4, 2005, pp.13–19.

Zhiguo Gao and Bingbing Jia, "The Nine-Dash Line in the South China Sea: History, Status and Implications," *The American Journal of International Law*, Vol. 107, No. 1, January 2013, pp.98–124.

Zhong Feiteng, "Three Strategic Issues in the Study of the South China Sea: Review and Reflection Based on Relevant Literature," *Foreign Affairs Review*, Vol. 29, No. 4, 2012, pp.21–36.

Zhou Fangyin, "The US Asia-Pacific Alliance System and China's Policy Options," *World Economics and Politics*, Vol. 27, No. 11, 2013, pp.4–24.

Zhou Qi, "The Origin and Evolution of the U.S. South China Sea Policy in the Post-Cold War Era," *World Economics and Politics*, Vol. 28, No. 6, 2014, pp.23–44.

Zhuang Guotu and Lu Qiuli, "Basic Stance of Australia Official on South China Sea Disputes in Recent Years," *Southeast Asian Affairs*, Vol. 40, No. 3, 2013, pp.97–102.Zuo Fengrong, "Preliminary Exploration of Russia's Maritime Strategy," *Foreign Affairs Review*, Vol. 29, No. 5, 2012, pp.125–139.

Zuo Fengrong, "Russia's New Asia-Pacific Strategy and Its Impact upon China-Russia Relations," *The Journal of International Studies*, Vol. 34, No. 2, 2013, pp.117–127.

Zou Keyuan, "The Chinese Traditional Maritime Boundary Line in the South China Sea and Its Legal Consequences for the Resolution of the Dispute over the Spratly Islands," *The International Journal of Marine and Coastal Law*, Vol. 14, No. 1, 1999, pp.27–55.

Index

www.ingramcontent.com/pod-product-compliance
Ingram Content Group UK Ltd.
Pitfield, Milton Keynes, MK11 3LW, UK
UKHW021009120926
8556IPUK00029B/361